MW01088033

John Wesley
ON CHRISTIAN PRACTICE

Richard Douglas's drawing of John Wesley as a frail old man.
Used by permission.

In 1999, Richard Douglas drew this portrait of John Wesley as a frail old man who was approaching the end of his long ministry. A wig covered his balding head. From mid February 1791, Wesley's physical powers declined rapidly. He preached his last sermon on 22 February 1791 at Leatherhead in the house of a family who had "lately begun to receive the truth." On the occasion illustrated by this portrait, Wesley was brought to his house and he asked to be left alone for half an hour. As soon as Wesley was by himself he began to pray for wisdom and strength.

John Wesley on Christian Practice

THE

STANDARD

SERMONS

IN

MODERN

ENGLISH

VOLUME III, 34-53

KENNETH CAIN KINGHORN

ABINGDON PRESS / Nashville

JOHN WESLEY ON CHRISTIAN PRACTICE
THE STANDARD SERMONS IN MODERN ENGLISH, VOL. 3

Copyright© 2003 by Abingdon Press

All rights reserved.
No part of this work may be reproduced or transmitted in any form or by any means, electronic or mechanical, including photocopying and recording, or by any information storage or retrieval system, except as may be expressly permitted by the 1976 Copyright Act or in writing from the publisher. Requests for permission should be addressed to Abingdon Press, P.O. Box 801, 201 Eighth Avenue South, Nashville, TN 37202-0801.

This book is printed on recycled, acid-free, elemental-chlorine–free paper.

Library of Congress Cataloging-in-Publication Data

Wesley, John, 1703-1791
[Sermons on several occasion.]
The standard sermons in modern English / [edited by] Kenneth Cain Kinghorn.
p. cm.
Includes bibliographical references and index.
Contents: v. 3. John Wesley on Christian Practice, 34-53
ISBN 0-687-02226-6 (alk. paper)
1. Methodist Church—Sermons. 2. Sermons, English. I. Kinghorn, Kenneth C. II. Title.
BX8217.W54 K56 2002
252'.07—dc21

2001055256

All scripture quotations unless noted otherwise are taken from the *New Revised Standard Version of the Bible,* copyright 1989, Division of Christian Education of the National Council of the Churches of Christ in the United States of America. Used by permission. All rights reserved.

Scripture quotations marked CEV are from the *Contemporary English Version,* © 1991, 1992, 1995 by American Bible Society. Used by permission.

Scripture quotations marked KJV are from the King James or Authorized Version of the Bible.

03 04 05 06 07 08 09 10 11 12—10 9 8 7 6 5 4 3 2

MANUFACTURED IN THE UNITED STATES OF AMERICA

Contents

Introduction

JOHN WESLEY ON CHRISTIAN PRACTICE

This book is volume 3 of a three-volume set containing John Wesley's Standard Sermons in modern English. Volume 1 in this series contains sermons 1-20, which deal with Wesley's teachings about Christian fundamentals. That book is titled *John Wesley on Christian Beliefs*. The sermons in volume 1 explain such Christian basics as the order of salvation, repentance, the work of Christ, the witness of the Spirit, sin in believers, holiness, and the final judgment. Underlying all these Christian fundamentals is a focus on the person of Jesus Christ and his redemptive work on the cross. Referring to belief in the centrality and finality of Christ, Wesley wrote that the saving work of Jesus is "*articulus stantis vel cadentis ecclesiæ* [the doctrine on which the church stands or falls]. . . . It is certainly the pillar and ground of that faith, of which alone cometh salvation—of that *catholic* or universal faith which is found in all the children of God, and which 'unless a man keep whole and undefiled, without doubt he shall perish everlastingly.'"[1] It is consistent with the ordered mind of Wesley for him to begin with biblical basics, which comprise volume 1 of his Standard Sermons.

Volume 2 of this series contains John Wesley's thirteen discourses on Christ's Sermon on the Mount. The main thrust of these sermons is Christian moral principles—guidelines that shape the way we live. That volume dealing with ethics is titled *John Wesley on the Sermon on the Mount.* Wesley defined ethics simply as "an art which treats of virtue and vice."[2] His texts for these discourses come from Matthew's Gospel, chapters 5–7. Concerning this section of scripture, Wesley said,

> Observe the benevolent condescension of our Lord. He seems, as it were, to lay aside his supreme authority as our legislator, that he may the better act the part of our friend and Saviour. Instead of using the lofty style, in positive commands, he, in a more gentle and engaging way, insinuated his will and our duty, by pronouncing those happy who comply with it.[3]

Wesley insisted that the ethical teachings of Jesus Christ constitute the sole basis for both holiness and happiness. Accordingly, Wesley included a course in ethics at his Kingswood School for Boys.[4] Commenting on Christ's teachings in the Sermon on the Mount, Wesley said that they are "the noblest compendium of religion which is to be found even in the oracles of God."[5] Wesley preached often from the Sermon on the Mount, and for the most part his hearers clung to his every word. Wesley's ethics brought a moral transformation to eighteenth-century England.[6] After Wesley's death in 1791, *Gentleman's Magazine* editorialized,

> A sense of decency in morals and religion was introduced in the lowest classes of mankind, the ignorant were instructed, and the wretched relieved and the abandoned reclaimed. . . . [Wesley] must be considered as one of the most extraordinary characters this or any other age has ever produced.[7]

Wesley's sermons on Christ's Sermon on the Mount are theologically precise, logically compelling, and existentially useful.[8] His articulation of plain truth for plain people presents an ethics of hope for persons of all conditions and in every circumstance of life.

This present volume contains discourses 34-53, completing John Wesley's Standard Sermons. The title of this volume indicates its content—*John Wesley on Christian Practice.* In these sermons Wesley explains how the inner life of the spirit expresses itself in our desires, decisions, and actions. He applies biblical truth to the practical issues of common life. Wesley shows how Christianity influences our responses to such considerations as the moral law, temptation, backsliding, depression, laziness, pain, gossip, money, stewardship, social challenges, and death. These homilies reflect the fundamental conviction of John Wesley that Christianity consists of a steady day-by-day obedience to Christ at all times, in all places, and under all circumstances. Accordingly, Wesley does not stress secondary matters, nor does he invest time "talking on useless, if not trifling subjects." He wrote, "Having no room to spend any time in . . . vain contention, we have our desire of spending and being spent, in promoting plain, practical religion."[9] These sermons embody that ideal.

It has been said of Wesley's theology that without God we *cannot*, and without us God *will not.* This epigram underscores Wesley's genius as a theologian of balance. He carefully avoided making one part of religion the whole of religion. Indeed, he referred to this practice as one of "Satan's devices." Wesley achieved an impressive synthesis of *revelation* and *reason*, *Scripture* and *tradition*, *grace* and *nature*, *faith* and *works*. Furthermore, he sought always to merge *theory* and *practice.* He drew his theology from the Bible and continually measured it in the living laboratories of daily life and common sense. He balanced innovations in ministry with the treasures of tradition.

Wesley interviewed thousands of people concerning their Christian experience, and these interviews helped him refine, clarify, and apply biblical truth. In his sermons, Wesley's logical mind combines with his remarkable grasp of Scripture, a familiarity with the centuries-old Christian tradition, and a keen understanding of the faith journeys of thousands of genuinely transformed people. John Wesley was an extraordinary man. As he advanced in age, he continued to produce sermons of undiminished power. In 1788, he wrote,

> I this day enter on my eighty-fifth year: And what cause have I to praise God, as for a thousand spiritual blessings, so for bodily

> blessings also! How little have I suffered yet by "the rush of numerous years!". . . [Nor] do I feel any such thing as weariness, either in travelling or preaching: And I am not conscious of any decay in writing sermons; which I do as readily, and I believe as correctly, as ever.[10]

From his scores of sermons, Wesley selected the fifty-three Standard Sermons as representing the doctrines he embraced and taught as "the essentials of true religion."[11] These sermons contain the marrow of Methodism. They articulate the distilled theological wisdom and practical genius of one of history's most effective preachers and remarkable saints.

Kenneth Kinghorn

I wish to express gratitude to the following people for assistance in this three-volume project, transcribing John Wesley's Standard Sermons into modern English. Dr. Christopher Armitrage, Professor of English at the University of North Carolina, offered suggestions pertaining to Wesley's eighteenth-century English. The Reverend Walter K. Price assisted in identifying the scripture references in Wesley's sermons. Lauren Porter helped translate Wesley's Latin. Student assistants Steve Kaynor, Dale Capron, Lamar Oliver, and Tiffany Reisz helped with the indexes.

Notes

1. Wesley's sermon, "The Lord Our Righteousness," ¶ 4. Wesley's quotation is from the Athanasian Creed [*Symbolum Quicunque*], §2. Philip Schaff, *The Creeds of Christendom* (New York: Harper & Bros., 1877), 2:66.
2. John Wesley, *The Complete English Dictionary, Explaining Most of Those Hard Words, Which Are Found in the Best English Writers* (London: R. Hawes, 1777). With a measure of overconfidence, Wesley wrote on the title page, "The author assures you, he thinks this is the best English Dictionary in the World."
3. *Notes upon the New Testament,* Matt. 5:2.
4. Thomas Jackson, ed., *The Works of John Wesley,* 14 vols. "A Farther Appeal to Men of Reason and Religion" (London: Wesleyan Conference Office, 1872), 13:283-301.
5. W. Reginald Ward and Richard P. Heitzenrater, eds., *The Works of John Wesley,* Bicentennial Edition, *Journal and Diaries* (Nashville: Abingdon Press, 1993), October 17, 1771, 22:293.

6. J. Wesley Bready, *England: Before and After Wesley: The Evangelical Revival and Social Reform* (London: Hodder and Stoughton, 1938), 331-422.

7. *Gentleman's Magazine* (1791), 61:282-84. This tribute is remarkable, given the anti-Methodist articles printed by this magazine while Wesley was alive.

8. See Leon O. Hynson, *To Reform the Nation: Theological Foundations of Wesley's Ethics* (Grand Rapids, Mich.: Francis Asbury Press, 1984), 142-47; and Ronald H. Stone, *John Wesley's Life and Ethics* (Nashville: Abingdon Press, 2001), 110-26.

9. Jackson, *Wesley's Works*, "A Farther Appeal to Men of Reason and Religion," 8:244.

10. Jackson, *Wesley's Works, Journal*, June 28, 1788, 4:427.

11. Preface to *Sermons on Several Occasions*, vol. 1 (London: Strahn, 1746), §1.

Introduction to Sermon 34

THE ORIGIN, NATURE, PROPERTIES, AND USE OF THE LAW[1]

During the span of John Wesley's ministry, the Methodists had to deal with two kinds of errors concerning the moral law. These errors were propagated by teachers who opposed John Wesley and the revival that moved forward under his leader-ship. On the one hand, some of Wesley's critics taught that Christians are not obligated to keep the moral law because they live under grace. This belief caused some Methodists to disparage the law, abandon the means of grace, and neglect good works. On the other hand, the error persisted that salvation is based on self-effort and good works. The first error led to Antinomianism, while the second led to legalism. In this sermon, Wesley corrects these two mistakes and clarifies the proper place of the moral law.

During the decade of the 1740s, Antinomianism in England threatened to undermine the gospel by declaring that faith cancels the need to obey the moral law. Wesley recorded a conversation he had with one of the antinomian teachers:

W. Do you believe you have nothing to do with the law of God?

A. I have not. I am not under the law. I live by faith.

W. Have you, as living by faith, a right to everything in the world?

A. I have. All is mine, since Christ is mine.

W. May you then take anything you will anywhere? Suppose, out of a shop, without the consent or knowledge of the owner?

A. I may, if I want it. For it is mine. Only I will not give offence.

W. Have you also a right to all the women in the world?

A. Yes, if they consent.

W. And is not that a sin?

A. Yes, to him that thinks it is a sin. But not to those whose *hearts are free.*

Wesley summed up his view of this exchange, "Surely these are the first-born children of Satan!"[2]

To another antinomian teacher, Wesley said, "All that is really uncommon in your doctrine is a heap of broad absurdities, in most of which you grossly contradict yourselves, as well as Scripture and common sense. In the meantime, you brag and vapour [boast], as if 'ye were the men, and wisdom should die with you.' I pray God to 'humble you, and prove you, and show you what is in your hearts!'"[3] This sermon corrects the antinomian error and clarifies "the origin, nature, properties, and use of the law."

Wesley also explains that when God created man and woman in his own image and likeness, he stamped the moral law upon their hearts. Due to the Fall, however, humankind forfeited this spiritual benefit, and now in its natural state humankind has only a faint sense of the moral law. Theologians call this condition "original sin." Wesley did not believe that original sin *erased* the image of God in us, but he did believe that image was *defaced.* Many people in Wesley's day, however, rejected or ignored the reality of original sin. The Deist and Enlightenment philosophers believed that humankind innately possesses an adequate understanding of right and duty. They insisted that we have both the inborn knowledge of what is right and the natural ability to do it.

Wesley refused to ground our ethical obligations in what human nature thinks or feels is right. He upheld his Church's teaching on the reality of original sin and sin's severe weakening of human understanding and ability. One of the requirements for ordination in the Church of England was agreement with its Articles of Religion. The article on original sin, in part, states that "original sin . . . is the fault and corruption of the Nature of every man, that naturally is engendered of the offspring of Adam; whereby man is very far gone from original righteousness, and is of his own nature inclined to evil."[4] Wesley affirms "the eternal fitness of things"—that is, humankind's innate sense of goodness and order.[5] Yet, Wesley insists that because of the Fall we can know what is right only as God reveals it. God has given this revelation to us through Scripture and Jesus Christ. We cannot determine what is right through intellectual reasoning or human intuition. We can know about God and God's will only as he communicates it to us and enables us to understand and live it.

In this sermon, Wesley states that the moral law convicts us of sin, points us to our need for Christ, and shows us how God wants us to live. The moral law originates in no other source than God. It constitutes the only way humankind can be holy and happy. God's law is holy, just, and perfect—and it accords with how God designed humankind to function. Yet, Wesley contends that obedience to the moral law does not earn our salvation. The law is invaluable as God's instruction to those who *are* saved. This sermon teaches us that Christian liberty is not the freedom to sin but the freedom *not* to sin.

Sermon 34

THE ORIGIN, NATURE, PROPERTIES, AND USE OF THE LAW

The law is holy, and the commandment is holy and just and good. *(Romans 7:12)*

1 Perhaps there are few subjects within the entire scope of religion that are so little understood as the moral law. Commentators usually tell the readers of St. Paul's Epistle to the Romans that by "the law," the apostle means the Jewish ceremonial law. Then, assuming that the Jewish law is not relevant to Christians, the commentators move on without giving further thought to the subject. Some are not satisfied with this explanation, however. They note that the Epistle is directed to the Romans and they suppose that, in the beginning of chapter 7, St. Paul is referring to the old Roman law. Because they have no more interest in this law than in the ceremonial law of Moses, they do not give much thought to it. They assume that St. Paul's occasional mention of the law is only to illustrate something else.

2. However, a careful observer of the book of Romans will not be content with these superficial explanations of the law. The more

one considers St. Paul's words, the more convinced one becomes that "the law" mentioned in this chapter does not mean the ancient law of Rome or the ceremonial law of Moses. This conclusion will certainly become clear to all who attentively consider the substance of St. Paul's Epistle to the Romans. He begins chapter 7, "Do you not know, brothers and sisters—for I am speaking to those who know the law—that the law is binding on a person only during that person's lifetime?" Is St. Paul referring to the law of Rome or to the ceremonial law? Neither one. He is concerned with the *moral law*.

Saint Paul clearly illustrates his point: "A married woman is bound by the law to her husband as long as he lives; but if her husband dies, she is discharged from the law concerning the husband. Accordingly, she will be called an adulteress if she lives with another man while her husband is alive. But if her husband dies, she is free from that law, and if she marries another man, she is not an adulteress." In this particular example, by parallel reasoning the apostle moves on to draw a general conclusion. He writes, "In the same way, my friends, you have died to the law [the entire Mosaic legal system] through the body of Christ [offered for you and bringing you under a new dispensation], so that you may belong to another [without any guilt], to him who has been raised from the dead [thereby proving his authority to make this change] in order that we may bear fruit for God."

Now, we *can* bear fruit, whereas before the coming of Christ, we could not. "While we were living in the flesh," we were under the dominion of our corrupt nature. It was natural that we were under its power because we had not yet benefited from the power of Christ's resurrection. Then, "our sinful passions were aroused by the law," and the law could not overcome our sin; it could only make sin worse for us. In various ways, our sinful desires "were at work in our members bearing the fruit of death." "But now we are discharged from the law"—that is, to the entire moral and ceremonial law. We are now "dead to that which held us captive." The entire Jewish law is now dead, and it has no more dominion over us than a deceased husband has over his wife. We are no longer slaves to the old written code, which consisted of outward obedience to the letter of the Mosaic law. Now, we have "new life of the Spirit."

3. Saint Paul proved that the Christian dispensation has set aside the Jewish dispensation. He showed how the moral law, although it can never pass away, now rests on a new foundation that differs from its former foundation. Next, St. Paul pauses to raise an objection and to answer it. He asks, "What then should we say? That the law is sin?" Some people might misconstrue these words to mean that the law produces sinful actions. Saint Paul answers his own question: "By no means is this the case!" The law is an irreconcilable enemy to sin, searching it out wherever it is. Paul testifies, "If it had not been for the law, I would not have known sin. I would not have known what it is to covet if the law had not said, 'You shall not covet.'" In the next four verses, St. Paul further explains his point of view. At that point, drawing from the example he uses, he adds a broad conclusion regarding the moral law: "The law is holy, and the commandment is holy and just and good."

4. These profound words are seldom discussed because they are so poorly understood. In order to explain and apply them, I will endeavor to clarify (1) the origin of the law, (2) the nature of the law, (3) the properties of the law (it is holy, just, and good), and (4) the uses of the law.

I. The Origin of the Law

1. First, I will endeavor to explain the origin of the moral law (often called "the law in its highest degree"). The origin of the moral law is not nearly so recent as the time of Moses, even though some people think so. Noah announced it to people long before Moses (and Enoch before him). We can trace its origin much further back, even prior to the foundation of the world. This period is indeed unknown to us mortals, but it is without doubt recorded in the chronicle of eternity "when the morning stars sang together," having been newly called into existence. It pleased the great Creator to make these his firstborn creatures intelligent beings so that they could know the one who created them. For this purpose God gave them understanding so that they could distinguish truth from falsehood and good from evil. As a necessary consequence, God endowed these angelic beings with freedom—the ability to choose

one thing and refuse the other. Because of this endowment, these beings were correspondingly enabled to offer free and willing service to God. This service in itself carried its own satisfying reward, and it was also entirely acceptable to their gracious Master.

2. To enable these angelic beings to use all the abilities he had given them—especially their intelligence and freedom—God gave them a law. This law was a complete reflection of all truth, so far as it could be understood by finite beings. The law mirrored all good, insofar as angelic minds were capable of grasping it. Through the law, their gracious Governor planned to provide a way for the ceaseless growth of the angels' happiness. Every act of obedience to God's law would add to the perfection of their nature and entitle them to a higher reward, which the righteous Judge would give at the appropriate time.

3. Then, according to his plan, God created a new order of intelligent beings—humankind. He formed the first human beings from the dust of the earth and breathed into them the breath of life, causing them to become living souls who were endued with power to choose good or evil. In the same way that he gave his law to the firstborn angelic beings, he also gave his law to humankind, as the free, intelligent creatures they were. God did not write this law upon tablets of stone or any permanent material substance. Rather, the finger of God engraved this law upon the inmost spirits both of angels and of human beings. God's purpose was that the law would never be far from us or difficult to understand. Instead, his moral law was always at hand, shining with clear light, just as the sun in the midst of heaven.

4. Such is the origin of God's law. With reference to humankind, this moral law was compatible with human nature. With reference to the older sons of God (the angels), the law shone in its full splendor "before the mountains were brought forth, or God had ever formed the earth and the world."

However, in the case of humankind, it was not long before the man and the woman rebelled against God. And by breaking this glorious law, the man and the woman almost obliterated it from their hearts: "They became darkened in their understanding and alienated from the life of God." Still, God did not spurn the work of his own hands. Because of the reconciling work of Jesus Christ, in some measure God rewrote his law on the hearts of his dark, sinful creatures. Once again, "He has told you, O mortal, what is good" (although not to the same extent as at first). "The Lord requires you to do justice, and to love kindness, and to walk humbly with your God."

5. God revealed this moral law to our first parents and to all their offspring. God spoke to us through Jesus Christ, "the true light, which enlightens everyone coming into the world." Nonetheless, as time passed, all people have walked away from this light and "all flesh corrupted its ways upon the earth." Then, God elected from out of humankind a chosen people—the Jews. He gave them a more perfect knowledge of his law. Due to their slowness in grasping this law, God wrote its main divisions—the Ten Commandments—on two tablets of stone. He commanded the parents to teach this law to their children through all succeeding generations.

6. God also revealed his law to those heathen who did not know him. Through their *consciences*, they "heard" God's law—those things that were "written in former days for our instruction." However, this way of learning God's law through our consciences is not adequate to allow us to comprehend "the breadth and length and height and depth" of his law. God alone can reveal this law by his Spirit. And as an outgrowth of that gracious promise given to all the Israel of God, the Holy Spirit does so in all who truly believe:

> The days are surely coming, says the LORD, when I will make a new covenant with the house of Israel. . . . This is the covenant that I will make. . . . I will put my law within them, and I will write it on their hearts; and I will be their God, and they shall be my people. (Jer. 31:31, 33)

II. The Nature of the Law

1. The second thing I propose to explain is the nature of the law that God originally gave to the angels in heaven and to the man and the woman in paradise. It is the same law that God has so mercifully promised to write afresh in the hearts of all true believers. To explain the nature of this law, first, I will point out that "the law" and "the commandments" are sometimes understood as

being different. Some believe that the commandments are only a part of the total law. However, in the text of this sermon, the terms "law" and "commandments" are used as equivalent terms, each meaning the same thing.

Neither of these terms refers to the ceremonial or the ritualistic laws. When St. Paul writes, "If it had not been for the law, I would not have known sin," it is easy to see that he is not referring to ceremonial law. It is not the ceremonial law that says, "You shall not covet." Therefore, the ceremonial law does not pertain to our present discussion.

2. Furthermore, in our text, the law does not refer to the Mosaic dispensation. It is true that the word is sometimes understood this way, as when Saint Paul writes to the Galatian Christians, "The law [the Mosaic dispensation] which came four hundred thirty years later [after Abraham] does not annul a covenant previously ratified." Even so, in Romans 7:12 (our text), "the law" cannot be understood to refer to the Mosaic law. Saint Paul never bestows such high commendations upon that imperfect and shadowy dispensation as he does in this text. The apostle nowhere affirms the Mosaic law to be a *spiritual* law; nor does he say that it is "holy, just, and good." It is not true that God will write that law on the hearts of those whose "iniquity and sin he no more remembers"? Again, in our text, "the law" refers to the *moral law*.

3. The moral law is a reliable reflection of "the high and lofty one who inhabits eternity, whose name is Holy." No mortal or angel has seen or can see the fullness of God's essence. We can see the unveiled face of God (and live) only if God manifests himself to give us life and not destroy it, enabling us mortals to receive the life he gives. The moral law is the heart of God disclosed to humankind. In some sense we may apply to this law what the apostle says about God's Son: He is "the reflection of God's glory and the exact imprint of God's very being."

4. The ancient heathen Cicero said, "If virtue could assume a form that we could see with our eyes, what wonderful love it would arouse within us!"[6] God's moral law has already accomplished whatever "virtue" might inspire if it were to take visible form! The law of God contains a summary of all virtues in a form

that people whose eyes God has enlightened can clearly apprehend with "unveiled faces" (2 Cor. 3:18). What is the law other than divine virtue and wisdom assuming a discernible form? What is it but God's own declaration of truth and good that from eternity were lodged in his uncreated mind? Now, in the moral law, these ideas of truth and good are available to us in a form that we can understand.

5. If we consider the law of God from another point of view, it is supreme and enduring good sense. It is the fixed moral virtue and the eternal suitability of everything that is or ever was. When we try to illustrate the depths of God with feeble analogies, I am aware of their inadequacy and impropriety. Nevertheless, we have no better language. Indeed, we have no other way to express ourselves so long as we are in our childlike state of existence. Because we know only in part, we are also obliged to speak only in part. We who live in houses of clay "cannot draw up our case because of darkness."[7] As long as I am a child, I must speak as a child, "but when the complete comes, the partial will come to an end."

6. Now, let us return to our immediate subject. The moral law of God (to use a human analogy) is a portrait of God's eternal mind; it is a copy of his divine nature. Yes, this law is the most beautiful demonstration of the will of the everlasting Father, the brightest emanation of his basic wisdom and the visible beauty of the Most High God. The law is the delight and amazement of the cherubim and seraphim and all the fellowship of heaven. It is the glory and joy of every wise believer who is an enlightened child of God upon earth.

III. The Properties of the Law

1. We have described the ever-blessed moral law of God. Now, in the third place, I will explain the characteristics of that law. I cannot describe all the law's properties because to do so would exceed the wisdom of an angel. I will, however, discuss those characteristics mentioned in the text, of which there are three—the law is holy, just, and good (Rom. 7:12). To begin, "the law is *holy*."

2. In this expression, St. Paul is speaking not of the law's effects, but of its nature. Referring to the law under another name,

St. James says, "The wisdom from above is first pure." James is referring to God's law written on our hearts. First, it is *pure*, meaning chaste, spotless, and inherently and essentially holy. Consequently, when the law is reproduced in our lives and souls, it is "religion that is pure and undefiled." Obeying the moral law is the pure, clean, unpolluted worship of God.

3. Indeed, this religion is pure, chaste, clean, and holy in the highest degree. Otherwise it could not be the direct offspring and explicit likeness of God, who is the essence of holiness. This religion is innocent of all sin; it is unstained and unblemished by any taint of evil. It is a chaste virgin, incapable of any defilement or mixture with what is corrupt or unholy. It has no association with any kind of sin because "what fellowship is there between light and darkness?" As in its very nature, sin is hostile to God, so God's law is antithetical to sin.

4. Therefore, with intense abhorrence, St. Paul rejects the blasphemous conjecture that the law of God is either sin or the cause of sin. By no means should we think that God's law produces sin! The law uncovers sin because it detects "things now hidden in darkness" and drags them out into daylight. The apostle observes that "sin is shown to be sin" because of the law. All of sin's disguises are ripped away, and it appears in its inherent ugliness. It is true that "through the commandment sin becomes sinful beyond measure." Because sin is shown to be set against light and knowledge, it is stripped even of the poor pretext of ignorance, and it loses both its excuse and its disguise. Through the law, sin becomes far more despicable both to God and to us.

Thus, it is true that the law, which in itself is pure and holy, "works death in us." Sin, when forced out into the light, rages all the more. When it is forbidden, sin breaks out with greater fury. Therefore, St. Paul, speaking for the person who is convinced of sin but not yet delivered from it, said, "Sin, seizing an opportunity in the commandment, produced in me all kinds of covetousness." That is, when one detects sin and tries to restrain it, one finds that the self dislikes the restraint. Consequently, so much the more, sin produces all kinds of temptations in us. Sin causes "many senseless and harmful desires" that the law tried to restrain. So Paul said, "when the commandment came, sin revived." Because of the law, sin fumed and rampaged all the more. However, this consequence of the law brings it no dishonor. We may abuse the law, but we cannot depreciate it. The law only proves that "the heart is devious above all else; it is perverse." Nonetheless, "the law of God is holy."

5. Second, the law is *just.* It returns to all people what is due them. God's law prescribes exactly what is right. It assigns precisely what should be done, said, or thought, with regard to us and our Creator and everyone he has created. In all respects, the law is suited to the nature of everything and everyone—the entire universe. It is suited to all our circumstances and mutual relationships, whether they exist from creation or have a beginning in a subsequent time. The law is exactly fitting for everything, whether essential or incidental. It does not clash with anything in any way; it is never irrelevant in any respect. Even though the law and all its parts depend completely on God's will, we can accurately say that there is nothing in it that is arbitrary. Therefore, the supreme universal law in heaven and earth is the prayer: "Your will be done."

6. Some people may raise the following questions: "Is the will of God the basis of his law? Is his will the source of right and wrong? Is something right because God wills it, or does he will it because it is right?"

I fear that these famous questions are more curious than useful. Probably posing the question in this way does not reflect the proper reverence that created beings should show toward the Creator and Governor of all things. It is not fitting for us mortals to call for the supreme God to explain to us his will or his ways! Nevertheless, with awe and reverence, we may comment on the matter. And may the Lord pardon us if we speak incorrectly!

7. It appears that the entire problem arises from considering God's will as something separate from God himself. Keeping God and his will together resolves the matter. No one can doubt that God is the source of his own law. The will of God corresponds with who God is. God's law is what God wills concerning what he has created. Consequently, it is one and the same thing to say that the law is the will of God, and that God himself is the cause of the law.

8. If God's law—the unchangeable rule of right and wrong—depends on the nature and necessary relationships of things to each other, then it must depend on God or his will. (I did not say their *eternal* relationships, because the eternal relationships of things that exist in time constitute a veritable contradiction.) Again, if God's law depends on the nature and relationships of things, then because all things and their relationships are the work of God's hands, the law arises out of God's will: "For God created all things, and by his will they existed and were created."

9. At the same time, it may be granted that in every particular case God wills something because it is right. He wills it because it corresponds to the rightness of things in their relationships. For example, we are to honor our parents because it is entirely appropriate and fitting to the structure of things.

10. Therefore, God's law is right and just concerning all things. As well as being pure and just, the law is also *good*. That God's law is good, we can conclude from its source. What source is there for God's law other than his goodness? What else other than goodness alone prompted God to impart to the holy angels his law as a divine reflection of himself? To what other source can we attribute God's bestowing upon humankind this reflection of his own nature? What else other than compassionate love constrained God still again to reveal his will to fallen mortals—either to Adam or any of his progeny, who like him "have sinned and fallen short of the glory of God"?

After human understanding became corrupted, was it not mere love that moved God to declare his law? God sent his prophets to disclose his law to blind and unthinking people. Doubtless, it was God's kindness that raised up Enoch and Noah to be preachers of righteousness and that caused Abraham (a friend of God), Isaac, and Jacob to bear witness to his truth. When "darkness covered the earth, and thick darkness the people," it was God's goodness alone that gave the written law to Moses and through him to the nation that God had chosen. Love prompted God to explain his living revelation through David and all the prophets that followed after him. At last, when the fullness of time had come, God sent his only-begotten Son. Jesus came "not to abolish the law, but to fulfill it." Christ confirmed every stroke of the letter of the law. He writes God's law on the hearts of all his children, and "he must reign until he has put all his enemies under his feet." And "when all things are subjected to him," he will present his mediatorial kingdom to the Father so that "God may be all in all."

11. God, out of his goodness, originally gave the law and preserved it through all the ages. As the fountain from which the law springs, the law is full of goodness and generosity. It is compassionate and kind. The psalmist paid respect to God's law by saying it is "sweeter . . . than honey, and drippings of the honeycomb." God's law is attractive and agreeable. It includes "whatever is true, whatever is honorable, whatever is just, whatever is pure, whatever is pleasing, whatever is commendable." It also pertains to whatever is excellent and worthy of praise before God and his holy angels. In God's law are hidden all the treasures of his wisdom, knowledge, and love.

12. If God's law is good in its nature, it follows that it is good in its consequences. As the tree is, so are its fruits. The fruit of God's law written in the heart is righteousness, peace, and trust forever. The law itself is righteousness, filling the soul with "the peace of God, which surpasses all understanding" and causing us to "rejoice always" in the testimony of a good conscience toward God.

God's law is not precisely a promise of things to come. It is a present installment of our purchased inheritance already begun within us. The law is God made manifest in our flesh, bringing with him eternal life and assuring us by that pure and perfect love that we are "marked with a seal for the day of redemption." "'They shall be mine,' says the LORD of hosts, 'my special possession on the day when I act, and I will spare them as parents spare their children who serve them.'" There remains for us "the crown of glory that never fades away."

IV. The Uses of the Law

1. Fourth and finally, we will examine the uses of the law. Without question, the first use of the law is to convince the world of sin. This responsibility is indeed the special work of the Holy

Spirit. He can accomplish his work without any means at all or by whatever method he pleases to use. To produce his work, God may even use means that seem inadequate or even ill-suited.

Accordingly, either in sickness or in health, some people's hearts have been broken down without any visible cause or outward means. On rare occasions, others have been awakened to a sense of God's wrath by hearing the message that "God was in Christ reconciling the world to himself." However, the usual method of the Holy Spirit is to convict sinners through the law. Ordinarily, it is the law brought to bear on the conscience that "breaks a rock in pieces." The law is the part of God's word that is "living and active" and "sharper than any two-edged sword."

This word in God's hand and in the hands of those whom he has sent pierces through all the layers of a deceitful heart and "divides soul from spirit" and, as it were, "joints from marrow." In this way, sinners discover their true condition. All their fig leaves are ripped away, and they see that they are "wretched, pitiable, poor, blind, and naked." The law brings flashes of lightning to convict throughout their souls. People feel themselves entirely sinful. They have nothing to pay. Their mouths are silenced, and they stand "accountable to God."

2. Thus, the first use of the law is to slay the sinner. The law destroys the life and power of those things in which sinners trust. The law convinces them that they are dead even while they live. We are not only under sentence of death, but actually dead to God and void of all spiritual life. As St. Paul stated, "We are dead through trespasses and sins."

The second use of the law is to bring sinners into life—into Christ—so that they can live. It is true that in convicting sinners and bringing them to Christ the Holy Spirit acts as a strict schoolmaster. It seems as though God's Spirit drives us by force rather than draws us by love. Yet love is the fountainhead of everything that God does. It is in the spirit of love that God uses painful means to separate us from our confidence in the flesh, thus leaving us no broken reed on which to lean. The law drives sinners, stripped of everything, to cry out in bitterness of soul, or groan from the depth of their hearts:

I give up every plea beside,
"Lord, I am damn'd,—but Thou hast died."[8]

3. The third use of the law is to maintain our spiritual life. The law is the foremost means by which the blessed Spirit prepares the believer for larger measures of the life of God.

I am afraid that this great and important truth is little understood by the world and by many Christians. The latter are genuine children of God by faith, and God has taken them out of the world. Many of them believe that when we come to Christ, the law has no further significance for us. In one sense, "Christ is the end of the law . . . for everyone who believes." In the sense that we are not saved by the law, the law does indeed come to an end. For all who believe, Jesus Christ becomes their righteousness and justification. The law justifies no one; it only brings them to Christ. In another respect, Christ is the end, or *goal*, of the law, toward which it constantly aims. However, after the law has brought us *to* Christ, it has yet a further office—to keep us *in* him. The more believers understand "the breadth and length and height and depth" of the law, the more the law constantly inspires them to encourage one another.

Closer and closer let us cleave
To His beloved embrace;
Expect His fulness to receive,
And grace to answer grace.[9]

4. Thus, every believer is free from the Jewish ceremonial law and the entire Mosaic dispensation. In this sense, Christ is "the end of the law." Yes, Christians are free from the moral law as a means of procuring their justification, because we "are now justified by his grace as a gift, through the redemption that is in Christ Jesus." In another sense, though, we are *not* free from the moral law. It still remains for us an indescribable benefit. First, the moral law works to convince us of the sin that remains in our hearts and lives, thereby keeping us close to Christ so that his blood can cleanse us every moment.

Second, from Christ our head we receive strength into ourselves as living members of his body. His strength empowers us to do what his law commands. Third, the moral law confirms our hope that whatever it requires, but which we have not yet attained, we can "receive grace upon grace" until we actually possess the fullness of his promises.

5. How certainly does this process agree with the experience of all true believers! They cry out, "Oh, how I love your law! It is my meditation all day long." Daily, in the divine mirror of the moral law, they understand more and more of their own sinfulness. They see ever more clearly that they are still sinners in everything and that neither their hearts nor ways are right before God. Moment by moment, this awareness drives them to Christ. These experiences reveal to them the meaning of what has been written: "You shall make a rosette of pure gold, and engrave on it, like the engraving of a signet, 'Holy to the LORD.'. . . It shall be on Aaron's forehead" (a type of Christ our High Priest), "and Aaron shall take on himself any guilt incurred in the holy offering that the Israelites consecrate as their sacred donations" (our prayers and religious activities cannot atone for our sins); "it shall always be on his forehead, in order that they may find favor before the LORD."[10]

6. A single illustration will explain this point: The law says, "You shall not murder." Our Lord applied this commandment not only to outward acts but also to every unkind word or thought. The more I explore this perfect law, the more I sense how far I come short of it. And the more I feel my shortcomings, the more I feel my need of Christ's blood to atone for all my sin. All the more I feel my need of the Holy Spirit to purify my heart and make me "mature and complete, lacking in nothing."

7. Consequently, I cannot for one moment omit the law any more than I can omit Christ. I need the law to keep me *in* Christ as much as I ever needed the law to bring me *to* Christ. Otherwise, my "evil, unbelieving heart" would cause me to "turn away from the living God." Indeed, God and his law each send me to the other. The law sends me to Christ, and Christ sends me to the law. On the one hand, the height and depth of the law compel me to

fly to the love of God in Christ. On the other hand, the love of God in Christ endears the law to me. God's commandments become for me "more than gold, more than fine gold," because I know that they are gracious promises that my Lord will fulfill in me in his time.

8. Who are you to "speak evil against the law and judge the law"? Who are you to compare the law with sin, Satan, and death, thereby assigning them all to hell? The apostle James considered "speaking evil against the law and judging it" as an enormous act of evil. He knew no better way to increase the guilt of judging our sisters and brothers than by explaining that it pertains to this truth. Concerning you who judge, James said, "You are not a doer of the law but a judge"—a judge of what *God* has established to judge *you*! In doing so, you have put yourself in the judgment seat of Christ and spurned the standard by which he will judge the world! Become aware of the advantage Satan has gained over you! From now on, never think or speak disparagingly of the moral law, the blessed instrument of the grace of God. Much less should we ever dress the law in ridiculous garments so as to satirize it. Indeed, love and value the law, for the sake of him from whom the law came and to whom it leads. Next to the cross of Christ, let the moral law be your glory and joy. Give it due respect and declare its value to everyone.

9. Do not reject the moral law if you are completely convinced that it comes from God, that it is a copy of all his perfections, and that it "is holy and just and good" (especially for Christian believers). Rather, cling to it ever more strongly. Never let mercy and truth; love for God and others; and the virtues of humility, meekness, and purity forsake you. "Bind them around your neck, write them on the tablet of your heart." If you want to keep close to Christ, keep close to the law. Cling to it, and never let it go. Let it continually lead you to the atoning blood and confirm your hope, until "the just requirement of the law is fulfilled" in you and you are "filled with all the fullness of God."

10. If your Lord has already fulfilled his word by "writing it on your heart," then stand firm in the freedom that Christ has given you. You have been made free from Jewish ceremonies, from the

guilt of sin, and from the fear of hell. These freedoms do not constitute the entirety of Christian liberty; they are the least of the liberties that Christ has given us.

Of infinitely greater importance is the freedom we have from the power of sin, serving the devil, and transgressing against God. O, stand firm in this liberty. By comparison, all your other freedoms are not even worthy to be mentioned. Remain steadfast in loving God with all your heart and serving him with all your strength. (His service leads to perfect freedom.) Being faithful means to "live blamelessly according to all the commandments and regulations of the Lord." "Do not submit again to a yoke of slavery." I do not mean the bondage of the Jewish law or even slavery to the fear of hell. I trust that these enslavements are far from having any hold on you.

I am warning against becoming entangled again in the bondage of inward or outward sin. Hate sin far more than death or hell. Despise the act of sin far more than the punishment of sin. Beware of the bondage of pride, lust, anger, and every evil attitude, word, or deed: "Look to Jesus." In order to do so, increasingly "look into the perfect law, the law of liberty, and persevere in it." By using the law in this way, daily you will "grow in the grace and knowledge of our Lord and Savior Jesus Christ."

Notes

1. In this sermon's title, the term *original* means "source" or "origin."
2. W. Reginald Ward and Richard P. Heitzenrater, eds., *The Works of John Wesley,* Bicentennial ed., vols. 18-23, *Journals and Diaries* (Nashville: Abingdon Press, 1988–95), March 23, 1746, 20:117-18.
3. Thomas Jackson, *The Works of John Wesley,* 14 vols. (Grand Rapids, Mich.: Zondervan Publishing House, 1872), 10:276.
4. Thirty-nine Articles of the Church of England, art. 9.
5. See sermons "The Circumcision of the Heart," II, 3; "The Original, Nature, Properties, and Use of the Law," II, 5.
6. Marcus Tullius Cicero [106 B.C.–43 B.C.], *Cicero in Twenty-eight Volumes,* Loeb Classical Library London (W. Heinemann; Cambridge, Mass.: Harvard University Press, 1900). *On Moral Obligations,* I, 5.
7. Job 4:10, 37:19.
8. George Osborn, ed., *The Poetical Works of John and Charles Wesley,* 13 vols. (London: Wesleyan-Methodist Conference Office, 1868–72), Hymn on Galatians 3:22, 1:85. (Hereafter, *Poet. Wks.*)
9. Charles Wesley, "At Parting," *Poet. Wks.*, 2:222.
10. Exod. 20:13; Deut. 5:17.

Introduction to Sermon 35

THE LAW ESTABLISHED THROUGH FAITH

Discourse 1

John Wesley did not write this sermon as an abstract exercise in theology. Rather, he addresses a concrete issue that divided Christians in the eighteenth century—the place of the moral law in the Christian life. As noted in the introduction to the previous sermon, Wesley encountered Christians who rejected the moral law on the basis that they were saved by faith, not by works. This position had led a number of them into Antinomianism. They relied on faith as "the only essential" and neglected good works as a necessary outcome of faith.

The *Doctrinal Minutes* of John Wesley's 1744 Conference of Preachers clearly described the Antinomian doctrine that had infected a segment of the Christian community. Using the customary Question and Answer method, that conference issued the following explanation:

Q. What is Antinomianism?

A. The doctrine which makes void the law through faith.

Q. What are the main pillars hereof?

> A. (1) That Christ abolished the moral law. (2) That, therefore, Christians are not obliged to observe it. (3) That one branch of Christian liberty is liberty from obeying the commandments of God. (4) That it is bondage to do a thing because it is commanded, or forbear it because it is forbidden. (5) That a believer is not obliged to use the ordinances of God, or to do good works. (6) That a preacher ought not to exhort to good works; not unbelievers, because it is hurtful; not believers, because it is needless.[1]

This sermon and the following one are good examples of theological discourse that is both doctrinal and practical. These two messages explain and "enforce" the importance of the moral law for Christian believers.

In correspondence with England's Moravian community, Wesley identified a serious error that had crept into their religious societies. He wrote,

> You undervalue good works (especially works of outward mercy), never publicly insisting on the necessity of them, nor declaring their weight and excellency. Hence, when some of your brethren have spoken of them, they put them on a wrong foot; viz., "If you find yourself moved, if your heart is free to it, then reprove, exhort, relieve." By this means you wholly avoid the taking up your cross, in order to do good; and also substitute an uncertain, precarious inward motion, in the place of the plain written word. Nay, one of your members has said of good works in general, (whether works of piety or of charity), "A believer is no more obliged to do these works of the Law, than a subject of the King of England is obliged to obey the laws of the King of France."[2]

Wesley was deeply distressed over such blatant disregard for Christ's clear teaching about the moral law.

The present sermon points out that false teachers set aside the moral law by (1) neglecting to preach it to their followers and (2) preaching a kind of faith that cancels the need for holiness and obedience to Scripture's commands. The principal reason that Antinomian teachers disparaged good works was that they feared people would depend on them for their salvation. These well-meaning teachers mistakenly concluded that faith in Christ forever canceled the need to obey the moral law. They relied entirely on the "merits of Christ" and denied the importance of faithful obedience and disciplined living.

In this sermon Wesley again shows that the Bible does not cancel the moral law. Wesley was in full agreement with the teaching of the Church of England about the need for good works. One of the Church's Articles of Religion states,

> Albeit that Good Works, which are the fruits of Faith, and follow after Justification, can not put away our sins, and endure the severity of God's judgment; yet are they pleasing and acceptable to God in Christ, and do spring out necessarily of a true and lively Faith; insomuch that by them a lively Faith may be as evidently known as a tree discerned by the fruit.[3]

In this sermon, Wesley declares that the moral law will never end—even in heaven.

The moral law is important because it instructs Christians in the ways that God intends for them to live. Furthermore, obedience to the moral law is the way to become both holy and happy. Wesley explains that God provides Christians with adequate grace to enable them to follow these instructions for righteous living. He also clarifies the truth that the moral law does not lead to salvation, and he demolishes the notion that we can earn our way to heaven. Yet, he insists that God intends for the moral law to be the standard by which all true believers pattern their lives. He declares,

> Are you now a believer in Christ? Do you have a faith that conquers the world? How remarkable! Are you less zealous for your Master now than you were when you did not know him? Are you less diligent in fasting, prayer, hearing his Word, and in calling sinners to God? O repent! See and feel your lamentable loss! Remember from what place you have fallen! Lament and deplore your unfaithfulness! Become zealous. Repent, and do the works you did at first, for fear that you will overthrow the law by faith. Do not allow God to cut you off, and put you with the unfaithful.[4]

Sermon 35

THE LAW ESTABLISHED THROUGH FAITH

Discourse 1

Do we then overthrow the law by this faith? By no means! On the contrary, we uphold the law. (Romans 3:31)

1 In the beginning of his Epistle to the Romans, St. Paul lays down his general proposition that "the gospel is the power of God for salvation to everyone who has faith." The gospel is the powerful means by which God makes every believer a partaker of present and eternal salvation. Next, St. Paul explains that "there is no other name under heaven given among mortals by which we must be saved." He speaks particularly of salvation from the guilt of sin, which he commonly calls justification. By various arguments addressed to the Jews and to the heathens, the apostle extensively proves that everyone stands in need of justification and that no one can appeal to his or her own innocence.

Consequently, St. Paul concludes that "every mouth" (Jew and Gentile) "must be silenced" (from self-justification), "and the whole world must be held accountable to God." Saint Paul further contends that "'no human being will be justified in God's sight' by deeds prescribed by the law." Now, "apart from law . . . God has disclosed the righteousness of God through faith in Jesus Christ for all who believe. For there is no distinction, since all have sinned and fallen short of the glory of God; they are now justified by his grace as a gift, through the redemption that is in Christ Jesus."

The apostle continues: "God put forward Jesus as a sacrifice of atonement by his blood, effective through faith. He did this to show his righteousness, because in his divine forbearance he had passed over the sins previously committed . . . to prove at the present time that he himself is righteous and that he justifies the one who has faith in Jesus." Without any repeal of his justice, for the sake of Christ's atonement God shows us mercy. Saint Paul then declares the main thesis that he has proved: "A person is justified by faith apart from works prescribed by the law."

2. It was easy for St. Paul to anticipate a problem that, in fact, has surfaced in every generation. The problem is that some people conclude that because we are justified apart from the works of the law, we should, therefore, abolish the law. Today, people continue to hold that view. Saint Paul does not engage in a formal dispute about this issue. Instead, he merely contradicts this way of thinking: "Do we then overthrow the law by this faith? By no means! On the contrary, we uphold the law."

3. Some people strangely suppose that when St. Paul said, "A person is justified apart from works prescribed by the law," he was referring to the Jewish ceremonial law. The apostle's very words refute that notion. Did St. Paul establish the ceremonial law? Obviously, he did not. By faith he overthrew the ceremonial law, and he publicly declared that he did so. It was only the *moral* law about which he could truly say, "Do we then overthrow the law by faith? By no means! On the contrary, we uphold the law."

4. However, not everyone holds the same conviction as St. Paul, and many people disagree with him. In all ages of the church, even among those who bore the Christian name, numbers of people have contended that "the faith that was once for all entrusted to the saints" canceled the entire law. They have refused to retain the

moral law as well as the ceremonial law. They have favored, as it were, "hewing both in pieces before the Lord." They have vehemently maintained, "If you uphold the law, 'Christ shall be of no benefit to you. . . . you have fallen away from grace.'"

5. But is the zeal of these people an enlightened zeal? Have they understood the proper relationship between the law and faith? Have they considered the close connection between the two? Do they comprehend that if we destroy one we certainly destroy both? Do they realize that to abolish the moral law is really to abolish faith and the law together, setting aside both and leaving no proper means for bringing us to faith or "rekindling the gift of God within our souls"?

6. Therefore, there is an obligation laid upon all who desire to come to Christ or to "continue to live their lives in him whom they have received." They must give attention to how it is possible for us to "overthrow the law by faith." We must effectively guard ourselves against this danger. First, let us investigate the most common ways of "overthrowing the law by faith." Second, we will explore how we can follow St. Paul and uphold the law by faith. Third, we will examine the power of grace.

I. The Relationship Between Faith and the Moral Law

1. First, let us look into the most common ways of "overthrowing the law through faith." One way for a preacher immediately to overthrow the law is never to preach the law. Such neglect is the same as demolishing the revelation of God. This failure is especially destructive when it is intentional, and it is truly dangerous when one makes it a practice never to preach the law. Sometimes the phrase "a preacher of the law" is used as a term of reproach, as though it meant a little less than "an enemy of the gospel."

2. A failure to preach the law proceeds from the deepest ignorance of the nature, attributes, and use of the law. This failure proves that those who do not preach the moral law do not know Christ, or they are utter strangers to living faith, or at the very least they are only infants in Christ and "unskilled in the word of righteousness."

3. Their main defense is that, in their judgment, "preaching the gospel" means speaking of nothing except the sufferings and merits of Christ. To them, this message constitutes all that is necessary to fulfill the aim of the law.

However, we utterly repudiate this contention. It does not satisfy the very first aim of the law, which is to convince people of sin and awaken those that are still asleep on the brink of hell. Occasionally, there may be exceptions. The preaching of Christ, without the preaching of the law, may have awakened perhaps one in a thousand. Even so, this result is not common.

Ordinarily, God convicts sinners through the law. Preaching grace alone is not the means that God has established to bring conviction of sin. It was not the means that our Lord himself used to awaken sinners. We have no authority in Scripture to present grace apart from the law, and we have no basis for thinking that this kind of preaching will prove effective. In addition, human nature does not give us any support for believing that we can preach grace without preaching the law. Jesus said, "Those who are well have no need of a physician, but those who are sick." It is absurd, therefore, to offer a physician to those who are whole, or who at least imagine themselves to be whole.

You must first convince people that they are sick. Otherwise, they will not respond favorably to your efforts. It is equally absurd to offer Christ to those whose hearts have not yet been broken. Accurately speaking, it is "throwing pearls before swine." Doubtless, "they will trample them under foot." You can reasonably expect them to "turn and maul you."

4. Someone may ask, "Although there is no command in Scripture to offer Christ to careless sinners, yet are there not scriptural precedents for it?" I do not know any such instances, and I do not believe that you can produce one, either from the four Gospels or from the Acts of the Apostles. Neither can you find any example of this practice in any of the writings of the apostles.

5. Someone may object, "Does not the apostle Paul say in 1 Corinthians, 'We proclaim Christ crucified,' and in 2 Corinthians, 'We do not proclaim ourselves; we proclaim Jesus Christ as Lord'?" The objector may go on to say, "We agree to rest the case.

We will walk in St. Paul's steps and follow his example. Just preach what St. Paul preached and the dispute is at an end."

We answer that we are certain that, as the very chief of the apostles, St. Paul preached Christ in a perfect way. Yet, who preached the law more than St. Paul? It is clear that he did not think that preaching the gospel served the same end as preaching the law.

6. Saint Paul's first recorded sermon concludes with these words:

> By this Jesus everyone who believes is set free from all those sins from which you could not be freed by the law of Moses. Beware, therefore, that what the prophets said does not happen to you: "Look, you scoffers! Be amazed and perish, for in your days I am doing a work, a work that you will never believe, even if someone tells you." (Acts 13:39-41)

Now, it is apparent that St. Paul's entire sermon was "preaching the law" in the sense that you understand the term. Most of his hearers, if not all of them, were either Jews or devout converts to Judaism; therefore, presumably many of them, at least in some degree, were already convinced of their sins. First, St. Paul reminded them that they could be justified not by the law of Moses, but only by faith in Christ. Then, he severely threatened them with the judgments of God. In the strongest sense, Paul was "preaching the law."

7. In St. Paul's next sermon (to the heathen at Lystra), we do not find so much as the name of Christ. The entire aim of that sermon was that his hearers would "turn from worthless [idols] to the living God." Now acknowledge the truth. Do you think that if you had been there you could have preached much more effectively than St. Paul? I would not wonder if you thought that the apostle's preaching was so inappropriate that his being mistreated and stoned was God's fair judgment upon him for not preaching Christ!

8. At Philippi, the jailer rushed in and fell down trembling before Paul and Silas and cried, "Sirs, what must I do to be saved?" Saint Paul immediately said, "Believe on the Lord Jesus." In the case of one so deeply convinced of sin, who would not have replied the same way? By contrast, you find St. Paul speaking to the men of Athens in quite a different manner. He rebuked their

superstition, ignorance, and idolatry. Out of consideration for a future judgment and the resurrection from the dead, he strongly pressed them to repent. Likewise, when Felix sent for St. Paul in order to "hear him speak concerning faith in Christ," the apostle did not preach Christ in the way you advocate. To do so would probably have caused the governor to mock or to oppose and revile him. Saint Paul "discussed justice, self-control, and the coming judgment," until "Felix [as hardened as he was] became frightened." Go, and march in the steps of St. Paul. To the careless sinner, preach Christ by "discussing justice, self-control, and the coming judgment!"

9. If you say, "But in his Epistles, St. Paul preached Christ in a different manner," I answer that (1) in his epistles, he did not preach at all, in the sense of which we are now speaking. In his Epistles, the apostle, as it were, was speaking before a congregation of Christian believers. However, setting aside this thought, I answer that (2) St. Paul's Epistles are directed not to unbelievers, such as those about whom we are now speaking. Rather, he was addressing "the saints of God" in Rome, Corinth, Philippi, and other places. Without doubt, St. Paul would speak more about Christ to the saints than to those who were without God in the world. (3) The Epistles of St. Paul are full of the law, even those to the Romans and the Galatians. In these Epistles, the apostle preaches the law (as you call it) to believers as well as to unbelievers.

10. If you disdain the law, it is clear that you do not know what it is to "preach Christ" in the way that St. Paul preached him. Certainly, he considered himself to be preaching Christ to Felix and to those at Antioch, Lystra, and Athens. Every thoughtful person can see from St. Paul's example that he proclaimed the love of Christ to sinners while also declaring that Christ will come from heaven "in flaming fire, inflicting vengeance on those who do not know God and on those who do not obey the gospel of our Lord Jesus." To the apostle, this message is also "preaching Christ" in the full scriptural meaning of the words.

To preach Christ is to preach what he has revealed in the Old and New Testaments. You are preaching Christ when you say, "The wicked shall depart to Sheol and all the nations that forget

God," as much as when you say, "Here is the Lamb of God who takes away the sin of the world."

11. Consider also that "to preach Christ" is *to preach everything that Christ has spoken*. It is to proclaim all his promises, warnings, and commands—all that is written in the Bible. When you preach the whole biblical message, you will know how to preach Christ without overthrowing the law.

12. Someone may ask, "Does not the greatest blessing accompany those sermons in which we particularly preach the merits and sufferings of Christ?"

I answer that probably it is so. When we preach the merits and sufferings of Christ to a congregation of penitents or believers, great blessings will follow. Such sermons are suited to the spiritual condition of the congregations. At the very least, these sermons will usually bring the most comfort. The greatest comfort, though, is not always the greatest blessing. I may sometimes receive a far greater blessing through a sermon that cuts me to the heart and humbles me to dust. I would not receive that comfort, however, if I were to preach or to hear sermons only on the sufferings of Christ. By constant repetition, these sermons would lose their force and grow more and more flat and lifeless. Eventually, they would become a dull repetition of words lacking spirit, life, or virtue. Only to preach Christ apart from the moral law would, in the process of time, make meaningless both the law *and* the gospel.

II. Upholding the Moral Law by Faith

1. A second way to "overthrow the law by faith" is to teach that faith replaces the need for holiness. This teaching takes a thousand smaller paths, and many there are who walk them. Indeed, there are hardly any who completely escape this error. There are few people who are convinced that we are "saved by faith" and are not sooner or later, or more or less, lured into this detour.

2. People are drawn into this alternative route when they accept the notion that faith in Christ entirely sets aside the need to keep his law. Also, there are other beliefs that lure people off the true path of Christ: (1) Some people think that holiness is less

necessary now than it was before Christ came. (2) Others think that a lesser degree of holiness is required for Christian believers. (3) Still others (Antinomians) think that holiness is less important for Christians than for others.

Also, there are some whose understanding is correct in general, but they think that in special circumstances they can take more liberty than they could have taken before they trusted in Christ. Indeed, their use of the term "liberty" to mean "freedom from obedience or holiness" immediately shows that their judgment is perverted. Their misuse of Christian freedom reveals that they are guilty of what they imagine to be far from them—overthrowing the law by faith. They imagine that faith replaces holiness.

3. The first appeal of those who explicitly teach this view is that we are now under the covenant of grace, not works. They draw the conclusion that we are no longer under the requirement to perform the works of the law.

Who has *ever* been under the covenant of works? No one but Adam and Eve before the Fall. They were completely and appropriately under the covenant that required perfect, universal obedience as the only condition of acceptance. The covenant of works allowed no place for pardon, even for the smallest transgression.

No one else has ever been under the covenant of works, however—neither Jew nor Gentile, not before Christ or since Christ. All of Adam and Eve's progeny have been and are still under the covenant of grace. Through the merits of Christ, God accepts them on the basis of his free grace. This grace grants pardon to those who believe with a faith that works by love and that leads to obedience and holiness.

4. Therefore, as some might suppose, it is not the case that people once were more obligated to obey God or his law than they are now. This notion is one that you cannot support. Moreover, if we had been under the covenant of works, we would have been obliged to do the works of the law before God accepted us. Now, however, all good works (although as necessary as ever) do not *precede* our acceptance by God. Good works *follow it.* Consequently, the covenant of grace gives you no basis or encouragement to disregard any part of the law or ignore any degree of obedience or holiness.

5. Someone may ask, "Are we not 'justified by faith apart from works prescribed by the law'?" Undoubtedly, we are justified apart from the works of the ceremonial or moral law. Would to God that everyone was convinced of this fact! A proper understanding of this truth would prevent innumerable evils—particularly Antinomianism. As a rule, it is the Pharisees who produce the Antinomians. By taking an extreme position so obviously contrary to Scripture, they cause others to move to the opposite extreme. Pharisees who seek to be justified by works frighten others away from allowing *any* place for good works.

6. The truth lies between both extremes. Without question, we *are* "justified by faith." This truth is the cornerstone of the entire Christian structure. "We are justified without the works of the law" as a prior condition of justification. Nonetheless, good works are an immediate fruit of the faith by which we are justified. If good works do not follow our faith in all inward and outward holiness, it is clear that "our faith is futile and we are still in our sins." Therefore, the fact that we are justified by faith without works is no basis for overthrowing the law by this faith. Nor is this fact a basis for imagining that faith exempts us from any kind or degree of holiness.

7. Someone may ask, "Does not St. Paul specifically say, 'To one who without works trusts him who justifies the ungodly, such faith is reckoned as righteousness'? And does it not follow that for believers, faith takes the place of righteousness? If faith does substitute for righteousness or holiness, what need is there for anything more than faith?"

One must admit that this theory comes to the point and constitutes the primary pillar for Antinomianism. The theory, however, does not require a long or labored response. We acknowledge these truths: (1) God "justifies the ungodly" who until that moment are completely ungodly, full of all evil, and empty of all good. (2) God justifies "the one who is without works," the one who until that moment has none. Indeed, he or she cannot do good works, because a bad tree cannot bear good fruit. (3) God justifies us by faith alone, apart from any goodness or righteousness preceding our justification. (4) Faith is reckoned to us prior to our becoming righteous. That is, through the merits of Christ, God accepts those who believe as if they had already fulfilled all righteousness.

Now, how do these statements speak to the point that faith, apart from works, is all that we need? Saint Paul does not say either in our text or anywhere else that this faith is counted to us for *subsequent* righteousness. He does teach that there is no righ-teousness *before* faith. But where does he teach that there is no righteousness *after* faith? He does assert that holiness cannot *precede* justification, but he does not teach that holiness does not need to *follow* it. Saint Paul therefore provides no support for "overthrowing the law" on the assumption that faith replaces the need for holiness.

III. The Power of Grace in Keeping the Law

1. There is still another way of "overthrowing the law by faith." It is more prevalent than any of the former ways of doing so. Although we may not overthrow the law in principle, we overthrow it in practice when we live as though faith is intended to excuse us from holiness.

Saint Paul earnestly protects us from this error. In well-known words he declares, "What then? Should we sin because we are not under law but under grace? By no means." We need to consider this caution thoughtfully, because it is of supreme importance.

2. Being "under the law" may mean several things: (1) being obligated to keep the ceremonial laws; (2) being obligated to conform to the complete Mosaic tradition; (3) being obligated to keep the entire moral law as the condition of our acceptance with God; or (4) being under the wrath and curse of God, the sentence of eternal death, a sense of guilt and condemnation, and being full of dismay and slavish fear.

3. A believer is not free from God's law, but is under Christ's law. Yet from the moment we believe, in any of the preceding senses, we are not "under the law." On the contrary, believers are "under grace," which is a more benevolent, gracious administration. Christians are no longer under the ceremonial law or the civil law of Moses. They are not even obligated to keep the moral law as the condition of God's acceptance. Believers are delivered from

the wrath and curse of God and from all sense of guilt and condemnation. They are free from all the fear and dread of death and hell, by which "all their lives they were held in slavery by the fear of death." Believers now perform a willing and universal obedience, which they could not do while "under the law." They do not obey from the motive of fear, but from a nobler principle, which is the grace of God ruling in their hearts and causing them to perform all their works in love.

4. What conclusion should we draw? Is the evangelical principle of action less compelling than the legal? Shall we be less obedient to God from the motive of filial love than we were from that of slavish fear? One hopes that the freedom of grace does not cause us to neglect the law. It is good if this practical Antinomianism—this overlooked way of "overthrowing the law by faith"—does not infect thousands of believers.

Has it not infected you? Examine yourself honestly and carefully. Do you not do things now that you dared not do when you were "under the law" or, as we commonly call it, when you were "under conviction" for sin? For instance, when you were under the law, you dared not overindulge yourself in food. You took just what you needed, and you ate the least expensive foods. Do you not allow yourself more liberty now? Do you not indulge yourself a little more than you did? O, beware that you do not "continue in sin in order that grace may abound."

5. When you were under conviction for sin, you dared not indulge the lust of the eye in any degree. You would not do anything, great or small, merely to gratify your curiosity. Whether in furniture or clothing, you focused only on purity and necessities, or at most very moderate conveniences. Excesses and elaborate embellishments of any kind, as well as fashionable elegance, were frightful and odious to you.

Is your attitude still the same? Is your conscience as sensitive now in these things as it was when you were still under the law? Do you still follow the same rule regarding both your furniture and your apparel, trampling under foot all decorative display, overabundance, useless belongings, and all things that are only ornamental, however fashionable they may be? Rather, have you not resumed what you had once laid aside and what you formerly could not use without injuring your conscience? Have you become used to saying, "I am no longer as meticulous as once I was"? I would to God that you were! If you were truly under grace you would not say, "I sin because I am not under the law, but under grace."

6. Also, you were once careful not to praise others, or still more to allow anyone to praise you. Receiving personal praise wounded your heart. You could not endure it. You sought "the glory that comes from the one who alone is God." You could not endure any kind of talk that was "useful for building up." You abhorred, hated, and dreaded all careless talk and worthless discourse. You were deeply conscious of the value of every precious fleeting moment of time. Also, you dreaded and abhorred wasteful spending; you valued your money only less than your time. Once, you shuddered for fear that you would be found an unfaithful steward of money.

Now today, do you still regard adulation as a deadly poison that you can give or receive only at the peril of your soul? Do you still dread and abhor all conversation that is not useful for building up yourself and others? Do you work to make the most of every moment, so that it will not pass without leaving you better than it found you? Regarding the value of both money and time, are you not less careful than formerly? Do you now permit yourself to spend money and time in ways that once you would not? What a pity! How the things that should have benefited your well-being have proved to become for you a cause of stumbling! How you have sinned because you were not under the law, but under grace!

7. God forbid that you should any longer continue in these ways to "pervert the grace of our God into licentiousness"! O bear in mind what clear and strong a conviction you once had concerning all these matters! At one time, you were completely comfortable that your convictions came from God. The world told you that you were deluded, but you knew that your beliefs came from the word of God. At that time you were not too careful in these matters, but now you are not careful enough. God kept you long in that painful school so that you might more perfectly learn those great lessons.

Now, have you already forgotten them? O, call them to memory before it is too late. Have you endured so many things for nothing? I trust that your labors have not been wasted. Now, use the conviction of sin without the former pain of guilt. Practice the lesson without the rod of discipline. Do not allow the mercy of God to count for less with you now than his fiery indignation formerly did. Is love a less powerful motive than fear? If not, let this rule constantly guide you: "Now that I am under grace, I will do nothing that I dared not to do when I was under the law."

8. I cannot conclude this point without entreating you also to examine yourself concerning sins of omission. Now that you are "under grace," are you as free from these sins as you were when you were "under the law"? How diligent you were then in listening to the word of God! Did you neglect any opportunity? Did you not consider it day and night? Would you have been deterred from listening to God's word by a small hindrance, a little business, a visitor, a slight ailment, a soft bed, or a dark or cold morning? Then, did you not fast often or practice abstinence to the best of your ability? While you were dangling over the mouth of hell, were you not often in prayer (as cold and drowsy as you were)? Without holding back, did you not call out for the God you did not yet know? Did you not boldly defend God's cause and reprove sinners? Did you not confess God's truth before an adulterous generation?

Are you now a believer in Christ? Do you have a faith that conquers the world? How remarkable! Are you less zealous for your Master now than you were when you did not know him? Are you less diligent in fasting, prayer, hearing his Word, and calling sinners to God? O repent! See and feel your lamentable loss! Remember from what place you have fallen! Lament and deplore your unfaithfulness! Become zealous. "Repent, and do the works you did at first," for fear that you will "overthrow the law by faith." Do not allow God to cut you off and "put you with the unfaithful."

Notes

1. Thomas Jackson, ed., Minutes of Some Late Conversations Between the Rev. Mr. Wesleys and Others, *Wesley's Works*, 8:278.

2. Nehemiah Curnock, ed., *The Journal of the Rev. John Wesley, A.M.*, 8 vols. (London: Epworth Press, 1938), 2:495.

3. Thirty-nine Articles of the Church of England, Art. 12.

4. Outler, *Wesley's Sermons*, 2:32.

Introduction to Sermon 36

THE LAW ESTABLISHED THROUGH FAITH

Discourse 2

This sermon continues the previous discourse, and it completes a cluster of three sermons dealing with the place of the law in the Christian life. Wesley begins this sermon by pointing out areas of agreement with the Antinomians. With them, he affirms that Christians are under the covenant of grace, not works. He also agrees that Jesus Christ is the sole source of our salvation. Wesley upholds the corollary truth that people are justified by faith apart from works prescribed by the law. Yet he restates and further articulates his conviction that we undermine the moral law if we live as though the purpose of faith is to exempt us from obeying it. In short, biblical holiness is impossible without obedience to the moral law.

As stated earlier, some of Wesley's Moravian friends had drifted toward Antinomianism. Their stress on grace and Christ's imputed righteousness caused them to disregard the moral law, or even to speak against it. In 1741, Wesley sent a letter to them in which he said,

> Above all permit *me,* even me, to press upon you, with all earnestness of love. First, with regard to your doctrine, that ye purge out from among you the leaven of *antinomianism,* wherewith you are

> so deeply infected, and no longer "make void the law through faith."[1]

In this sermon and the previous one, Wesley builds on Romans 3:31 to make the case that, far from *undermining* the moral law, faith *establishes* it.

The point of this discourse is that Christians are no longer under the Old Testament *ceremonial* law, but they will always be under the *moral* law. First, Wesley states that Christians uphold the law by "preaching, teaching, explaining, and applying every part of it in the same way that Christ our great teacher did while he was on the earth." Even if the Antinomians refused to preach the moral law, Wesley reminds us that Jesus and the apostles *did* preach and teach it. It is our duty to preach everything that Christ revealed, including his moral and ethical commands.

Second, Wesley declares that we uphold the moral law when we preach faith in Christ in a way that sustains the need to obey the law. Indeed, when faithful ministers preach the law, it produces holiness and good works. Such is the purpose of the moral law. Faith is not meant to replace the law of love, but to establish it.

Finally, Wesley explains that the moral law must be confirmed in the heart by faith. Faith goes beyond fulfilling the external aspects of the law; faith also works inwardly to purify the heart from evil inclinations. As well, genuine faith transforms the affections so that one loves what God loves and despises what God despises. Summarizing the meaning of the text of this sermon, Wesley insists, "We establish the law—Both the authority, purity, and the end of it; by defending that which the law attests: by pointing out Christ, the end of it, and by showing how it may be fulfilled in its purity."[2]

Sermon 36

THE LAW ESTABLISHED THROUGH FAITH

Discourse 2

Do we then overthrow the law by this faith? By no means! On the contrary, we uphold the law. (Romans 3:31)

1 The preceding sermon explained the most common ways of "overthrowing the law by faith." Let us review what I said. First, we invalidate the law by failing to preach it at all. With a single stroke, this neglect effectively destroys the law—which we do by claiming that we are "preaching Christ" and magnifying the gospel. In truth, however, we destroy both the law and the gospel when we fail to preach it.

Second, we nullify the law by teaching (directly or indirectly) that faith replaces the need for holiness, or that the full measure of holiness is not as necessary for those who trust Christ as it was for those who lived prior to his coming into the world. This theory holds that, because we now believe in Christ, holiness is not as necessary as it was before we believed in him! Another version of this notion is that Christian liberty brings freedom from any kind or degree of holiness. This assumption states several important truths—and then perverts them.

- we are now under the covenant of grace and not of works
- "a person is justified by faith apart from works prescribed by the law"
- "to one who without works trusts him who justifies the ungodly, such faith is reckoned as righteousness"

Third, if not in principle then in practice, we undermine the law by living or acting as though the purpose of faith is to exempt us from holiness. We allow ourselves to sin, claiming that "we are not under law but under grace." Now, it is important for us to examine how we can follow a better pattern and be able to say with St. Paul: "Do we then overthrow the law by this faith? By no means! On the contrary, we uphold the law."

2. Most certainly, we do not uphold the old ceremonial law. That law, of course, has been abolished forever. And even less so do we uphold the entire Mosaic dispensation. We know that our Lord has "nailed it to the cross." We certainly do not uphold the moral law if we believe that we have met the condition for our justification by fulfilling it. It is tragic that many people understand the moral law in this light. If it were true that we had to fulfill the moral law to be justified, then "no human being could ever be justified." Now that we have made this disclaimer about the moral law, we do uphold the moral law in the way taught by St. Paul.

I. Upholding the Moral Law

1. First of all, we "uphold the law" by preaching, teaching, explaining, and applying every part of it in the same way that Christ our great teacher did when he was on the earth. We uphold the moral law by following St. Peter's advice, "Whoever speaks must do so as one speaking the very words of God." We uphold the law by speaking as the ancient holy messengers—inspired by the Holy Spirit—spoke and wrote for our instruction. We endeavor to speak as the apostles of our blessed Lord who spoke under the

direction of the same Spirit. We uphold the law whenever we speak in the Lord's name, withholding nothing from those who listen. Without any limitation or reserve, we declare God's entire counsel to them.

In order more effectively to uphold the law, we will use very clear words. We do not peddle God's word like so many, who as clever merchants dishonestly tamper with their bad wines. We do not market, mix, contaminate, or weaken our message to suit it to the tastes of our hearers. "We refuse to practice cunning or to falsify God's word; but by the open statement of the truth we commend ourselves to the conscience of everyone in the sight of God."

2. Just as our blessed Lord and his apostles preached God's word, therefore, by our doctrine we uphold the law when we openly proclaim it to everyone in its completeness. We uphold the law when we declare it in its full "breadth and length and height and depth." We disclose every part of it—all its commandments in their complete, accurate, and spiritual sense. The law of God pertains to the outward actions that we should or should not do. God's law also concerns the inner disposition, thoughts, desires, and intents of the heart.

3. We diligently proclaim God's message because it is of the deepest significance. If the tree is bad, it will bear bad fruit; and if our hearts are not right before God, all our words and deeds will be evil. As important as words and deeds are, some people often misunderstand their significance, or else fail to ponder them. Most people are ignorant of God's law in its full spiritual meaning. To them, it is a "mystery that has been hidden throughout the ages and generations."

In the heathen world, God's law was completely hidden. With all their boasted wisdom, the heathen did not "find out the deep things of God," neither did they understand the letter or the spirit of his law. "They became futile in their thinking, and their senseless minds were darkened. Claiming to be wise, they became fools."

Moreover, the spiritual meaning of God's moral law was almost equally hidden from the majority of the Jewish nation. The Jews were quick to say of others, "The crowds, which do not know the law—they are accursed." Yet, in making this judgment about others, they pronounced condemnation upon themselves. They were under the same curse and shameful ignorance.

Consider our Lord's repeated rebuke of the wisest Jewish leaders for their glaring misinterpretations of God's law. Observe the presumption almost universally accepted among them that they needed only to "tithe mint, dill, and cumin." They thought that outward scrupulousness would atone for their lack of inner holiness and their complete neglect of "justice, mercy, and faith."

Worst of all, the Jewish leaders in the time of Jesus failed to love God. The spiritual meaning of the law was so completely hidden from the wisest of them that one of their most eminent rabbis gave the following commentary on these words of the psalmist: "If I had cherished iniquity in my heart, the Lord would not have listened." The scribe said, "If iniquity is only in my heart and I do not commit outward wickedness, the Lord will not regard the evil in the heart, and he will not punish me unless I commit the outward act!"[3]

4. It is a pity that the inward spiritual meaning of God's moral law is hidden not only from Jews and heathen, but also from what is called the Christian world. At least, it is unknown to the large majority of its citizens. The spiritual meaning of God's commandments remains a mystery to them. This fact can be observed in those countries that are covered with the darkness and ignorance of the medieval church. It is also certain that presently the far greater part of those who are called "Reformed Christians" are complete strangers to the purity and spirituality of Christ's law.

5. To this day, there are scribes and Pharisees who have the form but not the power of religion. They are generally wise in their own eyes and righteous in their own conceitedness. They take offense when they hear what Christ says, and they are deeply insulted when we speak about the religion of the heart. They become particularly upset when we explain that without religion of the heart, even giving away all our possessions has no benefit.

Even if others are offended, we must speak the truth as it is in Jesus. Whether they will listen or not, our duty is to save our own souls. We are called to proclaim everything that appears in the

Bible, "not to please mortals, but to please God." We must make known the promises and warnings of God that we find in Scripture.

At the same time that we proclaim all the blessings and privileges that God has prepared for his children, we are called also to "teach everything that he has said to us." And we know that everything that God has spoken has its benefit. The word of God awakens those who sleep, instructs the ignorant, and comforts the fainthearted, while building up and perfecting the saints. We know that "all scripture is inspired by God and is useful for teaching, for reproof, for correction, and for training in righteousness, so that everyone who belongs to God may be proficient, equipped for every good work."

6. It is our duty to "preach Christ" by proclaiming everything he has revealed. Without apology and indeed with a particular blessing from God, we can declare the love of our Lord Jesus Christ. We can speak in a more certain manner about "the Lord [who is] our righteousness." We should speak freely about the grace of God, who "was in Christ, reconciling the world to himself." At appropriate opportunities, we should dwell upon the praise of God who bore the iniquities of us all, was "wounded for our transgressions," "bruised for our iniquities," and by whose sufferings we can be healed.

Still, however, we would not be "preaching Christ" according to his word if we confined ourselves only to this truth. We cannot be innocent before God unless we proclaim Christ in *all* his offices. As workers who have no need to be ashamed, we are to preach Christ as our "high priest chosen from among mortals and put in charge of things pertaining to God."

In his office of *priest*, Christ "reconciled us to God by his blood" and "always lives to make intercession for us."

In the office of *prophet*, Christ "became for us wisdom from God" who by his word and his Spirit "is with us always," "guiding us into all the truth."

And in his office of *king*, forever he gives laws to all those whom he has bought with his blood. Furthermore, he restores to the image of God those whom he first reinstates in his favor. He reigns in all believing hearts until he "makes all things subject to himself," utterly casts out all sin, and "brings in everlasting righteousness."

II. Faith as the Means of Reestablishing Love

1. Second, we uphold the law when we preach faith in Christ—not faith replacing holiness, but producing holiness in all its fullness. We preach the negative and positive aspects of holiness—complete holiness of heart and life.

To this end, we constantly declare that Christian faith (the faith that God gives to his elect) remains only the servant of love. All those who do not want to "overthrow the law by faith" should deeply ponder this truth. As glorious and important as faith is, it is not the purpose of the law. God has given this honor to love alone. Love is the goal of all the commandments of God. From the beginning of the world to the consummation of all things, love is the only objective of every dispensation of God. Love will endure when heaven and earth flee away, because "love never ends."

Faith will completely cease. It will be swallowed up in sight, in the everlasting vision of God. However, love never ends.

> Its nature and its office still the same,
> Lasting its lamp and unconsumed its flame,
> In deathless triumph shall forever live,
> And endless good diffuse, and endless praise receive.[4]

2. Wonderful things are spoken of faith. And whoever has faith can properly say with St. Paul, "Thanks be to God for his indescribable gift!" Even so, faith loses all its prominence when compared to love. What St. Paul says about the gospel's superiority to the law can with utter correctness be said of the superior glory of love over faith: "Indeed, what once had glory has lost its glory because of the greater glory; for if what was set aside came through glory, much more has the permanent come in glory!" Before faith passes away, all its present glory arises from its service to love. Faith is the important but temporary means that God has ordained to promote the eternal goal of love.

3. Do not exaggerate faith to such proportions that it eclipses everything else. To do so is completely to misunderstand the nature of faith, as though it replaces love. We must consider that love will exist after faith, just as love existed long before faith. The

angels, from the moment of their creation, beheld the face of their Father who is in heaven. They had no cause for faith (as we commonly use the term) as "the conviction of things not seen." Neither did the angels need faith in its more particular meaning—faith in the blood of Jesus. They did not need this kind of faith because Jesus did not assume the nature of angels. Rather, he became a descendant of Abraham.

Therefore, before the foundation of the world, there was no need for faith, either in a general or particular sense. However there *was* a place for love. Love existed from eternity; it existed in God, the great ocean of love. And, from the moment of their creation, all the children of God have had a place for love. They received from their gracious Creator both their existence and the capacity to love.

4. It is not certain that faith, even in a general sense, had any place in paradise (even though many people have skillfully and impressively commented on this possibility). From the short and inconclusive account we have in the Bible, it is highly probable that Adam, before he rebelled against God, walked with him by sight and not by faith.

> For then their reason's eye was strong and clear,
> And (as an eagle can behold the sun)
> Could have approached th' Eternal Light as near
> As th' intellectual angels could have done.[5]

Then, Adam was able to talk with God face-to-face. Now, we cannot look upon his face and live. Consequently, Adam had no need for faith, because its purpose is to supply what we cannot see.

5. It is absolutely certain that faith in its special sense (faith in the blood of Christ) had no place in the time of Adam and Eve. This kind of faith necessarily presupposes sin and the wrath of God declared against the sinner. Without these conditions, there is no requirement for an atonement for sin to bring about the sinner's reconciliation with God. Accordingly, because there was no need of an atonement before the Fall of Adam and Eve, there was no occasion for faith in Christ's atonement. Humankind was then unstained by sin; Adam and Eve were holy as God is holy. Love then filled their hearts and reigned in them without a rival.

It was only when love was lost by sin that faith was added. Faith was given not for its own sake or with any intention that it would continue any longer than it was needed to serve the purpose for which God ordained it. This purpose was to restore mortals to the love from which they had fallen. Therefore, after the Fall, God added faith as "the conviction of things not seen." Prior to the Fall, this kind of faith was completely unnecessary. Confidence in Christ's redeeming love could not possibly have any place until God made the promise that the offspring of the woman would strike the serpent's head.

6. God originally intended that faith would reestablish the law of love. When we speak of faith in this way, we are not undervaluing it or taking away its due praise. On the contrary, we are explaining its real worth, elevating it to its proper position, and giving it the precise place that God's wisdom gave it in the beginning. Faith is the main means of restoring the holy love in which God originally created humankind.

It follows that although faith has no *independent* value (neither do any of the means of grace), yet faith is an indescribable blessing to humankind. Its value is that it leads to the goal of reestablishing the law of love in our hearts. In the present state of things, faith is the only means under heaven for bringing about love.

III. A Faith That Upholds the Law

1. Third, this consideration logically brings us to think about the most important way of "upholding the law" in our own hearts and lives. Indeed, without God's working in our hearts, what good is everything else? We might try to uphold the law by our doctrine or by preaching the law in its entirety and explaining and applying every part of it. We might unfold its most spiritual meaning and proclaim the secrets of God's kingdom. We might preach Christ in all his offices and declare that faith in Christ opens all the treasures of his love. At the same time, though, if the law we preach is not established in our hearts, we would be of no more value before God than "a noisy gong or a clanging cymbal." All our preaching would never benefit us; indeed, it would only multiply our damnation.

2. Accordingly, the main point we will now consider is how we can uphold the law in our own hearts so that it will have its full effect in our lives. We can uphold the law only by faith.

It is faith alone that effectively accomplishes this end. And we learn this truth by experience. As long as we walk by faith and not by sight, we proceed rapidly in the way of holiness. More and more, "we are crucified to the world and the world is crucified to us," only as "we look not at what can be seen but at what cannot be seen." Permit the eye of your soul to be steadily fixed not on the things that are temporary, but on those things that are eternal. More and more, "set your minds on things that are above, not on things that are on earth." In general, faith is the most direct and effective means of promoting righteousness and true holiness. Faith is what establishes God's holy and spiritual law in the hearts of those who believe.

3. Even more effectively, faith in a pardoning God establishes his law in our hearts. There is no motivation that more powerfully inclines us to love God than our awareness of his love for us in Christ. Nothing can inspire us to give our hearts to Christ like the acute awareness that he gave himself for us. Then, the power of our grateful love for God gives rise to our love for others as well. We cannot avoid loving our neighbor if we truly trust in the love with which God has loved us. This love for others that "does no wrong to a neighbor" comes from faith in, and love for, God.

Consequently, as St. Paul stated, "Love is the fulfilling of the law," in the sense of what the law says we should *not* do. In the following words, the apostle summed up the negative sense of the law of love:

> The commandments, "You shall not commit adultery; You shall not murder; You shall not steal; You shall not covet"; and any other commandment, are summed up in this word, "Love your neighbor as yourself." Love does no wrong to a neighbor; therefore, love is the fulfilling of the law. (Rom. 13:9, 10)

Neither is love content with doing no harm to our neighbor. On the positive side, love constantly induces us to do good. "Whenever we have an opportunity, let us work for the good of all." Love is, therefore, the fulfilling of both the positive and the negative laws of God.

4. Faith does more than fulfill the *external* negative and positive aspects of the law. Faith also works *inwardly*. Faith working by love purifies the heart and cleanses it from all evil affections. Saint John said, "All who have this hope purify themselves, just as he is pure." We are to purify ourselves of every earthly, fleshly desire and from all evil and inordinate affections. We are to purify ourselves of all carnality—yes, from "the mind that is set on the flesh which is hostile to God." At the same time, if faith working by love reaches its goal, it fills us with all goodness, righteousness, and truth. It brings all heaven into the soul and causes us to "walk in the light, even as God is in the light."

5. In this way, let us strive to uphold the law within ourselves. Let us not sin "because we are under grace." Rather, let us use all the power we receive through grace "to fulfill all righteousness." Remembering what light we received from God while his Spirit was convincing us of our sin, let us be careful not to extinguish that light. Let us hold fast to what we had then attained. Let nothing persuade us to build again what we once destroyed. Do not resume doing anything, large or small, that you once clearly saw was not for the glory of God or for the benefit of your own soul. Do not neglect anything minor or major that once you could not neglect without a stab of your conscience.

In order to expand, enlarge, and perfect the light we formerly possessed, let us now add the light of faith. By a greater tenderness of conscience and a more acute sense of sin, we confirm the former gift of God by a deeper understanding of the things that he revealed to us. Walking fearlessly and joyfully, with a clear, steady sight of eternal things, we will regard earthly pleasure, wealth, and praise as only bubbles upon the water. They count for nothing of significance. They are not desirable or deserving of any calculated thought. Rather, let us only look upon what is "behind the curtain," "where Christ is, seated at the right hand of God."

6. Are you able to say to God, "You are merciful toward my iniquities, and you remember my sins no more"? If so, from now on, determine to run away from sin, as you would flee from a

serpent. Now, how terribly wicked sin appears to you! How horrendous beyond expression! On the other hand, in how pleasant a light do you now see the holy and perfect will of God! From now on, therefore, strive so that God's purposes will be fulfilled *in* you, *by* you, and *through* you.

Stay awake, and pray that you will not sin and that you will see and avoid the slightest transgression of God's law. When the sun shines into a dark place, you see the specks that once you could not see. Likewise, you see the sins that you could not see before the sun of righteousness began to shine in your heart. Now, strive diligently in every respect to walk in the light you have received.

Ardently desire daily to receive more light, more of the knowledge and love of God, more of the Spirit of Christ, more of his life, and more of the power of his resurrection. Use all the knowledge, love, life, and power that you have already received. In this way, you will steadily go on from faith to faith. Daily, you will increase in holy love, until faith is swallowed up in sight, and the law of love will be established eternally.

Notes

1. Ward and Heitzenrater, *Wesley's Journal and Diaries,* 19:224.

2. *Explanatory Notes upon the New Testament,* Rom. 3:31.

3. Quoted in Matthew Henry [1662–1714], *A Commentary on the Holy Bible,* 6 vols. (New York: Funk, n.d.), commentary on Ps. 66:18.

4. Matthew Prior [1664–1721], "Charity," *A Collection of Moral and Sacred Poems from the Most Celebrated English Authors,* 3 vols. (Bristol: Printed and sold by Felix Farley, 1744), 1:87-89.

5. Sir John Davies [1559–1626], *The Original, Nature, and Immortality of the Soul: A Poem. With an Introduction Concerning Human Knowledge,* 3rd ed. (London: Printed for W. Mears and J. Browne, 1715), stanza 3, 1:15.

Introduction to Sermon 37

THE NATURE OF ENTHUSIASM

This sermon responds to numerous charges that the Methodists were infected with *enthusiasm* and that they were a danger to church and society. Today, the word *enthusiasm* usually suggests the desirable quality of inspired fervor. In the eighteenth century, however, the word *enthusiasm* meant *fanaticism,* ordinarily with regard to religion. Samuel Johnson's *Dictionary of the English Language* (1773 edition) offered several definitions of enthusiasm:

> 1. A vain belief of private revelation; a vain confidence of divine favour or communication. 2. Heat of imagination; violence of passion; confidence of opinion. 3. Elevation of fancy; exaltation of ideas.[1]

In 1744, the Rev. Thomas Church defined enthusiasm as "a false persuasion of an extraordinary divine assistance, which leads men on to such conduct as is only to be justified by the supposition of such assistance. An enthusiast is then sincere, but mistaken. His intentions are good, but his actions most abominable."[2]

Bishop Joseph Butler's often-quoted statement to John Wesley is well known: "Mr. Wesley, I will deal plainly with you. I once thought you and Mr. Whitefield well-meaning men: But I cannot think so now; for I have heard more of you; matters of fact, Sir." And Mr. Whitefield says in his Journal, "'There are promises still to be fulfilled in me.' Sir, the pretending to extraordinary revelations and gifts of the Holy Ghost is a horrid thing, a very horrid thing!"[3] Wesley replied, "My Lord, for what Mr. Whitefield says, Mr. Whitefield, and not I, is accountable. I pretend to no extraordinary revelations or gifts of the Holy Ghost; none but what every Christian may receive, and ought to expect and pray for."

Eighteenth-century fears of enthusiasm are understandable. Throughout English religious history, numerous cases of religious fanaticism had erupted. For example, during the Commonwealth period (1642–58), the Puritan Oliver Cromwell dissolved Parliament; and in the name of true religion, his followers beheaded King Charles I. The spectacle of the extremist seventeenth-century Ranters, Levellers, Diggers, and Fifth Monarchy Men had made the Church and the people wary of all species of religious enthusiasm. Wesley himself defined these kinds of enthusiasts as "religious madmen, those that fancy themselves inspired."[4]

Because the Methodists operated mostly outside the established Church, claimed the witness of the Holy Spirit, and used atypical methods (for instance, field preaching, lay preachers, extempore prayers, and class meetings), many people charged them with enthusiasm. Even so, Wesley denied that the Methodists were fanatics. In this sermon, he defines enthusiasm as expecting the end without using the proper means. Most definitely, that definition did not fit the Methodists. They were schooled in using the means of grace and in living disciplined lives. Wesley was methodical in his religious devotion, and the Methodist societies expected their members diligently to use the ordinances prescribed by Scripture. Wesley wrote in his journal, "I dislike something that has the appearance of *enthusiasm:* overvaluing *feelings* and *inward impressions;* mistaking the mere work of *imagination* for the voice of the Spirit; expecting the end without the means; and undervaluing *reason, knowledge*, and *wisdom,* in general."[5] On another occasion, Wesley wrote,

> I talked largely with a pious woman, whom I could not well understand. I could not doubt of her being quite sincere, nay, and much

> devoted to God: But she had fallen among some well-meaning enthusiasts, who taught her so to attend to the inward voice, as to quit the society, the preaching, the Lord's Supper, and almost all outward means. I find no persons harder to deal with than these. One knows not how to advise them. They must not act contrary to their conscience, though it be an erroneous one. And who can convince them that it is erroneous? None but the Almighty.[6]

This sermon is Wesley's public response to charges that the Methodists were enthusiasts. Calmly and constructively, he lays out his views. First, he agrees with his critics that enthusiasm is "a false persuasion of an extraordinary divine assistance." Then, he argues that the worst kinds of enthusiasts are those who are convinced they are Christians when they are not. He concludes that the kinds of enthusiasts to be reprimanded are the unenlightened and closed-minded zealots who assume that they are Christians because of their good works or because their feelings and intuitions give them false impressions. They conclude that they are true Christians because there are so many others like them. Wesley closes this sermon by saying, "Expect daily growth in that pure and holy religion which the world always did and always will call enthusiasm. Real religion, by which all are saved from actual enthusiasm and nominal Christianity, is 'the power of God and the wisdom of God.' It is the glorious image of the Most High."

Sermon 37

THE NATURE OF ENTHUSIASM

While [Paul] was making this defense, Festus exclaimed, "You are out of your mind, Paul!" *(Acts 26:24)*

1 All those in the world who do not know God say that those who follow St. Paul, as he followed Christ, are out of their minds. It is true that there is a type of religion (going by the name of Christianity) that can be practiced without any such reproach. This brand of religion is commonly accepted as a religion of "common sense." It is a religion of form, consisting of a series of outward duties performed in a proper, routine way. You can even add orthodoxy to this form of religion. It is a system of correct doctrines, and it has a level of morality that is also practiced by the heathen.

All the while, not many people will bring against those who practice this kind of Christianity the charge: "Much religion is driving you insane." But if you strive for the religion of the heart and talk about "righteousness and peace and joy in the Holy Spirit," it will not be long before others pass this judgment on you. They will say, "You are out of your mind."

2. People of the world obviously intend no compliment when they accuse you of lunacy. For once, they mean what they say.

They sincerely believe and declare that all people are out of their minds who say that "God's love has been poured into their hearts through the Holy Spirit that has been given to them." If you are indeed alive to God and dead to all things here on earth, and if you continually see "him who is invisible" and accordingly walk by faith and not by sight, the world will judge you. The people of the world regard it to be a clear case, beyond dispute, that too much religion is driving you insane.

3. It is easy to see that the world regards as madness the Christians' complete contempt for transient things, their steady pursuit of eternal things, their divine conviction of things not seen, and their rejoicing in God's favor. The world accounts as foolish those who testify to a holy love for God, and claim the witness of the Holy Spirit to their spirits that they are the children of God. In truth, the world disregards the entire spirit, life, and power of the religion of Jesus Christ.

4. The people of the world, however, will concede that in other respects, Christians act and talk like people of good sense. In many things Christians are regarded as reasonable people. It is only in religious matters that the world regards Christians to be muddled in the head. The world, therefore, concludes that Christians suffer only from a particular kind of insanity. Consequently, people of the world agree that the lunacy under which Christians labor is of a specific nature. Accordingly, the world is in the habit of calling this alleged insanity by a special name—*enthusiasm*.

5. This term is used very frequently, and it is hardly ever missing from the conversation of some people. Yet, even those people who use the term the most very rarely comprehend it. Therefore, serious people who wish to understand what they speak or hear may not object if I endeavor to explain this term and clarify the meaning of *enthusiasm*. My explanation may be an encouragement to those who are *unjustly* charged with enthusiasm. And my description may possibly be useful to some people who are *justly* charged with it (at least to those who might become enthusiasts if they are not counseled against it).

6. As to the word itself, *enthusiasm* is generally recognized to be of Greek extraction. But no one has yet been able to explain

its origin. Some have tried to trace the term to two Greek words that mean *in God*, because all enthusiasm has reference to him. But this explanation is quite forced. There is only a slight similarity between the two Greek words and the word derived from them.

Others would derive *enthusiasm* from a Greek term meaning *in sacrifice*, because many of the ancient enthusiasts became agitated in the most violent manner during the time of sacrifice. Perhaps *enthusiasm* is an imaginary word, invented from the clamor made by those who are emotionally affected.

7. It is likely that one reason this undignified word has been retained in so many languages is that people cannot agree on its origin or intent. Therefore, they adopted the Greek word because they did not understand its meaning. They did not translate it into their own languages because they did not know how. *Enthusiasm* is a word of imprecise, uncertain meaning to which no established sense has been fixed.

8. Therefore, it is not at all surprising that the word *enthusiasm* has so many meanings today, and people's understandings are quite incompatible with those of one another. Some use the word in a *positive* way to mean a divine impulse or impression that is superior to all our natural faculties, which for a time either partly or entirely suspends both the reason and the physical senses. Using the word this way, both the ancient prophets and the apostles were legitimate enthusiasts. At different times, they were so filled with the Holy Spirit and so moved by him who dwelt in their hearts that the exercises of their own reason, senses, and natural faculties were temporarily suspended. They were completely inspired by the power of God, and they spoke only as they were "moved by the Holy Spirit."

9. Others understand the word in a neutral sense, neither morally good nor morally evil. For instance, they speak of the enthusiasm of the poets, particularly Homer and Virgil. A late eminent writer went so far as to state that there is no one superior in his or her work, of whatever sort, who does not possess a strong tint of enthusiasm.[7] Those who hold this view regard enthusiasm as an exceptional power of thought, an unusual

excitement of spirit, vitality, and strength not found in ordinary people. These qualities elevate the soul to greater and higher things than calm reason could have attained.

10. Enthusiasm, however, is not commonly understood in either of these ways. Most people, if they agree no further, at least concur that enthusiasm is something *evil*. This view is clearly the attitude of all who designate the religion of the heart as "enthusiasm." Accordingly, in this sermon, I will consider enthusiasm as a vice or at least as a misfortune, if not a defect.

11. As to the nature of enthusiasm, many believe that it is undoubtedly a disorder of the mind that severely hinders the exercise of reason. Some think that enthusiasm completely cancels reason, not only confusing the mind, but also closing it. Given this understanding, enthusiasm may be considered a kind of insanity. Enthusiasm is seen as lunacy rather than folly, because fools *draw wrong conclusions from right premises*, whereas lunatics *draw right conclusions from wrong premises*.

Concede that the enthusiasts' assumptions are true, and their conclusions would necessarily follow. But the mistake of enthusiasts is that they are incorrect in their *premises*. They imagine themselves to be what they are not. Beginning wrong, therefore, the further they proceed, the more they go astray.

12. All true enthusiasts are necessarily deranged persons. Their insanity is not an ordinary type—it is a *religious* insanity. By the word "religious," I do not mean that enthusiasm is a part of genuine religion. It is quite the opposite. Religion is the spirit of a sound mind, and consequently true religion stands in direct opposition to every sort of mental confusion. I mean that enthusiasm is a derangement that focuses on religion as its main object. The enthusiasts are obsessed with religion, God, or the things of God. However, their focus on religion is such that every sensible Christian can discern the confusion of the enthusiasts' minds.

For the most part, enthusiasm may be described as a religious foolishness arising from some wrongly imagined influence or inspiration from God. At the very least, enthusiasm ascribes something to God that should not be attributed to him, or it expects something from God that we should not expect him to give.

13. There are many kinds of enthusiasm. In order to understand and avoid them, I will try to give a few general categories of those types that are the most common and, consequently, the most dangerous.

The first kind of enthusiasm I will specify is seen in those who imagine that they have grace that they do not really possess. When it is not actually the case, some imagine that through Christ they "have redemption and the forgiveness of sins." These people usually "have no root," no deep repentance or complete conviction. They "receive the word with joy," and "since they have no depth of soil," no deep work in their hearts, the seed "springs up quickly." There is an immediate change in them, but it is superficial. Their quick turn and easy joy combine with the pride of their unrepentant hearts and their excessive self-love. They are easily persuaded that they have already "tasted the goodness of the word of God and the powers of the age to come."

14. This pattern precisely illustrates the first sort of enthusiasm. It is a kind of delusion, arising from imagining that they have God's grace, which, in fact, they do not have. They deceive only themselves. We may properly call their delusion a kind of insanity. The reasoning of these poor souls would be correct if their assumptions were valid. Their premises, however, are merely products of their own imaginations. Therefore, everything built on them crashes to the ground. The foundation of all their fanciful ideas is their imagining themselves to have faith in Christ. If they truly did trust in Christ, they would indeed be kings and priests serving God and possessing "a kingdom that cannot be shaken." But they do not possess this kingdom. Consequently, all their conduct is as far from truth and moderation as that of ordinary maniacs who imagine that they are earthly kings, speaking and acting as if they really were!

15. There are many other varieties of enthusiasm. An example is that of flaming religious zealots. Most likely, these people fanatically contend for their opinions and styles of worship, which they dignify with the name "religion." They strongly imagine themselves to be believers in Jesus. Indeed, they think they are champions of "the faith that was once for all entrusted to the saints." Accordingly, all their conduct flows from that empty notion. If we

concede that their assumptions are accurate, they would have some justification for their behavior. Their actions, however, are apparently the result of confused minds and hearts.

16. The most common enthusiasts of this sort are those who imagine themselves to be Christians, but are not. These people abound in all parts of our land and throughout most parts of the habitable earth. If we believe the Bible, it is certain and undeniable that they are not Christians. Christians are holy; these people are unholy. Christians love God; these people love the world. Christians are humble; these people are proud. Christians are gentle; these people are hotheaded. Christians have the same mind that was in Christ; these people are at the furthermost distance from it.

Consequently, they are no more Christians than they are archangels. Yet, they *imagine* themselves to be Christians, and they can give several reasons for their claim. For as long as they can remember, they have been called Christians. They were "christened" many years ago. They embrace Christian opinions, commonly called the Christian or catholic faith. They use Christian modes of worship, as their predecessors did before them. They live what is called a "good Christian life," just as their neighbors do. Who will presume to think or say that these professors of religion are not Christians? Yet, they lack even one seed of true faith in Christ or genuine inner holiness. They have never tasted the love of God or "shared in the Holy Spirit."

17. Oh, you poor self-deceivers! You are not Christians—you are the worst kind of enthusiasts. Would-be doctors, cure yourselves! But first understand your disease. Your entire lives are fanatical because you base them on the fantasy that you have received the grace of God. But you have not. As a result of your fundamental mistake, you blunder on day after day, speaking and acting under a religious profession that in no way belongs to you. From your delusion arises the obvious, glaring inconsistency that runs through your entire behavior. It is a clumsy mixture of genuine heathenism and imaginary Christianity.

Because you belong to such a large company of people who side with you, you continue to assume that your numbers testify that you are the only ones with good sense. You think that all those who are not like you are lunatics. Your assumptions, however, do not alter the truth. In the sight of God and his holy angels—yes, and all the true children of God upon earth—you are merely deranged fanatics.

Are you not walking in an empty shadow of religion and imagined happiness? It is not "for nothing that you are in turmoil. Do you not suppose misfortunes as imaginary as your happiness or your religion? Do you not dream that you are great or good? Do you not believe that you are very intelligent and very wise? How long will you continue? Perhaps until death brings you back to your senses, and you lament your folly for all eternity.

18. A second kind of enthusiasm is seen in those who think they have received gifts from God that they have *not* received. Some have imagined themselves to be endued with the power to work miracles, heal the sick by a word or a touch, and restore sight to the blind. Some even claim the power to raise the dead (a notorious example of which is still fresh in our own memories). Others have taken it upon themselves to forecast things to come, and they make pronouncements with the utmost certainty and detail. The passing of time, however, usually convicts these enthusiasts. When the obvious facts run counter to their predictions, experience does what reason could not do—it brings them to their senses.

19. To the same class of fanatics belong those who preach or pray, while imagining themselves to be influenced by the Spirit of God when they are not. I am indeed aware that apart from God we can do nothing, especially in our public ministries. All our preaching is utterly useless unless it is accompanied by God's power; and all our prayers avail nothing unless the Holy Spirit helps us in our weaknesses. I know that if we do not preach and pray in the power of the Spirit, all is lost labor. God himself gives the help we need on the earth. It is God who "activates everything in everyone."

But this fact does not alter the case before us. Although there is a *real* influence of the Spirit of God, there is also an *imaginary* one. And there are many who mistake one for the other. Numerous people presume that they are under the influence of

God's Spirit when they are not. God is far from them. And many others imagine that they are more strongly under the Spirit's influence than they really are. Among this number, I fear, are all those who imagine that God dictates the very words they say. Consequently, they believe that it is impossible for them to speak any false thing—either *what* they say or *how* they say it. It is well known that many fanatics of this sort also have appeared during the present century. Some of them speak in a far more authoritative manner than St. Paul or any other apostle!

20. The same sort of fanaticism, although to a lesser degree, is often found in people who live private lives. In the same way, they imagine themselves to be influenced or directed by the Holy Spirit when they are not. I acknowledge that "anyone who does not have the Spirit of Christ does not belong to him." And I recognize that if we are ever to think, speak, or act correctly, it is through the assistance of the blessed Holy Spirit. Yet, there are many who attribute things to God's Spirit or expect things from him without any rational or scriptural basis! These people imagine that they either have received or will receive "particular directions" from God about important things and about inconsequential things concerning the most trifling circumstances. All the while, in these matters God would guide us through our own reason. Of course, God never excludes the personal help of his Spirit.

21. Those who expect God to direct them extraordinarily in spiritual things or in ordinary life are particularly susceptible to this kind of fanaticism. I mean they expect God to give them visions, dreams, strong impressions, or sudden flashes in their minds. I do not deny that in earlier times God has manifested his will in this way, and I grant that he can do so today. Indeed, I believe that he does in some very rare instances. Yet, how frequently people are mistaken in this regard. Pride and a vivid imagination deceive them. They attribute to God those impulses, impressions, dreams, or visions, which are completely unworthy of him. All this deception is absolute fanaticism. It is as far from religion as it is from truth and good judgment.

22. Perhaps some people will say, "Should we not ask for God's will in everything? Should not his will be the rule for all our

living?" I answer that undoubtedly it should. But how is a serious Christian to inquire about God's will? How can we know "the will of God"? Not by waiting for supernatural dreams. Not by expecting God to reveal his will in visions. Not by looking for any "particular impressions" or sudden impulses on our minds. No, not by these means. We seek God's will by *consulting the Bible.* We should look to its "teaching and instruction." Seeking the Lord's will through the Scriptures is the ordinary way to know his "holy and acceptable will."

23. Others might ask, "But how shall I know what is God's will in a particular case? What you propose is in itself unrelated to my need, and Scripture does not give me the specific guidance I want." I answer that in Scripture you find *general* rules that apply to all *individual* cases. For instance, St. Paul said, "This is the will of God, your sanctification." Thus, it is God's will for us to become inwardly and outwardly holy. He wills for us, to the best of our ability, to be good and do good in every circumstance. By understanding God's will in this way, we are walking on firm ground. This instruction is as clear as the radiance of the sun. Therefore, to know the will of God in a particular case, we only have to apply this general rule.

24. Suppose, for instance, it were suggested to a thoughtful man to marry or to enter into a new business. For him to know whether this suggestion is the will of God, he is already instructed, "It is God's will for you to be as holy as you can and to do as much good as you can." He needs only to ask, "In which of these states can I be most holy, and do the most good?"

The answer can be determined partly by reason and partly by experience. Experience tells him what advantages he has in his present state for being and doing good. Reason can tell him what he certainly or probably will have in the state suggested to him. By comparing Scripture, experience, and reason, he can judge which course of action may most help him to be and to do good. To the extent that he understands these things, he is certain of God's will.

25. All the while, during the entire process of searching for God's will, the seeker is confident that God's Spirit assists him. To be sure, it is not easy to say in how many ways God helps us. He

may bring many circumstances to mind, help us see others in a stronger and clearer light, unknowingly open our minds to receive certitude, and establish a conviction within our hearts. To the combination of many of these kinds of particulars that support his will concerning us, God may add an indescribable peace of mind. He may give us such an unusual degree of his love that we have no possibility of doubting what his will is for us.

26. This method is the clear, scriptural, and rational means of knowing God's will in a particular case. Consider how seldom this way is taken and what a flood of fanaticism necessarily erupts among those who try to know God's will by unscriptural and irrational methods. One wishes that the expression "seeking God's will" was used far more sparingly. It is a clear breach of the third commandment to use this expression on the most trivial occasions, as some do. It is a grievous way of taking the name of God in vain, and it shows remarkable irreverence toward him.

Would it not be far better to use other expressions that are not subject to such objections? For example, instead of saying on any particular occasion, "I want to know God's will," would it not be better to say, "I want to know what will most improve me and make me most useful"? This way of speaking is clear and inoffensive. It is putting the matter in a clear, scriptural way, and it avoids the danger of enthusiasm.

27. A third very common sort of enthusiasm (if it is not the same as the former) is found among those who think that we can attain the end without using the means. They set aside God's established means and look for his immediate power. If God were providentially to withhold the means he instituted, these people would not deserve the charge of enthusiasm. In such cases, God can and sometimes does exercise his direct power. True fanatics, however, are those who expect God to do so when they have the means he established but will not use them.

I am speaking about those who expect to understand the Holy Scriptures without reading and meditating on them. They do not use those available helps that would likely meet their needs. They make plans to speak in public assemblies without any preparation. I say "they make plans to speak," because sometimes there may be circumstances that make it necessary to speak without preparation. But whoever despises the importance of preparation is an enthusiast—that is, a fanatic.

28. One might expect that I would mention what some consider a fourth kind of enthusiasm—imagining things to be due to God's providence that are not. At the same time, I doubt if there is *anything* that is not due to God's providence in ordering or governing human affairs. I suspect that there is nothing except sin that is not within God's providence. I see God's providence working on my behalf, even in the sins of others. I do not use the term "general providence," because I take this term to be a catchphrase without meaning. If there is a particular providence of God, it must extend to all persons and things.

Our Lord understood God's providence this way. Otherwise, he would not have said, "Even the hairs of your head are all counted." He also declared, "Not one sparrow will fall to the ground apart from your Father." It has been said, "God watches over the whole universe as over every single person, and over every single person as over the whole universe."[8] What is there (except our sins) that we cannot ascribe to the providence of God? Therefore, I cannot charge anyone with fanaticism who assigns everything to God's providence.

29. Someone may say, "There is a charge of fanaticism here, because when you impute something to divine providence you imagine that you are the particular favorite of heaven." I answer that you have forgotten the words I just quoted: "God watches over the whole universe as over every single person." God's providence is over everyone in the universe as much as over any single person. Do you not see that the one who attributes to God's providence everything that happens to him is not making himself any more the favorite of heaven than he acknowledges everyone else to be? Therefore, on this ground you have no reason to charge anyone with enthusiasm.

30. With the utmost diligence, we should guard against every kind of fanaticism, considering the shameful consequences that naturally follow from it. The direct child of fanaticism is pride. And pride continually increases the source from which it springs,

separating us more and more from the favor and life of God. Pride dries up the very springs of faith, love, righteousness, and true holiness. All these benefits flow from grace, not human effort. Saint Peter said, "God opposes the proud, but gives grace to the humble."

31. Together with pride there naturally arises an unteachable and stubborn spirit. Consequently, whatever error or fault fanatics fall into, there is little hope of their restoration. Reason will have little sway with the fanatics who imagine a higher guide, namely the direct wisdom of God, which leads them. (People have often and correctly pointed out this fact.) And as fanatics grow in pride, they will also grow in autonomy and stubbornness. Fanatics will become less and less capable of being convinced, less susceptible to persuasion, and more and more fixed in their own discernment and self-will. Finally, they become completely immovable and inflexible.

32. When we become closed against the grace of God, as well as against all advice and help from others, we are entirely left to the guidance of our own hearts and of Satan, who is "king over all that are proud." It is no wonder that, daily, fanatics are increasingly rooted and grounded in scorn for all others, furious anger, every unkind attitude, and every earthly and devilish disposition. Neither should we wonder at the terrible outward consequences that have flowed from such attitudes in all ages. Fanaticism has spawned all kinds of evil and works of darkness committed by those who called themselves Christians. They have greedily done things such as were hardly named even among the heathen. Such is the nature and dreadful consequences of that many-headed monster, enthusiasm. From this consideration of fanaticism, we can now draw some simple inferences regarding our own behavior.

33. First, if enthusiasm is a frequently used term, it is also rarely understood. You should be careful not to talk about things that you do not comprehend. Do not use a word until you understand it. As in everything else, it is true with respect to "enthusiasm." Learn to think before you speak. First, know the meaning of this difficult word, and then use it if need requires it.

34. Second, few people of education and learning, and still fewer uneducated people, understand this murky and ambiguous word. They have no certain idea what it means. Be cautious, therefore, about judging others or calling anyone an enthusiast based on careless talk. Idle gossip by no means provides adequate grounds for condemning anyone. Unwise chatter provides the least tenable basis for judging someone to be an enthusiast. The more evil that a word implies, the more cautious you should be before applying it to anyone. To bring such a heavy accusation without full proof is not consistent with justice or mercy.

35. If enthusiasm is so great an evil, take caution that you are not entangled in it yourself. Stay awake and pray that you do not fall into this temptation, because it easily plagues those who fear and love God. O, be careful "not to think of yourself more highly than you ought to think." Do not assume that you have the grace of God if you have not attained it. You can have much joy, and you can have a measure of love and yet not have living faith. Cry out to God that he will not permit you, blind as you are, to stray out of his way. Pray that you will never imagine yourself to be a believer in Christ until Christ is revealed in you and his Spirit witnesses with your spirit that you are a child of God.

36. Be on guard that you are not an impassioned, persecuting fanatic. Do not imagine that God has called you to destroy people's lives, rather than to save them. (Doing so is contrary to the spirit of the one you call your Master.) Never dream of forcing others into the ways of God. Think and let think. Use no compulsion in matters of religion. Never force even those who are furthest out of the way to come to Christ by any means other than reason, truth, and love.

37. Be careful that you do not associate with the common crowd of fanatics, imagining that you are a Christian when you are not. Do not use the revered name of Christ unless you hold a clear scriptural title to it, have his very mind, and walk just as he walked.

38. Take caution that you do not fall into the second kind of enthusiasm, which is imagining that you have those gifts from God that you do not possess. Do not trust in visions, dreams, sud-

den impressions, or strong hunches of any kind. Remember, you are not to use these ways of seeking God's will for any particular occasion. Instead, apply the clear Scripture rule, assisted by experience, reason, and the regular support of the Holy Spirit. Do not carelessly use God's name. Do not speak of "the will of God" on every trifling occasion. Rather, let your words and actions be united with reverence and godly awe.

39. Finally, take care not to imagine that you will obtain the end without using God's means of achieving it. God can give the end without any means at all, but you have no reason to think that he will. Therefore, constantly and carefully use all the means that God has appointed as his ordinary channels of grace. Through the free love of God in Christ, use every means that reason and Scripture recommend for us to obtain, facilitate, and increase the gifts of God.

Expect daily growth in that pure and holy religion that the world always did and always will call enthusiasm. Real religion, by which all are saved from actual enthusiasm and nominal Christianity, is "the power of God and the wisdom of God." It is the glorious image of the Most High. It is righteousness, peace, and "a spring of water gushing up to eternal life"!

Notes

1. Samuel Johnson [1709–84], *A Dictionary of the English Language in which the words are deduced from their originals, and illustrated in their different significations by examples from the best writers*, 2 vols., 4th ed., rev. by the author (London: Printed for W. Strahan, 1773).

2. Quoted in Edward H. Sugden, *Wesley's Standard Sermons*, 2 vols. (London: Epworth Press, 1961), 2:85.

3. Jackson, *Wesley's Works*, 13:500.

4. John Wesley, *The Complete English Dictionary, Explaining Most of Those Hard Words, Which Are Found in the Best English Writers,* 3rd ed. (London: R. Hawes, 1777).

5. Ward and Heitzenrater, *Wesley's Journal and Diaries*, October 29, 1762, 21:396.

6. Curnock, *Wesley's Journal*, June 8, 1776, 6:111.

7. Wesley is referring to Anthony Ashley Cooper, the Earl of Shaftsbury.

8. See St. Augustine, *Confessions*, Bk. 3, chap. 11, §19. Philip Schaff, ed., *Nicene and Post-Nicene Fathers*, First Series, 14 vols. (Peabody, Mass.: Henrickson Publishers, 1994), 1:67. Augustine wrote, "O Thou Good Omnipotent, who so carest for every one of us as if Thou caredst for him only, and so for all as if they were but one!"

Introduction to Sermon 38

A CAUTION AGAINST BIGOTRY

The critics who branded John Wesley and the Methodists "enthusiasts" also accused them of bigotry. This allegation was based on several factors. To begin with, Wesley had ignored parish boundaries, preaching wherever he saw need and opportunity. In addition, the Methodists held their own class meetings and even erected their own buildings. These developments went against custom, and a number of Anglican bishops opposed the spread of Methodism. Critics, therefore, assumed that Wesley and his followers believed that the local parish priests were not adequately preaching the gospel and that the Methodists could do a better job. Also, Wesley selected and supervised unordained preachers, some of whom were not earnestly loyal to the Church of England. These lay preachers, of course, were not under the authority of the bishops of the Church. Furthermore, the Methodist societies were close-knit communities that tended to be more loyal to Methodism than to the established Church. Contrasting concepts of religion caused people to take sides and to oppose those who held differing views. Given these realities, detractors accused the Methodists of bigotry.

Wesley, however, was opposed to bigotry. Furthermore, he denied that Methodism spawned narrow-mindedness or intolerance. He contended that holding views different from those maintained by others did not make one a bigot. In his *Notes upon the New Testament,* he defined bigotry as "properly the [lack] of . . . pure universal love. A bigot only loves those who embrace his opinions, and receive his way of worship; and he loves them for that, and not for Christ's sake."[1] Wesley was determined that there would be no bigotry among the Methodists. He advised, "O be warned in time! Do not play with fire. Do not put your hand on the hole of a cockatrice's den. I entreat you, beware of bigotry. Let not your love or beneficence be confined to Methodists, so called, only; much less to that very small part of them who seem to be renewed in love."[2]

John Wesley was by background and inclination an Anglican, and he loved the Church's doctrines and traditions. He thought of himself as "a Church of England man," and he encouraged the Methodists to attend the Church's sacramental services.[3] Despite these loyalties, many Anglicans criticized him for ministering outside official ecclesiastical structures. At the same time, some within the dissenting churches reprimanded him for being too much an Anglican. In this sermon, Wesley reaches out to Christians in all theological circles. His message seeks to promote understanding and cooperation among sincere followers of Jesus Christ.

Wesley's tolerance by no means meant that he was a "latitudinarian," which he described as "one that fancies all religions are saving."[4] In general, the eighteenth-century English latitudinarians conformed to Anglican Church practices but attached relatively little importance to theology, liturgy, and ecclesiastical organization. Some of them, such as the Cambridge Platonists, sought to interpret the Christian faith in the light of Plato's philosophy. Wesley had little in common with their broad doctrinal tolerance. These people remained within the Anglican Church but stressed doctrinal latitude and championed reason as the final arbiter of truth.

On the occasion of the laying of the foundation for the new chapel on City Road in London, Wesley combined an attitude of tolerance with a firm commitment to biblical religion. He declared,

> Are you a lover of God and all mankind? Does your heart glow with gratitude to the Giver of every good and perfect gift? The Father of the spirits of all flesh, who giveth you life, and breath, and all things? Who hath given you his Son, his only Son, that you "might not perish, but have everlasting life?" Is your soul warm with benevolence to all mankind? . . . Do you "love, not in word only, but in deed and in truth"? Do you persevere in the "work of faith, and the labour of love"? Do you "walk in love, as Christ also loved us, and gave himself for us"? Do you, as you have time, "do good unto all men"? And in as high a degree as you are able? "Whosoever" thus "doeth the will of my Father which is in heaven, the same is my brother, and sister, and mother."[5]

Wesley's love for the progress of the gospel was by no means confined to the work of Methodism. He often published accounts of God's work in Great Britain and in other nations as it developed out of the ministries of Christians of diverse theological opinions and denominations.[6]

Wesley finds the root of bigotry at a level deeper than mere party jealously and strife. For him, the important question is whether Christians are wholeheartedly engaged in the all-important struggle of truth and righteousness against error and evil. Wesley encouraged Christians to unite in this warfare between Christ and the forces of the devil. Doing God's work in the battle against sin is more important than focusing on questions about denominational authority, ecclesiastical credentials, precise vocabulary or approved methods of ministry. Wesley argues in this sermon that those who are interested in building God's kingdom should rejoice in the successes of *all* ministries that bear good fruit. The ultimate measure of valid ministry is not proper form, but effective results.

Concerning the Methodists, Wesley insisted,

> They think, and let think. One condition, and one only, is required,—a real desire to save their soul. Where this is, it is enough: They desire no more: They lay stress upon nothing else: They ask only, "Is thy heart herein as my heart? If it be, give me thy hand." . . . Where, then, is there such another society in Europe? in the habitable world? I know none. Let any man show it me that can. Till then let no one talk of the bigotry of the Methodists.[7]

The text for this sermon comes from Mark 9:38-39, where Jesus and his disciples discuss casting out demons. Wesley begins with an affirmation of the reality of Satan and his work in the world. The penetrating analysis that follows is a classic example of balanced biblical theology. Wesley shows that in some people the devil works *overtly* to create superstition. These people live in fear of the devil's evil power. Satan dominates their thoughts and lives because he works openly in such terrifying ways.

In other people, however, the devil works *covertly* to foster unfaithfulness. These people live in peace because they remain oblivious to the devil's hidden activity, and many of them do not believe that Satan even exists. Wesley believes that every person is either under the influence of God or under the influence of the Enemy. Casting out demons means leading people from the kingdom of darkness into God's kingdom of light. The fruit of this transformation is holiness of heart and life. God alone can cast out demons, yet he uses his servants in this important work. In this sermon against bigotry, Wesley states that God uses human instruments, which many would regard as unlikely choices.

Wesley does not admonish critics to refrain from their prejudice against the Methodists. Rather, he exhorts the Methodists to avoid intolerance toward their critics! He insists that the principles of Methodism are incompatible with bigotry. The sermon ends with this advice: "Other people's failure to obey our Lord's instruction is no reason for you to fail as well. Let them have all the bigotry to themselves! If they try to hinder you do not try to hinder them. Instead, work, stay alert, and pray all the more, so as to strengthen your love toward them. If others say all kinds of evil against you, speak all kinds of good (which is true) about them."

Sermon 38

A CAUTION AGAINST BIGOTRY

John said to him, "Teacher, we saw someone casting out demons in your name, and we tried to stop him, because he was not following us." But Jesus said, "Do not stop him; for no one who does a deed of power in my name will be able soon afterward to speak evil of me." *(Mark 9:38-39)*

1 In the preceding verses, we read that the twelve had "argued with one another who was the greatest" among them. Next, Jesus "took a little child and put it among them; and taking it in his arms, he said to them, 'Whoever welcomes one such child in my name welcomes me, and whoever welcomes me welcomes not me but the one who sent me.'" Then, "John said to him, 'Teacher, we saw someone casting out demons in your name, and we tried to stop him, because he was not following us.' But Jesus said, 'Do not stop him.'" In effect, John was saying to Jesus, "If we accept the one who is not in our group, would we not be disloyal to you? Should we not forbid him? Should we have accepted him? Were we not in the right to stop this person from ministering?" Jesus replied, "Do not stop him."

2. In almost identical words, the same account appears in St. Luke's Gospel. Certain questions may arise: "Today no one casts

out demons, so what relevance does this story have for us? Has not the power of exorcism been withdrawn from the church for twelve or fourteen hundred years? How does this scriptural account and our Lord's response to it concern us today?"

3. Perhaps this Scripture is more relevant than we think. Examples of this kind are not unusual in our time. For us to reap the full benefit of this Scripture, first, I propose to show in what way people today can and do cast out demons. Second, I propose to explain what we may understand by the phrase "he was not following us." Third, I will explain our Lord's instruction, "Do not stop him." Finally, I will close with a conclusion drawn from all our considerations.

I. The Work of Casting Out Demons

1. In the first place, I will explain how people can and do cast out demons today. In order to understand clearly the meaning of "casting out demons," we should remember that, according to Scripture, God lives in, and works through, the children of light. Also, the devil lives in and works through the children of darkness. As the Holy Spirit occupies the lives of good people, so the evil spirit occupies the lives of the wicked.

Consequently, because of the unbridled power that Satan has over worldly people, St. Paul calls him "the god of this world." Our blessed Lord refers to the devil as "the ruler of this world." Therefore, St. John declared, "We know that we are God's children, and that the whole world lies under the power of the evil one." People of the world live and move in the devil, just as those who are not of the world live and move in God.

2. We should understand our adversary the devil as being more than a roaring lion who prowls around, looking for someone to devour, which he is. Satan is more than a subtle enemy who surprises poor souls and "holds them captive to do his will." He also lives in people and guides their steps. He rules the "powers of this present darkness" and governs worldly people and all their depraved plans and actions. The enemy does so by keeping control of their hearts, setting up his throne there, and bringing all

their thoughts into obedience to himself. He is "a strong man, fully armed, who guards his castle."

Even if this unclean spirit is driven out of a person, he often returns and "brings seven other spirits more evil than itself, and they enter and live there." He cannot be idle in the people he inhabits. He continually works among those who are disobedient. With great intensity, he works in them powerfully to transform them into his own likeness. He labors to efface all remnants of God's image, influencing those he controls for every evil word and work.

3. Therefore, it is an undeniable truth that to this day the god and ruler of this world still possesses all who do not know God. But today the *way* he possesses them differs from that of an earlier age. In former times, Satan frequently afflicted people's bodies as well as their souls. And he did so openly, without disguise. Today, he torments only their souls (except in some rare cases), and he works as quietly as possible.

The reason for this difference is clear. In an earlier time, his goal was to drive humankind into *superstition*. Accordingly, he worked as overtly as he could. Now, the devil's goal is to drive us into *unfaithfulness*. Therefore, he works as secretly as he can because the more hidden he is, the more he can control.

4. Still, if we can believe historians, there are countries even now in which Satan works as openly as previously. Someone may ask, "But why does he work in this fashion only in uncivilized and barbaric countries? Why does he not work openly in Italy, France, or England?" I answer that he works differently in these nations for a very simple reason—he understands his intended victims. He knows what he needs to do with each person. To Laplanders, he appears openly because he wants to establish them in superstition and deep idolatry. But with you, he pursues a different goal. He wants to cause you to idolize yourselves and to make you wiser in your own eyes than God and his revelation. In order to accomplish this goal, he does not dare appear openly as he really is. That strategy would defeat his plan. Instead, he uses all his skill to make you deny his existence, until he has you safely in his own domain.

5. Therefore, in different ways, Satan reigns as absolutely in one nation as in the other. He has the cheerful Italian infidel in his teeth as sure as he has the savage Mongolian. The deceived infidel, however, is fast asleep in the mouth of the lion, and the lion is too clever to awaken him from sleep. For the present, the devil only toys with him. And when it pleases the devil, he will swallow up his victim.

The god of this world holds his English worshipers in just as tight a grip as those in Lapland.[8] And it is not Satan's concern to frighten them because he fears that they would turn to the God of heaven. The prince of darkness, therefore, does not reveal himself while he rules over these willing subjects. The conqueror holds his captives all the more securely because they think they are free. Thus, while the "strong man, fully armed, guards his castle, his property is safe." Neither the Deist nor the nominal Christian suspects that the devil is present. Consequently, they are perfectly at peace with him.

6. All the while, the devil actively works in them with vigor. He has "blinded the minds of the unbelievers, to keep them from seeing the light of the gospel of the glory of Christ." He shackles their souls to the earth and hell with the chains of their own evil inclinations. He binds them to the earth by their love of the world, money, pleasure, and applause. Through pride, envy, anger, hate, and revenge, Satan causes their souls to draw closer to hell. They behave all the more securely and freely because they do not even know that the devil is at work.

7. How easy it is to determine the cause from the fruits it produces, which are sometimes glaring and obvious. It was so in the most refined of the heathen nations. Look no further than the admired and virtuous Romans. Even when they were at the height of their learning and glory, they were "filled with every kind of wickedness, evil, covetousness, malice. Full of envy, murder, strife, deceit, and craftiness, they were gossips, slanderers, God-haters, insolent, haughty, boastful, inventors of evil, rebellious toward parents, foolish, faithless, heartless, and ruthless."

8. The severest parts of this description of the heathen are confirmed by one whom some may think an undeniable witness—

Dion Cassius, one of their number. He observed that, prior to Caesar's return from Gaul, gluttony and sensuality of every kind were practiced openly and blatantly. Lying, injustice, and cruelty abounded in public courts and private families. In Roman society, the most outrageous robberies, destruction, and murders were so frequent throughout Rome that few people left their houses without making their wills. They did not know if they would return alive.[9]

9. The same flagrant and obvious works of the devil are found among many, if not all, modern heathens. The natural religion of the Creeks, Cherokees, Chickasaws, and all other Indians bordering on our southern American settlements authorizes them to torture their prisoners from morning to night until finally they roast them to death. This practice is true not only among a few individuals, but also among entire tribes. For the slightest unintended aggravation, they will ambush and shoot arrows at any members of their own tribes. Among these heathen, it is even common for a son to bash out the brains of his father if he lives too long. If a mother wearies of her children, she might fasten stones around their necks and systematically throw three or four of them into the river.

10. One wishes that none but the heathen practiced such obviously disgusting works of the devil. Regrettably, we dare not say that such is the case. Even in cruelty and bloodshed, how closely behind the heathen are some Christians! I am referring not only to the Spanish or Portuguese who butchered thousands in South America, or to the Dutch in the East Indies, or to the French in North America who did the same things as the Spanish. Our own countrymen have also carelessly wasted the blood of others and exterminated entire nations. All these offenses clearly demonstrate what sort of spirit lives and works in those who are disobedient to God.

11. These brutish people might almost make us overlook the works of the devil that are done in our own country. Sadly, it is to be lamented that even in England we cannot open our eyes without seeing Satan's works all around us. Is it not sufficient proof of the devil's power that ordinary blasphemers, drunkards, fornica-

tors, adulterers, thieves, robbers, homosexuals, and murderers are still found in every part of our land? How successfully the prince of this world governs in all these children of disobedience!

12. Less openly, but no less effectively, the devil works in hypocrites, gossips, liars, slanderers, despots, swindlers, false witnesses, and in those who betray friends, integrity, and nation. At the same time, these people talk about religion and conscience! They claim integrity, virtue, and patriotism. But they can no more deceive Satan than they can deceive God. The devil knows the ones who belong to him. They compose a great multitude, from every nation and people, all of which he presently controls.

13. If you consider these facts, you cannot avoid seeing today in what sense Christ's disciples also "cast out demons." Indeed, every minister of Christ casts them out, if "through him the work of the LORD prospers." By God's power accompanying his word, people today bring sinners to repentance, producing a complete inward and outward change from every evil to every good. In a proper sense, this ministry is to "cast out demons" from the souls in which they formerly lived. Satan, the "strong one," can no longer "guard his castle." One who is more powerful than he has come against him, cast him out, taken possession for himself, and made the former sinner a "dwelling place for God" through his Spirit.

Through the work of the Holy Spirit, the activity of Satan ends and the Son of God "destroys the works of the devil." Then, the understanding of sinners is enlightened, and their hearts are pleasantly drawn to God. Their desires are purified and their affections cleansed. Being filled with the Holy Spirit, they grow in grace until they are holy in heart and in every aspect of life.

14. This entire transformation is indeed the work of God, who alone is able to cast out Satan. And ordinarily he does this work through his servants on earth. They function as instruments in his hand, and by his power and authority they "cast out demons in his name." God sends those he chooses into this important work and he ordinarily uses those human instruments whom others would not have thought to choose.

Through Isaiah, God said, "My thoughts are not your thoughts, nor are your ways my ways, says the LORD." Accordingly, "God chooses what is weak in the world to shame the strong. He chooses what is foolish in the world to shame the wise." God works in this way for a simple reason: He establishes his own glory so that "no human being will be justified in his sight by deeds prescribed by the law."

II. Respecting the Ministries of Others

1. Someone may ask, "Should we not prohibit the ministries of those who 'cast out demons' if they are not in our religious circle?" This question was in the mind of St. John when he said to Jesus, "We saw someone casting out demons in your name, and we tried to stop him, because he was not following us." That apostle assumed that he had good reason for this action. Now, I will examine the meaning of the expression, "He was not following us."

The first meaning of this phrase that comes to mind is, "The one who casts out demons has no outward connection with our group, and we do not work together. He is not our colleague in the gospel ministry." Certainly, whenever our Lord sends many workers into his harvest, they cannot all act in subjection to, or connection with, one another.

Indeed, it is not possible for them all to have personal acquaintance with one another or even to know about the other workers. Of necessity, there will be many workers in different parts of the harvest. Not all of them can have mutual interchange. They may be complete strangers to one another, as though they had lived in different centuries. Considering the matter from this perspective, we can say about many of them, "They are not following us."

2. A second meaning of this expression may be, "He does not belong to our party." For all who "pray for the peace of Jerusalem," it has long been a matter of sadness that so many different parties still exist among those who are called Christians. These divisions have been especially conspicuous among our own countrymen. Many Christians have remained divided over points of no significance—matters that have nothing to do with genuine

religion. The most trifling circumstances have spawned different parties, which have continued for many generations. And each of these parties would be quick to object to those in another party, saying, "They are not following us."

3. Third, this expression can mean, "Others differ from us in religious opinions." At one time, all Christians were of one heart and soul. The great grace that rested on the early Christians unified all those who were filled with the Holy Spirit. This blessing, however, continued for only a short time. The unity of their hearts and souls soon disappeared. Differences of opinion sprang up in the church of Christ. Disagreements surfaced among genuine Christians as well as among nominal Christians.

Indeed, we even see a division of opinion pertaining to the chief of apostles—St. Paul. It does not appear that the division of opinion that began in his day has ever been completely removed. As long as those "pillars in the temple of God" remained upon the earth, we do not find complete agreement even among them. They were never entirely of one mind, especially regarding the Jewish ceremonial law. Therefore, it is not surprising that endless varieties of opinion would be found in today's Christian church.

A likely consequence of these differences of opinion is that whenever we see others "casting out demons," we will say about them, "They are not following us." That is, they do not hold our precise opinions. It is difficult to imagine that we would hold exactly the same opinions on all points, especially in religion. It is very probable that others may think differently than we think, even on several subjects of importance. We may differ on the nature and use of the moral law, the eternal decrees of God, the sufficiency and efficacy of his grace, and the continued perseverance of all his children.

4. Fourth, others may differ from us not only in matters of opinion, but also in particular customs. They may not favor the pattern of worship practiced by our congregation. They may consider certain worship styles that stem from traditions related to John Calvin or Martin Luther to be more spiritually profitable for them. They may have many objections to the form of liturgy that we favor above all others. They may have many doubts about the

form of church government that we consider as both apostolic and scriptural.[10] Perhaps they may move even further from us. For the sake of conscience, they may refrain from some of the ordinances that we regard as Christ's sacraments.[11]

Even if we agree that these sacraments come from God, nonetheless there may remain a difference between us regarding the method of administering the sacraments. We may disagree about the persons to whom we should administer them. The unavoidable consequence of any of these differences will be the decision to separate from fellowship. In this respect, therefore, one group might say of another, "They are not following us." As we phrase it, "They are not of our church."

5. There is even a far stronger sense in which we can say, "They are not following us." I refer to those who not only belong to a different church, but also adhere to a religious group that we consider unscriptural and unchristian. I am speaking about a church that we believe is completely and dangerously wrong in doctrine and practice. It is a religious organization that is guilty of massive superstition and idolatry; a church that has added many doctrines to "the faith that was once for all entrusted to the saints." This ecclesiastical body has dropped one entire commandment of God (about "graven images") and by her traditions made null and void several other commandments. This religious organization imagines that it has the highest reverence for, and strictest conformity to, the ancient church. Nonetheless, without any warrant from Scripture or the ancient church, it has introduced numberless innovations. Most certainly, we can say that those who stand at such a great distance from us "are not following us."

6. There may be an even wider difference than the ones I have described. Those who differ from us in judgment or practice may possibly stand at a still greater distance from us in their *affections*. This difference is a very natural and common consequence of the other variances. The disagreements that begin with opinions rarely end there. They usually spread into the affections, and they separate the best of friends. There are no antagonisms as deep and irreconcilable as those that spring from emotional disagreements about religion.

Religious differences cause even members of one's own household to become the bitterest of enemies. Because of religious discord, a father may oppose his own children. Children may turn against their fathers, and they may persecute each other, even to the death. All the while, they think that they are offering worship to God. It is to be expected that those who differ from us in religious opinions or practices will soon develop harsh feelings toward us, even an attitude of bitterness. As they become more and more prejudiced against us, in time they will despise *us* as much as our doctrines.

Almost inevitably, they will *speak* about us in the same way that they *think* about us. They will set themselves against us, and, as far as they are able, will impede our work. To them, our ministries do not appear to be God's work. Rather, they think of our work as merely human or even demonic. In the highest sense, those who think, speak, and act in this way "are not following us."

7. I do not at all believe that the person whom John and the disciples spoke about in our text went as far as I have described. (Yet, we have no specific account of him in this scriptural passage or in any other part of the Bible.) We have no basis to believe that there was any substantive difference between him and the apostles. And most certainly, he does not seem to have any ill will against the apostles or their Master. It appears that we can gather this much from our Lord's words, which immediately follow our text: "Do not stop him; for no one who does a deed of power in my name will be able soon afterward to speak evil of me."

I purposely put this matter in the strongest light, adding all the conditions that can reasonably be conceived. I have done so in order for us to be warned about the temptation to hinder the ministry of others. I hope that we will not yield to this error, and in so doing fight against God.

III. Supporting God's Work and Workers

1. Suppose that other people have no dealings with us; they do not belong to our group or church. Suppose they have separated from our religious company and widely differ from us in

understanding, practice, and affections. If we see these people "casting out demons," Jesus said, "Do not stop them." Now, in the third place, I will explain this important instruction of our Lord.

2. If we see a person casting out demons by bringing Christ into others' lives, it is good that we do not deny what we see with our own eyes. One does not need to be very familiar with human nature to grasp quickly how very unprepared we would be to believe that others could cast out demons if they did not agree with us in all or most of the ways that I have discussed above. I almost said, in *all* these ways, because, from experience, we know how unwilling we are to attribute anything good to those who do not agree with us in everything.

3. Someone might ask, "What is an adequate and reasonable proof that someone casts out demons?" (in the sense of bringing people to Christ). The answer is simple. First, is there abundant proof that those who were delivered from demons had been shameful, open sinners? Second, is there proof that they are no longer in that condition and have renounced their sins and now live a Christian life? Third, is there proof that the change took place through hearing this person preach? If these three points are clear and undeniable, you have adequate and reasonable proof that this person casts out demons. It is the kind of proof that you cannot deny without sinning willfully.

4. If others cast out demons, "do not stop them." Be careful not to obstruct them by your authority, arguments, or influence. Do not strive in any way to prevent them from exercising all the authority that God has given them. If you have supervision over them, do not use your position to stop the work of God. Do not give them cause to cease speaking in the name of Jesus.

If you do not oppose them, Satan will. Do not do his work for him. Do not influence these workers for Christ to cease their work. If they were to listen to the devil *and* to you, many souls might perish in wickedness. And God would require their blood at your hands.

5. You might ask, "What if the one who casts out demons is only a layperson and does not belong to the clergy? Should I not stop such a person?"

In response to your question, I ask whether the person has been successful in ministry. Is there reasonable proof that this person has or does cast out demons? If there is such proof, do not try to stop that ministry. To do so would imperil your soul. Will God not work by whomever he pleases to work? "No one can do these signs apart from the presence of God." People can cast out demons only if God has appointed them to do this very work. But if God has sent them, will you tell them to stop God's business? Will you forbid them to continue?

6. You might say, "But I am not certain that God has sent them." I answer that it is astonishing that you do not know who sent these servants. The seals of their ministries are that they have brought people from Satan to worship the living God. Any of those whom these people have helped will say, "How can you say that you do not know whether they come from God? Look, they have opened my eyes!" If God did not send them, they could do nothing. If you doubt the fact, send for the parents of those they have helped; send for their relatives, friends, and acquaintances. If you cannot doubt that a significant miracle has occurred, then in good conscience how can you "warn them to speak no more to anyone in the name of Christ"?

7. I concede that it is highly advisable for those who preach in the name of Christ to have an outward call (from the church) as well as an inward call (from the Lord). I do not say, though, that a call from the established church is absolutely essential for one to preach the gospel.

Is the Scripture not explicit? "One does not presume to take this honor, but takes it only when called by God, just as Aaron was." Numerous times, people have quoted this text to prove what they want it to prove. But surely there has never been a text that has been more abused. In the first place, Aaron was not called to preach at all. He was called on behalf of the people to offer gifts and sacrifices for sin. That assignment was Aaron's particular work. In the second place, the preachers we are discussing do not offer sacrifices at all. Their call is only to preach, a different calling than Aaron's. Therefore, one cannot find a single text in the entire Bible that misses the present point more than this one.

8. Someone may ask, "But what was the practice in the apostolic age?" You can easily see the answer to this question in the book of Acts. In the eighth chapter we read: "A severe persecution began against the church in Jerusalem, and all except the apostles were scattered throughout the countryside of Judea and Samaria. Now those who were scattered went from place to place, proclaiming the word." Did all these preachers have an official call from the church to engage in a preaching ministry? No one in his right mind can think so. Here is certain proof of the practice of the apostolic age. In the book of Acts, we see not just one "lay preacher," but a multitude of them. And the only call they had was from God.

9. Therefore, the practice of the apostolic age in no way suggests that it was unlawful for people to preach before they were ordained. We have no reason to think that the apostolic church required ordination before one began a preaching ministry. Without fail, the practice and the instruction of the apostle Paul was that one must be proven before he or she was set apart for ministry. He wrote, "Let them first be tested; then, if they prove themselves blameless, let them serve as deacons."

How were they proven? Did requiring them to interpret a Greek sentence prove them? Were they required to answer a few simple questions? Would these requirements be compelling proof that anyone is an effective minister of Christ? Not at all. They were tested as to whether their lives were holy and blameless (as is still done by most of the Protestant churches in Europe). They were tested as to whether they possessed the gifts that are absolutely and indispensably necessary to the building of the church of Christ.

10. Someone may object, "But what if a preacher has these qualities and has brought sinners to repentance? And yet the bishop will not ordain him." I answer by saying that if this is the case, then the bishop stops him from casting out demons. But I do not dare to stop him!

In my book *A Farther Appeal* (1745), I have published my reasons to the entire world.[12] Yet some people still insist that I should try to stop unordained people from preaching. All you who demand that I do, answer the reasons I gave in that book. I know of no one who has yet done so or even pretended to try. There have been a few people who have spoken of my arguments as weak and insignificant. This approach was convenient for them because it is much easier to despise (or pretend to despise) an argument than to answer it. Until someone answers my arguments, so long as I have reasonable proof that others are effectively "casting out demons," I will not obstruct them. Whatever others may do, I dare not try to stop them, for fear that I "may even be found fighting against God!"

11. If you reverence God, do not block these effective lay preachers, either directly or indirectly. There are many ways of hindering their ministries. You indirectly obstruct them if you reject, despise, or ridicule the work that God has done through them. You indirectly obstruct them when you discourage them in their work by drawing them into controversies about it. You hinder their work by raising objections against their ministries or by frightening them with repercussions (which very probably will never occur). You encumber them when you show them any unkindness by your words or deeds.

How much more you hinder their work when you speak to others about them in either a harsh or contemptuous manner or when you try to portray them in a hateful or detestable light. You are hampering their ministries every time you speak evil of them or discredit their labors. Do not hinder them in any of these ways or dishearten them by discouraging sinners from hearing the "implanted word that has the power to save [their] souls."

12. If you would follow our Lord's instruction in its complete meaning and to its full extent, you will remember his word: "Whoever is not with me is against me, and whoever does not gather with me scatters." Those who do not bring people into the kingdom of God certainly separate them from it. There can be no neutral person in this spiritual warfare. Everyone is either on God's side or on Satan's side.

Are you on God's side? If so, you not only will refrain from hindering those who cast out demons, but also will work to the limit of your ability to assist them in their ministries. If you are on God's side, you will quickly recognize his work and acknowledge its excellence. You will remove all the difficulties and objections that may appear. You will strengthen the hands of his workers by speaking justly about them before others and affirming what you have seen and heard. You will encourage others to listen to those whom God has sent. And you will not neglect to show affectionate love when God gives you an opportunity to demonstrate it.

IV. The Sin of Bigotry

1. If we willingly fail in any of these things by directly or indirectly hindering others in their ministries, "because they do not follow us," we are bigots. I draw this conclusion from what I have pointed out. I fear, however, that as frequently as people use the term *bigotry*, it is almost as poorly understood as the term *enthusiasm*.

Bigotry means to have too strong an attachment to, or love for, one's own party, opinion, church, or beliefs. Bigots are so stubbornly attached to any of these things that they hinder others from casting out demons. They hinder God's work only because of differences in any or all details.

2. First, be careful not to become a bigot by your unwillingness to believe that anyone who differs from you is casting out demons. If you are innocent on this count, then, second, ask yourself this question: Am I not guilty of bigotry directly or indirectly by forbidding others to minister? Do I not directly forbid them because they do not belong to my party, agree with my opinions, or worship God in the way I inherited from my predecessors?

3. Ask yourself if you do not at least indirectly hinder others from ministering on any of the following grounds. Do I regret that God would acknowledge and bless others who hold such mistaken opinions? Do I obstruct them because they do not belong to my church? Do I hinder them by debating with them about their work, raising objections, and encumbering them with possible consequences? Am I free from anger, contempt, or any kind of unpleasantness in my words or deeds? Do I speak behind the backs of others about their real or presumed faults, defects, or weaknesses? Do I keep sinners from hearing their words? If you do any of these things, you are a bigot.

4. You need to pray this prayer:

> Prove me, O LORD, and try me;
>   test my heart and mind.
> See if there is any wicked way in me,
>   and lead me in the way everlasting.
>   (Ps. 26:2; 139:24)

In order to examine ourselves thoroughly, let the matter be proposed in the strongest manner. What if I were to see a Roman Catholic, Arian, or Socinian casting out demons? If I did, I could not hinder that person without convicting myself of bigotry. Even if it could be imagined that I would see a Jew, Deist, or Muslim doing the same, if I were to hinder him or her, directly or indirectly, I would still be a bigot.

5. O, be innocent of bigotry. And do not merely be content with not hindering those who cast out demons. It is good to go this far, but do not stop here. If you want to be completely free from all bigotry, go further still. Whenever you see others casting out demons, whomever they may be, acknowledge that it is by the finger of God.

Do more than merely acknowledge their ministries. Also, rejoice with them and praise God's name with thanksgiving. Encourage those whom God decides to appoint to give themselves completely to his work. Wherever you are, speak well of them; defend their integrity and their mission. Do what you can to increase their areas of ministry. In word and deed, show them every kindness. On their behalf, unceasingly pray to God that they will be saved and save others.

6. I need to add only one caution. Never think that the bigotry of others is any excuse for your own bigotry. It is possible that others who cast out demons may forbid you to do the same. You will observe that this is the case in our text. The apostles tried to stop another from doing what they did themselves. Always beware of responding in kind. You are not to repay evil for evil.

Other people's failures to obey our Lord's instruction constitute no reason for you to fail as well. Let them have all the bigotry to themselves! If they try to hinder you, do not try to hinder them.

Instead, work, stay alert, and pray all the more, so as to strengthen your love toward them. If others say all kinds of evil against you, speak all kinds of good (which is true) about them. In this matter, imitate that celebrated saying of John Calvin (O, that he had always *practiced* the same attitude):

> Let Luther call me a hundred demons;
> I will still reverence him as a messenger of God.[13]

Notes

1. Wesley, *Explanatory Notes upon the New Testament,* 1 John 4:21.
2. Jackson, *Wesley's Works,* "A Plain Account of Christian Perfection," 11:431.
3. Frank Baker, *John Wesley and the Church of England* (Nashville: Abingdon Press, 1970).
4. John Wesley, *The Complete Dictionary, Explaining Most of Those Hard Words, Which Are Found in the Best English Writers,* 3rd ed. (London: R. Hawes, 1777).
5. Outler, *Wesley's Sermons,* 3:592.
6. Rupert Davies, *The Methodist Societies,* "A Plain Account of the People Called Methodists," 9:265-66.
7. Jackson, *Wesley's Works,* "Thoughts upon a Late Phenomenon," 13:266-67.
8. By speaking of those in Lapland, Wesley was referring to a very short and Mongoloid group of people in northern-most Scandinavia and parts of Russia who are nomadic fishers and hunters.
9. Cassius Dio Cocceianus, *Roman History,* 40, 44-50.
10. The Puritans did not have bishops or an episcopal form of church government.
11. The Quakers, of course, did not use the Christian sacraments.
12. Jackson, *Wesley's Works,* "A Farther Appeal to Men of Reason and Religion," 8:46-247.
13. John Calvin, *Opera Omnia,* 19 vols. (Amstelodami [Amsterdam]: Joannis Jacobi Schipperi, 1671), 11:774.

Introduction to Sermon 39

CATHOLIC SPIRIT

In the decades following the sixteenth-century Protestant Reformation, religious controversies plunged the European continent into persecution and war. Roman Catholics and Protestants quarreled and raised armies against each other. Protestants persecuted other Protestants. Doctrinal rigidity, suspicion, and intolerance did great harm to the Christian cause. The following hymn was actually sung in some Lutheran churches:

> Guard Thou Thy saints with Thy Word, O Lord,
> And smite the Calvinists with Thy sword![1]

Roman Catholics and Protestants martyred tens of thousands of Anabaptist Christians. In Geneva, John Calvin approved the burning of Michael Servetus for his views of the Trinity. Ulrich Zwingli died on the battlefield in a war against the Roman Catholic army. In 1555, theologians and church officials burned at the stake Hugh Latimer and Nicholas Ridley for their theological opinions. In the seventeenth century, the religious conflicts of the Thirty Years War (1618–48) cost the lives of millions of people. For centuries, intolerance and bigotry blighted the Christian witness.

Throughout his long ministry, John Wesley worked diligently to promote a "catholic spirit" among Christians. In *The Character of a Methodist*, he wrote,

> Whosoever . . . imagines that a Methodist is a man of such or such an *opinion* is grossly ignorant of the whole affair; he mistakes the truth totally. We believe, indeed, that "all Scripture is given by inspiration of God.". . . We believe Christ to be the Eternal Supreme God; and herein are we distinguished from [non-Trinitarians]. But as to all opinions which do not strike at the root of Christianity, we "think and let think."[2]

To be sure, John Wesley insisted on the cardinal doctrines of Christianity, such as those articulated in the ancient creeds of the ante-Nicene and post-Nicene church and in his own Anglican Church's Homilies and Thirty-nine Articles. Yet, he was deeply concerned that Christians demonstrate charity and tolerance for religious opinions different from their own, so long as they did not undermine Christianity's doctrinal foundations. In his *Explanatory Notes upon the New Testament*, Wesley declared,

> Would to God that all the party names and unscriptural phrases and forms which have divided the Christian world were forgot, and that we might all agree to sit down together, as humble, loving disciples, at the feet of our common Master, to hear His word, to imbibe His spirit, and to transcribe His life in our own![3]

Wesley believed that the unity of all Christians in Christ is not a future goal to be achieved, but a present fact to be recognized. Furthermore, he contended that the church is able fully to accomplish its mission only when Christians demonstrate oneness of mind and spirit in Christ. In 1763, he wrote,

> I desire to have a league offensive and defensive with every soldier of Christ. We have not only one faith, one hope, one Lord, but [we] are directly engaged in one warfare. We are carrying the war into the devil's own quarters, who therefore summons all his hosts to war. Come, then, ye that love Him, to the help of the Lord, to the help of the Lord against the mighty![4]

In Sermon #53, *On the Death of George Whitefield*, Wesley illustrated this catholic spirit:

> There are many doctrines of a less essential nature, [about] which even the sincere children of God (such is the present weakness of human understanding) are and have been divided for many ages. In these [minor doctrines] we may think and let think; we may "agree to disagree." But meantime, let us hold fast the essentials of "the faith which was once delivered to the saints," and which this champion of God [Whitefield] so strongly insisted on at all times and in all places.[5]

In this sermon, Wesley builds on the following Old Testament quotation: "If your heart is as true to mine as mine is to yours, give me your hand" (2 Kings 10:15). Wesley distinguishes between *doctrine* and *opinion*. In matters of doctrine that are essential to the integrity of Christianity, Wesley was unwavering. He declared,

> A catholic spirit is not *speculative latitudinarianism*. The catholic spirit is not (1) doctrinal indifference or (2) partisan bigotry concerning matters not central to the Christian faith. Such doctrinal indifference is the product of hell, not the offspring of heaven. Such unstable thought is being "tossed to and fro and blown about by every wind of doctrine," and it is a great curse, not a blessing. This vacillation is an irreconcilable enemy to true catholicism, not its friend. Persons of a truly catholic spirit are not still continuing to search for spiritual truth. In their understanding of the main tenets of Christian doctrine, they are as fixed as the sun.

The *Minutes* of Wesley's Methodist conferences reveal that while Wesley and his preachers were deeply concerned to maintain "sound doctrine," they sought to remain tolerant of "matters of opinion." Wesley urged his generation to overcome inconsequential differences between Christians in order for them to join together in their common faith and mission.

Wesley expressed his catholic spirit in a work titled *Plain Account of the People Called Methodists*:

> The thing which I was greatly afraid of all this time, and which I resolved to use every possible method of preventing, was a

> narrowness of spirit, a party zeal, a being straitened in our own bowels; that miserable bigotry which makes many so unready to believe that there is any work of God but among themselves. I thought it might be a help against this frequently to read, to all who were willing to hear, the accounts I received from time to time of the work which God is carrying on in the earth, both in our own and other countries, not among us alone, but among those of various opinions and denominations. For this I allotted one evening in every month. And I find no cause to repent my labour. It is generally a time of strong consolation to those who love God, and all mankind for his sake; as well as of breaking down the partition walls which either the craft of the devil or the folly of men has built up; and of encouraging every child of God to say (O when shall it once be?), "Whosoever doth the will of my Father which is in heaven, the same is my brother and sister and mother."[6]

Wesley closes this sermon by declaring, "Take caution that you do not vacillate in your understanding or limit your affections. Rather, keep a steady pace, rooted in the faith 'that was once for all entrusted to the saints.' Be grounded in true, catholic love until you are eternally taken up into love." Appended to the end of the sermon is Charles Wesley's hymn on Christian love and unity—a sublime expression of the catholic spirit.

Sermon 39

CATHOLIC SPIRIT

When [Jehu] . . . met Jehonadab son of Rechab coming to meet him; he greeted him, and said to him, "Is your heart as true to mine as mine is to yours?" Jehonadab answered, "It is." Jehu said, "If it is, give me your hand." (2 Kings 10:15)

1 Even those who do not love others as they should nevertheless acknowledge that it is our duty to love all humankind. The "royal law"—"You shall love your neighbor as yourself"—is self-authenticating to everyone who hears it. The biblical law of love should not receive the wretched interpretation given by certain ancient zealots. They said, "You shall love your relatives, acquaintances, and friends, but you should hate your enemies." This interpretation is clearly incorrect. Our Lord said,

> You have heard that it was said, "You shall love your neighbor and hate your enemy." But I say to you, Love your enemies and pray for those who persecute you, so that you may be children [and appear so to others] of your Father in heaven; for he makes his sun rise on the evil and on the good, and sends rain on the righteous and on the unrighteous. (Matt. 5:43-45)

2. Certainly, there is a particular love that Christians owe to those who love God. The psalmist David said, "As for the holy ones in the land, they are the noble, in whom is all my delight." And our Lord declared, "I give you a new commandment, that you love one another. Just as I have loved you, you also should love one another. By this everyone will know that you are my disciples, if you have love for one another."

The apostle John frequently and strongly acclaimed this kind of love. "This is the message you have heard from the beginning, that we should love one another. . . . We know love by this, that he laid down his life for us—and [if circumstances require] we ought to lay down our lives for one another." Saint John also said, "Beloved, let us love one another, because love is from God; everyone who loves is born of God and knows God. Whoever does not love does not know God, for God is love. . . . In this is love, not that we loved God but that he loved us and sent his Son to be the atoning sacrifice for our sins. Beloved, since God loved us so much, we also ought to love one another."

3. Everyone *commends* the principle of love, but does everyone *practice* it? Daily experience shows that they do not. Where are the Christians that even "love one another, just as Christ has commanded us"? There are many obstacles that lie in the way! For the most part, the two general hindrances to love are (1) Christians cannot all think alike, and, consequently, (2) they cannot all behave the same way. Even in the smaller details of their behavior, Christians differ in proportion to the disparity of their opinions.

4. Although differences in beliefs or modes of worship may prevent a perfect external union, do these things need to prevent our unity in affection for each other? Though we cannot think alike, can we not love alike? Can we not become one in heart, although we are not of one in opinion? Without any doubt, we can. All the children of God can unite in love, despite their lesser differences. Although our diversity remains, Christians can encourage one another in love and good deeds.

5. In this regard, surely the example of Jehu (even though his character was by no means perfect) is for every serious Christian quite worthy of attention and imitation: "When [Jehu] . . . met

Jehonadab son of Rechab coming to meet him; he greeted him, and said to him, 'Is your heart as true to mine as mine is to yours?' Jehonadab answered, 'It is.' Jehu said, 'If it is, give me your hand.'"

This biblical text naturally divides itself into two parts: (1) the question proposed by Jehu to Jehonadab, "Is your heart as true to mine as mine is to yours?" and (2) the offer given to Jehonadab, "If it is, give me your hand."

I. The Question: "Is Your Heart as True to Mine as Mine Is to Yours?"

1. First, let us consider the question proposed by Jehu to Jehonadab, "Is your heart as true to mine as mine is to yours?"

The first thing we can observe in these words is that Jehu does not ask about Jehonadab's *opinions*. It is certain that he held some views that were very unusual; indeed, they were quite unique. Some of these views had an immediate influence on his practice. Jehonadab stressed them so strongly that he required them of his children's children, to the last descendants. This fact is apparent from the prophet Jeremiah's account many years after Jehonadab's death:

> So I took Jaazaniah son of Jeremiah son of Habazziniah, and his brothers, and all his sons, and the whole house of the Rechabites. . . . Then I set before the Rechabites pitchers full of wine, and cups; and I said to them, "Have some wine." But they answered, "We will drink no wine, for our ancestor Jonadab son of Rechab commanded us, 'You shall never drink wine, neither you nor your children; nor shall you ever build a house, or sow seed; nor shall you plant a vineyard, or even own one; but you shall live in tents all your days, that you may live many days in the land where you reside.' We have obeyed the charge of our ancestor Jonadab son of Rechab in all that he commanded us, to drink no wine all our days, our wives, our sons, our daughters, or ourselves and not to build houses to live in. We have no vineyard or field or seed; but we have lived in tents, and have obeyed and done all that our ancestor Jonadab commanded us." (Jer. 35:3, 5-10)

2. Jehu's tendency in things secular and religious was to "drive like a maniac." However, when Jehu met Jehonadab, he was not concerned with any of the opinions that he held so closely. Rather, he allowed Jehonadab to "follow his own opinion." Neither Jehu nor Jehonadab seem to have given the other the slightest opposition to the beliefs he held.

3. It is very likely that today there are many good people who also hold peculiar beliefs. Some of these people may hold views as eccentric as those of Jehonadab. It is certain that as long as "we know only in part," we will not all see everything alike. It is a necessary result of the present deficiencies and limits of human understanding that people will hold different views in religion and in ordinary life. It has been this way since the beginning of the world, and it will continue "until the time of universal restoration."

4. Furthermore, we all believe that each of our particular beliefs is true. (To hold any view that we do not think is true is, of course, not to hold it at all.) Yet, none of us can be certain that all our beliefs are absolutely true. Indeed, every thinking person is assured that everything we believe cannot be true. It is necessary for every human being to err in some things. To be ignorant of many things and mistaken in others is the necessary condition of humanity. Wise people admit that this imperfection is true of themselves. They know that, in general, they are bound to misunderstand some things. However, they do not always know their precise mistakes, and perhaps they cannot ever know them all.

5. I say that perhaps they cannot know all their errors. Who can know the full extent of the scope of ignorance? Or, what amounts to the same thing, who understands the farthest reaches of intolerance? Prejudice is often so firmly implanted in young minds that later in life it is impossible to extract because it has gained such a deep root. Who can say (unless they know every aspect of the matter) just how responsible anyone is for his or her errors? Because all culpability must entail some confirmation of the will, only God who searches the heart can be the final judge.

6. Therefore, wise people will allow others the same freedom of thought they want others to allow them. They will no more insist that others embrace their opinions than they would want others

to impose opinions on them. Wise people are patient with those who differ from them. They only ask one question of those with whom they want to unite in love: "Is your heart as true to mine as mine is to yours?"

7. Second, we can see that Jehu does not ask about Jehonadab's *mode of worship.* (It is highly probable that in this regard they differed widely.) We may well believe that Jehonadab and his offspring worshiped God at Jerusalem, whereas Jehu did not. Jehu was more concerned about government policy than religion. He put to death those who worshiped Baal, and he "wiped out Baal from Israel." Still, Jehu did not turn aside from the sin of worshiping the golden calves.

8. Even among people of upright hearts who desire "to have a clear conscience toward God and all people," as long as there are different beliefs, there will be different ways of worshiping God. A difference of opinion necessarily leads to a difference of practice. In all ages, people have differed in their views about God more than in anything else. Consequently, in their practice they have differed most in the way they worship him. If these differences were limited to the heathen world, it would not surprise us. We know that the heathen "did not know God through wisdom," and it follows that they could not know how to worship him. The people of the Christian world all agree on the general truth that "God is spirit, and those who worship him must worship in spirit and truth." Nevertheless, among Christians, the individual modes of worshiping God are almost as different as they are among the heathen.

9. And how will we select from among so much variety? No one can choose for (or dictate to) another. In "holiness and godly sincerity," all people must follow the convictions of their own consciences. All must be "fully convinced in their own minds" and follow the best light they have. We do not have the authority to force others to walk according to our own customs. God has given no authority to any of us to control the consciences of our sisters and brothers. But we all must judge for ourselves, and "each of us will be accountable to God."

10. By the very nature of the Christian tradition, every follower of Christ is obligated to be a member of a congregation and some denomination. These affiliations entail a specific way of worshiping God. You do not have fellowship with others unless you agree with them. Yet, excepting one's own conscience, none can be obligated by any power on earth to choose one congregation over another, or one form of worship instead of another.

I am aware that it is usually assumed that the place of our birth determines the church to which we belong. We assume that someone who is born in England should be a member of the Church of England and accordingly worship God in the particular way this Church prescribes. I once passionately affirmed this assumption. Now, however, I find many reasons to moderate such a zealous viewpoint. I fear that this outlook is accompanied by too many problems for reasonable people to be able to surmount them. Not the least of these problems is that if this rule had been maintained there would never have been a reformation from the papal system. This notion completely undermines the right of private judgment on which the Protestant Reformation stands.

11. Therefore, I dare not presume to force my form of worship on any other person. I believe that the Anglican Church is truly ancient and apostolic. My belief, however, is not a conclusive guide for another person. Consequently, I do not ask others with whom I wish to unite in love, "Do you belong to my church or my congregation?" I do not ask whether they accept the same form of ecclesiastical government and acknowledge the same church officials that I do.

Nor do I ask, "Do you participate in the same form of prayer I use to worship God?" I do not inquire, "Do you receive the Lord's Supper in the same posture and manner that I do?" I do not explore whether their view of baptism or mode of baptism agrees with mine. I do not ask the age of those to be baptized or whether others even recognize the sacraments of baptism and the Lord's Supper (as clear as I am in my own mind about these questions). Let all these matters wait for a future discussion at a better time (if we even need to discuss them at all). For the present, I have only one question: "Is your heart as true to mine as mine is to yours?"

12. What does Jehu's question suggest for us today? I am not presently concerned with what Jehu meant in his time. I am asking what Christ's present-day disciples should mean when they ask others this question.

In the first place, Jehu's question means, "Is your heart right with God? Do you believe in his existence and perfect attributes? Do you believe in God's eternity, vastness, wisdom, power, justice, mercy, and truth? Do you believe that he now 'sustains all things by his powerful word'?" Does God have control of even the smallest and most abject things and use them for his own glory and the good of those who love him? I want to know if you have a divine, supernatural conviction of the truth of God's rule. Do you "walk by faith, not by sight"? Do you "look not at what can be seen but at what cannot be seen"?

13. Do you trust in the Lord Jesus Christ "who is over all, God blessed forever"? Has he been revealed in your soul? Do you "know Jesus Christ and him crucified"? Does he "abide in you and you in him"? Is Christ formed in your heart by faith? Having absolutely disallowed all your own good works and your own righteousness, have you "submitted to God's righteousness through faith in Jesus Christ"? Are you "found in him, not having a righteousness of your own, but one that comes through faith in Christ"? Through him are you "fighting the good fight of the faith" and "taking hold of eternal life"?

14. Is your faith filled with the power of love? Do you adore God? I do not add "above all things," because this phrase is an unscriptural and ambiguous expression. Rather, I ask whether you love God "with all your heart, and with all your soul, and with all your mind, and with all your strength." Do you seek all your happiness in him alone? And do you find that for which you are searching? Does your soul continually "magnify the Lord and your spirit rejoice in God your Savior"?

Have you learned to "give thanks in all circumstances"? Do you find "how good it is to sing praises to our God"? Is God the center of your soul and the sum of all your desires? Accordingly, are you "storing up for yourselves treasures in heaven" and "regarding everything else as loss"? Has God's love taken the love of the world from your soul? If so, you are "crucified to the world." Have you died, and is your life hidden with Christ in God?

15. Are you engaged not in doing your "own will, but the will of him who sent you"? Do you serve the one who sent you briefly to sojourn in the world, to spend a few days in a strange land until you finish the work he assigned you to do and return to your Father's house? Is it your food and drink to do the will of your Father who is in heaven? Is your eye clear in all things and constantly fixed on him, continually "looking unto Jesus"? Do you always refer to him in everything you do? Is Christ central in all your work, business, and manner of life? Do you aim only at God's glory in everything? "And whatever you do, in word or deed, do you do everything in the name of the Lord Jesus, giving thanks to God the Father through him?"

16. Does the love of God compel you to "serve the LORD with fear" and reverently rejoice in him? Are you more afraid of displeasing God than of sinking into death or hell? Is nothing more fearful to you than the thought of "defying his glorious presence"? With this attitude, do you "hate every false way" and every transgression of his holy and perfect law? Do you "do your best always to have a clear conscience toward God and all people"?

17. Is your heart right toward others? Without exception, do you "love all your neighbors as yourself"? "If you love those who love you, what credit is that to you?" Do you "love your enemies"? Is your soul full of goodwill and kind affection toward them? Do you love even the enemies of God, the unthankful, and the unrighteous? Do you compassionately have hope for them? Are you willing even to wish that you were temporarily "accursed" for their sakes? Do you demonstrate your compassion for others by "loving your enemies and praying for those who persecute you"?

18. Do you confirm your love by your works? When you have time and opportunity, do you truly "work for the good of all" whether for neighbors, strangers, friends, or enemies—good or bad? Do you do them all the good you can? Do you attempt to supply all their needs and to the uttermost of your ability assist

them in body and soul? If you have his disposition or even strive toward it, then "your heart [is] as true to mine as mine is to yours."

II. The Response: "If It Is, Give Me Your Hand"

1. "If your heart is as true to mine as mine is to yours, give me your hand." By this response, I do not mean, "Hold my beliefs." You need not believe everything I believe. I do not expect it or desire it. Neither do I mean, "I will adopt your beliefs." I cannot do so. My beliefs are not entirely contingent on my choice. I can no more think as I will than I can see or hear as I will. Keep your opinion, and I will keep mine—as steadfastly as ever. You need not make an effort to come over to my views or bring me over to yours. I do not ask you to debate those points or to hear or say a word about them. On both sides, let us leave our beliefs alone. I only ask you to "give me your hand."

2. By this statement, I do not mean "Embrace my ways of worship." Nor do I mean "I will embrace yours." Our preference for a mode of worship also is something that does not depend either on your choice or on mine. We must both act as we are "fully convinced in our own minds."

Cling to what you believe is most pleasing to God, and I will do the same. I believe that the Episcopal form of church government is scriptural and apostolic. If you think the Presbyterian or Congregational form is better, continue to think so and act accordingly. I believe that infants should be baptized and that this rite may be done either by dipping or by sprinkling. If you are persuaded otherwise, stay with your opinion, and follow your own persuasion. It appears to me that liturgies of prayer are excellent worship aids, especially in formal corporate services. If you think extemporaneous prayer is more helpful, act appropriately according to your own judgment.

My opinion is that I should not refuse to baptize people and that I should eat bread and drink wine as a memorial of my dying Master. But, if you are not convinced of my convictions, then act according to the light you have. I have no desire to debate with you a minute about any of the preceding points. Let all these lesser matters stay in the background and never come to the forefront. "If your heart is as my heart—if you love God and all humankind—I ask no more: 'Give me your hand.'"

3. By this statement, I mean, first, love me for who I am. I am not speaking of the general love you have for all humankind, the love you have for your enemies or God's, the love you have for those who hate and persecute you, or the love you have for strangers about whom you do not know anything good or bad. I am not satisfied with this love alone. Not at all.

If your heart is as true to mine as mine is to yours, then love me with a very kind affection, as "a true friend who sticks closer than one's nearest kin." Love me as a brother in Christ, an equal citizen of the new Jerusalem, and a fellow soldier engaged in the same warfare under the same "pioneer of our salvation." Love me as a companion in "the kingdom and the patient endurance" of Jesus and as a joint heir of his glory.

4. Love me to a higher degree than you love the mass of humankind. Love me with a love that is "patient and kind." If I am ignorant or mistaken, do not increase my burden; rather, bear it for me. Love is gentle, pleasant, and compassionate with me when I am in the wrong. Love is not envious, if ever it pleases God to prosper me in his work more than he prospers you. Love me with a love that "is not irritable or resentful" about my follies or infirmities.

Love endures, even if I fail to act according to God's will (as you see it). Love does not assume evil of me). Love lays aside jealousy and evil speculation. Love me with a love that covers all things and never divulges my faults or infirmities. Love believes all things, is always willing to think the best, and puts the highest construction on all my words and actions. Love hopes all things—either that the evil thing reported was never done, not done under the alleged circumstances, or at least that it was done with good intention or during the sudden stress of temptation. Love hopes to the end that whatever is wrong will by God's grace be corrected, and whatever is lacking will be supplied through the riches of his mercy in Christ Jesus.

5. Second, by saying, "Give me your hand," I mean, commit me to God in all your prayers. Wrestle in prayer with God on my behalf, asking him speedily to correct what he sees wrong in me and supply what is lacking in me. In your times of deepest prayer, plead with God who is near you that my heart will be more like your heart toward God and others. Pray that I will have a fuller conviction of things not seen and a stronger view of God's love in Christ Jesus.

Ask God that I will more consistently walk by faith, not by sight, and pray that I will more earnestly hold to eternal life. Pray that love for God and all humankind will be poured into my heart in a larger measure. Ask God that I may be more earnest and active in "doing the will of my Father who is in heaven," more "zealous for good deeds," and more careful to "abstain from every form of evil."

6. Third, when I invite you to give me your hand, I mean, awaken me to love and good deeds. As you have opportunity, follow up your prayer for me by speaking to me in love about whatever you believe will benefit the health of my soul. Enable me in the work that God has given me to do, and instruct me in how to do it more perfectly. Yes, when it appears that I am doing my own will instead of the will of he who sent me,

> Let the righteous strike me;
> let the faithful correct me. (Ps. 141:5; John 6:38)

O speak and do not withhold from me whatever you believe may help amend my faults, strengthen my weakness, build me up in love, or make me in any way more fit for the Master's use.

7. Finally, by asking for your hand, I mean, Love me "not in word or speech, but in truth and action." Insofar as your conscience allows (while still keeping your own beliefs and ways of worship), join with me in God's work and let us go forward hand in hand. At the least, you are free to go this far. Wherever you are, speak honestly about God's work, regardless of the workers, and say good things about them. If you possibly can, console them when they are in difficulty or distress. Offer them cheerful and effective support so that they will glorify God on your behalf.

8. We need to consider two things about offering our hand of fellowship to others. (1) Whatever love, good deeds, or spiritual and practical help I expect from those whose hearts are true to mine as mine is to theirs, by God's grace and to the best of my ability I am ready to give the same to them. (2) I have not spoken about myself only, but about all whose hearts are right toward God and others, that we may all love one another as Christ has loved us.

III. The Importance of Balance

1. From what we have seen, we can learn the meaning of the term "catholic spirit." Hardly any expression has been more greatly misunderstood and dangerously abused than the term "catholic spirit." However, any who calmly consider the foregoing explanations can correct any misconceptions of the term and avert misapplications.

First, we can learn that a catholic spirit is not *speculative latitudinarianism.* The catholic spirit is not indifference toward all beliefs. Such doctrinal apathy is the product of hell, not the offspring of heaven. Such unstable thought means being "tossed to and fro and blown about by every wind of doctrine." It is a great curse, not a blessing. This vacillation is not a friend to true catholicism; it is an irreconcilable enemy. Persons of a truly catholic spirit do not continually search for spiritual truth. In their understanding of the main tenets of Christian doctrine, they are as fixed as the sun. Of course, they are always ready to hear and consider whatever challenges their religious principles. This openness, however, does not indicate any uncertainty of mind and does not result in religious vacillation. The person who is doctrinally stable does not limp between two opposite opinions or vainly try to blend them together.

Keep this truth in mind, you people who do not know what you believe and yet claim to have a catholic spirit. You make this claim only because you are people with cloudy minds and confused understandings. You have no settled, consistent principles. Rather, you approve the muddling together of all opinions. Know definitely that you have completely missed your way. You do not realize where you are. You think you are into the very spirit of Christ, when in truth you are nearer the spirit of antichrist. Go first and learn the basic truths of the gospel of Christ, and then you will learn how to be of a truly catholic spirit.

2. Second, from what we have considered we can learn that a catholic spirit is not any kind of *practical latitudinarianism*—that is, accepting of almost every practice. The catholic spirit is not unconcerned about the practice and mode of public worship. Such indifference would not be a blessing; it would be a curse. Far from being a help to "worshiping the Father in spirit and in truth," an indifferent attitude is an indescribable obstacle to true worship. Persons of a truly catholic spirit have carefully thought about all things pertaining to public worship and have no doubt or reluctance concerning the particular form of worship in which they join. They are clearly convinced that their way of worshiping God is both scriptural and wise. They know of no other form of worship that is more biblical and sensible. Consequently, without wandering here and there, they cling closely to their form of worship. Moreover, they praise God for the opportunity to worship as God has led them.

3. Third, a catholic spirit is not apathetic about other ways of worship. This kind of tolerant "broad mindedness" is no less preposterous and unscriptural than the other kinds of latitudinarianism we have examined. Such indifference is far from a truly catholic spirit. Those who really are catholic in spirit are as settled in their congregation as they are in their beliefs. They are united to one congregation in spirit and in all the outward ties of Christian fellowship. There, they partake of all the ordinances of God, receive holy communion, pour out their souls in common prayers, and join in public praise and thanksgiving. In their congregation, they rejoice to hear the message of reconciliation and the gospel of the grace of God. On solemn occasions, these people and their nearest companions seek God by fasting.

They have special loving concerns for the members of their congregations, and the commitment is mutual. They admonish, encourage, comfort, reprove, and in every way strengthen one another in the faith. They regard one another as members of the same family. According to the abilities God has given them, they unhesitatingly care for others and provide for them so that they will have "everything needed for life and godliness."

4. Steadfast, they hold firmly to their religious principles—those things they believe to be the truth as it is in Jesus. They unwaveringly adhere to the worship forms that they consider most acceptable in God's sight, and they unite to a particular congregation in the kindest and closest ties.

At the same time, their hearts reach out to everyone they know and do not know. With strong and cordial affection, they embrace neighbors and strangers, as well as friends and enemies. This kind of love is catholic (universal) love. Those who have this love possess a catholic spirit. Love alone validates its character, and a catholic spirit is universal love.

5. If then we understand catholic love in its true sense (that is, in the way we have described in this sermon), those who have a catholic spirit offer their hands to all whose hearts are at one with their hearts. Those people have catholic spirits who know how to value and praise God for all the advantages they enjoy. They understand the things of God—the true, scriptural manner of worshiping him. Above all, they are members of a congregation that "fears God and does what is right and acceptable to him." They hold on to these blessings with the greatest care, guarding them as the apple of the eye.

At the same time, they love all who believe in the Lord Jesus Christ, regardless of their opinions, form of worship, or congregational membership. People of a catholic spirit regard all fellow believers who love God and others as members of Christ and children of God who are joint partakers of the kingdom of God and fellow heirs of God's eternal kingdom. People of a catholic spirit rejoice to please God and fear to offend him. They are careful to abstain from evil and are zealous for good deeds.

Christians who truly have a catholic spirit keep their sisters and brothers in Christ in their hearts. They have an indescribable affection for them, yearn for their welfare, ceaselessly entrust them to God in prayer, and intervene with others on their behalf.

They speak encouragingly to them, and in all their words they work to strengthen them in God. To the utmost of their abilities, in everything spiritual and temporal, they help their Christian sisters and brothers. They are ready "to spend and be spent" for others and even to "lay down their lives" for their sakes.

6. You, O saint of God, think on these things. If you are already living in this way, continue doing so. If up to this time you have taken the wrong path, bless God who has brought you back. Now, in the royal way of universal love, run the race that is set before you. Take caution that you do not vacillate in your understanding or limit your affections. Rather, keep a steady pace, rooted in the faith "that was once for all entrusted to the saints." Be grounded in true, catholic love until you are taken up into God's eternal love.

John Wesley first published this sermon in 1750 in volume 3 of his Sermons on Several Occasions. *In 1755, H. Cock republished the sermon separately and added the following hymn written by Charles Wesley. The hymn, consisting of 7 six-line stanzas, highlights love, respect, and unity among Christian believers.*

1.

Weary of all this wordy strife,
These notions, forms, and modes, and names,
To Thee, the Way, the Truth, the Life,
Whose love my simple heart inflames,
Divinely taught, at last I fly
With Thee and Thine to live and die.

2.

Forth from the midst of *Babel* brought,
Parties and sects I cast behind;
Inlarged my heart, and free my thought,
Where'er the latent truth I find,
The latent truth with joy to own,
And bow to Jesus' name alone.

3.

Redeem'd by Thine almighty grace,
   I taste my glorious liberty.
With open arms the world embrace,
   But *cleave* to those who cleave to Thee;
But only in Thy saints *delight*.
Who walk with God in purest white.

4.

One with the little flock I rest,
   The members sound who hold the Head;
The chosen few, with pardon blest,
   And by th' anointing spirit led
Into the mind that was in Thee,
In to the depth of Deity.

5.

My brethren, friends, and kinsmen these,
   Who do my heavenly Father's will,
Who *aim* at perfect holiness,
   And all Thy counsels to fulful,
Athirst to be whate're Thou art,
And love their God with all their heart.

6.

For these, howe're in flesh disjoin'd,
   Where'er dispersed o'er earth abroad,
Unfeigned, unbounded love I find,
   And constant as the life of God;
Fountain of life, from thence it sprung,
As pure, as even, and as strong.

7.

Join'd to the hidden church unknown
  In this sure bond of perfectness,
Obscurely safe, I dwell alone,
  And glory in th' uniting grace,
To me, to each believer given,
To all Thy saints in earth and heaven.

Notes

1. Andrew Landale Drummond, *German Protestantism Since Luther* (London: The Epworth Press, 1951), 20.

2. Davies, *The Methodist Societies: History, Nature, and Design,* "The Character of a Methodist," 9:33-34.

3. Wesley, *Explanatory Notes upon the New Testament,* Preface. See also his commentary on Matthew 5:47.

4. Telford, *Wesley's Letters*, 4:218.

5. Outler, *Wesley's Sermons,* "On the Death of George Whitefield," 2:341.

6. Davies, *The Methodist Societies: History, Nature, and Design,* "A Plain Account of the People Called Methodists," 9:265-66.

Introduction to Sermon 40

CHRISTIAN PERFECTION

The doctrine of Christian perfection is the most distinguishing theological feature of John Wesley's thought and the Methodist movement that he founded. Explaining this doctrine, Wesley wrote, "By that perfection, to which St. Paul directs [us] to go on, (Heb. 6:1,) I understand neither more nor less, than what St. John terms 'perfect love' (1 John 4:18;) and our Lord, 'loving the Lord our God with all our heart, and mind, and soul, and strength.'"[1]

Due to misunderstandings of this teaching, some have contended that it is unsound and indefensible. Some have charged that Christian perfection is not a Protestant doctrine. Wesley, of course, was very much a Protestant. Concerning the sixteenth-century Protestant Reformers, Wesley wrote, "They were not only reformed from very many erroneous opinions, and from numberless superstitious and idolatrous modes of worship, till then prevailing over the western church; but they were also exceedingly reformed with respect to their lives and tempers. More of the ancient, scriptural Christianity was to be found, almost in every part of Europe."[2] Wesley was in full accord with the Reformation doctrines of biblical authority, justification, and adoption. However, he emphasized regeneration and sanctification to a greater extent than did the Reformers.

A hallmark of Wesleyan theology is God's call to holiness of heart and life, a teaching that appears throughout the Scriptures. For example, the Pentateuch records God's declaration to his people:

> For I am the LORD your God; sanctify yourselves therefore, and be holy, for I am holy. You shall not defile yourselves. . . . For I am the LORD who brought you up from the land of Egypt, to be your God; you shall be holy, for I am holy. (Lev. 11:44, 45)

The theme of holiness also permeates the writings of the prophets. Ezekiel delivered God's message: "I will give them one heart, and put a new spirit within them; I will remove the heart of stone from their flesh and give them a heart of flesh, so that they may follow my statutes and keep my ordinances and obey them. Then they shall be my people, and I will be their God" (Ezek. 11:19, 20). God's ancient commands and promises to Israel are echoed and developed more fully in the New Testament. Saint Paul prayed, "May the God of peace himself sanctify you entirely; and may your spirit and soul and body be kept sound and blameless at the coming of our Lord Jesus Christ. The one who calls you is faithful, and he will do this" (1 Thess. 5:23). The apostle Peter echoed this theme: "As he who called you is holy, be holy yourselves in all your conduct; for it is written, 'You shall be holy, for I am holy'" (1 Pet. 1:15, 16). Wesley took very seriously the biblical call to live righteously, which is summed up by the writer of Hebrews: "Pursue . . . holiness without which no one will see the Lord" (Heb. 12:14).

One important factor that has contributed to a misunderstanding of John Wesley's teaching on holiness is *context.* The sixteenth-century Protestant Reformers corrected the confused belief of many that we gain salvation through human merit. In opposition to this concept, the Reformers powerfully championed the biblical doctrines of justification and adoption, which are works of grace that God does for us to change our position before God. The Reformers emphasized *relative righteousness*, which God *imputes* to believers to give them a new *standing.*

In the eighteenth century, Wesley faced a contrasting challenge to the gospel—the incorrect belief that faith cancels the need for good works or personal holiness. To be sure, Wesley agreed with the Protestant Reformers that salvation is based entirely on the atonement of Christ and the unmerited grace of God. Yet, given England's eighteenth-century drift toward Antinomianism, Wesley also accentuated a *realized righteousness,* which God *imparts* to believers to change their *state.* The different contexts and needs respectively in the sixteenth and eighteenth centuries called for different emphases. The Reformers addressed the need to understand that "by grace [we] have been saved through faith, and this is not [our] own doing" (Eph. 2:8, 9). Wesley addressed the need to take seriously the biblical statement, "Pursue . . . the holiness without which no one will see the Lord" (Heb. 12:14). He called for a faith that works through love (Gal. 5:6). Wesley sought to avoid the two errors of positing works without faith, and faith without works.

Another factor that has contributed to a misunderstanding of John Wesley's teaching on Christian perfection is *terminology.* The Reformers understood the Latin word *perfectus* ("perfect") in static terms. The word *perfectus* means an absolute perfection that is finished and complete—a "perfected perfection."[3] By definition, this perfection cannot be improved. Understood in this way, it is obvious that perfection can be ascribed only to God. John Wesley, however, by no means taught absolute perfection. He was aware of the early church fathers who wrote in Greek and Latin, and he read them in the original languages. He was especially familiar with the ante-Nicene writers who wrote in Greek. They used the New Testament Greek word *teleiosis* ("perfect"), which is not static, in contrast to the static Latin term *perfectus. Teleiosis* is a dynamic term that implies continuing growth and ongoing movement toward an ever-greater maturity. In this light, a small growing apple in the month of June can be described as a "perfect" apple—even if in the following months it will become increasingly mature and perfect. Because many in Wesley's day understood the term *perfect* in its Latin meaning rather than in its Greek meaning, we can understand how Wesley's theological opponents and even some of his followers could have easily misunderstood him. The perfection that Wesley taught was not a stationary or completed perfection. It was a *relative* perfection—a perfection of *love* that leads to ever greater and greater degrees of holiness.

A third cause for misunderstanding Wesley's view of Christian perfection pertains to the word *sin*. The Protestant Reformers defined sin as any act that falls short of the absolute perfection of God. Given that concept of sin, we can understand why they insisted that Christians sin continually in thought, word, and deed. John Wesley, however, understood sin as a willful transgression of a known law of God. He did not regard unintentional or involuntary transgressions as "sin properly so called." (Even so, he taught that unintentional transgressions and human errors of judgment needed Christ's atonement.) Thus, it is easy to see why others misunderstood Wesley's call to Christian perfection.

In John Wesley's treatise *A Plain Account of Christian Perfection,* he further clarified his view on the subject of sin:

> To explain myself a little farther on this head: (1.) Not only sin, properly so called, (that is, a voluntary transgression of a known law,) but sin, improperly so called, (that is, an involuntary transgression of a divine law, known or unknown,) needs the atoning blood. (2.) I believe there is no such perfection in this life as excludes these involuntary transgressions which I apprehend to be naturally consequent on the ignorance and mistakes inseparable from mortality. (3.) Therefore *sinless perfection* is a phrase I never use, lest I should seem to contradict myself. (4.) I believe, a person filled with the love of God is still liable to these involuntary transgressions. (5.) Such transgressions you may call sins, if you please: I do not, for the reasons above-mentioned.[4]

Wesley never taught that we could achieve perfect performance, but he did insist that God gives Christians the grace and power not to sin deliberately and willfully.

Wesley championed the Christian perfection that he found in the Scriptures, the Church Fathers, the Homilies of the Church of England, and writers such as Thomas à Kempis (1380–1471), Jeremy Taylor (1613–67), and William Law (1686–1761). These writings helped him understand holiness in terms of our affections, intentions, and motives. Wesley believed that God wills for us to demonstrate the kind of love that Jesus commanded: "'You shall love the Lord your God with all your heart, and with all your soul, and with all your mind.' This is the greatest and first commandment. And a second is like it: 'You shall love your neighbor as yourself.' On these two commandments hang all the law and the prophets" (Matt. 22:37-40).

Wesley explained the origin of the present sermon:

> I think it was in the latter end of the year 1740, that I had a conversation with Dr. Gibson, then Bishop of London, at Whitehall. He asked me what I meant by perfection. I told him without any disguise or reserve. When I ceased speaking, he said, 'Mr. Wesley, if this be all you mean, publish it to all the world. If any one then can confute what you say, he may have free leave.' I answered, 'My Lord, I will'; and accordingly wrote and published the sermon on Christian perfection. In this I endeavoured to show, (1.) In what sense Christians are not, (2.) In what sense they are, perfect.[5]

Wesley's interest in God's imparting righteousness to us was consistent with his approval of the hymn written by one of his contemporaries, Augustus Toplady, in 1776:

> Rock of Ages, cleft for me,
> Let me hide myself in thee;
> Let the water and the blood,
> From thy wounded side which flowed,
> Be of sin the double cure;
> Save from wrath and make me pure.

It was Charles Wesley, however, who excelled in expressing holiness and Christian perfection through hymns. To this day, Christians sing such hymns of Charles Wesley as the following:

> O for a heart to praise my God.
> A heart from sin set free,
> A heart that always feels thy blood
> So freely shed for me.

A heart resigned, submissive, meek,
My great Redeemer's throne,
Where only Christ is heard to speak,
Where Jesus reigns alone.

A humble, lowly, contrite heart,
Believing, true, and clean,
Which neither life nor death can part
From him that dwells within;

A heart in every thought renewed
And full of love divine,
Perfect and right and pure and good,
A copy, Lord, of thine:

Thy nature, gracious Lord, impart;
Come quickly from above;
Write thy new name upon my heart,
Thy new, best name of Love.[6]

Explaining Christian perfection more formally, John Wesley described it as "loving God with all our heart, mind, soul, and strength. This implies that no wrong temper, none contrary to love, remains in the soul; and that all the thoughts, words, and actions, are governed by pure love."[7] In 1764, Wesley summarized his teaching on the doctrine of Christian perfection:

> (1.) There is such a thing as perfection; for it is again and again mentioned in Scripture. (2.) It is not so early as justification; for justified persons are to 'go on unto perfection.' (Heb. 6:1) (3.) It is not so late as death; for St. Paul speaks of living men that were perfect. (Philip. 3:15) (4.) It is not absolute. Absolute perfection belongs not to man, nor to angels, but to God alone. (5.) It does not make a man infallible: None is infallible, while he remains in the body. (6.) Is it sinless? It is not worth while to contend for a term. It is 'salvation from sin.' (7.) It is 'perfect love.' (1 John 4:18.) This is the essence of it; its properties, or inseparable fruits, are, rejoicing evermore, praying without ceasing, and in everything giving thanks. (1 Thess. v. 16, &c.) (8.) It is improvable. It is so far

> from lying in an indivisible point, from being incapable of increase, that one perfected in love may grow in grace far swifter than he did before. (9.) It is amissible, capable of being lost; of which we have numerous instances. But we were not thoroughly convinced of this, till five or six years ago. (10.) It is constantly both preceded and followed by a gradual work.[8]

As to the question of *when* one may judge himself or herself to have attained this experience, Wesley responded,

> When, after having been fully convinced of inbred sin, by a far deeper and clearer conviction than that he experienced before justification, and after having experienced a gradual mortification of it, he experiences a total death to sin, and an entire renewal in the love and image of God, so as to rejoice evermore, to pray without ceasing, and in everything to give thanks. Not that 'to feel all love and no sin' is a sufficient proof. Several have experienced this for a time, before their souls were fully renewed. None therefore ought to believe that the work is done, till there is added the testimony of the Spirit, witnessing his entire sanctification, as clearly as his justification.[9]

In 1790, shortly before his death, Wesley wrote that the doctrine of Christian perfection was "the grand depositum which God has lodged with the people called Methodists; and for the sake of propagating this chiefly He appeared to have raised us up."[10] This sermon constitutes one of Wesley's clearest explanations of this doctrine. Printed after the sermon is a poem by Charles Wesley, titled "The Promise of Sanctification."

Sermon 40

CHRISTIAN PERFECTION

Not that I have already obtained this or have already reached the goal. *(Philippians 3:12)*

1 In Holy Scripture, scarcely any expression has given more offense than the term *perfection. Perfect* is a word that many people cannot tolerate. The very mention of it is an abomination to them. Whoever "preaches perfection" (as they refer to it) and asserts that it is attainable in this life runs the great danger of being considered worse than a heathen or petty tax collector.

2. Consequently, some people advise against ever using the words *perfect* and *perfection* because they claim that they give "such great offense." But are these words not found in the Bible? Because they *are* found there, by what authority can any of God's messengers set them aside, even if everyone would be offended by their use? That is not the way we learned Christ, and we will not make room for the devil. Whatever God has spoken, we will speak, whether others hear or refuse to hear. Only by speaking God's truth can any of Christ's ministers "not be responsible for the blood of any, because they do not shrink from declaring to them the whole purpose of God."

3. We cannot set aside the words *perfect* and *perfection*. They are the words of God, not of mortals. But we can and should explain their meaning so that the sincere of heart will not err to the right hand or to the left and miss "the goal for the prize of the heavenly call." An explanation is needed all the more because in our text, St. Paul speaks of himself as *not* perfect: "Not that I have already obtained this or have already reached the goal." Yet, immediately after making this statement, the apostle speaks of himself and many others as being perfect: "Let those of us then who are mature [perfect] be of the same mind."

4. I want to remove the dilemma arising from this seeming contradiction to give light to those who are pressing forward to the mark and to prevent "what is lame from being put out of joint." I will endeavor to explain (1) in what sense Christians *are not* perfect and (2) in what sense Christians *are* perfect.

I. In What Sense Christians Are Not Perfect

1. In the first place, I will attempt to show in what sense Christians are not perfect. First, from both experience and Scripture it becomes clear that they are not perfect in *knowledge*. In this life, Christians are not perfect to the extent that they are free from ignorance. As well as all others, they know many things about the present world. And, with regard to the world to come, they understand the general truths that God has revealed. They also know spiritual truths that unspiritual people do not know because these truths are spiritually discerned.

Christians understand "what love the Father has given us, that we should be called children of God." They know the powerful working of God's Spirit in their hearts and the wisdom of his providence directing all their paths and causing all things to work together for their good. Indeed, in every circumstance of life they know what the Lord requires of them and how "to have a clear conscience toward God and all people."

2. Yet there are countless things that Christians do not know. In the book of Job, we read,

> The Almighty—we cannot find him;
>   he is great in power and justice,
> These are indeed but the outskirts of his ways;
>   and how small a whisper do we hear of him!
> But the thunder of his power who can understand?
> (Job 37:23; 26:14)

As is the case with everyone else, Christians do not understand these mysteries. I cannot explain how there are three that testify—the Father, the Son, and the Holy Spirit—and how these three agree. I do not fathom how the eternal Son of God "emptied himself, taking the form of a slave." I cannot understand a single attribute of God or any detail of his divine nature.

Christians do not know "the times or periods" when God will work his great works upon the earth. We cannot grasp even the things that God has partly revealed to his servants the prophets from the time the world began. Much less do Christians know when God, for the sake of the elect, will cut short the days and bring in his kingdom, or when "the heavens will pass away with a loud noise, and the elements will be dissolved with fire."

3. Christians do not even understand the reasons for many of God's present dispensations with regard to humankind. The Christian is compelled to wait here on earth for God's further revelation.

> Clouds and thick darkness are all around him;
> righteousness and justice are the foundation of his throne.
> (Ps. 97:2)

Indeed, in God's dealings with Christians, he often says to them, "You do not know now what I am doing, but later you will understand." How little do God's children comprehend even what they see before them—the visible works of God's hands! They do not fathom how God "stretches out the North over the void, and hangs the earth upon nothing" or how he unites all the parts of this vast cosmos by a hidden chain that cannot be broken. Even the best of people have vast incomprehension and small understanding. Therefore, no one in this life is so perfect as to be free from ignorance.

4. Second, Christians are not perfect to the extent that they are free from *making mistakes*. Errors are almost an unavoidable consequence of limited human understanding. "We know only in part," and we are always subject to being mistaken about the things that we do not know. It is true, though, that God's children do not err regarding the things that are essential to salvation. They do not "put darkness for light and light for darkness." "They do not invite death by the error of their lives, or bring on destruction by the works of their hands."[11] Christians "are all taught by God." The path that God teaches them is the way of holiness, and it is so clear that "no traveler, not even fools, shall go astray."

In matters that are not essential to salvation, however, Christians make frequent mistakes. The best and wisest people are frequently wrong about facts. They believe some things did not happen, when they really did; they think some things have been done that were not done. Even if they are not mistaken about a fact, they may be wrong about its details. They believe many or all the details to be quite different from what they really are.

These kinds of mistakes are certain to produce many additional errors. Consequently, Christians may believe that some evil things are good and that some good things are evil. As a result, they may not correctly assess the integrity of others. They may assume that good people are better than they are or that evil people are worse than they are. They may believe that a wicked person is good or that a holy and righteous person is wicked.

5. With regard to understanding the Bible, the best of people daily err about its meaning (as careful as they try to avoid doing so). They may especially misunderstand those passages that do not directly relate to their lives. Therefore, even God's children do not always agree on the interpretation of many passages of the Bible. These differences of interpretations are no proof that the people on both sides of an issue are not equally God's children. Contrasts in understanding only prove that we can no more expect any mortal to be infallible than to be omniscient (all knowing).

6. Some may object to what I have said on the basis of what St. John wrote to his sisters and brothers in the faith: "You have been

anointed by the Holy One, and all of you have knowledge." The answer to this objection, however, is obvious: Christians know everything necessary for the health of their souls. It is clear that the apostle never intended to expand further the application of this statement.

First, he did not describe the disciple as being "above his teacher." Christ himself, in human form, did not know all things. Concerning his return and the close of the age, he said, "About that day and hour no one knows . . . but only the Father." Second, St. John's later words are clear: "I write this to you about those who would deceive you." Other scriptures also frequently caution, "Let no one deceive you." This counsel would have been pointless if those who had an anointing from the Holy One were not subject to ignorance and mistakes. Christians, therefore, are not so perfect as to be free from ignorance or error.

7. Third, we can add that Christians are not free from *infirmities*. It is important to understand this word correctly. Let us not use this unclear word, *infirmities*, to refer to sins, as some do. A person might say, "Everyone has his infirmity, and mine is drunkenness." Given this understanding of *infirmities*, another person has the "infirmity" of immorality, another the "infirmity" of taking God's holy name in vain, and still another the "infirmity" of calling his sister or brother a fool, or returning "reviling for reviling." It is clear that if those of you who speak this way do not repent, you will all go quickly into hell, along with your "infirmities."

When I use the word *infirmity*, I mean both "physical infirmities" and those inward or outward imperfections that are not of a moral nature. Included in these infirmities are slowness of understanding, dull or confused perception, muddled thought, uneven ability to respond, and a sluggish mind. A poor memory falls into this category (not to mention other infirmities).

Another variety of infirmity includes the consequences of these limitations. Among them are slowness of speech, incorrect grammar, and unpolished pronunciation. To these flaws, one could add a thousand nameless defects in speech or manners. To a greater or lesser degree, these infirmities appear in the best of people. None of us can hope to be perfectly free of these defects until our spirits return to God who gave them.

8. Pending our return to God in eternity, we cannot expect until that time to be completely rid of temptation. We will not have such perfection in this life. It is true that some people are eager to "practice every kind of uncleanness." They scarcely recognize the temptations that they do not resist. In this sense, they seem to be without temptation.

In addition, there are many who Satan, the wise enemy of souls, sees to be fast asleep in a dead form of godliness. He does not tempt them to outrageous sin, for fear that they would awaken before they drop into everlasting flames. I also know that there are children of God, being now justified freely, "through the redemption that is in Christ Jesus," who for the present feel no temptation. God has said to their enemies, "Do not touch my anointed ones; do my children no harm." During this period, perhaps for weeks or months, God "sets them atop the heights of the land" and "bears them on eagles' wings" above "all the flaming arrows of the evil one."

This state of freedom from temptation, however, will not last. We learn this fact from the single example of the Son of God himself. So long as he was on earth, he was tempted to the end of his life. Therefore, let his servants also expect to be tempted: "It is enough for the servant to be like the master."

9. Despite what some may claim, Christian perfection does not mean exemption from ignorance, mistakes, infirmities, or temptations. In truth, Christian perfection is only another name for holiness—as it were, two names for the same thing. Therefore, everyone who is perfect is holy, and everyone who is holy is, in the scriptural sense, perfect.

Finally, we can observe that there is no *perfection of degrees* (as it is termed). There is no holiness that does not allow for continuous growth. However holy one may become or to whatever high degree of holiness we may have reached, we still need to "grow in grace" and daily to advance in the knowledge and love of God our Savior.

II. In What Sense Christians Are Perfect

1. In the second place, I will consider in what sense Christians *are* perfect. At the outset, it should be seen that there are several stages in the Christian life as well as in the natural life. Some of God's children are newborn infants, and others have attained a greater maturity. Accordingly, in his first Epistle, St. John speaks to those he calls "little children," to those he refers to as "young people," and to those he designates "fathers."

First, he said, "I am writing to you, little children, because your sins are forgiven." "You have been justified," and "have peace with God through our Lord Jesus Christ." Second, St. John also said, "I write to you, young people, because you are strong and the word of God abides in you, and you have overcome the evil one." You have "quenched all the flaming arrows of the evil one"—those doubts and fears through which Satan disturbed their first peace. The witness of God that their sins were forgiven "remains in their hearts." Finally, John said, "I write to you, fathers, because you know him who is from the beginning." "You have known the Father, Son, and Holy Spirit in your inmost soul. You have come to maturity (perfection), to the measure of the full stature of Christ."

2. In the second part of this sermon, I am speaking about those "fathers" to whom St. John wrote. They are truly and authentically Christians. Yet even "infants in Christ" "have been born of God and do not sin." If anyone doubts this privilege of the children of God, we cannot resolve the question by theoretical thinking. Arguments can be drawn out endlessly without settling a matter. Neither can we put an end to the matter by referring to the experience of this or that particular person. Many people may presume that they do not commit sin, when in fact they do. But their claims do not settle anything one way or another. Instead, we appeal to the teaching and instruction (or to the "law and to the testimony") in the Bible. "Although everyone is a liar, let God be proved true." By God's word alone we will live, and by his word we shall be judged.

3. The word of God clearly discloses that even those who are justified (newly born again) do not "continue in sin." They

cannot "go on living in sin." They are "united with him in a death like his." "Their old self was crucified with him so that the body of sin might be destroyed, and we might no longer be enslaved to sin. For whoever has died is freed from sin." They are "dead to sin and alive to God." "For sin has no dominion over them, because they are not under law but under grace." "Having been set free from sin, they have become slaves of righteousness."

4. At the very least, we can learn from these verses that those whom I have described (all genuine Christians who trust in Christ) are set free from outwardly sinful deeds. The same freedom that St. Paul describes in these verses is reaffirmed by St. Peter: "Whoever has suffered in the flesh has finished with sin, so as to live . . . no longer by human desires but by the will of God." Certainly, being finished with sin in one's outward behavior must mean ceasing from the outward transgression of the law.

5. The most explicit statement about being finished with sin is found in the familiar words of St. John in the third chapter of his first Epistle:

> Everyone who commits sin is a child of the devil; for the devil has been sinning from the beginning. The Son of God was revealed for this purpose, to destroy the works of the devil. Those who have been born of God do not sin, because God's seed abides in them; they cannot sin, because they have been born of God. (1 John 3:8, 9)

Saint John also said, "We know that those who are born of God do not sin, but the one who was born from God (Jesus Christ) protects them, and the evil one does not touch them."

6. Some say that these verses mean that Christians do not sin *willfully* or *habitually*, or that they do not sin to the extent that others do, or that they do not sin as they once did. Who says this? Does St. John? No, he does not. There are no such qualifying words in the text, the chapter, the Epistle, or in any of his writings at all. The best way to answer an audacious opinion is simply to deny it. If there are those who can prove this notion from the Word of God, let them present their strongest reasons.

7. To support the outlandish claims that Christians must continue to sin, some people have advanced a sort of reasoning that they extract from certain examples in the Bible. They say, "Look! Did not Abraham himself commit sin by lying and denying that he was married to Sarah? Did not Moses commit sin when he became angry with God at the waters of Meribah? To give a comprehensive illustration, did not even David, a man after God's heart, commit the sins of adultery and murder against Uriah the Hittite?"

I answer that it is certainly obvious that David did sin. But what are you inferring about the future? First, it is absolutely true that in the general course of David's life he was one of the holiest among the Jewish people. Second, we concede that the holiest of the Jews did sometimes commit sin. But if you deduce that all Christians *must* and *do* commit sin for as long as they live, we utterly reject this conclusion. Such a deduction cannot be drawn from those premises.

8. Those who argue that of necessity Christians must sin continually seem never to have considered the words of our Lord. He declared: "Truly I tell you, among those born of women no one has arisen greater than John the Baptist; yet the least in the kingdom of heaven is greater than he." I really fear that there are some who have hypothesized that in this passage, "the kingdom of heaven" refers to the kingdom of glory. This interpretation alleges that the Son of God was revealing to us that the least glorified saint in heaven is greater than anyone upon the earth! To state this view is adequately to refute it. Sufficient refutation can doubtless be presented. Here, "the kingdom of heaven" (or "the kingdom of God," as St. Luke calls it) refers to God's kingdom on earth, to which belong all who truly trust in Christ.

In the following verse, it is said that we are to take this kingdom "by force." In these words, our Lord declares two things. First, prior to his coming in the flesh among us mortals, there had never been one greater than John the Baptist. It evidently follows that neither Abraham, David, nor any Jew was greater than John.

Second, our Lord declares that one who is least in the kingdom of God is greater than John (in the kingdom that Jesus came to set up on earth and that the aggressive now began "to take by force"). The obvious conclusion is that the least of those who now have Christ as their king are greater than Abraham or David or any Jew there ever was. And none of those Old Testament saints ever exceeded the greatness of John. But the least of those who trust Christ are greater than John. They are not greater prophets (as some have interpreted these words) because it is evident that they are not. They are, however, greater in the grace of God and the knowledge of our Lord Jesus Christ.

Therefore, we cannot measure the privileges of real Christians by those previously given to the Jews. We acknowledge that their ministry (or dispensation) was glorious. Ours, however, *abounds* in glory. Those who would lower the Christian dispensation to the Jewish standard are in error. It is completely inaccurate to gather examples of weaknesses recorded in the Old Testament and conclude from them that those who have "clothed themselves with Christ" are endued with no greater strength than they were. Those who teach this theory "are wrong, because they know neither the scriptures nor the power of God."

9. Someone may ask, "If we cannot infer from examples in the Bible that Christians must and do sin constantly, are there not scriptural assertions that prove this point? Does not the Bible explicitly say, 'Even a just man sins seven times a day?'"

I answer this question by saying, "Not at all! Scripture says no such thing. There is no analogous text in the Bible. What you have in mind is found in the book of Proverbs: 'Though [the righteous] fall seven times, they will rise again.' This verse speaks to something entirely different. First, the words *a day* are not in the text. This verse can apply to a righteous person who falls seven times during his *lifetime*."

Second, this verse contains no mention at all of "falling into sin." These words refer to "falling into earthly affliction." The preceding verse is clear at this point: "Do not lie in wait like an outlaw against the home of the righteous; do no violence to the place where the righteous live." Next, we read, "Though the righteous fall seven times, they will rise again; but the wicked are overthrown by calamity." It is as though the writer had said, "God will deliver the righteous out of their trouble. But when the wicked fall, there will be no one to deliver them."

10. The objectors still continue: "In other places, Solomon clearly asserts, 'There is no man who does not sin.' Indeed, Solomon said, 'Surely there is no one on earth so righteous as to do good without ever sinning.'" I answer that doubtless in the days of Solomon it was as he stated—there is no one who did not sin. This state of affairs was true from Adam to Moses, from Moses to Solomon, and from Solomon to Christ. During that period, there was no one who did not sin. From the day sin entered into the world, "surely there is no one on earth so righteous as to do good without ever sinning."[12]

Then, in the fullness of time, the Son of God "was revealed to take away sins." It is certainly true that "heirs, as long as they are minors, are no better than slaves." All the ancient holy ones who were under the Jewish dispensation were "minors" during that infant state of the community of God. While they were minors, they were enslaved to the elemental spirits of the world.

But when the fullness of time had come, God sent his Son, born under the law, in order to redeem those who were under the law, so that we might receive adoption as children. God planned that we might receive the grace that "has now been revealed through the appearing of our Savior Christ Jesus, who abolished death and brought life and immortality to light through the gospel." These "are no longer slaves but God's children." Whatever the conditions that prevailed under the law, with St. John, we can now safely affirm that since the gospel was given, "those who are born of God do not sin."

11. More thoroughly than usual, it is highly important for us to consider the far-reaching difference between the Jewish and Christian dispensations. It is important to see the basis of the Christian dispensation, which St. John reports in his Gospel. There, it is recorded that Jesus declared, "As the scripture has said, 'Out of the believer's heart shall flow rivers of living water.'" The apostle immediately added, "Now Jesus said this about the Spirit, which believers in him were to receive; for as yet there was no Spirit, because Jesus was not yet glorified." By these words, the

apostle does not mean (as some have taught) that the miracle-working power of the Holy Spirit had not yet been given.

Our Lord had already granted miraculous powers to all his apostles when he first sent them forth to preach the gospel. At that time, he had given them "authority over unclean spirits, to cast them out" and to "cure the sick" and even "raise the dead." Still, the Holy Spirit was not yet given in his sanctifying graces, as he was after Jesus was glorified. God sent the fullness of the Holy Spirit after Jesus "ascended the high mount, leading captives in his train and received gifts from people, even from those who rebelled against the LORD." And "when the day of Pentecost had come," for the first time those who "waited for the promise of the Father" were made more than conquerors over sin by the Holy Spirit given to them.

12. In addition, St. Peter clearly testifies that this important salvation from sin was not given until Jesus was glorified. He spoke about his Jewish sisters and brothers who had now "received the outcome of their faith, the salvation of their souls." Next, the apostle added more:

> Concerning this salvation, the prophets who prophesied of the grace [God's gracious dispensation] that was to be yours made careful search and inquiry, inquiring about the person or time that the Spirit of Christ within them indicated when it testified in advance to the sufferings destined for Christ and the subsequent glory [God's glorious salvation]. It was revealed to them that they were serving not themselves but you, in regard to the things that have now been announced to you through those who brought you good news by the Holy Spirit sent from heaven. (1 Pet. 1:10-12)

At the day of Pentecost, God sent these blessings to all true believers and to all generations to come. On this foundation, the apostle based the following persuasive exhortation: "Therefore prepare your minds for action. . . . As he who called you is holy, be holy yourselves in all your conduct."

13. Those who have adequately considered these things must acknowledge that we cannot measure the privileges of Christians by what the Old Testament tells us about those who were under the Jewish dispensation. The fullness of time has now arrived. The

Holy Spirit has now been given, and the revelation of Jesus Christ has brought God's wonderful salvation to humankind. The kingdom of heaven has now been established on earth.

Because King David fell far short of the pattern and standard of Christian perfection, in ancient times God's Holy Spirit announced: "On that day the LORD will shield the inhabitants of Jerusalem so that the feeblest among them on that day shall be like David, and the house of David shall be like God, like the angel of the LORD, at their head."[13]

14. If you want to disprove St. John's words, "Those who are born of God do not sin," and deny that they should be understood in their clear, natural, and obvious meaning, you must find proof in the New Testament. Otherwise, you will "box as though beating the air." And the first of these assumed "proofs" is taken from the examples recorded in the New Testament. Some may say, "The apostles themselves committed sin—even Peter and Paul, the greatest of them. Saint Paul had a sharp disagreement with Barnabas, and St. Peter showed hypocrisy at Antioch."

I answer, "Let us assume that both Peter and Paul did commit sin. What do you want to conclude from that assumption? Do you assume that all the other apostles sometimes committed sin? There is no trace of proof for that assumption. Or would you therefore presume that all the other Christians of the apostolic age committed sin?" It grows worse and worse. Those who are in control of their reason would never imagine this inference.

Again, there are those who will argue this way: "If two of the apostles once committed a sin, then all other Christians in all ages can and do commit sins as long as they live."

I answer, "What a pity, my brother! A person of ordinary intelligence would be ashamed of such logic. Least of all can you validly argue that we *must* sin at all." Such is not the case. God forbid that we should speak this way! None of us must sin of necessity. The grace of God was surely sufficient for the apostles, and it is sufficient for us today. The apostles were able to overcome the temptations they faced, and we also have the same power to resist them as well. Whoever is tempted to any sin need not yield to it because no one is tested beyond his or her strength.

15. An objector might say, "But three times St. Paul appealed to the Lord, and still he could not escape from his temptation."

I reply that we should consider a literal translation of the apostle's own words:

> A thorn was given me in the flesh, a messenger of Satan to torment me, to keep me from being too elated. Three times I appealed to the Lord about this, that it would leave me, but he said to me, "My grace is sufficient for you, for power is made perfect in weakness." So, I will boast all the more gladly of my weaknesses, so that the power of Christ may dwell in me. Therefore I am content with weaknesses . . . for whenever I am weak, then I am strong. (2 Cor. 12:7-10)

16. Because this scripture is one of the strongholds of those who insist that we *must* sin, we need to consider it carefully. First, let it be noticed that Paul's "thorn" (whatever it was) by no means caused him to commit sin, much less made it necessary for him to do so. Therefore, from these verses it can never be proved that any Christian *must* sin.

Second, the early church fathers tell us that St. Paul's thorn was a physical pain. Tertullian (160–225) reported that this thorn was a violent headache. Both St. Chrysostom (347–407) and St. Jerome (c. 342–420) agree. Saint Cyprian (d. 258) expressed it in more general terms as "many and grievous tortures of the flesh and body."[14]

Third, the apostle's own words agree exactly, "A thorn was given me in the flesh . . . to torment me . . . for whenever I am weak, then I am strong." The word *weakness* (of the body) appears no less than four times in these two verses.

Fourth, whatever trial St. Paul endured, it could not be either inward or outward sin—not inward stirrings of pride, anger, or lust or outward expressions of these attitudes. From the words that immediately follow, this fact is apparent beyond all possible doubt: "I will boast all the more gladly of my weaknesses, so that the power of Christ may dwell in me." Think! Did St. Paul boast of his pride, anger, or lust? Was it through these "weaknesses" that the power of Christ dwelled in him? The apostle continued:

"Therefore I am content with weaknesses, for whenever I am weak, then I am strong." He was saying that when he was physically weak, he was spiritually strong.

By contrast, would anyone dare say, "When I am weak by pride or lust, then I am spiritually strong"? Today, I call you all who find the power of Christ dwelling in you to say if you are boasting in your anger, pride, or lust. Can you take pleasure in these so-called infirmities? Do these weaknesses strengthen you? If it were possible, would you not leap into the fire to escape them? Judge for yourselves, then, whether the apostle could boast and take pleasure in them!

Finally, let us recognize that this thorn was given to St. Paul more than fourteen years before he wrote this Epistle, which he composed several years before he finished his earthly work. After receiving his thorn in the flesh, he had a long course to run, many battles to fight, and many victories to gain. He had much more to receive with regard to God's gifts and the knowledge of Jesus Christ. We cannot conclude that any of St. Paul's spiritual weaknesses (if that is what he was referring to) could ever have made him strong. Nor can we conclude that he (an elderly father in Christ) continued to suffer from spiritual weakness and that, until the day of his death he never became spiritually strong. From all that we know about St. Paul, such a notion is quite out of the question. His life and experience do not contradict the assertion of St. John that "those who have been born of God do not sin."

17. Some people might object: "But does not St. James directly contradict what you are teaching? He said, 'All of us make many mistakes.' Is not making mistakes the same as committing sin?"

I answer that in this instance I concede that you are correct. I acknowledge that the persons here spoken of *did* commit sin, even many sins. But who are the persons St. James spoke about? He was speaking about those teachers whom God had not sent. These teachers were probably the same "senseless persons" who taught "faith without works," a doctrine that St. James so sharply condemned. In saying that "all of us make many mistakes," the apostle was not referring to himself or to any genuine Christian. The word "we" was commonly used as a figure of speech in all writing, including the inspired writings of the Bible. For several reasons, it is clear that St. James was not including himself or any other true believer.

First, he uses the same word *we* to refer to two different things: "With the tongue we bless the Lord and Father, and with it we curse others. From the same mouth come blessing and cursing." This statement is true, but St. James is not including himself or anyone who is a new creation in Christ.

Second, the apostle said, "Not many of you should become teachers, my brothers and sisters, for you know that we who teach will be judged with greater strictness. For all of us make many mistakes." *We*! Who are *we*? Not St. James, the apostles, or true believers. The apostle was referring to those who know that, because of many offenses, they "will be judged with greater strictness." This statement does not apply to the apostle himself or to any who followed his example. "There is therefore now no condemnation for those who are in Christ Jesus, who walk not according to the flesh but according to the Spirit."

Third, the very verse containing the phrase "all of us make many mistakes" proves that these words do not apply to all people or all Christians. Immediately, the verse mentions those who "make no mistakes," and the word "we" applies to both kinds of people. The apostle contrasted those who make many mistakes with those who are "perfect."

18. Saint James clearly explained himself and established the meaning of his words. If anyone still remains in doubt, St. John (who wrote many years after St. James) put the matter entirely out of dispute by the explicit statements already quoted—1 John 3:5, 8, 9; 5:18. At this point a new difficulty may arise: How will we reconcile St. John with himself? On one hand, he declares, "Those who have been born of God do not sin." "We know that those who are born of God do not sin." On the other hand, St. John wrote, "If we say that we have no sin, we deceive ourselves, and the truth is not in us." "If we say that we have not sinned, we make him a liar, and his word is not in us."

19. As many difficulties as these verses may seem to raise, these difficulties vanish if we consider the following points. First, 1 John

1:10 explains the meaning of the eighth verse: "If we say that we have no sin" is explained by, "If we say that we have not sinned"—that is, *never* sinned. Second, the point being considered in this sermon is not whether up until now we have or have not sinned. Neither of these verses asserts that we *presently* sin. Third, the ninth verse explains both the eighth and tenth verses: "If we confess our sins, he who is faithful and just will forgive us our sins and cleanse us from all unrighteousness."

It is as though the apostle John said, "I have already affirmed that 'the blood of Jesus his Son cleanses us from all sin.'" Yet, let no one say, "I do not need Christ's cleansing blood, because I do not have any sin that needs to be cleansed." If we say that we have not sinned, we deceive ourselves and make God a liar. If we confess our sins, however, God who is faithful and just will forgive us our sins and cleanse us from all unrighteousness, so that we do not sin anymore.

20. In this light, St. John is completely consistent with himself and with the other writers of Holy Scripture. This agreement comes more clearly into view when we gather all of St. John's statements on this subject:

(1) He announced, "The blood of Jesus his Son cleanses us from all sin" (1 John 1:7).
(2) No one can honestly say, "I have not sinned, and I have no sin from which to be cleansed."
(3) We can declare, "God is ready to forgive our past sins and to save us from them in the future."
(4) St. John said, "My little children, I am writing these things to you so that you may not sin. But if anyone does sin (or has sinned), we have an advocate with the Father, Jesus Christ the righteous" (1 John 2:1).

So far, St. John's message is clear.

Nonetheless, for fear that any question would remain about a matter of such vast importance, the apostle continues this subject in the third chapter, in which he carefully explains his message. Saint John wrote, "Little children, let no one deceive you (as if I had given any encouragement to continue sinning). Everyone who does what is right is righteous, just as Christ is righteous. Everyone who commits sin is a child of the devil, for the devil has been sinning from the beginning. The Son of God was revealed for this purpose, to destroy the works of the devil.

"Those who have been born of God do not sin, because God's seed abides in them; they cannot sin, because they have been born of God. The children of God and the children of the devil are revealed in this way." Although some people of dull understanding might possibly have had questions about St. John's message, here the apostle (the last of the inspired biblical writers) resolutely settles the matter in the clearest manner. This message accords with the entire direction of the New Testament: Christians are perfect to the extent that they do not commit sin.

21. This state of being in Christ is the glorious privilege of every Christian—even those who are "infants in Christ." Second, however, becoming perfect by freedom from evil thoughts and attitudes is known only by those who are "strong in the Lord" and have "conquered the evil one." These are the ones who "know him who is from the beginning."

To begin with, they have freedom from evil and sinful thoughts. Here, it must be said that thoughts about evil are not always "evil thoughts." A thought about sin and a sinful thought are widely different things. For instance, someone might think about a murder that another person has committed, without it being an evil or sinful thought. Our blessed Lord himself doubtless thought about, or understood, the devil's meaning when he said, "All these I will give you, if you will fall down and worship me." Yet Christ entertained no evil or sinful thought—nor indeed was he capable of having such thoughts.

It follows that genuine Christians likewise do not have these thoughts, because "everyone who is fully qualified will be like the teacher." Therefore, if Christ the teacher was free from evil or sinful thoughts, so are his true disciples.

22. Indeed, from what source would evil thoughts proceed in the servant who is "like the teacher"? Jesus said, "It is from within, from the human heart, that evil intentions come." If one's heart is no longer evil, it follows that evil thoughts can no longer come

from it. If a tree is bad, so will be its fruit. If the tree is good, however, so will be its fruit. Our Lord himself gave witness to this truth: "Every good tree bears good fruit, but the bad tree bears bad fruit. A good tree cannot bear bad fruit, nor can a bad tree bear good fruit."

23. Saint Paul, from his own experience, affirms the same happy privilege of real Christians: "The weapons of our warfare are not merely human, but they have divine power to destroy strongholds. We destroy arguments and every proud obstacle raised up against the knowledge of God, and we take every thought captive to obey Christ."

24. Second, just as Christians are freed from evil thoughts, they are also freed from evil attitudes. This truth is evident from the statement of our Lord, which I quoted above: "A disciple is not above the teacher, but everyone who is fully qualified will be like the teacher." Immediately prior to making this statement, Jesus had been delivering some of Christianity's most sublime teachings (and some of the most upsetting). He declared: "I say to you that listen, Love your enemies, do good to those who hate you. . . . If anyone strikes you on the cheek, offer the other also." Jesus knew that the world would not accept this teaching. Therefore, immediately he added: "Can a blind person guide a blind person? Will not both fall into a pit?"

In effect, Jesus was saying, "Do not confer with any human being about these matters. Do not consult with people who are devoid of spiritual discernment and whose eyes of understanding God has not opened. If you do, you all will perish together."

Then, in the next verse, Jesus eliminated the two main objections with which these "wise fools" meet us at every turn. They say, "These are heavy burdens, too hard to bear," and "such knowledge is so high that we cannot attain it." Jesus said to them, "A disciple is not above the teacher." In effect, Jesus meant, "If I have suffered, be content to walk in my steps. And do not doubt that then I will fulfill my word to you—'everyone who is fully qualified will be like the teacher.'" The teacher was free from all sinful attitudes, and so are his disciples—that is, all genuine Christians.

25. With St. Paul, every Christian can say, "I have been crucified with Christ; and it is no longer I who live, but it is Christ who lives in me." These words clearly describe deliverance from inward and outward sin. Negatively, this truth is expressed this way: "It is no longer I who live"—my evil nature, the body of sin, has been destroyed. Positively, St. Paul said, "Christ lives in me"—and he is everything that is holy, righteous, and good. Both facts are necessarily and inseparably connected: "It is no longer I who live" and "Christ lives in me." "What fellowship is there between light and darkness? What agreement does Christ have with Belial?"

26. Christ who lives in true believers has "cleansed their hearts by faith." All who have Christ, "the hope of glory," within them also "purify themselves, just as he is pure." They are cleansed of pride because Christ was humble in heart. They are purified of self-will and lust because Christ hungered only to do the will of his Father and to complete his work. They are cleansed from anger in the ordinary sense of the word because Christ was meek, gentle, patient, and forbearing.

I say in the ordinary sense of the word, because not all anger is evil. We read that our Lord himself once "looked round about on them with anger." But what kind of anger did Jesus have? The following words tell that at the same time he was "grieved at their hardness of heart." Jesus was angry at the sin, and, at the same time, he grieved for the sinners. He was angry and displeased at the offense but sad for the offenders. He looked upon the offense with fury and even hatred; yet, he felt grief and love for the persons. You who are perfect, "go and do likewise." "Be angry but do not sin." Feel displeasure at every offense against God, but toward the offender have only love and tender compassion.

27. Jesus "will save his people from their sins"—outward sins, sins of the heart, evil thoughts and dispositions. Some reply, "It is true that we will be saved from our sins, but not until we die. Freedom from sin cannot come in this world."

I answer by asking how are we to reconcile this denial with the explicit words of St. John. He declared, "Love has been perfected among us in this: that we may have boldness on the day of judgment, because as he is, so are we in this world." Beyond all contradiction, the apostle speaks here of himself and other living Christians, of whom he clearly affirms that they are as their teacher, not only at or after death, but also "in this world." It is as if St. John had expected this very evasion, and he determined to overturn it from the beginning.

28. Parallel to this verse are St. John's words in the first chapter of this Epistle: "God is light and in him there is no darkness at all. If we walk in the light as he himself is in the light, we have fellowship with one another, and the blood of Jesus his Son cleanses us from all sin. If we confess our sins, he who is faithful and just will forgive us our sins and cleanse us from all unrighteousness." It is evident that in these verses the apostle is speaking of deliverance accomplished "in this world." Saint John did not say, "The blood of Christ *will* cleanse in the future" (at the hour of death or on the day of judgment). Rather, Christ's blood "cleanses [at the present time] us [living Christians] from all sin."

It is equally evident that if *any* sin remains, we are not cleansed from *all* sin. If some sin continues in the soul, the soul is not cleansed from all unrighteousness. Let no sinners speak against their own souls by saying that this cleansing relates only to justification, which is cleansing from the *guilt* of sin, but not from its *power*. To begin with, this understanding confuses what the apostle clearly separates. He spoke about both "forgiveness for sins" and "cleansing from all unrighteousness."

Second, to deny present cleansing from all sin is in the strongest possible sense to assert justification by works. It makes all inward and outward holiness a necessary requirement for justification. If the cleansing of which St. John here speaks is limited to cleansing the *guilt* of sin, then we are not justified except on the condition of "walking in the light, as he is in the light." Therefore, we conclude that St. John teaches that Christians are saved in this world from all sin and unrighteousness. Christians are perfect in the sense that they do not commit sin, and they are freed from evil thoughts and dispositions.

29. God has fulfilled the things he "spoke through the mouth of his holy prophets from of old." In particular, God declared through Moses: "The LORD your God will circumcise your heart

and the heart of your descendants, so that you will love the LORD your God with all your heart and with all your soul." Again, the Lord spoke through David who prayed, "Create in me a clean heart, O God, and put a new and right spirit within me." Most notably, God spoke through the prophet Ezekiel:

> I will sprinkle clean water upon you, and you shall be clean from all your uncleannesses, and from all your idols I will cleanse you. A new heart I will give you, and a new spirit I will put within you . . . and make you follow my statutes and be careful to observe my ordinances. . . . You shall be my people, and I will be your God. I will save you from all your uncleannesses. . . . Thus says the Lord GOD: On the day that I cleanse you from all your iniquities . . . then the nations that are left all around you shall know that I, the LORD, have rebuilt the ruined places. . . . I, the LORD, have spoken, and I will do it. (Ezek. 36:25-36)

30. "Since we have these promises, beloved, let us cleanse ourselves from every defilement of body and of spirit, making holiness perfect in the fear of God." These promises appear both in the law and in the prophets, and our blessed Lord and his apostles have confirmed them to us in the gospel. "Therefore, while the promise of entering his rest is still open, let us take care that none of you should seem to have failed to reach it." "Those who enter God's rest also cease from their labors." This one thing let us do: "Forgetting what lies behind and straining forward to what lies ahead, let us press on toward the goal for the prize of the heavenly call of God in Christ Jesus." Night and day, let us cry out to God until we are "set free from bondage to decay and obtain the freedom of the glory of the children of God."

In the first edition of Wesley's sermons (1741) at the end of John Wesley's sermon Christian Perfection, *the following poem by Charles Wesley was included. Also in 1742, it appeared in* Hymns and Sacred Poems *(pp. 261-64). In several subsequent editions of Wesley's sermons the poem was omitted. Then, in the 1771 edition of Wesley's* Works, *the poem was restored, and since that time it has usually appeared with this sermon.*

The Promise of Sanctification
Ezekiel 36:25, etc.
By the Reverend Mr. Charles Wesley.

1. God of all power, and truth, and grace,
   Which shall from age to age endure;
 Whose word, when heaven and earth shall pass,
   Remains, and stands for ever sure.

2. Calmly to thee my soul looks up,
   And waits thy promises to prove;
 The object of my stedfast hope,
   The seal of thine eternal love.

3. That I thy mercy may proclaim,
   That all mankind thy truth may see,
 Hallow thy great and glorious name,
   And perfect holiness in me.

4. Chose from the world if now I stand,
   Adorned in righteousness divine,
 If brought unto the promised land
   I justly call the Saviour mine;

5. Perform the work thou hast begun,
   My inmost soul to thee convert:
 Love me, for ever love thine own,
   And sprinkle with thy blood my heart.

6. Thy sanctifying Spirit pour
   To quench my thirst, and wash me clean;
 Now, Father, let the gracious shower
   Descend, and make me pure from sin.

7. Purge me from every sinful blot;
   My idols all be cast aside:
 Cleanse me from every evil thought,
   From all the filth of self and pride.

8. Give me a new, a perfect heart,
 From doubt, and fear, and sorrow free;
The mind which was in Christ impart,
 And let my spirit cleave to thee.

9. O take this heart of stone away,
 (Thy rule it doth not, cannot own)
In me no longer let it stay:
 O take away this heart of stone.

10. The hatred of my carnal mind
 Out of my flesh at once remove;
Give me a tender heart, resigned,
 And pure, and filled with faith and love.

11. Within me thy good Spirit place,
 Spirit of health, and love and power;
Plant in me thy victorious grace,
 And sin shall never enter more.

12. Cause me to walk in Christ my way,
 And I thy statutes shall fulfil;
In every point thy law obey.
 And perfectly perform thy will.

13. Hast thou not said, who canst not lie,
 That I thy law shall keep and do?
Lord, I believe, though men deny:
 They all are false; but thou art true.

14. O that I now, from sin released,
 Thy word might to the utmost prove!
Enter into the promised rest,
 The Canaan of thy perfect love!

15. There let me ever, ever dwell;
 By thou my God, and I will be
Thy servant: O set to thy seal;
 Give me eternal life in thee.

16. From all remaining filth within
    Let me in Thee salvation have:
From actual, and from inbred sin
    My ransomed soul persist to save.

17. Wash out my old orig'nal stain:
    Tell me no more, It cannot be,
Demons or men! The Lamb was slain,
    His blood was all poured out for me.

18. Sprinkle it, Jesus, on my heart!
    One drop of thy all-cleansing blood
Shall make my sinfulness depart,
    And fill me with the life of God.

19. Father, supply my every need:
    Sustain the life thyself hast given;
Call for the corn, the living bread,
    The manna that comes down from heaven.

20. The gracious fruits of righteousness,
    Thy blessings' unexhausted store,
In me abundantly increase;
    Nor let me ever hunger more.

21. Let me no more in deep complaint
    "My leanness, O my leanness!" cry,
Alone consumed with pining want
    Of all my Father's children I!

22. The painful thirst, the fond desire
    Thy joyous presence shall remove,
While my full soul doth still require
    Thy whole eternity of love.

23. Holy, and true, and righteous Lord,
    I wait to prove thy perfect will:
Be mindful of thy gracious word,
    And stamp me with thy Spirit's seal.

24. Thy faithful mercies let me find
 In which thou causest me to trust;
Give me the meek and lowly mind,
 And lay my spirit in the dust.

25. Show me how foul my heart hath been,
 When all renewed by grace I am;
When thou hast emptied me of sin,
 Show me the fullness of my shame.

26. Open my faith's interior eye,
 Display thy glory from above;
And all I am shall sink and die,
 Lost in astonishment and love.

27. Confound, o'erpower me with thy grace!
 I would be by myself abhorred,
(All might, all majesty, all praise,
 All glory be to Christ my Lord!)

28. Now let me gain perfection's height!
 Now let me into nothing fall!
Be less than nothing in thy sight,
 And feel that Christ is all in all!

Notes

1. Jackson, *Wesley's Works,* 10:407.
2. Outler, *Wesley's Sermons,* "On Attending the Church Service," 3:470.
3. See Kenneth Kinghorn, *The Gospel of Grace* (Nashville: Abingdon Press, 1992), 107-9.
4. Jackson, *Wesley's Works,* 11:396.
5. Ibid., 11:374.
6. Franz Hilderbrandt, Oliver A. Beckerlegge, and James Dale, eds., *The Works of John Wesley,* Bicentennial ed., vol. 7, *A Collection of Hymns for the Use of the People Called Methodists* (Nashville: Abingdon Press, 1983), 7:490-91, #334. Also, *The United Methodist Hymnal* (Nashville: The United Methodist Publishing House, 1989), #417.
7. Jackson, *Wesley's Works,* 11:394.
8. Ibid., 11:441-42.
9. Ibid., 11:401-2.
10. Telford, *Wesley's Letters,* September 15, 1790, 8:238.
11. Wisd. of Sol. 1:12.
12. Eccles. 7:20.
13. Zech. 12:8.
14. St. Cyprian, *On Mortality,* 13. Ante-Nicene Fathers, First Series, 14 vols. (Peabody, Mass.: Hendrickson Publishers, 1994), 5:472.

Introduction to Sermon 41

WANDERING THOUGHTS

This sermon addresses a question that arises out of the doctrine of Christian perfection. In Wesley's sermon on that subject (Sermon 40), he asserts that Christians can be "freed from evil thoughts and dispositions." Most Christians, however, find that they are not entirely liberated from "wandering thoughts." Wesley's critics complained that he set the standard for the Christian life much higher than had either Jesus Christ or his apostles. They charged that Wesley required "such degrees of perfection as are not in the power of human nature, in its present state of infirmity, to attain to." In this sermon, Wesley explains that although wandering thoughts can lead us into spiritual harm, a large number of our wandering thoughts are not sinful and do not bring God's condemnation. Wesley distinguishes between those wandering thoughts that are sinful and those that are not. He contends that the only evil thoughts that are blameworthy are those that we welcome, embrace, and act upon. In a letter of counsel and encouragement, Wesley wrote, "Nothing is sin, strictly speaking, but a voluntary transgression of a known law of God. Therefore every voluntary breach of the law of love is sin; and nothing else, if we speak properly. . . . There may be ten thousand wandering thoughts and forgetful intervals without any breach of love."[1]

In this message, Wesley contends that a major reason for our having wandering thoughts is that we have both souls and bodies—each with different needs. Pain in the body, for instance, can interrupt our concentration and cause our thoughts to wander. Pressing concerns easily interrupt our prayers and draw our thoughts away from God. Yet wandering thoughts of this sort are not sinful unless we allow them to become so. The sermon closes with a discussion of the extent to which we can expect to be delivered from wandering thoughts. This message provided such significant help for so many people that the British Conference *Minutes* of 1766 instructed Wesley's preachers to disperse it throughout the Methodist societies.

In this sermon Wesley explains that, on the one hand, involuntary and unwanted evil thoughts can be welcomed, accepted, and acted out. On the other hand, those minds that are completely submitted to God's will can reject such thoughts and rise above them. The sanctifying work of the Holy Spirit can so fill Christians with love for God that their desires and attitudes can be subordinated at all times to God's perfect will. We cannot in every instance prevent wandering thoughts from temporarily drawing our attention away from God. Nevertheless, we can overcome wandering thoughts that threaten to take precedence over God's will for our attitudes and actions.

In a letter to Sarah Ryan, Wesley wrote, "Do you . . . find any wandering thoughts in prayer or useless thoughts at other seasons? Does the corruptible body . . . press down the soul and make it muse about useless things? Have you so great a command over your imagination as to keep out all unprofitable images?"[2] He advised Sarah to banish such thoughts the moment they appear and refuse to allow them "to trouble [or] sully the soul."

Toward the end of this discourse, Wesley states that to pray for deliverance from wandering thoughts would be to pray that God would take them away while we are still in the body. He declares, "It is as if we should pray to be at the same time angels and human beings—mortal and immortal. This cannot be." In sum, this sermon does not suggest that sanctified Christians never have wandering thoughts. Still, those disciples who are entirely devoted to Christ can bring every consideration into captivity to him and find victory over wandering thoughts that hinder their walk with God. In Wesley's *Collection of Forms of Prayer, For Every Day of the Week*, first published in 1733, he wrote the following prayer:

> Let thy Holy Spirit, who, on the first day of the week, descended in miraculous gifts on thy Apostles, descend on me thy unworthy servant, that I may be always "in the spirit on the Lord's day." Let his blessed inspiration prevent and assist me in all the duties of this thy sacred day, that my wandering thoughts may all be fixed on thee, my tumultuous affections composed, and my flat and cold desires quickened into fervent longings and thirstings after thee.[3]

Sermon 41

WANDERING THOUGHTS

We take every thought captive to obey Christ.
*(2 Corinthians 10:5*b*)*

1 Some people have vigorously maintained that even while we remain in the body, God will "take every thought captive to obey Christ." They think that no wandering thought will ever enter the mind. These teachers maintain that we are not perfected in love unless we are perfected to the point that God eliminates all wandering thoughts. They insist that every affection and disposition must be holy, just, and good and that our every thought must be wise and consistent.

2. This claim raises a question of great importance. Many people who honor and love God with all their hearts have been deeply concerned about this issue. They have been confused about wandering thoughts, and they are deeply wounded in their souls! They have been driven into futile and harmful thinking, which has weakened their progress with God and hindered their running the race that is set before them. Indeed, because of misunderstandings about wandering thoughts, many people have even thrown away God's precious gift of salvation. They have been influenced first to doubt and then to deny the work that God formed in their souls.

Doing so, they have grieved the Spirit of God to the point that he withdrew from them and left them in complete darkness.

3. Among the profusion of books that have been recently published on almost all subjects, why is it that we have none on the subject of "wandering thoughts"? At least we have none that begin to satisfy a sensible and serious mind. In order in some measure to address this need, I intend to look into the following questions: (1) What are the different kinds of wandering thoughts? (2) What causes wandering thoughts? (3) Which of these thoughts are sinful, and which are not? (4) From which of our wandering thoughts can we expectantly pray for God to deliver us?

I. The Different Kinds of Wandering Thoughts

1. First, I will examine the different kinds of wandering thoughts. Although we can name uncounted varieties, in general there are two kinds: (1) those that wander from God and (2) those that wander from the particular details on our minds.

2. It is a natural thing for our thoughts to stray from God. Human nature tends continually to wander from God and ignore him. He is not in all our thoughts. As the apostle said, all of us are "without God in the world." We think about those things that *we* love. We do not properly cherish God, so we do not think about him.

Even if from time to time we are forced to think about God, we drive out these thoughts as soon as we can and return to deliberating about what we love. We do not find pleasure in thinking about God; our thoughts about him are lifeless, displeasing, and tedious. The world and the things of the world take up our time and wholly occupy all our thoughts. We think about what we will eat and drink, what we will wear, see, hear, and attain. We focus on what will please our feelings and fantasies. As long as we are in our natural state, we will love the world. From morning to evening, our minds are fixed on random thoughts that wander widely.

3. There is in every person by nature a "mind that is set on the flesh and hostile to God." Often, we are not only "without God

in the world," but also "fighting against God." It is no wonder, therefore, that people overflow with skeptical thoughts. They say in their hearts, "There is no God." They question (if they do not deny) God's power, wisdom, mercy, justice, and holiness. No wonder they so often distrust his providence or at least doubt that it extends to all events.

Even if they acknowledge God's providence, they still nourish critical or gloomy thoughts. Closely akin to these musings and often connected with them are thoughts that are proud and pointless. Yet again, people are sometimes absorbed with angry, hateful, or vindictive thoughts. At other times, they are preoccupied with frivolous images of physical or mental pleasure. Due to these wandering thoughts, their worldly and fleshly minds grow more fixed in their ways. Through these thoughts, they wage outright war with God. These wandering thoughts are the worst kind.

4. Widely different from the random thoughts I just described are wandering thoughts of an entirely different sort. These thoughts do not wander from God, but the mind *does* wander from the particular point it had in view. For instance, I sit down to ponder the words in the verse preceding the text of this sermon: "The weapons of our warfare are not merely human, but they have divine power." I think that everyone who is called a Christian should have this power. Yet, it is very much to the contrary!

Observe almost every part of what is called the Christian world! What kind of spiritual weapons are the people using? In what kind of warfare are they engaged?

> Our earth we now lament to see
>   With floods of wickedness o'erflow'd,
> With violence, wrong, and cruelty
>   One wide extended field of blood,
> Where men, like fiends, each other tear,
>   In all the hellish rage of war.[4]

Observe just how it is that these Christians "love one another"! How is the love of Christians any better than the love of Muslims and pagans? What abominations can be found among Muslims or heathen that are not also found among Christians?

And before I am aware of it, my mind wanders from the point and strays from one circumstance to another. In some sense these are wandering thoughts. They do not wander from God, much less fight against him. Nonetheless, they drift from the particular point I was pondering.

II. The Causes of Wandering Thoughts

I have described the nature and kinds of wandering thoughts (to speak practically rather than philosophically). Now, in the second place, we will consider what causes them.

1. First, it is easy to see that the causes of the thoughts that oppose God or wander from him come from our sinful attitudes. For instance, why is God not in all the thoughts, or in any of the thoughts, of humankind? There is a simple reason. Whether people are rich or poor, educated or uneducated, they are in effect atheists who neither know nor love God.

Why are their thoughts continually wandering after the world? Because they are idolaters. To be sure, they do not worship an image or bow down to the trunk of a tree. Nonetheless, they are equally mired in idolatry that is just as damnable. They love and worship the present world. They look for happiness in the things that are seen and in the pleasures that perish with use. Why is it that their thoughts continuously wander from the very purpose of their being—the knowledge of God in Christ?

Their thoughts wander from God because they are unbelievers. They have no faith, or at least no more faith than a demon. All these wandering thoughts effortlessly and naturally spring from the bitter root of unbelief within us.

2. This tendency can be applied to other areas, such as the presence of pride, anger, revenge, conceit, lust, and covetousness. Every one of these things causes thoughts that are consistent with their own nature. So does every sinful attitude of which humankind is capable. It is not possible or necessary to list the details. It is enough to recognize that however many evil attitudes reside in the soul, in those many ways the soul will stray from God through the worst kinds of wandering thoughts.

3. The causes of these types of wandering thoughts are exceeding varied. The natural union of soul and body causes multitudes of them. A diseased body directly and deeply affects one's comprehension. If the blood moves unevenly in the brain, all regular thinking ceases. Delirious insanity follows, and logical thinking ceases. Even if one's spirit becomes distraught or agitated to a certain level, temporary mental illness or frenzy prevents all rational thinking. Furthermore, does not every nervous disorder interrupt our process of reasoning?

> A perishable body weighs down the soul,
> and this earthy tent burdens the thoughtful mind.[5]

4. Does our body work against the mind only in times of sickness or extraordinary disturbances? No. Even when we are in perfect health, our physical beings more or less constantly work against us. Every twenty-four hours even, a very healthy person will become somewhat irrational. Do we not fall asleep? And while we sleep, are we not likely to dream? So then, who of us are the masters of our own thoughts, and who can keep them ordered and consistent? Who is able to keep the mind focused on any one point, or who can prevent his or her thoughts from wandering from pole to pole?

5. But suppose we are awake. Are we always so alert that we can constantly govern our thoughts? Is not the very nature of our bodies such that they subject us to extreme emotions? Sometimes we are too depressed, dull, and lethargic to follow a train of thought. At other times we are too excited to think clearly. The imagination involuntarily leaps back and forth, carrying us where it will. Our thoughts range from here to there, whether or not we want them to do so; and this experience comes solely from the natural stirrings of our emotions and nerves.

6. Furthermore, many of our wandering thoughts arise from the various interactions of our ideas that occur entirely without our knowledge and independently of our choices. We cannot understand how these connections are formed, and they take place in a thousand different ways. The wisest and holiest of people lack the power to stop the flow of their mental associations or prevent

their necessary consequences. (Daily, we see this happening.) Let the fire touch one end of the fuse and it immediately runs to the other end.

7. Let us fix our attention on any subject as intently as we can. If pleasure or pain enters in (especially if they are intense), they will demand our immediate attention and capture our thoughts. These factors will interrupt the most intense contemplations and divert the mind from its most preferred subject.

8. These causes of wandering thoughts reside within us as a part of our human nature. Wandering thoughts also naturally and necessarily arise from the numerous impressions of external things. Whatever strikes upon the physical senses (such as the eye or ear) will create a perception in the mind. Accordingly, whatever we see or hear will interrupt our train of thought. Any one who does something that we can see, or says anything that we can hear, causes our mind to wander (more or less) from its point of concentration.

9. There is no question that the demonic spirits that continually "look for someone to devour" make use of all these opportunities to agitate and distract our minds. They will harass and confuse us by one or more of these means. To the extent that God allows, demonic spirits will interrupt our thoughts, especially when we are thinking about the most exalted subjects.

This strategy is not at all strange. These demonic spirits well understand the very beginnings of thought. They know which physical organs directly affect our imagination, understanding, and every other mental faculty. They understand that by impressing those parts of our physical beings they can influence the actions that depend on them. Even without any of these means they can implant a thousand thoughts in our minds. It is as easy for spirit to act upon spirit, as it is for matter to act upon matter. All these things considered, we cannot be surprised that we have wandering thoughts.

III. Distinguishing the Kinds of Wandering Thoughts

1. Third, we will consider what kinds of wandering thoughts are sinful and what kinds are not. To begin with, all the thoughts

that wander from God and leave him no room in our minds are, without doubt, sinful thoughts. Such thoughts are a kind of practical atheism, and they verify that we are without God in the world. Even more to the point are all those thoughts that are contrary to God and prompt opposition or animosity toward him.

These thoughts include all grumbling and discontentment that in effect say, "We do not want God to rule over us." These thoughts also encompass all unbelieving notions about God's being, attributes, and providence. I am referring to God's particular providence over all things as well as all people in the universe. Apart from God "not one sparrow will fall to the ground," and "even the hairs of our heads are all counted." Distinctions between general providence (commonly so called) and particular providence (sometimes called special providence) are only harmless, high-sounding words that signify nothing.

2. Again, all thoughts that arise from sinful attitudes are undoubtedly evil. I am speaking about those thoughts, for instance, that spring from vindictive passions, pride, lust, or conceit. "A bad tree cannot bear good fruit," so if the tree is evil so also must be its fruit.

3. Those thoughts that produce or nourish sinful attitudes must also be evil thoughts. Thoughts that lead to pride, conceit, anger, and love for the world are evil thoughts. The same is true for those thoughts that confirm and increase any other unholy attitude, emotion, or affection. Not only what flows from evil is evil, but also whatever leads to the evil itself. These things tend to separate the soul from God and to make the soul or keep the soul "earthly, unspiritual, and devilish."

4. Consequently, by the law of cause and effect, even those thoughts that are caused by physical weakness or disease (such as the natural functions of the body) become sinful when they produce or aid the growth of any sinful attitude. These evil urges are "the desire of the flesh, the desire of the eyes, the pride in riches." However innocent these urges may be in themselves, they nevertheless can become sinful.

In the same way, wandering thoughts that are caused by the words or actions of others become sinful if they cause or feed any wrong attitude. We can say the same thing about those things that the devil suggests or implants. They foster earthly or devilish dispositions whenever we make room for them, by which decision we make them our own. They are equally as sinful as the attitudes they nourish.

5. Let us consider the following instances of wandering thoughts. When our attention is drawn away from the matter on which we are concentrating, wandering thoughts are no more sinful than the coursing of the blood in our veins or the ideas that stir in our minds. If such wandering thoughts arise from poor health or some accidental weakness or sickness, wandering thoughts are as blameless as a weak or sick body. Surely no one doubts that innocently we can have a bad state of nerves or a fever. A temporary or permanent mental disturbance can exist without our being guilty of sin.

Even if these things arise in a soul that is united with a healthy body, they may be completely innocent. Wandering thoughts can arise from the natural union of body and soul or from any of ten thousand changes that can occur in those organs of the body that influence our thinking. Yet, they are not evil thoughts. They are as innocent as the causes that produced them. Likewise, they are guiltless when they spring from the incidental, involuntary connection of ideas.

6. If in various ways other people affect our thoughts, causing them to break our concentration, our thoughts are still innocent. It is no more a sin to become aware of what we see and hear (and often we cannot prevent seeing, hearing, and perceiving) than it is to have eyes and ears.

Someone may ask, "If the devil introduces wandering thoughts, are those thoughts not evil?" I answer that they are troublesome—and in that sense harmful—but they are not sinful. I do not know if Satan spoke to our Lord audibly. Perhaps Satan only spoke to our Lord's heart when he said, "All these I will give you, if you will fall down and worship me." But whether the devil spoke inwardly or outwardly, our Lord doubtless understood what he promised. Consequently, our Lord had a thought that corresponded to the tempter's words.

But was it a sinful thought? We know that it was not. "In him there is no sin"—not in word, thought, or deed. And there is no sin in a thousand similar thoughts that Satan can implant in any of our Lord's followers.

7. None of these kinds of wandering thoughts are inconsistent with perfect love, regardless of what impulsive persons may have affirmed. By false accusations, some people grieve those whom the Lord has not grieved. Indeed, if these kinds of wandering thoughts are inconsistent with perfect love, then sharp pain and sleep would also be inconsistent as well. Whenever sharp pain comes in, it interrupts our thoughts and draws them into another channel. And when we sleep, we fall into a condition of unconsciousness and absurd musings. In this state, our thoughts—loose, wild, and incoherent—wander over the earth. Nonetheless, these wandering thoughts are consistent with perfect love, as are all wandering thoughts of this kind.

IV. Deliverance from Wandering Thoughts

1. From what has been observed, it is easy to give a clear answer to our final question: "What kind of wandering thoughts can we expect and pray to be delivered from?" We can pray and expect to be delivered from the first kind of wandering thoughts. We can be freed from thoughts by which the *heart* wanders from God. We can know freedom from all thoughts contrary to his will, or those thoughts that leave us without God in the world. All who are perfected in love are unquestionably delivered from these wandering thoughts. We can expect this kind of deliverance—and we should pray for it.

These kinds of wandering thoughts imply unbelief and hostility toward God. God, however, wants to destroy both altitudes, and totally destroy them. Furthermore, we can indeed be completely delivered from all sinful wandering thoughts. All who are perfected in love are delivered from these thoughts. Otherwise, they are not saved from sin. In all kinds of ways, other people and demons will tempt them, but they cannot defeat them.

2. With regard to the second kind of wandering thoughts, the case is much different. Until the cause of these wandering thoughts is removed, we cannot reasonably expect that the consequences will cease. Still, for as long as we remain in the body, these causes will remain. Consequently, we have every reason to believe that the effects will also remain.

3. Let us be more specific. Suppose a soul (however holy) resides in a person's sick body, and suppose that the mind is so completely deranged that this person rages insanely. Will not all of that person's thoughts be wild and unconnected for as long as the disorder continues? Suppose a fever causes a temporary derangement that we call a delirium. Until the delirium is removed, can a person's thoughts be rightly ordered? Suppose what we call a nervous disorder reaches the point of causing at least a partial delusion. Will not such a person have a thousand wandering thoughts? Will not these irregular thoughts continue for as long as the disorder that causes them?

4. Is it not the same with those thoughts that inevitably arise from violent pain? By the unchanging order of nature, these thoughts will more or less continue for as long as the pain exists. In the same way, this consequence will occur whenever one's thoughts are troubled, broken, or interrupted by any flaws in understanding, judgment, or imagination, which come from the natural constitution of the body. And how many interruptions of our thoughts will result from the unexplainable and involuntary associations of our ideas! Directly or indirectly, all these things come because "a perishable body weighs down the soul." We cannot expect them to be removed until "this perishable body puts on imperishability."

5. Only after we die will we be delivered from the wandering thoughts that are caused by what we see and hear among those who surround us. To avoid these interruptions we would "need to go out of the world." As long as we remain in the world with people around us, and as long as we have "eyes to see, or ears to hear," the things that we daily see and hear will certainly affect our minds. To a greater or lesser degree, they will interrupt our thoughts.

6. Furthermore, as long as evil spirits roam back and forth in this fallen and disordered world, they will assault every inhabitant of flesh and blood. Whether or not they can succeed, they will persist. They will continue to harass those whom they cannot destroy. They will attack, even if they cannot conquer. From these attacks of our restless and unwearied enemies, we must not look for a complete deliverance until we are sheltered where "the wicked cease from troubling, and there the weary are at rest."

7. Let us sum up the whole matter. To expect deliverance from those wandering thoughts caused by evil spirits is to expect that the devil would die or fall asleep. Or, at least, it is to think that no longer "your adversary the devil prowls around, looking for someone to devour." To expect deliverance from those wandering thoughts that are caused by other people is to believe either that people would vanish from the earth or that we could be absolutely isolated from them and have no dealings with them.

Or, it is to assume that we would neither see with our eyes nor hear with our ears. We would be as unconscious as tree trunks or stones. To pray for deliverance from wandering thoughts that are caused by the body is in effect to pray that we may leave the body. Otherwise, it is to pray for impossibilities and nonsense. It would be to pray that God would take away wandering thoughts though keeping us in union with a mortal body without experiencing the natural and necessary consequences of that union. It is as if we should pray to be at the same time angels and human beings—mortal and immortal. This cannot be. Only when this perishable body puts on imperishability will our mortal bodies be set aside.

8. Instead, let us pray with both the spirit and the mind "that all things will work together for good." Let us pray that we will be "more than conquerors," even as we endure all the infirmities of our bodies, all human interruptions, and all the assaults and suggestions of evil spirits. Let us pray that we will be delivered from all sin, that it will be destroyed both root and branch. Let us pray that we will be cleansed from "every defilement of body and of spirit" and from every evil attitude, word, and deed. Let us pray that we will "love the Lord our God with all our heart, and with all our soul, and with all our mind, and with all our strength."

Let us also pray that all "the fruit of the Spirit" may be found in us. Let us pray not only for "love, joy, and peace," but also for "patience, kindness, generosity, faithfulness, gentleness, and self-control." Pray that all these things may increase among you more and more, until "entry into the eternal kingdom of our Lord and Savior Jesus Christ will be richly provided for you"!

Notes

1. Telford, *Wesley's Letters*, June 16, 1772, 5:322.
2. Ibid., December 14, 1757, 3:243.
3. Jackson, *Wesley's Works*, 11:203-4.
4. Charles Wesley, "For Peace," *Poet. Wks.*, 6:112.
5. Wisd. of Sol. 9:15.

Introduction to Sermon 42

SATAN'S DEVICES

Wesley recognized that Satan relentlessly tempts God's children. Writing to Elizabeth Bennis, Wesley said, "You cannot be without temptation unless you would go out of the world."[1] In another of his sermons, Wesley declared,

> Besides evil men, do not evil spirits also continually surround us on every side? Do not Satan and his angels continually go about seeking whom they may devour? Who is out of the reach of their malice and subtlety? Not the wisest or the best of the children of men. "The servant is not above his Master." If then they tempted him, will they not tempt us also? Yea, it may be, should God see good to permit, more or less to the end of our lives. "No temptation" therefore "hath taken us" which we had not reason to expect, either from our body or soul, either from evil spirits or evil men, yea, or even from good men, till our spirits return to God that gave them.[2]

Wesley was convinced that unless Christians knew that they faced a battle with the devil, they would not be in a position to overcome him. For example, he wrote in his journal, "I took a list of the present society in Norwich, consisting of one hundred and sixty members. But I have far more comfort in it now than when it consisted of six hundred. These know what they are about, and the greater part are not ignorant of Satan's devices."[3] Wesley often warned individuals about ignorance of "Satan's devices," although insisting that Christians can resist the devil and overcome his wiles. Writing to Elizabeth Ritchie, Wesley said,

> Be not ignorant of Satan's devices: he will assault you on every side; he will cast temptations upon you
>
> Thick as autumnal leaves that strew the ground.4
>
> But with every temptation there shall be a way to escape; and you shall be more than conqueror through Him that loves you. You can do, you can suffer His whole will. Go on in His name and in the power of His might; and fulfil the joy of,
>
> Yours affectionately, John Wesley.[5]

The present sermon begins by explaining that the devil, who is the god of this world, works constantly to overthrow God's children and to torment those whom he cannot destroy. One of Satan's principle theological devices is to fracture the Christian gospel by pitting one aspect of it against another. For example, some people champion faith to the point of undervaluing the significance of good works. Others may emphasize good works to the point of undermining the doctrine of salvation by grace alone. Satan schemes to cause us excessively to emphasize one gospel truth to the point of neglecting or denying its balancing truth.

In 1745, the conference of Wesley's preachers dealt with the matter of balance between justification and sanctification. The conference formulated the following questions and answers:

> **Q.** 20. Should we not have a care of depreciating justification, in order to exalt the state of full sanctification?
>
> **A.** Undoubtedly we should beware of this; for one may insensibly slide into it.
>
> **Q.** 21. How shall we effectually avoid it?
>
> **A.** When we are going to speak of entire sanctification, let us first describe the blessings of a justified state, as strongly as possible.[6]

Wesley's sermons emphasize the fundamental importance of Christian conversion. Through the new birth, believers enter God's kingdom and partake of the blessings of righteousness, peace, and joy in the Holy Spirit. New believers have passed from spiritual death into spiritual life; they have become new creations in Christ. To deny any of the benefits of the new birth is to become a victim of one of Satan's devices. Although justification brings repentant sinners into a right standing with God, the future holds even more for them. God calls his newborn children to victory over sin and to maturity and holiness.

Wesley states the importance of understanding another of Satan's devices. The enemy tempts Christians to focus so much on the areas in which they need to grow that they deny the work that God has already accomplished in them. This ploy is one of the most common of Satan's strategies. Wesley explains that expectations for the future should not cause Christians to disparage God's present blessings.

In the first part of this sermon, Wesley develops the several ways that Satan works to destroy the first work that God has already done in Christians' lives: (1) Satan seeks to undermine the joy of Christians by causing them to mourn over sins that God has forgiven. (2) The tempter attacks the peace of Christians by urging them to ponder their unworthiness. (3) The devil tries to convince people that they are not really Christians because they do not yet manifest all the fruit of the Spirit in their lives. (4) The Evil One attacks Christians in times of physical weakness. (5) The enemy points to Christians' defects in an effort to move them away from their trust in Christ.

The second part of this sermon explains how Christians can repel Satan's attacks. Wesley urges believers to turn their attention away from the sins that God has forgiven and focus on Christ who is their present advocate. John Fletcher, one of Wesley's most gifted and trusted colleagues, echoed Wesley's advice in a letter he wrote to a friend:

> You do not forget, I hope, that you have need of patience, as well as I, to inherit the promises; the best and greatest of which are not sealed, but to such as keep the word of Christ's patience, and such

> as persevere with him in his temptations. Hold on, then, patient faith and joyful hope! If I were by you, I would preach to your heart and my own a lecture on this text, "We are saved by hope," and by a faith which is never stronger than when it is contrary to all the feelings of flesh and blood.[7]

This sermon counsels Christians always to keep the hope of heaven before them, while remaining grateful for the work that God has already done in their lives. Wesley encourages his readers to receive courage from the godly examples of others and to make good use of every opportunity to press forward to claim all the blessings that God is prepared to give them.

Sermon 42

SATAN'S DEVICES

We are not ignorant of his designs. (2 Corinthians 2:11)

1 Satan, "the god of this world," uses many devices to destroy the children of God, or to torment those he cannot destroy. He employs as many strategies as the stars of heaven or the sands on the seashore to perplex and hinder believers from running the race that is set before them. Yet I am proposing to discuss only one of them (Satan employs this strategy in a variety of ways). The devil uses this scheme to divide the gospel and use one part of it to destroy the other.

2. The inward kingdom of heaven that God establishes in the hearts of all who "repent and believe in the good news" is nothing other than "righteousness and peace and joy in the Holy Spirit." Every new convert to Christ understands that we are made partakers of these blessings at the very hour we believe in Jesus. But these blessings constitute only the firstfruits of his Spirit. The full harvest is yet to come. Although these blessings are inconceivably grand, we expect to see even greater ones. We expect to "love the Lord our God" more than we do now, which is with a sincere affection—although it is presently weak. We also expect to love him with "all our heart, and with all our soul, and with all our

mind, and with all our strength." We anticipate power to "rejoice always, pray without ceasing, and give thanks in all circumstances," knowing that it is "the will of God in Christ Jesus for us."

3. We expect to be "made perfect" in the love that casts out all painful fear as well as every desire except to glorify the God we adore, and to love and serve him more and more. We anticipate the kind of growth in the experiential knowledge and love of God our Savior that will enable us always to "walk in the light as he himself is in the light." We believe "the same mind will be in us that was in Christ Jesus." We expect to love all people to the extent that we will be ready "to lay down our life for their sakes." We anticipate being freed from anger, pride, and every unkind affection. We expect to be cleansed from our idols and from every defilement of body and spirit and to be saved from all inward and outward uncleanness and to be "purified as he is pure."

4. We trust the promise of God (who never lies) that the time will surely come when in every word and work we will do his will on earth as it is done in heaven. We anticipate the time when all our speech will be "seasoned with salt," serving to "give grace to those who hear." We expect "whether we eat or drink, or whatever we do, to do everything for the glory of God." We look forward to when "whatever we do, in word or deed, we will do everything in the name of the Lord Jesus, giving thanks to God the Father through him."

5. Satan's main design is to destroy the first work of God in the soul (or at least to impede its growth) by our expectation of a greater work of God still to come. Therefore it is my present intent, first, to enumerate the several ways that the devil tries to accomplish his plan. Second, I will explain how we can hurl back the fiery darts of the wicked one and use his strategy for our downfall as an opportunity to rise all the higher.

I. Understanding Satan's Devices

1. First, I will point out the various ways by which Satan tries to destroy the first work of God in the soul, or at least to impede its growth through our expectation of a still greater work of God in the future. To begin with, the devil tries to quench our joy in

the Lord by causing us to dwell on our own degeneracy, sinfulness, and unworthiness. Satan tempts us to think that God will have to work a far greater change in us, or else we cannot see the Lord. If we knew that we must remain as we are to the day of our death, we might possibly draw a kind of comfort, even if it is a weak comfort. Satan wants us to contemplate the assurance that we do not need to remain in our present state because we are assured that there is still a greater change to come. He menaces us with the thought that unless sin is completely removed in the present life, we will not see God in heaven. By distorted representations of what we have not yet attained (and the absolute necessity of attaining it), the subtle adversary Satan often stifles the joy that we should feel in what we have already attained. The devil works to prevent our rejoicing in what we now have, on the grounds that there is more that we do not yet have.

The aim of this strategy is that we cannot properly taste the goodness of God who has already done so much for us because there are much greater things yet to be done. Correspondingly, the deeper the conviction that God works in us of our present unrighteousness and the more fervent the longing we have for the complete holiness he has promised, the more Satan tempts us to think lightly of God's present gifts. We undervalue what we have already received because we focus on what we have not yet received.

2. If Satan can win this struggle and quench our joy, he will also quickly attack our peace. He will suggest, "Are you fit to see God? 'His eyes are too pure to behold evil.' How then can you flatter yourself by imagining that God regards you with approval? God is holy, and you are evil. 'What fellowship is there between light and darkness?' How is it possible that you, as unclean as you are, can have God's acceptance? You see indeed 'the prize of the heavenly call.' But do you not see that the prize is far off? How can you presume then to think that all your sins are already blotted out? You cannot have God's forgiveness and be brought nearer to him until you resemble him more."

In this way, Satan will try to disturb your peace and even tear down its very foundation. Gradually and without your noticing it, the devil will try to bring you back to the point at which you first began to move toward God. Satan will even tell you to seek for justification by good works or your own righteousness. He wants you to believe that something in you is the ground of your justification or that you must be righteous before God accepts you.

3. Let us assume, however, that we hold fast to the truth that "no one can lay any foundation other than the one that has been laid; that foundation is Jesus Christ." Let us assume that we trust that "we are now justified by his grace as a gift, through the redemption that is in Christ Jesus." Nevertheless, the devil will not cease to say, "'The tree is known by its fruit.' So, do you have the fruit of justification? Is 'the same mind in you that was in Christ Jesus'? Are you 'dead to sin and alive to God in Christ Jesus'? Have you '[become] like him in his death,' and do you know 'the power of his resurrection'?" Such is Satan's device.

When we compare the small amount of fruit we feel in our souls with the fullness of God's promises, we will be ready to conclude, "Certainly, God has not said, 'your sin is blotted out'! Surely, I have not received the remission of my sins. What place do I have among those who are sanctified?"

4. Especially in times of sickness and pain, Satan will press this accusation with all his force. He will say, "Is it not the word of God who cannot lie who says that 'without holiness no one will see the Lord'? You are not holy, and you know it. You understand that holiness includes being made into the full image of God. Look how far this standard is beyond you! You cannot reach it. Therefore, all your labor has been in vain. Everything that you have endured has been wasted. You have spent your strength for nothing. You are yet in your sins, and in the end you will perish."

Thus, if your eye is not steadily fixed on him who has borne all your sins, the devil will bring you again under the "fear of death," by which you were so long "held in slavery." Satan will use this device to spoil your peace and joy in the Lord, if not completely destroy it.

5. However, the devil's masterpiece of subtlety is yet to come. He is not content to strike against your peace and joy. He will carry his attempts still further by assaulting your righteousness also. Through your expectation of receiving more holiness and of

attaining the full image of God, the devil will try to shake (and if possible, to destroy) the holiness that you have already received.

6. From what we have previously seen, we can partly understand the method that Satan uses. First, by impairing our joy in the Lord, he also undermines our holiness. The devil uses this device because joy in the Holy Spirit is a precious means of promoting every holy disposition. Joy is a choice means of God, through which he accomplishes much of his work in believing souls. Joy is a considerable help to inward and outward holiness. It strengthens our hands to continue in "our work of faith and labor of love." Joy helps us courageously "fight the good fight of the faith and take hold of eternal life." God especially intends joy to be a power against inward and outward sufferings. It "lifts our drooping hands and strengthens our weak knees." Consequently, whatever stifles our joy in the Lord proportionately obstructs our holiness. Therefore, to the extent that Satan disturbs our joy, he also hinders our holiness.

7. The devil can accomplish the same effect if he can in any way destroy or unsettle our peace because the peace of God is another precious means God uses to advance his image within us. There is scarcely a greater help to holiness than peace. It is a continuous serenity of spirit, consistency of a mind stayed on God, and a calm rest in the blood of Jesus. And without this kind of peace, it is hardly possible to grow in grace and in the vital knowledge of our Lord Jesus Christ. All fear (except the filial respect befitting a son or daughter) freezes and paralyzes the soul. Fear clogs all the springs of spiritual life and stops all movement of the heart toward God. And doubt, as it were, encumbers the soul, so that it becomes mired in the deep clay. Therefore, to the extent that doubt and fear gain control in our lives, our growth in holiness decreases.

8. Through our doubts and fears, therefore, our clever adversary the devil tries to use the certainty of our need for perfect love as a means of disturbing (or destroying) both our peace and our faith. Indeed, peace and faith are inseparably connected, and they must stand or fall together. As long as faith exists, we remain in peace and our heart stands fast while it trusts in the Lord. But if we lose our faith and our filial confidence in a loving, pardoning

God, our peace ceases. Its very foundation has been destroyed. Faith is the only foundation of holiness and peace. Consequently, whatever strikes at faith strikes at the very root of all holiness. It is impossible for me to love God without faith, which is an abiding sense that Christ "loved me and gave himself for me" and a continuing conviction that God for Christ's sake is merciful to me a sinner. "We love him because he first loved us," and our love is in proportion to the strength and clarity of our conviction that God has loved us and accepted us in his Son.

Unless we love God, it is not possible for us to love our neighbors as ourselves. If we do not love God and others, we cannot have a right disposition toward either. It obviously follows that whatever weakens our faith must impede our holiness to the same degree. Undermining our faith is Satan's most effective and concise way to destroy all holiness. The loss of faith does not merely affect a single Christian attitude, specific grace, or fruit of the Spirit. As our faith diminishes, this loss pulls up the very root of God's entire work.

9. Therefore, it is no wonder that Satan, the ruler of this world's "present darkness," exerts all his strength to undermine us. Experience confirms that the devil works in this way. The indescribable violence with which Satan attacks those who hunger and thirst after righteousness is far easier to believe than it is to explain. On the one hand, people can see in a strong and clear light the desperate wickedness of their own hearts. On the other hand, they understand the spotless holiness to which they are called in Christ Jesus. They see the depth of their own corruption and complete alienation from God, and also they see the height of the glory of God—the image of the Holy One, in whose likeness they are called to be renewed.

As a result, many times there is no spirit left in them. They could almost cry out, "It is not possible for God to change me." They are ready to give up faith and hope and to abandon the very confidence by which they can overcome every trial and by which they can "do all things through Christ who strengthens them." They come to doubt that having done God's will they will "receive what was promised."

10. If Christian believers "hold their first confidence firm to the end," they will undoubtedly receive the promise of God, which extends through time and eternity. Here, Satan lays another trap for our feet. While we earnestly long for the part of God's promise that is to be fulfilled on earth—"the freedom of the glory of the children of God"—we may be drawn away from that part of God's promise that will ultimately be revealed in heaven. Our eye may gradually be diverted from "the crown of righteousness, which the Lord, the righteous judge, will give on that day to all who have longed for his appearing." We can be drawn away from seeing the "inheritance that is imperishable kept in heaven for us." Losing sight of the glorious future would be a loss to our souls and a hindrance to our holiness. For us to run the race that is set before us, we need to walk in the constant vision of our goal.

In ancient times, it was "looking ahead to the reward" that encouraged Moses "to share ill-treatment with the people of God" rather than "to enjoy the fleeting pleasures of sin." "He considered abuse suffered for the Christ to be greater wealth than the treasures of Egypt." It is explicitly said of Jesus Christ that "for the sake of the joy that was set before him endured the cross, disregarding its shame," until he took "his seat at the right hand of the throne of God." From these examples we can easily conclude how much more necessary it is for us to hold the vision of the joy set before us. Doing so, we can endure whatever cross God's wisdom assigns to us. Keeping the goal of the future before us, through holiness we can press onward to glory.

11. Although we are moving toward our goal and the glorious freedom that is preparatory for it, we may be in danger of falling into another trap of the devil that he uses to confuse God's children. We can "worry about tomorrow," to the extent that we neglect to develop the present. We can anticipate "perfect love" so as to fail to use the love that has already "been poured into our hearts." There is no lack of instances of Christians who have greatly suffered from this mistake. They became so interested in what they would obtain hereafter that they completely neglected what they had already received. In hope of getting five additional talents, they buried their one talent in the ground. At least, they

did not increase it as they could have for the glory of God and the good of their own souls.

12. Through these devices, the deceptive adversary of God and humankind works to undermine God's instruction. He divides the gospel against itself and uses one part of it to undermine the other. By tempting us to expect God's perfect work, which is yet future, the devil undercuts what God has already done in our lives. We have seen several devices by which Satan tries to defeat us by his undermining the sources of holiness. The devil also more directly accomplishes his purpose by twisting our blessed hope for the future into a source of unholy attitudes.

13. Whenever our hearts are eagerly yearning for all of God's "precious and very great promises," Satan will not neglect the opportunity to tempt us to murmur against God. The devil pushes us toward discouragement when we thirst for the fullness of God "as a deer longs for flowing streams." Satan wants us to become discouraged when our soul breaks out in the fervent longing, "Why is his chariot so long in coming?" If possible, in an unguarded hour, Satan will use all his wisdom and strength to influence us to fume against our Lord for his delays in meeting our expectations. At the least, the devil will try to arouse within us some degree of irritability or impatience.

Perhaps he will tempt us to envy those that we believe to have already attained "the prize of the heavenly call." Satan knows well that by giving way to any of these attitudes, we are pulling down the very thing we want to fortify. By seeking after absolutely perfect holiness, we become more unholy than we were! Indeed, there is a great danger that "the last state of that person is worse than the first." One becomes as those about whom the apostle Peter spoke in those terrible words: "It would have been better for them never to have known the way of righteousness than, after knowing it, to turn back from the holy commandment that was passed on to them."

14. Next, Satan hopes to gain another advantage, which is to create a bad name for the gospel. He is aware of how few people are able (and too many are not even willing to try) to distinguish between the *natural inclination* of a doctrine and the *incidental abuse* of that doctrine. With regard to the doctrine of Christian

perfection, the devil constantly confuses these two distinctions in order to influence the minds of careless people against the magnificent promises of God. And how often and commonly (I almost said how universally) has Satan prevailed through this device! Who are they that recognize any of these accidental ill effects of the doctrine of Christian perfection and do not immediately conclude, "This is its natural tendency"? Who are those that do not quickly cry out, "See, these are the fruits [meaning the *natural* and *necessary* fruits] of such doctrine!"

This conclusion is not valid, however. The ill effects are fruits that may incidentally spring from the *abuse* of a great and precious truth. The abuse of this or any other scriptural doctrine by no means destroys its usefulness. Human unfaithfulness can neither pervert God's right way nor "nullify his promise." "By no means! Although everyone is a liar, let God be proved true." The word of the Lord will stand. "The one who has promised is faithful," and "he will do it." Therefore, let us not ever "shift from the hope promised by the gospel." Rather, let us look at how we can answer these flaming arrows of the wicked one and rise even higher by what he intends as a cause of our falling. This consideration constitutes the second part of this sermon.

II. Resisting Satan's Devices

1. First, does Satan attempt to quench your joy in the Lord through a consideration of your sinfulness and God's requirement that without absolutely perfect holiness no one will see the Lord? You can turn this arrow back at Satan's own head. Through the grace of God, the more you feel your own evil, the more you rejoice in confident hope that God will take it all away. While you cling to this hope, every evil disposition you feel (although you hate it with a perfect hatred) can become a means not of decreasing your humble joy, but rather of enlarging it. You can say, "As wax melts before the fire," this and that weakness will "perish before the Lord." By this means, the greater the change that remains to be worked in your soul, the more you can "exult in the God of your salvation." He has already done many wonderful things for you, and he will do even greater things than these.

2. Second, Satan will all the more zealously assault your peace with the following thought: "God is holy, but you are unholy. You are very far away from the holiness without which you cannot see God. Therefore, how can you be in God's favor? How can you imagine that you are justified?"

To respond to this accusation, give more earnest attention to holding firmly to the truth that "we are found in him," "not because of any works of righteousness that we have done." We are "accepted in the Beloved One," "not having a righteousness of our own" as the cause of all or part of our justification before God. Rather, we have the righteousness "that comes through faith in Christ, the righteousness from God based on faith." O, bind this truth around your neck; write it on the tablet of your heart; wear it as a bracelet on your arm, and as an emblem on your forehead. The following verse contains that truth: "I am now justified by his grace as a gift, through the redemption that is in Christ Jesus." Increasingly value and treasure the precious reality that "by grace you have been saved through faith." To a greater and greater extent, appreciate the free grace of God who "so loved the world that he gave his only Son, so that everyone who believes in him may not perish but may have eternal life."

In this way, the sinfulness you feel on the one hand and the holiness you expect from God on the other hand will help establish your peace and make it flow as a river. Your peace will flow with an even current, despite all the mountains of ungodliness. These mountains will become level in the day the Lord returns to take full possession of your heart. In that day, neither sickness, pain, nor the approach of death will cause any doubt or fear. You know that for God a day, an hour, or a second is like a thousand years. God cannot be restricted to a period of time in which to work whatever remains to be done in your soul. God's time is always the best time. Therefore, "do not worry about anything, but in everything let your requests be made known to God." And do not pray with doubt or fear, but with thanksgiving. We have already been assured that God does not withhold any kind of good thing from you.

3. Third, the more you are tempted to lay down your shield or cast away your faith and confidence in God's love, that much

more you are to give attention to clinging to the sound teaching you have followed. So much the more, labor to "rekindle the gift of God that is within you." Never forget this truth: "We have an advocate with the Father, Jesus Christ the righteous." Remember that you can say, "The life I now live in the flesh I live by faith in the Son of God, who loved me and gave himself for me." Let this truth be your glory and crown of rejoicing. Make sure "no one seizes your crown." Steadfastly maintain:

> I know that my Redeemer lives,
> and that at the last he will stand upon the earth.
> (Job 19:25)

You are able to claim, "I have redemption in his blood, the forgiveness of sins." Consequently, being filled with "all joy and peace in believing," press on to be "renewed in knowledge according to the image of your creator." All the while, continually ask God for the ability to see the prize of the heavenly call, not as Satan represents it as being dreadful, but in its genuine inherent beauty. Look on redemption not as something that you *must* have or go to hell, but as something that you *can* have to lead you to heaven. Look upon your salvation as the most desirable gift among the provisions of God's rich mercies. See redemption in this true light, and you will hunger after it more and more. Your entire soul will thirst for God and for the glorious conformity to his likeness. Having received a sturdy hope of this gift and strong comfort through grace, you will no more be weary or faint-hearted. You will continue onward until you "receive the outcome of your faith."

4. In the same strength of faith, press on to glory. Indeed, God established this hope from the beginning. From the start, he joined pardon, holiness, and heaven. Why should we separate them? Beware of doing so. Do not allow one link of this golden chain to be broken: God for Christ's sake has forgiven me. He is now renewing me in his own image. Soon, he will make me fit for himself and bring me to stand before his face. I, whom he has justified through the blood of his Son and completely sanctified by his Spirit, will soon ascend to "the city of the living God, the heavenly Jerusalem." Then, I will come to "the assembly of the firstborn

who are enrolled in heaven, and to God the judge of all, and to Jesus, the mediator of a new covenant."

How quickly will these shadows flee and the day of eternity will dawn upon me! How soon will I drink of "the river of the water of life, flowing from the throne of God and of the Lamb." There, "his servants will worship him; they will see his face, and his name will be on their foreheads. And there will be no more night; they need no light of lamp or sun, for the Lord God will be their light, and they will reign forever and ever."

5. If once you "have tasted the goodness of the word of God and the powers of the age to come," you will not complain against God just because you are not yet fully "enabled to share in the inheritance of the saints in the light." Instead of grieving because you are not yet entirely delivered, you will praise God for delivering you this far. You will praise God for what he *has* done and take it as a foretaste of what he *will* do. You will not be angry with him because you are not yet completely renewed.

Instead, you will bless him because one day you will be complete and because "salvation is nearer to us now than when we became believers." Instead of pointlessly tormenting yourself because the time has not fully come, you will calmly and quietly wait for it, knowing that it "will come and will not delay." All the more cheerfully, you can endure the burden of sin that remains in you because it will not always remain. In only a little while, it will be completely gone.

> Wait for the LORD;
> be strong, and let your heart take courage;
> wait for the LORD! (Ps. 27:14)

6. So far as a mortal can judge (God alone searches the hearts), do you see any who appear now ready to be partakers of their hope, having "reached perfection in love"? Far from being jealous of the grace of God in them, let their example cheer and comfort your heart. Glorify God for them. "If one member is honored, all rejoice together." Instead of jealousy or evil speculation, praise God for the encouragement others provide. Rejoice in having a current proof of God's faithfulness in fulfilling all his promises.

Rouse yourself all the more to "make it your own, because Christ Jesus has made you his own."

7. In order to accomplish this task, "make the most of the time." Take advantage of every opportunity to grow in grace and do good. Do not permit the thought of receiving more grace tomorrow make you neglectful of today. You have one talent now. If you expect five more talents in the future, work so much the more to better what you already possess. And the more you expect to receive beyond this life, all the more labor for God in the present. Today's grace is enough for today. God is now pouring his benefits upon you. Therefore, just now validate yourself as a faithful steward of the present grace of God. Whatever may come tomorrow, make every effort today to support your faith with courage, self-control, patience, mutual affection, and the fear of God until you attain pure and perfect love. Let these things be in you and increase among you; do not be lazy or unfruitful: "For in this way, entry into the eternal kingdom of our Lord and Savior Jesus Christ will be richly provided for you."

8. Finally, if in the past you have abused this blessed hope of being holy as he is holy, do not on this cause abandon your hope. Cease the abuse, and retain the use. Use today your blessed hope to the greater glory of God and profit to your own soul. In unwavering faith, calm serenity of spirit, full assurance of hope, and rejoicing evermore for what God has done, "go on toward perfection." Daily, "grow in the grace and knowledge of our Lord and Savior Jesus Christ." "Go from strength to strength" in submission, patience, and humble thankfulness for what you have attained and for what you will attain. Run the race that is set before you, "looking to Jesus" until through perfect love you enter into God's glory.

Notes

1. Telford, *Wesley's Letters*, December 1, 1773, 6:56.
2. Outler, *Wesley's Sermons*, "On Temptation" (I, 7), 3:162.
3. Ward and Heitzenrater, *Wesley's Journal and Diaries*, February 25, 1767, 22:71.
4. Wesley's quotation, "Thick as autumnal leaves that strew the ground," is from John Milton's *Paradise Lost*, 1:302.
5. Telford, *Wesley's Letters*, June 3, 1774, 6:89.
6. Jackson, *Wesley's Works*, 8:284.
7. Ibid., 11:325.

Introduction to Sermon 43

THE SCRIPTURE WAY OF SALVATION

This sermon contains John Wesley's broad overview of the way of salvation—including prevenient grace, the new birth, and sanctification. Decades of Bible study, observation, and experience had led Wesley to a settled conviction of the truth of what he taught. Moreover, the fires of controversy repeatedly forced him to examine and refine his teaching. This sermon is one of Wesley's most frequently read discourses and one of the most useful.

Wesley recommended this sermon as a clear exposition of the teaching of the Bible about the way of salvation. In a letter to Mary Bishop, the proprietor of private schools in Bath, he wrote,

> Certainly simple faith is the very thing you want [need], that faith which lives upon Christ from moment to moment. I believe that sermon *The Scripture Way of Salvation* might at this time be particularly useful to you. It is a great thing to seize and improve the *very now.* What a blessing you may receive at this instant! Behold the Lamb of God! What, if even before this letter comes to your hands; the Lord should come to your heart! Is He not nigh? Is He not now knocking at the door? What do you say? "Come in, my

> Lord, come in." Are you not ready? Are you not a mere sinner, and stripped of all? Therefore, all is ready for you. Fear not; only believe, and enter into rest. How gracious is it in the kind Physician to humble you, prove you, and show you what is in your heart! Now let Christ and love alone be there.[1]

This sermon combines and summarizes the thoughts of several other sermons by Wesley, including *Salvation by Faith*, *Justification by Faith*, and *The Circumcision of the Heart*. History has judged this message as one of Mr. Wesley's most helpful discourses. Indeed, of all Wesley's sermons, *The Scripture Way of Salvation* is his best summary of "the order of salvation."

The immediate object of this printed discourse is to counter the doctrine that saving faith is a mere intellectual assent to the truth of the Christian gospel. In an earlier sermon, Wesley had stated,

> With regard to the nature of this faith, [it] is not (as some have fondly conceived) a bare assent to the truth of the Bible, of the articles of our creed, or of all that is contained in the Old and New Testament. The devils believe this, as well as I or thou; and yet they are devils still.[2]

Those who relied solely on cognitive assent to the truth taught by the Bible tended to regard religion as a legal contract. They failed to experience Christianity as a personal relationship with Jesus Christ.

Some of Wesley's own preachers (for instance, Thomas Maxfield and George Bell) had accepted the view that the death of Christ on the cross in itself secured salvation, quite apart from individual faith or personal trust. This view led Maxfield and Bell into odd suppositions. By claiming that the death of Christ had already sealed their salvation, they denied the need for faith and good works in the Christian life. In 1763, Maxfield and Bell broke all fellowship with Wesley and drew some out of the Methodist societies. These teachers held the curious notion that people who were "only" regenerated were not yet saved. They contended that "merely justified" Christians cannot please God or grow in grace and that only "sanctified" Christians have God's favor. Maxfield and Bell alleged that "entirely sanctified" Christians are wholly perfect, infallible, above temptation, and secure from ever falling from grace. They also presumed that as the recipients of God's grace they were not required to obey the moral law.

The present sermon counteracts these eccentric teachings. The sermon also issues a call to sanctification through faith in and obedience to Christ. Before the sermon's publication, Methodism had seen five years of remarkable visitations of the Holy Spirit that resulted in the conversion of many people, a number of whom had made significant progress in their sanctification. In the living laboratory of God's powerful working among the people, Wesley observed and conversed with a host of genuine Christians. The theology in this sermon, rooted in Scripture, had been confirmed in thousands of converts whose lives God had profoundly transformed. This sermon continues to be widely read because it contains the mature and practical insights that Wesley had gained as a Bible scholar, teacher, leader, theologian, and preacher.

Sermon 43

THE SCRIPTURE WAY OF SALVATION

You have been saved through faith. *(Ephesians 2:8)*

1 Nothing can be more intricate, complex, and difficult to understand than "religion," as many comprehend it. Vagueness of understanding is true of heathen religions, even many of the most rational of them. It is also true of the religion of those who are in some sense Christians, even among persons who are "acknowledged pillars" of the church.

Yet, the genuine religion of Jesus Christ is a clear and simple thing that is easy to understand! That is, we can comprehend it if we look at it in its original form, just as the Bible describes it. The wise Creator and Governor of the world revealed Christianity in a form that can be comprehended by the small capacity of human understanding in its present state. We can readily observe Christianity's purpose and its means to accomplish its purpose. In a single word, the purpose of Christianity is *salvation*. And the means by which to attain salvation is *faith*.

2. It is easy to see that the substance of the entire Bible is summed up in two plain words—*faith* and *salvation*. These terms,

as it were, constitute the essence of all Scripture. Therefore, we should take every possible caution to avoid all mistakes concerning faith and salvation. We need to form a true and accurate understanding of them both. Therefore, let us seriously examine: (1) What is salvation? (2) What is the faith by which we are saved? (3) How are we saved by faith?

I. The Nature of Salvation

1. First, we will examine the question, "What is salvation?" The salvation spoken of in our text is often misunderstood to mean just going to heaven and possessing eternal happiness. In this text, salvation does not refer to going to paradise, which our Lord called going to "Abraham's bosom." Salvation is not a blessing that lies only on the other side of death—or, as we usually say, in the other world. The very words of the text verify what I am saying: "You *have been* saved." Salvation is not limited to the distant future. It is a present reality, a blessing, which (through God's free mercy) we can presently possess. The words of the text are clear: "You have been saved." The salvation spoken of in our text can be extended to include the entire work of God—from the first dawning of grace in the soul until it is consummated in glory.

2. If we take this understanding of salvation to its fullest extent, it will include all that is formed in the soul by what is frequently termed "natural conscience." This work is more properly called "preventing grace," or "prevenient grace." Prevenient grace includes all the "drawings" of God the Father to bring us to Christ. Prevenient grace creates within us the desire for God, and if we respond to God's bringing us to himself, our desire increases more and more.

Prevenient grace includes the "true light, which enlightens everyone" that comes in to the world. This grace teaches us to "do justice, and to love kindness, and to walk humbly with God." Prevenient grace imparts all the convictions that, from time to time, the Holy Spirit works in every human being. It is true, however, that the majority of people suppress the impressions of the

Holy Spirit as soon as possible. In time, they forget, or at least deny, that they ever had them at all.

3. In this sermon, however, we are concerned only with the salvation about which the apostle is directly speaking. And this salvation consists of two inherent components—*justification* and *sanctification.*

Justification is a synonym for pardon. It is the forgiveness of all our sins and (what is necessarily implied) our acceptance by God. The price paid for our forgiveness is the blood and righteousness of Christ. To state it a little more clearly, the price of our forgiveness consists of everything that Christ has done and suffered for us until "he poured out himself to death, and was numbered with the transgressors." The price that Jesus Christ paid for us is commonly called the "meritorious cause" of our justification. The immediate effects of justification are the peace of God (a peace that "surpasses all understanding") and a rejoicing in the "hope of sharing the glory of God" "with an indescribable and glorious joy."

4. In the very moment we are justified, there begins the process of sanctification. In that instant we are "born again." That is, we are "born from above" or born of the Spirit. We experience a *real* change as well as a *relative* change. We are inwardly renewed by the power of God. We sense that "God's love has been poured into our hearts through the Holy Spirit that has been given to us." This experience produces love for all humankind, and especially for the children of God. It expels love for the world, pleasure, comfort, fame, money, pride, anger, self-will, and every other evil attitude. In a word, God changes our minds that were "earthly, unspiritual, and devilish," into the "same mind that was in Christ Jesus."

5. It is natural and understandable that those who experience such a change imagine that all sin is gone. They assume that sin is completely rooted out of their hearts and has no place in them anymore. How easy is it for them to think, "I *feel* no sin; therefore I *have* no sin." They assume that because sin does not agitate within them (at the moment), it does not exist. They think that because it has no stirring, it has no being.

6. It is seldom long, however, before their experience sets them straight. They find that sin was suspended but was not destroyed. Temptations return and sin revives, revealing that sin was only stunned, not annihilated. Now, they feel two principles in themselves, manifestly contrary to each other: "What the flesh desires is opposed to the Spirit." Their human nature opposes the grace of God.

They cannot deny that they still feel the power to believe in Christ and to love God, and his "Spirit bears witness with their spirits that they are children of God." Nevertheless, they sometimes feel in themselves pride, self-will, anger, or unbelief. They find one or more of these tendencies frequently stirring in their hearts, although these sinful impulses do not overpower them. Perhaps these inclinations "push hard at them to cause them to fall, but the LORD helps them."

7. Fourteen hundred years ago, Macarius (300–390) described the present experience of the children of God:

> When grace operates in inexperienced people, they immediately imagine that they have no more sin. While on the contrary, those that have discernment cannot deny that even we who have the grace of God may be assailed again. . . . We have often had examples among the sisters and brothers of those who have experienced such grace as to declare that they had no sin in them. Yet, despite their claim, when they imagined themselves entirely free from sin, the evil that lurked within was stirred up anew, and they were almost consumed by sin.[3]

8. From the time we are born again, the gradual work of sanctification begins to take place within us. "By the Spirit we put to death the deeds of the flesh"—that is, of our evil nature. And as we become increasingly dead to sin, we become more and more alive to God. We continue from grace to grace, careful to "abstain from every form of evil" and "zealous for good deeds." "Whenever we have an opportunity, we work for the good of all." We "live blamelessly according to all the commandments," and through them we "worship the Father in spirit and truth." We take up the cross and deny ourselves every pleasure that does not lead us to God.

9. Being justified, we anticipate entire sanctification, which is a full salvation from all our sins. It is freedom from pride, self-will, anger, and unbelief. As the apostle expresses it, "Let us go on toward perfection." Now, what is perfection? The word has various meanings, and here it means perfect love. It is love that excludes sin, fills the heart, and occupies the whole capacity of the soul. It is love that "rejoices always, prays without ceasing, and gives thanks in all circumstances."

II. The Faith by Which We Are Saved

The second question that we will consider is: "What is the faith by which we are saved?"

1. In general, the apostle defined faith as "the assurance of things hoped for, the conviction of things not seen." Faith perceives those things that are not visible by sight or by any of the other external senses. Saving faith involves a supernatural conviction regarding God and the things of God. It is a kind of spiritual light apparent to the soul. Saving faith is a supernatural seeing or perceiving God. Accordingly, Scripture sometimes speaks of God giving us light, and sometimes Scripture speaks of faith as our ability to discern this light. Saint Paul declared, "God who said, 'Let light shine out of darkness,' has shone in our hearts to give the light of the knowledge of the glory of God in the face of Jesus Christ."

Elsewhere, St. Paul spoke about "the eyes of our hearts being enlightened." By this twofold operation of the Holy Spirit, we have the eyes of our hearts opened and enlightened. Consequently, we can see the things that in our natural selves "no eye has seen, nor ear heard, nor the human heart conceived." We can see the invisible things of God. We comprehend the spiritual world that surrounds us, which our natural faculties can no more discern than if it did not exist. We see the eternal world piercing through the veil that hangs between time and eternity. Clouds and darkness no more hide it, and we now see "the glory about to be revealed to us."

2. To define faith more specifically, it is a divine conviction and manifestation that "God was in Christ reconciling the world to himself." It is also the assurance that "the Son of God loved me and gave himself for me." By faith (whether we call it the *nature* of faith or the *property* of faith), we "receive Christ." We receive him in all his offices—as our prophet, priest, and king. It is by faith that Christ "became for us wisdom from God, and righteousness and sanctification and redemption."

3. Someone may ask, "Is this the 'faith of assurance' or the 'faith of affiliation'?" I answer that Scripture makes no distinction of this kind. Saint Paul said, "There is one body and one Spirit, just as you were called to the one hope of your calling, one Lord, one faith, one baptism, one God and Father of all, who is above all and through all and in all." It is certain that faith necessarily involves assurance. (Here, *assurance* is only another word for *conviction;* it is difficult to see the difference between them.) Faith is the assurance that Christ "loved me and gave himself for me." "Those who believe in the Son of God have the testimony in their hearts." The Holy Spirit "bears witness with our spirits that we are children of God." "And because we are his children, God has sent the Spirit of his Son into our hearts, crying, 'Abba! Father!'" He gives us an assurance that he is our Father, and we have a childlike confidence in him.

It needs to be noticed that in the very order of things, assurance goes before confidence. We cannot have a childlike confidence in God until we *know* we are God's children. Therefore, as some have supposed, assurance (or confidence, trust, reliance, affiliation, or whatever else it may be called) is not the first aspect of faith. Assurance is the *result* of saving faith.

4. It is by this kind of faith that "we have been saved." That is, by faith we are justified and sanctified (taking faith in its highest sense). Now, the third division of our inquiry is the question of how we are justified and sanctified by faith. Because this issue is the main concern of this sermon (and a matter of great importance), it is appropriate to give the matter a special and focused consideration.

III. How We Are Justified by Faith

1. First, let us consider the question, "How are we justified by faith?" In what sense should we understand justification? I answer that faith is the condition, and the only condition, for justification. None are justified other than those who believe; apart from faith no one is justified. Faith is the *only* condition; faith alone is sufficient for justification. All who believe are justified, whatever else they have or do not have. In other words, no one is justified until he or she believes, and everyone who does believe is justified.

2. You may raise the question, "Does God not also command us to repent? And does he not expect us to 'Bear fruit worthy of repentance'? Are we not expected to 'cease to do evil, and learn to do good'? Are not repentance and good works of the utmost necessity, and if we willingly neglect either one can we reasonably expect to be justified at all? If these requirements are necessary, how can you say that faith is the only condition for justification?"

I answer that God does undoubtedly command us to repent and to bear fruit worthy of repentance. And if we deliberately neglect repentance and appropriate works, we cannot reasonably expect to be justified at all. Therefore, both repentance and fruit worthy of repentance are in some sense necessary for justification. Yet they are not necessary in the same sense as faith, nor are they of the same importance. They are not necessary in the same proportion because they are only conditionally necessary, if there is time and opportunity for them. If these conditions are not present, one can be justified without them.

As an example, I mention the thief on the cross beside Jesus. (We call this man a thief, but a recent writer has detected that he was not a thief, but a very honest and respectable person.) Even so, it was not possible that he could have been justified without faith. Similarly, allow that we have ever so much repentance, or ever so many of the fruits worthy of repentance. Without faith, these things will not benefit us at all. One is not justified until one believes. With or without this fruit, however, the instant we believe we are justified (even with more or less repentance). Repentance and its fruits are only secondarily necessary for faith, whereas faith is immediately and directly necessary for justification. The truth remains that faith is the only condition that is immediately and strictly required for justification.

3. Someone may ask, "Do you believe that we are sanctified by faith? We know that you believe we are justified by faith, but do you not believe and teach that we are sanctified by our good works?"

I answer that for twenty-five years, people have openly and fervently charged that I believe and teach that our works sanctify us. However, I have steadfastly declared just the contrary, and in all kinds of ways I have clarified my views. I have continuously testified in private and in public that we are both justified and sanctified by faith. Indeed, one of these great truths clearly illustrates the other. Just as we are justified by faith, so are we sanctified by faith.

Faith is the only condition for sanctification, just as it is for justification. Faith is the condition, and no one is sanctified except the one who believes. Apart from faith, no one is sanctified. Faith alone is the only condition sufficient for sanctification. Everyone who believes is sanctified, whatever else he or she has or does not have. In other words, no one is sanctified until he or she believes, and everyone who believes is sanctified.

4. Perhaps you are thinking, "Is there not a repentance that results from, as well as a repentance prior to, justification? And is it not compulsory for all who are justified to be 'zealous for good deeds'? Indeed, are not good deeds so necessary that if we deliberately neglect them we cannot reasonably expect ever to be fully sanctified—that is, 'made perfect in love'? In fact, without good works, can we 'grow in the grace and knowledge of our Lord and Savior Jesus Christ'? Can we even keep the grace that God has already given us? Can we continue in the faith or in the favor of God that we have received? Do you yourself not acknowledge all this to be true, and do you not constantly assert it? Now, if this is true, how can you say that faith is the only condition of sanctification?"

5. I respond by acknowledging that I do say all these things, and I constantly maintain them as God's truth. I maintain that

there is a repentance that both precedes and follows justification. It is obligatory for all who are justified to be zealous for good deeds. Good works are so necessary that if we willingly neglect them, we cannot reasonably expect ever to be sanctified. Without them, we cannot "grow in grace," advance in the image of God, and have "the same mind that was in Christ Jesus." No, we cannot retain the grace that we have received or continue in faith or in God's favor.

What conclusion must we draw from what we have said? We deduce that both repentance (rightly understood) and the practice of all good works (works of inward piety and outward mercy), because they come from faith, are in some sense necessary for sanctification.

6. I say "repentance rightly understood" because the repentance needed for sanctification is not the same as that needed for justification. The repentance that follows justification is widely different from the repentance that precedes it. Repentance after justification presupposes no guilt, sense of condemnation, or consciousness of God's wrath. It does not have any doubt of God's favor or any fear of punishment.

Precisely this kind of repentance is a conviction, formed by the Holy Spirit, that sin remains in our hearts. It is the awareness of "the mind that is set on the flesh" that still remains "even in them that are regenerate."[4] Sin remains in justified Christians, although it no longer reigns in them or holds dominion over them.

The repentance we are discussing is a conviction that we are prone to evil and that we have hearts "bent on turning away from God." It is an awareness that "what the flesh desires is opposed to the Spirit." Unless we continually stay alert and pray, the flesh will reveal pride, anger, love of the world, love of comfort, love of praise, or "the love of pleasure more than the love of God." Repentance is a conviction of our hearts' tendencies toward self-will, skepticism, idolatry, and, above all, unbelief. In a thousand ways and under a thousand deceptions, we are more or less continuously "turning away from the living God."

7. With the conviction of sin remaining in our hearts is linked a clear conviction of sin remaining in our lives, still clinging to all

our words and deeds. In the best of justified Christians, we notice a mixture of sin, in either their spirits, their actions, or their attitudes. We observe something that is not able to withstand the righteous judgment of God.

> If you, O LORD, should mark iniquities,
> Lord, who could stand? (Ps. 130:3)

Where we least suspect it, we find a pollution of pride and self-will, or unbelief and idolatry.

Justified Christians are more ashamed of their best services than their former worst sins. Consequently, they cannot help feeling that their best works are far from having anything meritorious in them or from being able to stand the scrutiny of divine justice. If it were not for the blood of the covenant, we would be guilty before God for even our good works.

8. Experience shows that one more thing must be added to the conviction that sin remains in our hearts—clings to all our words and actions—and that we would be guilty if we were not constantly cleansed by Christ's atoning blood. This additional thing is that our repentance must include a conviction of our helplessness and complete inability in ourselves. We must have God's free, almighty grace preceding us and accompanying us every moment. In our powerlessness, without God's help, we cannot think one good thought, form one good desire, speak one correct word, or perform one good deed.

9. You may ask, "But what are the good works that you claim are necessary for sanctification?" I answer, first, that our works of piety should include public, family, and private prayer; receiving the Lord's Supper; searching the Scripture by hearing, reading, and meditating; and fasting or abstinence as our health permits.

10. Second, our works of mercy should include ministering to people's bodies and souls. These good deeds entail such things as feeding the hungry, clothing the naked, showing hospitality to the stranger, and visiting imprisoned, sick, and suffering people. Our good deeds should also include instructing the ignorant, awakening foolish sinners, stirring up the lukewarm, confirming the timid, comforting the fainthearted, supporting those who are

being tested, and in every way helping save souls from death. The repentance and the fruits worthy of repentance that are necessary to full sanctification consist of these things. God has ordained that his children do these works while they wait for full salvation.

11. Therefore, we can see the dangerous harm of the seemingly innocent opinion of some people. They say, "There is no sin in a believer.[5] The moment one is justified, all sin is destroyed, root and branch." This view completely undermines the repentance of believers and totally blocks the way to sanctification. There is no place for repentance in those who believe that they have no sin in their hearts or lives. Consequently, there is no need to be "perfected in love." To this end, the repentance of believers is fundamentally necessary.

12. In like manner, it is clear that there is no possible danger in expecting full salvation. Suppose we were mistaken, and suppose no such blessing ever has been or can be attained. We lose nothing by hoping. The very anticipation of sanctification arouses us to use and develop all the gifts that God has given us. In doing so, when our Lord returns he will "receive what is his own with interest."

13. Let us now return to our subject. Although we acknowledge that both repentance and its fruits are necessary for full salvation, they are not essential in the same sense or to the same degree as faith. They are not necessary in the same degree because the fruits of repentance are only conditionally required—there must be time and opportunity for them. Otherwise, one can be sanctified without them. However, we can never be sanctified without faith.

Let someone have ever so much repentance or ever so many good works; these virtues will never benefit as means of sanctification. Faith is sanctification's indispensable requirement. The instant one believes—with or without the fruits of repentance, and even with a greater or lesser degree of repentance—that one is sanctified. Repentance and its fruits are not necessary in the same sense as faith. They are only distantly necessary for the continuation and increase of faith. By contrast, faith is immediately and directly essential for sanctification. Faith is the only condition that is closely and necessarily tied to sanctification.

14. The following question may arise: "By what kind of faith are we sanctified—that is, saved from sin and perfected in love?"

First, I answer that this faith is a divine assurance and conviction that God has promised our sanctification in Holy Scripture. Until we are thoroughly satisfied that God did pledge this gift to us, we cannot move one step further. One would think that a reasonable person needs no further word to confirm this promise than the ancient word in Deuteronomy: "The LORD your God will circumcise your heart and the heart of your descendants, so that you will love the LORD your God with all your heart and with all your soul." How clearly this promise expresses being perfected in love! How powerfully it indicates that we can be saved from all sin! As long as love fills the entire heart, what room does it have for sin?

15. Second, faith is a divine assurance and conviction that God is able to perform what he has promised. We concede that for mortals, it is impossible to bring something that is clean out of something that is unclean and to purify the heart from all sin and fill it with all holiness. Yet, human helplessness creates no obstacle in this matter, because "for God all things are possible." Certainly, no one ever imagined that this work was possible to any power other than that of God Almighty! If the Lord speaks, it will be done. "God said, 'Let there be light'; and there was light."

16. Third, sanctifying faith is a divine assurance and conviction that God is able and willing to do it *now*. And why not? With God, is not a moment the same as a thousand years? God does not need more time to accomplish whatever is his will. And he does not need to wait for any more worthiness or fitness in the persons whom he is pleased to bless. Therefore, at any point in time we can boldly say, "Now is the day of salvation." "Today, if you hear his voice, do not harden your hearts." "Look, everything is ready; come to the wedding banquet."

17. We need to add one more thing to the confidence that God is both able and willing to sanctify us now. We must have the divine assurance and conviction that he *does it*. In the very hour that you believe, God completes the work. He speaks to the inmost soul: "According to your faith let it be done to you." Then,

the soul is pure from every spot of sin, and it is "cleansed from all unrighteousness." At that point, the believer experiences the deep meaning of these solemn words: "If we walk in the light as he himself is in the light, we have fellowship with one another, and the blood of Jesus his Son cleanses us from all sin."

18. This question may arise: "But does God accomplish this great work in the soul gradually or instantaneously?"

I respond by saying that perhaps it can be gradually worked in some people. By this statement, I mean that they do not refer to the particular moment when sin ceased. But it is certainly desirable (if it is God's will) that we should be sanctified instantaneously and that the Lord would destroy sin "by the breath of his mouth"—"in a moment, in the twinkling of an eye." Ordinarily, God does so. And for any unprejudiced person there is quite enough evidence to confirm this fact. Therefore, in every moment, look for your sanctification. Look for it in the way we have described—namely, while doing all those "good works" for which you have been created anew in Christ Jesus.

There is no danger in your expecting God's work. If you are no better for expecting it, you can be no worse. Even if you were to be disappointed in your hope, you still lose nothing. But you will *not* be disappointed in your hope: "It will come and will not delay." Look for your sanctification every day, every hour, every moment. Why not this hour, in this moment? Certainly, if you believe that sanctification comes by faith, you can look for it now. In this way, you can know with certainty whether you are seeking it by faith or by works.

If you are seeking sanctification through your good deeds, you are looking to prior conditions before God sanctifies you. You may think, "I must first *be* this or *do* that." If so, you are seeking sanctification by your works. If you seek it by faith, you may expect it as you are. If so, you can expect it now. It is important to observe that there is an inseparable connection between these three points:

Expect it by faith.
Expect it as you are.
Expect it now!

To deny one of these points is to deny them all, and to acknowledge one of them is to allow them all.

Do you believe that we are sanctified by faith? Then be true to your belief and look for this blessing just as you are, neither better nor worse than you are. As a poor sinner, you have nothing to pay or plead except "Christ died for me." And if you look for sanctification as you are, then expect it now. Wait for nothing. Why should you? Christ is ready. And he is all you want. He is waiting for you. He stands at the door! Let your inmost soul cry out,

> Come quickly in, Thou heavenly Guest;
> Nor ever hence remove,
> But sup with us, and let the feast
> Be everlasting love.[6]

Notes

1. Jackson, *Works*, 13:22.
2. Outler, *Wesley's Sermons*, "The Way to the Kingdom" (11, 10), 1:230.
3. Paraphrase of Macarius in *The Homilies of the Church of England*, 1721, 17, p. 267.
4. Rom. 8:7 and the Thirty-nine Articles, art. 9, "Of Original or Birth Sin."
5. See Wesley's standard sermon #13, "On Sin in Believers."
6. Charles Wesley, *Hymns on God's Everlasting Love, Poet. Wks.*, 3:66.

Introduction to Sermon 44

ORIGINAL SIN

Many of those who influenced the shape of eighteenth-century culture believed in the essential goodness of humankind. Following the lead of Enlightenment philosophers, a number of Wesley's contemporaries denied the Christian doctrine of original sin. They trusted in education and self-discipline as the primary means of improving human nature. Leading intellectuals championed the optimistic view that humankind could create an ideal society based on reason and common sense. Many in Wesley's day rejected the biblical account of the Fall and disallowed the scriptural teaching that all people naturally tend toward evil.

This deistic philosophy even insinuated itself into the Church of England, and even a number of Church leaders disagreed with the traditional teaching that original sin had greatly marred human minds and souls. "Enlightened" thinkers, they insisted, should focus on human possibilities because God was too remote and uninvolved in our lives for us to know him in personal experience. The Deists considered any claim of having the awareness of God in one's life was beneath the dignity of "respectable" people. They enjoyed quoting a supposed conversation between an inquirer and Anthony Ashley Cooper, First Earl of Shaftesbury:

> C: People differ in their discourse and profession about these matters [religion], but men of sense are really but of one religion.
>
> I: Pray, my lord, what religion is that which men of sense agree in?
>
> C: Madam . . . men of sense never tell it.[1]

Deists regarded the vagueness of their beliefs as an advantage because they believed that the use of broad generalities would head off religious controversy.

The Deists pronounced it blasphemous to preach that God is a judge who will hold all people accountable for their sins. For Deism, the highest social virtue was tolerance toward all religious opinions (except those of the leaders of the Evangelical Revival). The Deists conceived of God as a dignified, benign being, who left people to work out their own futures. They believed that humankind had the inherent wisdom and ability to live sensibly; and living a respectable life was for them the sum of religion.

Deism necessarily rejected the biblical account of the Fall. This philosophy also ignored the Epistles of St. Paul, which emphasized the inherent sinfulness of humankind and the need for a crucified savior to atone for the sins of the world. Deists within the Church of England also rejected the ninth article of the church's Thirty-nine Articles of Religion, titled "Of Original or Birth Sin." That article describes original sin as

> The fault and corruption of the nature of every man, that naturally is engendered of the offspring of Adam; whereby man is very far gone from original righteousness, and is of his own nature inclined to evil, so that the flesh lusteth always contrary to the spirit; and therefore in every person born into this world, it deserveth God's wrath and damnation.

In contrast to the Deists, who rejected many of the Church's Articles of Religion, John Wesley embraced them all, including the recognition of the reality of original sin. He wrote, "We have all testified before God, 'that all and every [one of] the Articles of our Church, as also the Book of Common Prayer . . . are agreeable to the word of God.'"[2]

In Wesley's day, a major opponent of the Church's doctrine of original sin was John Taylor, a clergyman and president of a theological college. Taylor also denied the divinity of Christ. Wesley recorded in his journal an account of the pernicious effects of the teachings of Taylor regarding the doctrine of original sin:

> We came to Shakerley, six miles further, before five in the evening. Abundance of people were gathered before six, many of whom were disciples of Dr. Taylor, laughing at original sin, and consequently at the whole frame of scriptural Christianity. O what a providence is it which has brought us here also, among these silver-tongued antichrists! Surely a few, at least, will recover out of the snare, and know Jesus Christ as their wisdom and righteousness![3]

In 1756, Wesley addressed this debate about original sin in a formal treatise titled *The Doctrine of Original Sin: According to Scripture, Reason, and Experience*.[4] Many people did not take the time to read this 272-page work. Therefore, in 1759, Wesley published the present sermon, which is essentially a summary of the first part of that lengthier treatise on the subject of original sin. This sermon sold for two pence; and in 1760, Wesley added it to his Standard Sermons.

In this sermon, Wesley avoids two opposites—salvation through human effort and salvation by divine predestination. The Deists, of course, placed the responsibility for salvation entirely on the shoulders of each individual. Wesley disagreed. He concurred with Calvinism in that we cannot do any good thing apart from the grace of God. However, he denied the article in the Westminster Catechism, which states that because of Adam's sin, God imputes *guilt* to all newborn infants. Wesley did affirm that all people do indeed sustain the *consequences* of Adam's sin, but he did not accept the teaching that they carry Adam's *culpability*. Wesley wrote,

> That all men are liable . . . for Adam's sin alone, I do not assert; but they are so, for their own outward and inward sins, which, through their own fault, spring from the infection of their nature. And this, I think, may fairly be inferred from Rom. [6:23]: "The wages of sin is death". . . its due reward; death, temporal, spiritual, and eternal. God grant that we may never feel it so![5]

Wesley adds, "But with regard to parents and their posterity, God assures us, children 'shall not die for the iniquity of their fathers.' No, not eternally. I believe none ever did, or ever will, die eternally, merely for the sin of our first father."[6]

This sermon teaches that original sin is universal; it is present in every newborn infant. We do not merely acquire sin's tendencies—we inherit them. Wesley concludes,

> Know your disease! Know your cure! You were born in sin; therefore you must be born from above, that is, born of God. By nature you are completely corrupted; by grace you will be wholly renewed. As all die in Adam, so all will be made alive in Christ. You who were dead through your trespasses, Christ has made alive. God has already given you a prescription for life: We live by faith in the Son of God, who loved us and gave himself for us! Therefore, let us go on through faith for faith, until your whole sickness be healed, and the same mind is in you that was in Christ Jesus.

Sermon 44

ORIGINAL SIN

The LORD saw that the wickedness of humankind was great in the earth, and that every inclination of the thoughts of their hearts was only evil continually. *(Genesis 6:5)*

1 The Bible's description of human nature is vastly different from the favorable pictures that people have drawn throughout the ages. The writings of many of the ancients abound with bright descriptions of human dignity. People have pictured human nature as being composed of all virtue and happiness—or that these qualities are within our grasp, without our drawing on any power other than human ability. People have believed that we are self-sufficient and only slightly inferior to God himself. They think that we are able to live by our own resources.

2. This elevated view of human nature is not limited to the heathen people who were guided in their inquiries by little more than the dim light of reason. Also, many who bear the name of Christ and who are entrusted with the revelation of God have spoken optimistically about human nature, as if it is completely composed of innocence and perfection. The present century, in particular, has abounded in this understanding. Perhaps no part of

the world is more optimistic about human nature than our own country. Here, numbers of people of substantial understanding and extensive learning have used their greatest abilities to display what they call "the fair side of human nature." It must be acknowledged that if their accounts of human nature are accurate, we are only "a little lower than the angels"—or as the Hebrew biblical text can be more literally rendered, "a little less than God."

3. Is it any wonder that these accounts of human nature are very willingly accepted by the largest part of humankind? Who is not easily persuaded to think approvingly of himself or herself? Accordingly, writers who hold such high views of human nature are almost universally read, admired, and applauded. They have made innumerable converts, not only among frivolous people, but also among those of learning. In our time, it is quite out of fashion to say anything disparaging about human nature. Most people admit that we do have a few infirmities, yet they think that in general we are very innocent, wise, and virtuous.

4. Now, what are we to do with the teaching of the Bible? Scripture will never agree with such optimistic accounts of human nature. Even though these views are pleasant to flesh and blood, they are completely irreconcilable with the Bible. Scripture declares that "by the one man's disobedience the many were made sinners." The Bible teaches that in Adam, we all died. We died spiritually and forfeited the life and image of God. Then, the fallen, sinful Adam "became the father of a son in his likeness." It was not possible for him to sire anyone different, because "who can bring a clean thing out of an unclean?" All Adam's offspring (we and everyone else) are "by nature dead through trespasses and sins."

We "have no hope and are without God in the world." Consequently, we are "by nature children of wrath." Everyone can say, "Indeed, I was born guilty, a sinner when my mother conceived me." "For there is no distinction, since all have sinned and fall short of the glory of God." We have fallen short of that glorious image of God, in which humankind was originally created.

Consequently, the psalmist David declared:

> The LORD looks down from heaven on humankind
> to see if there are any who are wise,
> who seek after God.
> They have all gone astray, they are all alike perverse;
> There is no one who does good,
> no, not one. (Ps. 14:2, 3)

In confirmation of this declaration, we read in Genesis that "the LORD saw that the wickedness of humankind was great in the earth, and that every inclination of the thoughts of their hearts was only evil continually."

These scriptures show us *God's* explanation of human nature. From the biblical account, (1) I will describe humankind as it existed prior to the flood; (2) I will explore the question of whether we are the same today, and (3) I will offer some conclusions.

I. Humankind Prior to the Great Flood

1. First, I will refer to the opening words of our sermon text to clarify what people were like before the flood. We can completely depend on this account because it comes from God who cannot be deceived. We read that "God saw that the wickedness of humankind was great." This verse does not refer only to this or that person, or a few people, or most people. The verse includes *all* people universally. This scripture takes in every person in the entire human race. It is not easy for us to compute their numbers or to say how many thousands and millions there were.

In that time, the earth retained much of its primeval beauty and original fruitfulness. The surface of the earth was not fractured and torn as it now is. Spring and summer were united, and it is likely that the earth provided food for considerably more inhabitants than it can now sustain. The number of people must have been greatly multiplied during the seven or eight hundred years when people gave birth to sons and daughters.

Yet, among this unimaginable number of people, only Noah "found favor in the sight of the LORD." He alone (perhaps including a part of his household) was the exception in the midst of the universal wickedness of the day. In only a short time, this evil caused God in righteous judgment to send universal destruction. All the rest of humankind that was guilty together also received punishment together.

2. The Lord saw "every inclination of the thoughts of their hearts." God discerned their souls, inner selves, and spirits. He saw into the sources of all their inward and outward actions. He observed every inclination of their hearts. It is not possible to find a word of greater significance than the term *inclinations.* The word encompasses whatever is formed, shaped, and created within us. Our inclinations touch everything that is in, or progresses from, our souls—every preference, affection, emotion, appetite, attitude, plan, and thought. One's inclinations necessarily pertain to all words and actions, which naturally flow from the fountain. They are either good or evil, depending on the fountain from which they come.

3. God saw that the people's inclinations were all evil. They were contrary to moral virtue and opposed to God's nature, which necessarily includes every good. The people's inclinations were contrary to the divine will, the eternal standard of good and evil. Their attitudes were opposed to the pure, holy image of God, in which humankind was originally formed. After God's original creation, he surveyed the works of his hands and saw them to be "very good." Humankind once stood in perfection before God. Now, people's hearts were contrary to justice, mercy, and truth. Their inclinations undermined the fundamental relationships that all people once had with the Creator and with their fellow human beings.

4. Some might wish to raise the question: "Was there not good intermingled with the evil? Was there not light mixed with the darkness?" The answer is that there was no good at all in humankind. God saw that "*every* inclination of the thoughts of their hearts was only evil." It cannot be denied that many of them (perhaps all of them) had good stirrings in their hearts. We read

that God's Spirit strove with mortals, with the hope that they would repent. God especially called to people during the 120 years of grace, more particularly during that merciful extension of his patience while Noah built the ark. Still, "nothing good dwelled within them"; they were entirely evil throughout. The evil was unrelieved and not joined with anything having the nature of good.

5. We may ask a further question, "Was there no pause in this evil? Were there no bright intervals when something good might be found in human hearts?" Here, we are not considering what the grace of God might occasionally work in human life. Disregarding this consideration, we have no reason to believe there was any interlude in their evil. For God, who "saw that every inclination of the thoughts of their hearts was only evil," also saw that it was uninterrupted and that the people were evil *continually*. Every year, every day, every hour, every moment, they never moved into the good.

II. Human Nature as It Is Today

God "knows what is in everyone" and "he searches the minds and hearts." Also, for our instruction he gave us an authentic account of the entire population of the earth. Before God sent the flood upon the earth, everyone was continuously evil. Now, second, we will examine whether humankind is the same today.

1. It is certain that people are the same in our day. Scripture gives us no reason to think any differently about the present state of humankind. In fact, all the scripture passages cited above refer to people who lived *after* the flood. More than a thousand years after the flood, God spoke through the psalmist David the following judgment concerning human nature:

> They have all gone astray, they are all alike perverse;
> there is no one who does good,
> no, not one. (Ps. 14:3)

Everyone has strayed from the path of truth and holiness. Not one person is good.

In their different generations, all the prophets bear witness to the same truth. The prophet Isaiah spoke about God's special people (and certainly the heathen were in no better condition):

> The whole head is sick,
>   and the whole heart faint.
> From the sole of the foot even to the head,
>   there is no soundness in it,
> but bruises and sores and bleeding wounds. (Isa. 1:5, 6)

All the apostles gave the same account of human nature. Indeed, this judgment is found throughout the entire Bible.[7] From all these biblical passages we learn that in their natural state, unassisted by God's grace, all people come under this judgment—"Every inclination of the thoughts of their hearts was only evil continually."

2. Daily experience confirms this account to be an accurate description of human nature in our time. It is true that people in their natural state do not discern their sinful condition. We should not be surprised at this fact. For as long as those who are born spiritually blind continue in that condition, they are hardly aware of their need. Much less could we assume that in a place in which everyone was blind that any of them would be aware of their lack of sight. Similarly, as long as people remain in a natural blindness to spiritual perception, they are not aware of their spiritual needs, particularly their lack of spiritual understanding. As soon as God opens the eyes of their hearts, however, they see the state they are in. Then, they are deeply convinced that "everyone goes about like a shadow"—that is, in folly, ignorance, sin, and wickedness.

3. When God opens our eyes, we see that we were formerly "without God in the world." That is, according to the original text, we were practical atheists. In our natural selves, we had no knowledge of God or familiarity with him. As soon as we gained the use of reason, "through the things he has made," we learned about the invisible attributes of God such as "his eternal power and divine nature." From the things we see, we deduced the existence of an eternal, powerful being whom we cannot see. Even

though we recognized God's existence, we had no intimacy with him. Just as we know that there is an Emperor of China (whom, as yet, we do not know), so we knew there is a King of all the earth. Still, we did not know him.

Indeed, we could not know God through any of our natural faculties. By none of our human attributes could we gain the knowledge of God. We could no more understand him through our natural comprehension than we could see him with our physical eyes. Jesus said, "No one knows the Son except the Father, and no one knows the Father except the Son and anyone to whom the Son chooses to reveal him."

4. We read of an ancient king who wanted to know what was the natural language of humankind. In order to reach a conclusion, he experimented by ordering two newborn infants to be taken to a place and reared without any teaching. They could not even hear the sound of a human voice. What was the outcome of the experiment? Finally, the two children were brought out of their isolation—and they spoke no language at all! They could only utter unintelligible sounds, like those of animals.[8]

Similarly, if two infants from the time of their birth were reared without being instructed in any religion, there is little room to doubt that the outcome would be the same (unless the grace of God interposed). They would have no religion at all. They would have no more understanding of God than the beasts of the field or a wild donkey's colt. Such is the character of natural religion apart from the Christian religion and the influences of God's spirit!

5. If we have no knowledge of God, we cannot have any love for him. We cannot love someone whom we do not know. Certainly, most people talk about loving God and perhaps imagine that they do love him. Only a few people will admit that they do not love him. Even so, the facts are too obvious to deny. No one naturally loves God any more than we love a stone or the earth we walk on.

What we love, we delight in. People do not inherently delight in God, though, because they do not know him. In our natural state, we cannot comprehend how anyone could delight in him. We find no pleasure in him at all; God is completely uninteresting to us. Loving God is far above us, completely out of our sight. In our natural selves, we cannot acquire a love for him.

6. By nature, we have no love for God, and "there is no fear of God before [our] eyes." Admittedly, sooner or later, most people develop a kind of undiscerning, irrational fear of God, which is best described as "superstition." The misdirected Epicureans gave it a name—"religion." This fear is not a natural fear; it is acquired, mainly through conversation or from examples. In our natural state, "God is not in all our thoughts." We leave God to manage his own affairs, which we think is to sit quietly in heaven and leave us here on earth to manage ours. Thus, we have no more reverence for God before our eyes than we have love of God in our hearts.

7. So, all people are "without God in the world." They are practical atheists. But atheism does not protect us from worshiping false gods. In our natural state, we all are born into the world as gross idolaters. Of course, we may not be idolaters in the ordinary sense of the word. We do not worship molded or sculptured images, as the idolatrous heathen do. We do not bow down to the trunk of a tree or to the work of our own hands. We do not pray to the angels or saints in heaven any more than we pray to the saints upon the earth.

But what *do* we worship? We have set up our idols in our hearts, and we bow down and worship them. We venerate ourselves when we give honor to ourselves although that honor is due to God alone. This attitude is *pride.* All pride is idolatry; it is giving to ourselves the veneration that is due only to God. Although God did not intend for us to have pride, what living person is without it? Through pride, we rob God of his intrinsic sovereignty, and, as idolaters, we usurp God's glory.

8. But pride is not the only kind of idolatry of which, by nature we are all guilty. Satan has also stamped another aspect of his image on our hearts—*stubbornness.* Before the devil was cast out of heaven, he said, "*I* will sit on the mount of assembly of the far north." By that statement, he was saying in effect, "I will do my own will and pleasure, independent of my Creator."

Everyone born into the world says the same thing thousands of times. People even earnestly declare this objective without ever blushing and without fear or shame. Ask people why they assumed this attitude, and they will reply, "Because I wanted to." What is this outlook other than, "I will do what I want to do"?

For all intents and purposes, this attitude is the same as saying, "The devil and I are agreed, because Satan and I govern our actions by the same principle." All the while, God's will is not in their thoughts and they do not consider it in the slightest. Nonetheless, God's will ought to be the supreme rule of every intelligent person in heaven or earth. The supremacy of God's will follows as the essential, fixed relationship that all living beings have with their Creator.

9. In our natural state, we bear the image of the devil and follow in his steps. But next, leaving Satan out of consideration, we plunge into an idolatry of which he is not guilty—*the love of the world*. The love of this world is as natural to every person as the love of one's own will. What is more natural to us than to seek happiness in what is created rather in the one who created it? Is it not natural to seek in the works of one's own hands the satisfaction that can be found in God alone? What is more natural than the desire of the flesh? I am speaking about finding gratification in all kinds of fleshly pleasures.

Some people (particularly those of learning and education) indeed talk majestically about their disdain for these low forms of sensual pleasure. They pretend to give no value to the gratification of those appetites that bring them down to the same level as the animals that perish. These claims are sheer pretense, however, because all people are conscious that in this matter they are, by nature, as the animals. Sensual appetites, even those of the lowest kind, have, more or less, dominion over them. Despite people's vaunted intellect, their fleshly desires lead them into captivity and drive them uncontrollably.

Humankind, with all its good breeding and other accomplishments, has no moral superiority over the goats. Indeed, the animals may have moral superiority over us in our natural state! Certainly they do if we give ear to a modern statement, which very fittingly states:

Once in a season, beasts too taste of love:
Only the beast of reason is its slave,
And in that folly drudges all the year.[9]

To be sure, it must be acknowledged that there are considerable differences among people (beside those distinctions produced by prevenient grace). These differences are due to differences of physical characteristics and education. Nevertheless, other than those who are completely ignorant of themselves, who will be the first to throw a stone at another? Who can endure the test of our blessed Lord's comment on the seventh commandment: "Everyone who looks at a woman with lust has already committed adultery with her in his heart"?

One does not know what to marvel at most—the *ignorance* or the *insolence* of those who speak with such disdain about others and who are overcome by desires that all people have felt in their own hearts! The desire of every sensual pleasure, innocent or not, is natural to every human being.

10. Similarly, we are all subject to *the desire of the eyes*—the craving for the pleasures of the imagination. These desires arise either from noteworthy, beautiful, or rare objects (if indeed these objects are not linked with each other). On careful examination, perhaps it would appear that magnificent and beautiful objects please us only as long as they are new. And when their newness has passed, most of the pleasure they gave is gone. In proportion to their becoming familiar, they become dull and empty. No matter how often we experience this fact, our desire for new things still remains.

The inbred "pleasures of imagination" continue to be fixed in the soul. Indeed, the more we indulge the "desire of the eye," the more it increases. This lust incites us to follow after more and more objects, even though we abandon all of them with abortive hope and deluded expectations. A poet has written:

The hoary fool, who many days
  Has struggled with continued sorrow,
Renews his hope, and fondly lays
  The desperate bet upon tomorrow!

Tomorrow comes! 'Tis noon! 'Tis night!
This day like all the former flies:
Yet on he goes, to seek delight
Tomorrow, till tonight he dies![10]

11. There is a third symptom of the fatal disease of original sin and the love of the world—*pride in riches*. This sinful tendency is "the desire for praise," and "the glory that comes from human beings." Those who have a high view of human nature regard this disposition as strictly normal—as natural as sight, hearing, or any of our physical senses. Are even educated, refined, and highly intelligent people ashamed of this human tendency? They are so far from feeling embarrassed about this inclination that they applaud themselves for their love of applause!

Even distinguished Christians (so called) have no difficulty in adopting the saying of an ancient, vain heathen: "Not to regard what others think of us is the mark of a wicked and amoral mind."[11] For these Christians, to remain calm and unmoved "in honor and dishonor, in ill repute and good repute" is a negative mark. Such a one deserves this judgment: "Away with such a fellow from the earth! For he should not be allowed to live."

Can one even imagine that these people have ever heard of Jesus Christ or his apostles? Do they even know who it was that said, "How can you believe when you accept glory from one another and do not seek the glory that comes from the one who alone is God?" It is truly impossible to trust and please God as long as we accept (or seek) glory from one another and do not seek the glory that comes from God alone.

What then is the true condition of all humankind—the Christian as well as the heathen? They all seek "glory from one another"! In their opinion, it is as natural for them to act this way as it is to see the light that enters the eye or hear the sound that comes into the ear. They regard it as a mark of virtue to seek glory from others, and they regard it as improper to be content with "the glory that comes from the one who alone is God."

III. Concluding Observations on Human Nature

1. Now, I move on to draw a few conclusions from what has been said. First, we can learn a chief, fundamental doctrinal difference between Christianity and the most refined heathenism. Many of the ancient heathen have abundantly described the vices of particular people. They have spoken a great deal against their covetousness, cruelty, opulence, or extravagance. Some heathen writers have dared to say, "No one is born without vices of one kind or another." Yet, because none of them was informed about the Fall of humankind, they did not know the *extent* of human depravity. They failed to understand that everyone is void of all good and filled with all types of evil. The ancient heathen were wholly ignorant of the total depravity of the whole of human nature. They did not understand the extent of the evil in everyone born into the world, in every faculty of the soul. This depravity lies not so much in the particular vices that reign in individual persons as it does in the general deluge of atheism, idolatry, pride, self-will, and love of the world.

Therefore, the doctrine of original sin is the first distinguishing difference between heathenism and Christianity. Heathenism acknowledges that many people are infected with vices and even born with an inclination toward them. Heathenism assumes, however, that in some people, their natural good greatly outweighs the evil in them.

By contrast, Christianity maintains that all people are "born in sin" and "formed in wickedness." Scripture teaches that within every person exists a "mind that is set on the flesh, which is hostile to God," and it cannot submit to God's law. This carnal mind infects the entire soul to the extent that in our "flesh" (our natural state), "nothing good dwells within us." "Every inclination of the thoughts of the heart is only evil continually."

2. Second, we can learn that all who deny the presence of "original sin" (or whatever name we give it) are still heathenish in the fundamental point that distinguishes heathenism from Christianity. They may even admit that we have many vices, some of which are inborn, and that as a consequence we are not born nearly as wise or virtuous as we should be. There are few people, however, who

will openly affirm that we are born with as much inclination to good as to evil or that we are all naturally as virtuous and wise as Adam and Eve were when God created them. But in a word, this is what they ask: "Are we naturally filled with all sorts of evil? Are we empty of all good? Are we completely fallen? Are our souls totally corrupted? Is 'every inclination of the thoughts of our hearts only evil continually?'" Acknowledge that this is so, and to this extent you are a Christian. Deny it, and you are still a heathen.

3. In the third place, we can determine the correct character of the religion of Jesus Christ. It is God's means of healing a sick soul. Through his own method of spiritual healing, the great physician of souls applies medicine to heal this sickness and restore humankind's totally corrupt nature. Through the knowledge of himself and Jesus Christ whom he has sent, God heals all our unbelief. He gives us faith, a divine assurance and conviction of the reality of God and of the things of God.

God leads us to understand the important truth that "Christ loved me and gave himself for me." Through our repentance and humility, God removes the deadly disease of pride. And through our meek and thankful submission to God's will, he heals us of self-will. Love for God is his sovereign remedy for our love of the world in all its forms. This kind of healing is true religion; it is faith made effective through love. By a loving, thankful compliance with, and conformity to, the word and will of God, faith leads to genuine humility and death to the world.

4. Indeed, if humankind were not depraved, there would be no need for this redemption. There would be no requirement for God's work in our hearts and no need for us "to be renewed in the spirit of our minds." If we were not such complete sinners, the phrase "excess godliness" would be a better expression than "excess wickedness." In that case, for all intents and purposes, a religion of externals, without inner holiness, would be enough.

Accordingly, in the judgment of those who deny original sin, outward religion is adequate. These people make very little more of religion than the famous Thomas Hobbes made of reason. According to Hobbes, reason is only "a well-ordered train of words."[12] According to those who deny original sin, religion is only a well-ordered train of words and actions. Truly, they are consistent. If the inside is not "full of wickedness," but already clean, what need is there to "clean the outside of the cup"? If their assumption that we have no original sin is correct, it follows that outward reform is all that people need.

5. But that notion is not what you learned from the Bible. You know that the one who sees "what is in everyone" gives a far different explanation of nature and grace and of our Fall and recovery. You know that the chief aim of religion is to renew our hearts in the image of God and to rectify the total loss of righteousness and true holiness that we suffered through the sin of our first parent, Adam. You know that all religion that does not satisfy this purpose stops short of the renewal of our soul in the image of God after the likeness of him who created it. Such religion is nothing more than a poor sham and a mere mockery of God. It leads only to the destruction of our own souls.

O, stay on guard against all those teachers of falsehood who would impose this religion upon you in the place of genuine Christianity! Do not pay attention to them, even if they would come to you with every kind of wicked deception, polite speech, respectability, and charming and elegant language. They may speak declarations of earnest goodwill to you and even profess reverence for the Holy Scriptures. Comply with the simple, cherished "faith that was once for all entrusted to the saints" and delivered by God's Spirit to your hearts.

Know your disease! Know your cure! You were born in sin; therefore "you must be born from above"—that is, "born of God." By nature, you are completely corrupted; by grace, you will be wholly renewed: "As all die in Adam, so all will be made alive in Christ." You "who were dead through your trespasses, Christ has made alive." God has already given you a prescription for life: "We live by faith in the Son of God, who loved us and gave himself for us"! Therefore, let us go on "through faith for faith," until your whole sickness be healed, and "the same mind is in you that was in Christ Jesus."

Notes

1. Gilbert Burnet [1643–1715], *Burnet's History of My Own Time*, 2 vols. (Oxford: Clarendon Press, 1897–1900), vol. 1, book 2, chap. 1.

2. Jackson, *Wesley's Works,* 7:461.
3. Ward and Heitzenrater, *Wesley's Journal and Diaries,* August 28, 1748, 20:245-46.
4. Jackson, *Wesley's Works,* 9:192-464.
5. Ibid., 9:286.
6. Ibid.
7. Gen. 6:5; Prov. 20:9; Isa. 53:6, 64:6; Rom. 3:23; 1 John 1:8.
8. This story is found in Herodotus, *The Histories: History of the Greco-Persian Wars* (New York: Penguin Books, 1996), ii.2.
9. Thomas Otway, *The Orphan* (1680), act 5, scene 1.
10. Matthew Prior, "To the Honourable Charles Montague," stanzas 4 and 5.
11. Cf. Cicero, *On Moral Obligation,* I, xxviii, 99.
12. Thomas Hobbes's actual words were, "The general use of speech is to transfer our mental discourse into verbal, or the train of our thoughts into a train of words" (Thomas Hobbes, *Leviathan* [New York: Dutton, 1950], I.iv.12).

Introduction to Sermon 45

THE NEW BIRTH

John Wesley had a deep appreciation for the Christian sacraments, which were a part of the Anglican tradition into which he was born and from which he drew spiritual benefit. In the eyes of Wesley's Anglican critics, his ministries of evangelism and Christian nurture used irregular *methods*. However, one could not fairly accuse Wesley of departing from the Church's stated *doctrines*, including its sacramental theology. In this regard, he was in every way "a Church of England man." Wesley believed that Christ instituted the sacraments and that they have great value in Christian initiation, confirmation, and nurture. He wrote that God "hath appointed [baptism] as an outward and visible sign of an inward and spiritual grace; which grace is 'a death unto sin and a new birth unto righteousness.'"[1] In 1758, Wesley published *A Treatise on Baptism*, which links baptism with God's saving act in Jesus Christ.[2] Yet, as this sermon explains, we forfeit this grace when we quench the Holy Spirit. And because all people have sinned, everyone needs the new birth.

As Wesley traveled across Great Britain, it became obvious to him that large numbers of people who had been baptized as infants were very far from living as true Christians. This reality brought into tension the liturgical and the evangelical aspects of

Wesley's thought. Although Wesley retained a high view of baptism, he did not believe that baptism was necessary for salvation, nor did he believe that it was a substitute for the new birth. In 1750, he wrote a letter in which he clearly makes these points: "You think the mode of baptism is 'necessary to salvation': I deny that even baptism itself is so; if it were, every Quaker must be damned, which I can in no wise believe. I hold nothing to be (strictly speaking) necessary to salvation but the mind which was in Christ."[3]

As the eighteenth-century Methodist revival progressed, it accentuated the contrast between those who had vital faith in Christ and those who were Christians in name only. The attitude and actions of these two categories of people differed significantly, and Wesley saw that people needed much more than the sacrament of baptism. In Sermon 18, *The Marks of the New Birth*, he wrote,

> Lean no more on the staff of that broken reed, that ye *were* born again in baptism. Who denies that ye were then made "children of God, and heirs of the kingdom of heaven"? But, notwithstanding this, ye are now children of the devil; therefore ye must be born again. And let not Satan put it into your heart to cavil at a word, when the thing is clear. Ye have heard what are the marks of the children of God; all ye who have them not on your souls, baptized or unbaptized, must needs receive them, or without doubt ye will perish everlastingly. And if ye have been baptized, your only hope is this: that those who were made the children of God by baptism, but are now the children of the devil, may yet again receive "power to become the sons of God"; that they may receive again what they have lost, even the "Spirit of adoption."[4]

In the present sermon, Wesley declares, "Whether or not you have been baptized, you must be born again. Otherwise, it is not possible for you to become inwardly holy. And without inward and outward holiness you cannot be happy in this world or in the world to come."

This discourse explains that the main consequence of original sin is not *guilt*, but *depravity*. As Wesley emphasized in the previous sermon, again he insists that newborn infants are inclined toward evil, but they are not guilty. Although God made Adam and Eve in his own image and likeness, the Fall *effaced* (but not *erased*) that image and subjected all people to sin and death. Because people are born in a state of spiritual death, they need the new birth, which brings them into an experience of spiritual life. In the closing section of this sermon, Wesley declares, "If you have not already experienced this inward work of God, let your continual prayer be, 'Lord, add this to all your blessings: let me be born again. Deny me anything you please, but do not deny me this: let me be born from above. Take away whatever seems good to you—reputation, fortune, friends, or health. Only give me this: I want to be born of the Spirit! I want to be received among the children of God.'"

Sermon 45

THE NEW BIRTH

You must be born from above. *(John 3:7)*

1 Within the entire scope of Christianity, if any doctrines can be correctly called fundamental, without doubt there are two—justification and the new birth. Justification refers to the main work that God does *for* us in forgiving our sins. The new birth refers to the grand work that God does *in* us by renewing our fallen nature. In their sequence, neither of these works comes before the other. In the same moment that we are justified by the grace of God through "the redemption that is in Christ Jesus," we are also "born of the Spirit." However, in logical order (as we say) justification precedes the new birth. First, we believe that God turns away his judgment, and then we trust his Spirit to work in our hearts.

2. It is of enormous importance for everyone fully to understand these two basic doctrines. Being convinced of this importance, many excellent authors have written extensively about justification, explaining every point of this doctrine by opening the relevant scriptures. Similarly, many have written about the new birth, some of them extensively, yet not as clearly, profoundly, or accurately as could be wished. Some discussions of the new birth are obscure and complex, while others are trivial and shallow.

Therefore, a complete yet clear account of the new birth still seems necessary. We can do with an explanation that will enable us to give satisfactory answers to three questions. With God's help, I will briefly and clearly answer them: (1) Why must we be born again, and what is the foundation of this doctrine? (2) How should we be born again, and what is the nature of the new birth? (3) For what reason must we be born again, and what is its purpose? (4) I will add a few conclusions that naturally follow from these points.

I. The Foundation of the New Birth

1. First, why must we be born again? What is the foundation of this doctrine? The foundation of the new birth begins almost as early as the creation of the world. In the scriptural account of creation, we read: "God said, 'Let us make humankind in our image, according to our likeness. . . .' So God created humankind in his image, in the image of God he created them." God made humankind in his *natural image*, as a portrait of his immortality, a spiritual being endowed with understanding, free will, and numerous affections. God also made humankind in his *political image*, as the governor of earth and as exercising "dominion over the fish of the sea, and over the birds of the air, and over the cattle, and over all the wild animals of the earth." Principally, however, God made humankind in his *moral image*, which, according to the apostle Paul, is "true righteousness and holiness." This image is the primary image of God in which he made us.

"God is love." Therefore, at the creation, God made the man and the woman full of love. Love was the single principle governing all their attitudes, thoughts, words, and actions. God is full of justice, mercy, and truth, and so were the man and the woman as they came from the hands of their Creator. God is spotless purity. Accordingly, the original man and woman were free from every sinful stain.

Otherwise, God would not have pronounced humankind (and all the other works of his hands) as being "very good." The man and the woman could not have been "very good" if they were not free from sin and filled with righteousness and true holiness. Humankind is the only earthy agency for expressing God's character. If we assume that intelligent creatures do not love God and are without righteousness and holiness, we necessarily assume that they are not good at all, much less "very good."

2. Although God made us in his own image, we were not created unchangeable. To be created changeless would have been inconsistent with the probationary state in which it pleased God to place the man and the woman. God created them with the ability to stand, and yet they were susceptible to falling. God himself informed the man and the woman of this possibility, and he gave them a solemn warning against it.

Despite the human ability to stand and despite God's warning, the man and the woman did not retain their glory. They fell from their exalted position. They ate "of the tree about which God commanded, 'You shall not eat of it.'" They willfully disobeyed their Creator and openly rebelled against his sovereignty.

By these acts, the man and the woman flagrantly declared that they would no longer have God as their ruler. They would be governed by their own wills, not the will of God who created them. They would not seek happiness in God, but in the world and in the works of their own hands. God had already said to them, "In the day that you eat of it you shall die." And the Lord's word cannot be broken. Accordingly, the day the man and woman disobeyed God, they did die.

They died to God, which is the most terrible of all deaths. They forfeited the life of God and became separated from him who is the only source of spiritual life. As the body dies when it is separated from the soul, the soul dies when it is cut off from God. In the very day and hour that they ate the forbidden fruit, Adam and Eve became disunited from God. Their actions demonstrated immediate proof of this estrangement. Their behavior revealed that God's love was extinguished in their souls, which were now "alienated from the life of God." Instead of living the life of God, they were now under the power of cowering fear, and they "fled from the presence of the LORD."

They retained such a small trace of the knowledge of the One who fills the heavens and the earth that they "hid themselves from the presence of the LORD God among the trees of the garden." Thus, the man and the woman lost both the knowledge and the love of God, and without these virtues, God's image could no longer exist in them. Consequently, when they lost God's knowledge and love, they also lost his image. They became unholy and unhappy. Instead of retaining these blessings, they plunged into pride and self-will, the very image of the devil. They embraced fleshly appetites and desires, which is the picture of the animals that perish.

3. Someone may say, "God's threat ('In the day that you eat of it you shall die') refers only to the physical death of the body." The answer to this theory is clear. To assert this view is precisely and obviously to make God a liar; it is to declare that the God of truth really affirmed something contrary to the truth. It is obvious that Adam and Eve did not physically die in the day that they ate the fruit. Instead of dying, they lived more than nine hundred additional years. Therefore, without impeaching God's truthfulness, we cannot possibly understand his warning to Adam and Eve to pertain to the death of the body. We must understand that warning to pertain to spiritual death and the loss of the life and image of God.

4. Saint Paul taught that "all die in Adam." That statement refers to all the posterity descended from Adam and Eve. The natural consequence is that everyone who comes from Adam and Eve enters the world spiritually unresponsive to God, completely "dead in sin." We are all totally empty of God's life and image. We are deprived of the "true righteousness and holiness" in which God created Adam and Eve.

Instead of being in a state of righteousness and holiness, everyone is born into the world in pride and self-will, which are characteristics of the devil. In our fleshly appetites and desires, we have the image of animals. Therefore, the total corruption of human nature forms the basis for our need of the new birth. Because we are "born in sin," we "must be born anew." Everyone born in the flesh must be born of the Spirit of God.

II. The Nature of the New Birth

1. The second question we will consider is, "How must one be born anew?" What is the nature of the new birth? This question is the most significant one that we can conceive. Therefore, in such an important matter we should not be satisfied with a meager investigation. Rather, we should explore this question with the greatest possible care and ponder it in our hearts. We need to understand fully this important issue so as to comprehend clearly how we should be born anew.

2. Of course, we should not expect a detailed philosophical account of the new birth. Our Lord sufficiently shields us from any such expectation by the words that immediately follow our text. He reminded Nicodemus of a fact that is as certain as anything in the world. The wisest person under the sun is not fully able to explain this marvel. Jesus said,

> The wind blows where it chooses (not because of *your* power or wisdom), and you hear the sound of it (you are certain that it *does* blow). But you do not know where it comes from or where it goes. (No one can *explain* the precise way the wind begins and ends, rises and falls.) So it is with everyone who is born of the Spirit.

You can be as absolutely certain of the new birth as you are certain of the movement of the wind. But, neither you nor the wisest person can explain how the wind moves or how the Holy Spirit effects the new birth in the soul.

3. For every rational and Christian purpose, it is enough for us to give a clear scriptural account of the nature of the new birth without descending into intricate and meticulous scrutiny. This explanation will satisfy all reasonable people whose only desire is the salvation of their souls.

In his conversation with Nicodemus, our Lord's expression "being born again" was not the first use of this term. The phrase was well known before that time, and it was commonly used among the Jews when our Savior appeared among them. When the adult heathen became convinced that the Jewish religion had come from God and they wanted to embrace it, the custom was first to baptize them before admitting them to the rite of circumcision. After they were baptized, the Jews said that they were "born again." By this term, they meant that the one who had been a child of the devil was now adopted into the family of God and regarded as one of God's children.

Our Lord used this expression with Nicodemus who was "a teacher of Israel," and he ought to have understood it well. However, Jesus used the phrase in a stronger sense than Nicodemus was accustomed to understanding. Perhaps our Lord's new meaning of the phrase prompted Nicodemus to ask, "How can these things be?" The words of Jesus cannot be understood *literally*. "Can one enter a second time into the mother's womb and be born?" The words, however, can be understood *spiritually*. One can be "born from above," "born of God," or "born of the Spirit" in a way that closely corresponds to a natural birth.

4. Before children are born into the world they have eyes, but they cannot see; they have ears, but they cannot hear. They are greatly limited in the use of their senses. They have no comprehension of any of the things of the world, and they have no natural understanding. We do not call that mode of existence "life," as we ordinarily understand it. It is only when children are born that we are accustomed to saying that life begins. As soon as they are born, they begin to see light and the various objects that surround them. Their ears are then opened, and they hear sounds. In addition, all the other organs of sense begin their appropriate functions. Newborn infants breathe and live in an entirely different way. All these parallels between physical and spiritual birth are convincing!

In a spiritual sense, prior to the new birth when people are in a purely natural state, they have spiritual eyes, but they cannot see. A thick impenetrable veil lies upon them. They have spiritual ears, but they cannot hear; they are completely deaf to what they hunger most to hear. Their other spiritual senses are closed, and they are in the same condition as if they were altogether dead. Consequently, they have no knowledge of, or communion with, God. They do not know him at all. They have no real understanding of the spiritual or eternal things of God. Although they are living persons, they are dead to authentic Christianity.

As soon as they are born of God, however, there is a total change in this state of affairs. In the language of the apostle Paul, the "eyes of their hearts are enlightened." "God who said, 'Let light shine out of darkness,' shines in their hearts to give the light of the knowledge of the glory of God in the face of Jesus Christ." Their ears are opened, and they are now able to hear the inner voice of God, saying, "Take heart; your sins are forgiven"; "Go your way, and from now on do not sin again."

This message (if not in those exact words) is what God speaks to the hearts of those who are born anew. Now, they are prepared to hear whatever "he who teaches knowledge to humankind" is pleased from time to time to reveal to them. In the language of the church, we "feel in our hearts the mighty working of the Spirit of God."[5] This sense does not refer to a sensual, fleshy emotion, as people of the world foolishly and deliberately misunderstand the term. They fail to comprehend, even though again and again they have been told what we mean by "feeling God at work in the heart." We mean that one is inwardly aware of the graces that God's Spirit works in the heart.

One consciously senses "the peace of God, which surpasses all understanding." Many times, one feels "an indescribable and glorious joy." Newborn Christians sense that "God's love has been poured into their hearts through the Holy Spirit that has been given to them." After the new birth, the Christian's spiritual senses have been "trained by practice to distinguish good from evil." By the use of these spiritual abilities, they daily increase in the knowledge of God, of Jesus Christ whom God has sent, and of all the things pertaining to his inward kingdom.

After the new birth, it is accurate to say that we have come alive. God, by his Spirit, "brings us to himself" and makes us "alive to God in Christ Jesus." Christians live a life that the world cannot understand—it is a life "hidden with Christ in God." As it were, God is constantly breathing upon their souls, and their souls are continually breathing toward God. Grace descends into their hearts, and prayer and praise ascend to heaven. Through this vital union between God and his children, the communion with the Father and the Son is a type of spiritual breathing, by which the life of God continues in the soul. God's children mature until they come "to the measure of the full stature of Christ."

5. From what has been said, the nature of the new birth becomes clearly evident. God works this momentous change in the soul, bringing it into life and raising it from the death of sin to the life of righteousness. It is the change worked in the soul by the almighty Spirit of God, who "creates us anew in Christ Jesus, according to the image of the creator."

The new birth is being born anew "in true righteousness and holiness" when love for the world is changed into love for God. Pride is changed into humility; anger into meekness; and hatred, envy, and hostility into a sincere, tender, unbiased love for all humankind. In a word, the new birth is the change by which the "earthly, unspiritual, devilish" mind is turned into "the same mind that was in Christ Jesus." This is the nature of the new birth, and "so it is with everyone who is born of the Spirit."

III. The Purpose of the New Birth

1. It is not difficult for those who have considered these things to see the necessity of the new birth and to answer the third question: What is the purpose of the new birth? First, it is very easy to see that the new birth is necessary for holiness. Now, according to the Bible, what is holiness? It is not a simple external religion that consists of a series of outward duties, no matter how many they may be or how precisely we perform them. No, these things are not holiness.

Gospel holiness is nothing less than the image of God stamped upon the heart. Holiness is having "the same mind that was in Christ Jesus." It consists of all the heavenly affections and attitudes combined. Holiness involves a continuous, thankful love to God, who did not withhold his only son from us. It becomes both natural and necessary for us to love everyone. Holiness fills us with "compassion, kindness, humility, meekness, and patience." It is the kind of love for God that teaches us to "be holy in all our conduct."

Holiness enables us to present everything we are and have—souls, bodies, thoughts, words, and deeds—as a continuous living sacrifice, acceptable to God through Christ Jesus. It is not possible for this holiness to exist until we are first renewed in our minds. This transformation cannot begin in the soul until the change is accomplished and the power of the highest overshadows us and brings us "from darkness to light and from the power of Satan to God." That is to say, our transformation begins with the new birth, which is absolutely necessary for holiness.

2. "Without holiness, no one will see the Lord" or behold God's face in glory. Therefore, the new birth is absolutely necessary for eternal salvation. So perverse and devious are human hearts, people may delude themselves that they can live in their sins until they draw their last breath and then go to live with God when they die. Thousands of people really do believe that they have found an easy road that does not lead to destruction. They say, "What danger can there be for such a harmless and virtuous woman?" They ask, "What fear is there that such an honest man of such strict morality could miss heaven?" These people constantly think this way, especially if they regularly attend church and sacrament.

One of them will ask with complete confidence, "What? Will I not do as well as my neighbors?" The answer is, "Yes, you will do as well as your *unholy* neighbors, and you will do as well as those who die in their sins. Together, you will all drop into the pit—that is, into the bottommost hell. You will all be together in 'the lake of fire that burns with sulfur.'" At last, you will then see the necessity of holiness for heaven. May God grant that you see it sooner rather than later! You will then see the need for the new birth because we cannot be holy unless we are born anew.

3. Moreover, unless we are born anew, none of us can even be happy in this present world. In the nature of things, it is not possible for us to be happy if we are not holy. Even the poor, ungodly Roman poet could tell us,

No bad person can be happy.[6]

The reason is obvious: All unholy attitudes are unsettled attitudes. Hostility, hatred, envy, jealousy, and revenge create a present hell in the heart. At the same time, so do even the more gentle passions, if they are not kept within proper bounds. They give a thousand times more pain than pleasure. Even "hope deferred makes the heart sick"—and how often this is the case.

Every desire that does not accord with God's will is prone to "pierce us with many pains." To the extent that the common sources of sin, pride, self-will, and idolatry prevail in our lives, to the same degree they are the common causes of unhappiness. Therefore, as long as these attitudes hold sway in any soul, happiness has no place in us. Evil attitudes must all reign until our perverted natures are changed—that is, until we are born again. Consequently, the new birth is absolutely necessary for happiness in this world and in the world to come.

IV. Conclusions About the New Birth

Finally, I will add a few conclusions that naturally follow from the preceding explanations.

1. First, the new birth is not *baptism*. The two are not the same thing. To be sure, many people seem to imagine that both are essentially alike. At least they speak as if they think the two are identical. Yet, I do not know that this belief is publicly professed by any Christian denomination at all. Certainly no church within the British Empire holds this view—not the established Church or any of the dissenting churches. The judgment of a dissenting church was clearly declared in 1647:

> **Q.** What are the parts of a sacrament?
>
> **A.** The parts of a sacrament are two: the one, an outward and visible sign. . . . The other is an inward and spiritual grace.
>
> **Q.** What is baptism?
>
> **A.** Baptism is a sacrament . . . in which Christ has ordained the washing with water . . . to be a sign and seal of . . . regeneration by his Spirit.[7]

Here it is apparent that baptism, *the sign*, is distinct from regeneration, *the thing signified.*

Likewise, the judgment of our national Church is stated with the utmost clarity in the Catechism.

> **Q.** What do you mean by the word "sacrament"?
>
> **A.** I mean an outward and visible sign of an inward and spiritual grace.
>
> **Q.** What is the outward part or form in baptism?
>
> **A.** Water, in which the person is baptized, "in the name of the Father, Son, and Holy Spirit."
>
> **Q.** What is the inward thing signified?
>
> **A.** A death to sin, and a new birth unto righteousness.[8]

In the Church of England, nothing is more clear than that baptism is *not* the new birth. Indeed, the logic is so clear and apparent that we do not need to cite any other authority. What can be more obvious than that the application of water is an *external* work, and the coming of the Holy Spirit is an *internal* work? It is clear that the one is a *visible* thing and the other is an *invisible* thing. The two are entirely distinct from each other. One is a human act that washes the body, and the other is an act of God done in the soul. The rite of baptism is just as separable from regeneration as the body is from the soul, or water is from the Holy Spirit.

2. Second, from the preceding considerations we can say that because the new birth is not the same thing as baptism, it does not always accompany baptism. The two do not always go together. It is possible for people to be "born of water" and yet not be "born of the Spirit." Sometimes, there can be the outward sign without the inward grace. At this point, I am not speaking about infants. It is sure that our national Church assumes that all who are baptized in their infancy are at the same time born anew. The entire ritual for the baptism of infants is based on this premise. The fact that we can-

not comprehend how this work can be done in infants is not a substantive objection against it. For that matter, we cannot understand how this work is done in a person of more mature years. Yet, whatever may be the case with infants, it is certain that the baptisms of those of more mature years are not identical to the new birth.

Jesus said, "The tree is known by its fruit." And by this test it becomes too obvious to be denied that many people who were children of the devil before they were baptized remain the same after their baptism. They continue to do the works of their father, the devil. They continue to be servants of sin, without any pretense of being inwardly or outwardly holy.

3. From what has been said, the third conclusion that we can draw is that the new birth is not the same as sanctification. Nonetheless, the union of justification and sanctification is certainly taken for granted by many people. This mistake is seen particularly in the recent monograph of a distinguished writer.[9] Setting aside several other important objections that can be made to his treatise, the error of confusing regeneration and sanctification is obvious. The pages of that work constantly speak of regeneration as a progressive work carried on in the soul by slow degrees from the time we first turn to God. This process is undeniably true about sanctification. However, it is not true about regeneration, the new birth. The new birth is a part of sanctification, but not the whole of it.

Justification is the gate of entrance into the process of sanctification. When we are born again, our sanctification (inward and outward holiness) begins. From this point, we are gradually to "grow up in every way into him who is the head, into Christ." This expression of the apostle commendably illustrates the difference between justification (the new birth) and sanctification, and it points out the exact analogy that exists between natural and spiritual things: A child is born in a moment, or at least in a very short time. Then, the child gradually and slowly grows until he or she attains the stature of an adult. Comparably, a child is born of God in a short time, if not in a moment. Then, by slow degrees, that person grows up "to the measure of the full stature of Christ." The same relationship exists between our natural birth and growth as between our new birth and our sanctification.

4. We can learn one more point from the preceding discussion. It is a matter of such immense importance that we may be excused if we consider it carefully and argue it at some length. I am speaking about those who love human souls and are grieved at the thought that any should perish. What shall these concerned Christians say to those whom they observe desecrating the Lord's day, or engaging in drunkenness or in any other willful sin? What can they say if it is true that we must be born anew? A passionate person might object: "No. You must not confront him. How can you talk so uncharitably to someone? Has he not already been baptized? He cannot be born again *now*, because he was born again when he was baptized."

Here is my answer to your objection: Do you really believe that such a person cannot be born again? If so, he cannot be saved. Although one is as old as Nicodemus was, nevertheless, "no one can see the kingdom of God without being born from above." Therefore, in saying "He cannot be born again," in effect you assign him to damnation.

Where now is the uncharitable attitude? On my side, or on yours? I say, "He can be born again, and so become an heir of salvation." You say, "He cannot be born again." If what you say is true, he must inevitably perish. So you completely block his way to salvation and send him to hell out of mere "charity"!

Suppose that in genuine charity we say to the sinner, "You must be born again." Assume, however, that the sinner has been taught to say, "I defy your new doctrine; I do not need be born again. I was born again when I was baptized. What! Do you want me to deny my baptism?"

First, I answer that there is nothing under heaven that can change a lie. Otherwise, I would say to an unapologetic sinner, "If you have been baptized, do not admit it! How greatly your profession deepens your guilt! How terribly will it increase your damnation! Were you dedicated to God when you were eight days old, and all these years have you been dedicating yourself to the devil? Even before you had the ability to reason, were you consecrated to God the Father, God the Son, and God the Holy Spirit? And since the time you have been able to reason for yourself, have you been rebelling against God and giving yourself to Satan?"

Does reckless sacrilege, the love of the world, pride, anger, lust, foolish desires, and a whole sequence of evil affections stand where it should not stand? Have you set up all these accursed things in the soul that was once a "temple of the Holy Spirit"? At your baptism, were you not set apart as "a dwelling place for God"? Indeed, were you not solemnly dedicated to him? Now, do you not boast that you once belonged to God? O, be ashamed of yourself, blush with remorse, hide yourself in the earth! Never boast about those things that ought to fill you with humiliation—things that should shame you before God and others!

Second, I answer your claim that you have been born again with the reminder that you have already betrayed your baptism. And you have done so in a most effective manner. You have denied it thousands of times, and daily you continue to do so. In your baptism, you "renounced the devil and all his works." Whenever, therefore, you make room for the devil and do his works, you are spurning your baptism. Therefore, you renounce your baptism with every willful sin or impure act. You reject the Lord in your drunkenness, revenge, or obscene or irreverent talk, and by every blasphemy that comes from your mouth. Every time you defile the Lord's day, you thereby deny your baptism. Indeed you do so every time you do anything to another person that you would not have that person do to you.

Third, I respond to your claim to be a Christian by insisting that whether or not you have been baptized, you must be born again. Otherwise it is not possible for you to become inwardly holy. And without inward and outward holiness, you cannot be happy in this world or in the world to come.

Perhaps you will reply, "But I harm no one; I am honest and fair in all my dealings; I do not curse or take the Lord's name in vain; I do not defile the Lord's day; I am not a drunkard; I do not slander my neighbors; I do not live in any willful sin." If these claims are true, we wish that everyone went as far as you do. But, if you want to be saved, you must go even farther—you must be born again.

You may add to your claim, "I do go farther still. I not only do no harm, but also do all the good I can." I doubt that claim. I fear that you have had a thousand opportunities to do good that you have permitted to pass without taking advantage of them. For this neglect, you are accountable to God. But even if you had taken advantage of all your opportunities to do all the good you could to everyone, this achievement does not change things at all. Still, you must be born again. Without the new birth, nothing will profit your poor, sinful, polluted soul.

Perhaps you will say, "But I regularly attend all the ordinances of God. I am faithful to my church and the sacrament." I answer that it is good that you do. However, unless you are born again, all these works will not keep you from hell. Attend church twice a day, go to the Lord's table every week, and say ever so many prayers in private. Hear ever so many good and excellent sermons, even the best that have ever been preached. Read ever so many good books. Still, you must be born again. None of these good things will substitute for the new birth. No, there is nothing under heaven that will take its place.

Therefore, if you have not already experienced this inward work of God, let your continual prayer be, "Lord, add this to all your blessings: let me be born again. Deny me anything you please, but do not deny me this blessing: Let me be born from above. Take away whatever seems good to you—reputation, fortune, friends, or health. Only give me this: I want to be born of the Spirit! I want to be received among the children of God. Let me be born, 'not of perishable but of imperishable seed, through the living and enduring word of God.' Daily, let me 'grow in the grace and knowledge of our Lord and Savior Jesus Christ.'"

Notes

1. Jackson, *Wesley's Works,* 9:494.
2. Ibid., 10:188-201.
3. Frank Baker, *The Works of John Wesley,* Bicentennial Ed., *Letters,* vol. 26 (Oxford: Clarendon Press, 1982), May 22, 1750, 26:425.
4. Outler, *Wesley's Sermons,* "The Marks of the New Birth" (IV, 5), 1:430.
5. Anglican Elizabethan Homilies, "Rogation Week," 438.
6. Juvenal [Decimus Junius Juvenalis, 60–127], *Sixteen Satires,* iv, 8-9.
7. Westminster Larger Catechism, Questions 163 and 165.
8. Book of Common Prayer, Catechism, 581.
9. William Law, *The Works of the Reverend William Law,* 9 vols. (London: Printed for J. Richardson, 1762), Grounds and Reason of Christian Regeneration or the New Birth, vol. 5.

Introduction to Sermon 46

THE WILDERNESS STATE

Through personal experience and observation, Wesley fully understood that Christians sometimes fall into uncertainty and depression. Experience confirms that sometimes God seems far removed. Christ's disciples rarely avoid going through spiritual valleys. This sermon addresses the reality that Christians will experience low points in their lives.

In Wesley's day, the doctrine of Christian assurance brought comfort to many Methodists. Yet, this doctrine also caused some of them to experience consternation and worry. When, at times, they lacked a conscious experience of the witness of the Spirit, they lost their peace and joy. In such periods, they wondered if the Holy Spirit had abandoned them. This sermon and the one that follows ("Heaviness Through Manifold Temptations") speak to the questions Christians ask when they find themselves downcast, lacking in zeal, confused, or without joy.

In the eighteenth century, it was common for Christians to compare the pilgrimage of Christ's disciples to Israel's difficult trek in the desert. They saw themselves as passing through the world's wilderness on their way to heaven's promised land. Wesley drew upon the experience of Israel to illustrate that Christians sometimes experience trials in the "wilderness." "The wilderness state" was also a term that referred to the temptation of Jesus during his testing in the wilderness for forty days and forty nights.[1] Christ's wilderness temptation came immediately after his baptism and anointing with the Holy Spirit, which was symbolized by the descent of the dove. Wesley taught, "After the clearest light and the strongest consolation, let us expect the sharpest temptations."[2] In Wesley's generation, most people immediately understood the implications of the sermon's title, "The Wilderness State."

Wesley was sympathetic to Christians whose joy was diminished due to their being in a spiritual valley. He wrote in his journal an account of his preaching from this text:

> From these words, "Then was Jesus led by the Spirit into the wilderness to be tempted of the devil," I took occasion to describe that wilderness state, that state of doubts, and fears, and strong temptation, which so many go through, though in different degrees, after they have received remission of sins.[3]

He wrote a member of a Methodist society, "From what not only you but many others likewise have experienced, we find there is very frequently a kind of wilderness state, not only after justification, but even after deliverance from sin; and I doubt whether the sermon upon that state might not give you light in this case also."[4]

William Law and other mystics had made the experience of being in a wilderness state into a *virtue*. They advanced the theory that those who lived in radiant Christian assurance were in a lower state of grace than those who suffered in the "dark night of the soul." These mystic teachers contended that Christians can rise to spiritual heights only when they leave "perceptible comforts" and live by "naked faith" in a wilderness state of anxiety and depression. They taught that God purifies us more quickly and completely by sorrow than by joy and that we are comforted more by anxiety than by peace. These mystics insisted that, spiritually, we are better off when God takes away our sense of peace and joy. Some went so far as to say that radiant faith belongs to a "lower dispensation."

Wesley strongly rejected this notion. He insisted that the Bible never teaches this doctrine that the mystics advanced. Indeed, he pointed out many times that "the kingdom of God is . . . righteousness and peace and joy in the Holy Spirit."[5] He celebrated Christ's promise to give us joy that the world can neither give nor remove. God never withdraws from us what he has given us. The wilderness state is not the consequence of God's departing from us, as some mystics claimed, but rather the result of our departing from him.

Wesley opposed the idea that spiritual darkness purifies us more fully than spiritual light. In this sermon, he declares, "Scripture nowhere says that God's *absence* best perfects his work in the heart! Rather, God perfects his work in us through his *presence*. . . . A strong consciousness of God's inner presence will do more in an hour than his absence can accomplish in an entire generation."

This sermon and the next one, *Heaviness Through Manifold Temptations,* deal with separate and distinct spiritual conditions. The wilderness state—in which God is absent—is the consequence of sin, disobedience, unfaithfulness, or neglect. The wilderness state stems from the loss of faith, love, peace, and joy. In a different vein, the heaviness that comes from trials—in which God is present—stems from the sufferings Christians may face in their lives. These ordeals include sickness, pain, emotional afflictions, calamity, poverty, grief, sorrow for the lost, and persecution. Christians who suffer such trials continue to hold on to their faith, and they retain love, peace, and joy. Wesley insists that although Christians can expect to suffer trials, they must tenaciously avoid the wilderness state and its accompanying darkness. This sermon shows how one can steer clear of, and recover from, the desolate misery of being in the wilderness state.

Sermon 46

THE WILDERNESS STATE

So you have pain now; but I will see you again, and your hearts will rejoice, and no one will take your joy from you. *(John 16:22)*

1 After God had worked a great deliverance for Israel by bringing the people "out of the house of slavery," they did not immediately enter into the land that he had promised to their fathers. Instead, they "wandered in trackless wastes," and in different ways they met with trials and fears. In the same way, after God has delivered those who fear him from the bondage of sin and Satan, not many of them immediately enter the "rest that remains for the people of God."

Even after they are "justified by God's grace as a gift, through the redemption that is in Christ Jesus," they experience trials and fears. To some degree, most Christians wander out of the good way into which God has brought them. As it were, they come into a "howling wilderness waste," in which they are tried and afflicted in various ways. Alluding to the experience of the Israelites, some have called these trials "a wilderness state."

2. Certainly, those who are in this condition deserve the kindest compassion. They suffer under an evil and painful loss of faith,

a condition that is not usually understood. For this very reason, it is all the harder for them to find a remedy. Because they are themselves in the wilderness, they cannot be expected to understand the nature of their own anxiety. And few of their sisters and brothers (perhaps even their teachers) are able to understand their trials or know how to heal them. Therefore, we need all the more (1) to examine the nature of this affliction, (2) to look into its cause, and (3) to find a cure for it.

I. The Nature of the Wilderness State

1. First, what is the nature of this affliction into which so many descend after they have believed? What are the components of the wilderness state, and what are its authentic symptoms? It consists of the loss of the faith that God once worked in the heart. Those in the wilderness lack the divine "assurance" and satisfactory "conviction of things not seen," which they once enjoyed. They no longer have the inner testimony of the Spirit, which once enabled them to say, "The life I now live in the flesh, I live by faith in the Son of God, who loved me and gave himself for me." The light of heaven no longer "shines in their hearts," and they do not "see him who is invisible."

Instead, darkness covers their souls, and blindness veils their understanding. The Holy Spirit no longer "bears witness with their spirits that they are children of God." God's Spirit does not witness as the Spirit of adoption, crying, "Abba! Father!" They no longer have a confident trust in God's love and the freedom to approach him with holy boldness. The expression of their hearts is no longer, "Though he slay me, yet will I trust in him." Rather, in the same way as Samson, their hair has been shaved, and they have become as weak as any other person.

2. Second, this depressed state leads to the loss of love, because love rises or falls with genuine, living faith. Accordingly, those who are deprived of their faith are also deprived of their love for God. They can no longer say, "Lord, you know everything; you know that I love you." Those who are in a wilderness state are not happy in God; happiness belongs to those who truly love him.

They do not "smell the fragrance of the costly perfume" and delight in the Lord as they formerly did. At one time, all their desires were "God's name and his renown." But now, even their desires are cold and dead, if not completely lifeless.

Just as their love for God has "grown cold," so has their love for their neighbors. They no longer have a passion for the souls of others. They now lack a yearning for their welfare. They do not have the ardent, enthusiastic, and active desire for others to be reconciled to God. They feel no compassion for the sheep that are lost; they no longer "deal gently with the ignorant and wayward." Once, they were "kind toward everyone," "correcting them with gentleness." If others were detected in a transgression, they restored the transgressors in a spirit of gentleness.

But after a period of uncertainty—perhaps of many days—anger begins to regain its power. When we lose our faith and joy, irritability and impatience crowd in, driving us toward a fall. In this state, it is good if we escape "repaying evil for evil or abuse for abuse."

3. Third, due to the loss of faith and love, we lose joy in the Holy Spirit. If the loving consciousness of pardon no longer exists, the joy of our pardon cannot remain. If the Holy Spirit does not "bear witness with our spirits that we are children of God," the joy that once flowed from that inward witness must also cease.

Similarly, those who once "rejoiced with an indescribable and glorious joy" are now deprived of the "hope that is full of immortality" and the joy that this hope brings. They also lose the joy that comes from a consciousness of "God's love, which has been poured into their hearts." If the cause is removed, so is its result. When the fountain is dammed up, its living waters no longer refresh the thirsty soul.

4. Fourth, with the loss of faith, love, and joy is also the loss of peace. The peace that once "surpassed all understanding" is no longer present. The pleasant serenity of mind and calmness of spirit is gone. Agonizing doubt returns. When in a wilderness state, we question whether we ever did, or perhaps ever will, believe. We begin to doubt whether we ever had the genuine witness of the Spirit in our hearts. We ask ourselves if we did not

deceive our own souls and mistake the voice of nature for the voice of God. Perhaps we question whether we will ever hear his voice and find his favor.

Then, our doubts combine with slavish fear. It is a "fear that has to do with punishment." We dread the wrath of God, just as we did before we believed. We fear that God will reject us from his presence. And from that time, we sink into anxiety about death, from which we were once completely delivered.

5. This loss of peace, however, is accompanied by still more injury—the loss of power. We know that everyone who has peace with God through Jesus Christ has power over all sin. But whenever we lose God's peace, we also lose the power over sin. As long as God's peace continues with us, so does his power. God gives us strength even over "besetting sins"—whether they arise from our nature, body, education, or vocation. Indeed, God gives us power over those sinful dispositions and desires that we cannot conquer until he comes into our lives. In Christ, "sin will have no dominion over us."[6]

In the wilderness state, however, we no longer have any dominion over sin. We may truly struggle against sin, but we cannot overcome it. The crown has fallen from our heads. Now, our enemies again prevail over us and more or less bring us into slavery. The glory has departed, along with the kingdom of God, which was in our hearts. We are devoid of righteousness and peace and joy in the Holy Spirit.

II. The Cause of the Wilderness State

1. We have examined the nature of what many have termed (and with good reason) "the wilderness state." Now, second, we can more fully understand the wilderness state by asking the question, "What are its causes?" There are indeed many causes. And I would never dare to list among them the arbitrary sovereign will of God. In truth, God "delights in the *welfare* of his servants." "He does not willingly afflict or grieve anyone."

The unchanging will of God for us "is our sanctification," accompanied by "righteousness and peace and joy in the Holy

Spirit." He generously gives these gifts. And Scripture assures us that "the gifts of God are irrevocable." God never withdraws the things he has given, nor does he desire to take them back from us. Therefore, he never withdraws himself from us, as some contend. It is only we who withdraw from him.

(i) Sin and the wilderness state

2. The most common cause of the wilderness state is sin of one kind or another. Our transgressions usually bring about the confusion that causes iniquity and misery. First, there is the sin of *commission.* We often observe that this kind of sin darkens the soul in an instant, especially if it is a known, willful, or presumptuous sin. For instance, suppose a person who is walking in the clear light of God's presence would be influenced to commit a single act of drunkenness or immorality. It would not be any surprise that in that very hour he or she falls into a complete loss of faith. It is true that there have been some very rare cases in which God prevented this loss of faith by an extraordinary exhibition of his pardoning mercy, almost in the very instant of our sinning. Usually, however, such an abuse of God's goodness and so great a contempt for his love causes an immediate alienation from God and "a darkness that can be felt."

3. We can hope that this example does not occur very frequently. We trust that there are not many Christians who so spurn the riches of God's goodness, that, while walking in his light, flagrantly and presumptuously rebelling against him. God's light is much more frequently lost by giving in to sins of *omission.* Omissions of duty do not immediately quench the Spirit, but gradually and slowly they will do so. Sins of *commission* can be compared to pouring water on a fire; sins of *omission* can be compared to withdrawing fuel from the fire.

God's Spirit will many times reprove our neglect of duty before he departs from us. He gives us many inward checks and secret warnings before he withdraws his influences. Consequently, only a series of willfully persistent omissions will bring us into the complete darkness of a wilderness state.

4. Perhaps no sin of omission more frequently causes the loss of faith than the *neglect of private prayer*. The need for private prayer cannot be satisfied by any other religious exercise. Nothing can be more certain. God's life in the soul does not continue, much less grow, unless we use every opportunity to commune with him and pour out our hearts before him. Therefore, we must not neglect prayer by allowing business, visitors, or any pastime to prevent these secret activities of the soul (or by rushing through them in a slight and careless manner). To neglect private prayer is to decline in our relationship with God. If we frequently or for long periods suspend our prayers, God's life within us will progressively decline.

5. There is another sin of omission that frequently brings the soul of a believer to a loss of faith and joy. It is the neglect of *ministering to others*. Even in the Jewish dispensation, God strongly commanded, "You shall not hate in your heart anyone of your kin; you shall reprove your neighbor, or you will incur guilt yourself." If we do not reprove others when we see them in a fault, such neglect will soon bring leanness into our own souls. By our silence, we are taking part in their sins. By neglecting to reprove our neighbors, we make their sins our own. We become accountable to God for them because we saw their danger and gave them no warning. So "if they perish in their iniquity," God may justly "require their blood at our hands." Therefore, it is no wonder that by grieving the Spirit this way, we forfeit the light of God's countenance.

6. A third cause of our losing the sense of God's presence is our *giving in to some inward sin*. For example, even if inward pride does not reveal itself in outward conduct, we know that "all those who are arrogant are an abomination to the LORD." How easy it is for one who is filled with peace and joy to fall into this snare of the devil! How instinctive it is for us to imagine that we have more grace, wisdom, or strength than we really have! How prone we are "to think of ourselves more highly than we ought to think"! It is natural for us to rejoice over a gift that we have received, as though it had not been given to us. Because God always "opposes the proud" and only "gives grace to the

humble," our pride will certainly obscure, if not destroy, the light that once shone in our hearts.

7. The same result comes from yielding to anger, regardless of the provocation or cause. Anger can even be disguised in the name of a passion for the truth or the glory of God. Indeed, all passion that comes from anything other than the flame of love is "earthly, unspiritual, and devilish." Worldly zeal can become the flame of fury. It is unadorned, sinful anger—neither more nor less. Nothing is a greater enemy to the mild, gentle love of God than anger.

Anger and love never have, and never will, exist together in the same heart. To the degree that anger predominates, love and joy in the Holy Spirit will decline. This truth is particularly noticeable when we become angry with any of our Christian sisters or brothers or any who are united with us by civic or religious ties. If we yield to the spirit of anger for only an hour, we lose the sweet influences of the Holy Spirit. Instead of changing others for the good, we destroy ourselves and become an easy prey for any enemy that assails us.

8. Let us assume that we are conscious that anger is Satan's snare. We can come under attack from still another source. When cruelty and anger are asleep and love alone is awake, we may be no less endangered by *unhealthy desires*. These cravings equally tend to cast a shadow on the soul. The loss of faith is the certain consequence of any "harmful desire," or proud or excessive fondness. The jealous God will surely contend with us if we set our minds on the things of the earth or on any person or thing under the sun other than God and what inclines us toward him. Nor should we seek happiness in any created thing.

God will not allow any rival. The "god of this world" will blind and darken our minds if "we will not listen to God's voice" of warning, and return to him with all our hearts. If we continue to grieve him with our idols and pursuing other gods, we shall soon become cold, barren, and dry.

9. Satan often blinds us, even when we do not yield to any definite sin. We need only to become *slothful*. It gives the devil sufficient advantage if we fail to "rekindle the gift of God that is within us." The enemy takes advantage of us if we do not continually

"agonize to enter through the narrow door," earnestly "strive for the crown," and "take the kingdom of heaven by force."

We need only to stop our spiritual warfare, and Satan will certainly conquer us. We need only to become careless or "grow weary or lose heart" and become comfortable and lazy. Our natural depravity will soon return and envelop our souls. To fail, it is enough that we give in to spiritual sloth because laziness will effectively cast a shadow over the soul. If not as quickly as murder or adultery, sloth will just as surely destroy the light of God within us.

10. It is important to observe that the cause of a wilderness state (whether it results from omission or commission, or inward or outward sin) is not always near at hand. Sometimes the sin that caused the present distress may have been committed in the distant past. It might have occurred days, weeks, or months previously.

The fact that God now withdraws his light and peace from us because of what was done so long ago is not (as one might at first imagine) an example of his harshness. Rather, our very distress proves his patient and tender mercy. He waited all this time because of the possibility that we would see, admit, and correct what was wrong. And when we fail to repent and amend the wrong, God finally reveals his displeasure so that our unhappiness will at last bring us to repentance.

(ii) Ignorance and the wilderness state

1. *Ignorance* is another general cause of the various kinds of the wilderness state. Some people do not know the Scriptures. They imagine that there are passages (either in the Old or New Testament) that state all believers without exception must sometimes become depressed. This ignorance will naturally bring upon them their anticipated loss of faith. How common is this very thing among us! How few people there are who do not *expect* to be depressed! It is not surprising, because they are taught to anticipate it. Their leaders influence them into this way of thinking.

We find this tendency in the mystical writers of the Church of

Rome, but also in many of the most spiritual and experiential teachers in our own Church (although there were a few exceptions in the last century). These teachers instruct us to expect a loss of faith and joy. And they teach this expectation as a clear, unquestionable scriptural doctrine. They even cite many texts to "prove" it.

2. Also, our ignorance of the nature of God's work in the soul frequently causes this wilderness state. People think that they are not always supposed to walk in "radiant faith." Particularly, writers of the Church of Rome have taught them this belief. And, without adequate examination, too many Protestants have accepted these incorrect assertions. These instructors teach that "radiant faith" (termed "luminous faith") belongs to a "lower dispensation." They contend that we will rise higher when we leave "perceptible comforts" and live by "naked faith." If one's faith is stripped of love, peace, and joy in the Holy Spirit, it is "naked" indeed!

These teachers say that living in a state of light and joy is good, but living in a state of "lost faith" and "drought" is even better. They contend that only by the wilderness state can we be "purified" from pride, love of the world, and excessive self-love. They teach that we should not desire or expect always to "walk in the light."[7] Although other reasons may coincide, this teaching has caused the main body of pious people in the Church of Rome generally to walk in a dark and despondent way. If they ever receive God's light, they soon lose it.[8]

(iii) Temptation and the wilderness state

1. A third general cause of the wilderness state is *temptation.* When the candle of the Lord first shines on us, frequently temptation flees and totally disappears. All is calm within us and perhaps around us as well. God "causes even our enemies to be at peace with us." It is very natural for us to assume that we will not see any more spiritual warfare. There are instances when this spiritual calm continues for weeks, months, or years. Ordinarily, however, this tranquility does not last. Soon again "the rain falls, the floods come, and the winds blow."

When God slackens his bridle in the teeth of those who "do not know either the Son or the Father" (and consequently hate God's children), their antagonism will show itself in various circumstances. As in ancient times, "the child who was born according to the flesh persecuted the child who was born according to the Spirit, and so it is now also." The same cause still produces the same effect. The evil that remains in the heart will stir yet again. Anger and many other "roots of bitterness" will try to spring up. At the same time, Satan will not fail to hurl his flaming arrows. The newborn soul will be required to struggle against opposition from both the world and family.

Also, new Christians must "struggle against the rulers, against the authorities, against the cosmic powers of this present darkness, against the spiritual forces of evil in the heavenly places." At this point, when such varieties of assaults come all at once and perhaps with undiminished violence, it is not strange if they cause fragile believers to experience anxiety and a loss of faith. These distresses might come more especially if we are not alert, and if the assaults come in an unexpected hour. Especially, believers are subject to the wilderness state if they naively tell themselves, "The day of disaster will no more return."

2. If prior to temptation we think too highly of ourselves (as if we had been cleansed from all sin), temptation's force within us will be exceedingly strengthened. During the warmth of our "first love" for God, we instinctively imagine that we are invulnerable! How ready are we to believe that God has already "fulfilled in us every good resolve and work of faith"! Because we *feel* no sin, we think that we *have* no sin.

We assume that our soul is nothing but love! It might be that a biting attack from an enemy that we supposed had been conquered and killed will plunge us into a wilderness state, or even a complete loss of faith. We can especially become depressed when we reason with the enemy instead of immediately calling upon God. By simple faith, we should cast ourselves on him who alone "knows how to rescue the godly from trial."

III. The Cure for the Wilderness State

We have examined common causes of believers' loss of faith. Now, we will consider the question, "What is the cure for the wilderness state?"

1. It is a fundamental and fatal mistake to think that there is one single cure for every experience of a wilderness state. Yet, this assumption is very common even among many who are regarded as experienced Christians. Indeed, some people assume the role of "teachers of Israel"—that is, spiritual guides of others. As such, they know and use only one spiritual medicine, whatever might be the cause of the sickness.

Immediately, they begin to apply the promises of good news. In their words, they "preach the gospel." Their only concern is to give comfort. Therefore, they say many agreeable and compassionate things about God's love to poor, helpless sinners. They talk only about the power of the blood of Christ.

Clearly, this approach to ministry is nothing but spiritual sham. Indeed, it is the worst kind of spiritual fraud because it tends to destroy both soul and body in hell (if not to kill people's bodies) without the singular mercy of God. It is difficult to speak the kind of words that are appropriate to those promise-mongers who "smear whitewash" over human hurts. They well deserve the title that they have ignorantly given to others—"spiritual charlatans." In effect, they have "profaned the blood of the covenant." They obscenely desecrate the promises of God by applying them to everyone, without making any distinctions. In reality, the cure for spiritual and bodily diseases must be as diverse as their causes. Therefore, we must discover the cause of the wilderness state, and this insight will point to the cure.

2. For instance, is it sinning that causes the darkness or depression? If so, what sin? Is it any kind of outward misdeed? Does your conscience accuse you of committing any sin by which you are grieving the Holy Spirit of God? Is it because of sin that God as well as his joy and peace have departed from you? How can you expect that God's joy and peace will return unless you forsake the loathsome transgression? "Let the wicked forsake their way." "Cleanse your hands, you sinners," and "remove the evil of your

doings." "Then, your light shall rise in the darkness," and our God will return and "abundantly pardon."

3. If after your closest examination you cannot find a sin of commission that causes the cloud upon your soul, next probe to see if there is some sin of omission that separates you from God. Do you "hate in your heart anyone of your kin"? Do you admonish those who sin in your sight? Do you walk in all God's ordinances, including public, family, and private prayer? If you regularly neglect any one of these known duties, how can you expect that the light of God's face will continue to shine upon you?

Hasten to "strengthen what remains," and then your soul will live. "Today, if you will listen to his voice," by God's grace, "complete what is lacking." When you "hear a word behind you, saying, 'This is the way; walk in it,'" "do not harden your hearts." No longer be "disobedient to the heavenly vision." Until you remove your sin (whether of omission or commission), all comfort is false and deceitful. Deceptive comfort only covers the wound that still festers and poisons beneath the scab. Expect no inner peace until you have peace with God, which you cannot have without "fruits worthy of repentance."

4. Perhaps you are not even conscious of any sin of omission that impairs your peace and joy in the Holy Spirit. Then, is there no inward sin, which in your heart is "a root of bitterness springing up and causing trouble"? Is your dryness and barrenness of soul caused by your "unbelieving heart that turns away from the living God"? Has "the foot of arrogance come against you"? Do you "think of yourself more highly than you ought to think"?

Have you in any respect "worshiped your net or made offerings to your seine"?[9] Have you ascribed your success in any undertaking to your own courage, strength, or wisdom? Have you bragged about something you have received, as though it were not a gift? Have you boasted of anything except the cross of our Lord Jesus Christ? Have you loved or desired human praise more than God's approval? Have you taken pleasure in human praise?

If so, the way you should take is clear. If you have fallen through pride, "humble yourselves therefore under the mighty hand of God, so that in due time he may exalt you." Have you driven God away by giving in to anger? Have you "fretted because of the wicked" or "been envious of wrongdoers"? Have you been angry with any of your sisters or brothers? Have you looked at their sin (real or imagined) so as to withdraw your heart from them and sin against the royal law of love?

If so, look to the Lord so that you can renew your strength. Allow God to take away all your disrespect and coldness, so that love, peace, and joy may all return. Pray that you will be unfailingly "kind to one another, tenderhearted, forgiving one another, as God in Christ forgave you." Have you given in to any foolish desire or to any kind or amount of excessive affection? Until you put away your idols, how can God's love have a place in your heart? "Do not be deceived; God is not mocked." He will not dwell in a divided heart. As long as you (as Samson) cherish "Delilah" in your heart, God has no place there.

It is useless to hope to recover God's light until you "tear out your right eye and throw it away." O, let there be no more delay! Pray to the Lord that he may enable you to do so! Mourn your own inadequacy and helplessness. The Lord being your helper, "enter by the narrow gate," and take the kingdom of heaven by violence! Cast out every idol from God's sanctuary, and "the glory of the LORD will appear to you."

5. Perhaps it is spiritual sloth and the lack of striving that keeps your soul in darkness. You dwell at ease in the land. There is no war within your coasts, and so you are tranquil and indifferent. You continue in the same routine of outward duties, and you are content to stay where you are. Meanwhile, do you wonder why your soul is dead?

O, wake up! Stir up yourself before the Lord! Arise, and shake off the dust from your soul. Wrestle with God for his mighty blessing. Pour out your heart unto God in prayer, and continue praying at all times. Stay alert! Wake up from your sleep, and keep awake! Otherwise, you can expect nothing except to become more and more separated from the light and life of God.

6. After your most complete and honest self-examination, if you cannot see that you are presently giving in to spiritual sloth or to any inward or outward sin, then think back to the past. Think

about your former attitudes, words, and actions. Have they been upright before the Lord? "Ponder it on your beds, and be silent." Ask God to examine the motives of your heart and cause you to remember anything that has ever "defied his glorious presence." If the guilt of any unrepented sin remains on your soul, you will continue in darkness until you are renewed by repentance. By faith, you must be cleansed in the "fountain opened for sin and impurity."

7. If the cause of your affliction is not sin, but ignorance, the method of healing is entirely different. Your problem might be ignorance of the meaning of Scripture, perhaps caused by uninformed commentators. You may be ignorant of the wilderness state, however wise or educated you may be about other points. And in your case, this ignorance must be eliminated before we can remove the depression it causes.

We must clarify the true meaning of misinterpreted biblical texts. Here, my purpose does not permit me to consider all the scripture passages that have wrongly been used to support the necessity of the wilderness state. I will just mention two or three that are frequently used to prove that all believers must, sooner or later, "walk in gloom."

8. One of these scriptures is Isaiah 50:10:

> Who among you fears the LORD
> and obeys the voice of his servant,
> who walks in darkness
> and has no light,
> yet trusts in the name of the LORD
> and relies upon his God?

How is it clear from this text or its context that the persons addressed here ever had light? This scripture does not refer to one who is "convicted of sin" and "fears the LORD and obeys the voice of his servant." We should advise such persons, even if they are in spiritual darkness and have never seen the light of God's face, to "trust in the name of the Lord, and rely upon God." This text does not prove that a believer in Christ must sometimes "walk in darkness."

9. Another text that has been reputed to support the need to walk in a wilderness state is Hosea 2:14: "Therefore, I will now allure her, and bring her into the wilderness, and speak tenderly to her." Some have concluded from this scripture that God will bring every believer "into the wilderness"—that is, into a state of paralysis and loss of faith. It is certain, though, that this text says no such thing. The passage does not at all speak about individual believers. It clearly refers to the Jewish nation, and probably to it alone. Even if the text is applied to individuals, its clear meaning is: "I will draw them by love; I will next convince them of sin; and I will comfort them by my pardoning mercy."

10. A third scripture used to support the necessity of a wilderness state is the text for this sermon: "So you have pain now; but I will see you again, and your hearts will rejoice, and no one will take your joy from you." Some have taken this verse to suggest that, after a time, God will withdraw himself from all believers. It is alleged that not until God's children have lived in this sorrow can they have the joy that no one can take from them.

Yet, the entire context shows that here our Lord is speaking personally to the apostles, and to no one else. He is referring to particular events connected with his own death and resurrection. He said, "A little while, and you will no longer see me (while I am in the tomb), and again a little while, and you will see me (after I have risen from the dead)." Then, Jesus said, "You will weep and mourn, but the world will rejoice . . . but your pain will turn into joy. You have pain now (because I will be taken away); but I will see you again (after my resurrection), and your hearts will rejoice, and no one will take your joy from you (the joy that I will give you)." We know that these words were literally fulfilled in the particular case of the apostles. We cannot infer, however, that these verses refer to God's dealings with all believers in general.

11. A fourth text (to mention no more) that has been frequently cited in proof of the necessity of living in a wilderness state is 1 Peter 4:12; "Beloved, do not be surprised at the fiery ordeal that is taking place among you." This text, however, is as far from supporting the point as the preceding text. Literally translated, the verse says, "Beloved, do not wonder at the fire that is among you, which is for your affliction." In whatever way this verse might be

applied to inward afflictions (in a secondary sense), its primary meaning undoubtedly refers to martyrdom and the sufferings connected with it. Therefore, there is nothing at all in this text to support the view for which it is sometimes cited. We will challenge everyone to produce a single Old Testament or New Testament text that applies to the wilderness state any more than this text in St. Peter's first Epistle.

12. Someone might ask the questions, "But is not spiritual darkness much more profitable to us than light? Is not the work of God in the heart most rapidly and effectively carried on during a state of inward suffering? Is not a believer more quickly and completely purified by sorrow than by joy, by anxiety, pain, distress, and spiritual martyrdom than by continual peace?"

I answer that the mystics take this position, and it is found in their books. However, this view is not present in the Bible. Scripture nowhere says that God's *absence* best perfects his work in the heart! Rather, God perfects his work in us through his *presence.* God matures us through our clear communion with the Father and the Son. A strong consciousness of God's inner presence will do more in an hour than his absence can accomplish in an entire generation. The presence of joy in the Holy Spirit will far more effectively purify the soul than the lack of God's joy. God's peace is the best means of refining the soul from the rubbish of earthly affections.

Away, then, with the worthless notion that the kingdom of God is divided against itself! Away with the foolish belief that the peace of God and joy in the Holy Spirit *hinder* holiness! Away with the thought that we are saved not by faith, but by unbelief! Away with the idea that we are saved not by hope, but by despair!

13. As long as people fantasize this way, they may well "walk in darkness." The effect will not cease until the cause is removed. However, we must not think that the wilderness state will end immediately when the cause is removed. When ignorance or sin has led to spiritual darkness, one or the other may be removed, but the light that they blocked out might not immediately return. Because spiritual light is God's free gift, he can restore it sooner or later, as it pleases him. When sin is removed, we cannot reasonably

expect that the light will return instantly. The sin began before its consequence, and the consequence might fittingly continue after the sin has ended. Even in the natural process of things, a wound cannot be healed while the arrow remains in the flesh. Neither is the wound healed as soon as the arrow has been removed. Tenderness and pain may remain long afterward.

14. Finally, if spiritual darkness is caused by numerous, intense, and sudden temptations, the best way to remove and prevent it is to teach believers always to anticipate temptation. We live in an evil world among wicked, subtle, malevolent spirits. In addition, our own hearts are capable of every kind of evil. To help cure the wilderness state, convince believers that the entire work of sanctification is not accomplished at once (as they imagined). When they first believe, they are like newborn infants. They need gradually to grow up, and they can expect many storms before they come to the full stature of Christ.

Above all, instruct Christians that when the storm comes upon them not to debate with the devil, but to pray. Tell them to pour out their souls before God and tell him about their trouble. These are chiefly the persons to whom we are to apply God's "precious and very great promises." These promises do not pertain to the ignorant, until the ignorance has been removed. Much less do they apply to the impenitent sinner. We can liberally and affectionately declare to these people the loving-kindness of God our Savior and enlarge upon his eternal and tender mercies. Here, we can dwell upon the faithfulness of God, whose "promise is well tried." We can expand upon the virtue of the blood that was shed for us to cleanse us from all sin. Then, God will confirm his word and bring their souls out of trouble. God will say, "Arise, shine; for your light has come, and the glory of the LORD has risen upon you." Indeed, if you walk humbly and closely with God, this light will "shine brighter and brighter until full day."

Notes

1. Matt. 4:1, 2.
2. *Notes upon the New Testament,* Matt. 4:1.
3. Ward and Heitzenrater, *Wesley's Journal and Diaries,* March 28, 1740, 19:141.

4. Telford, *Wesley's Letters,* October 13, 1765, 4:270.
5. Rom. 14:17.
6. Rom. 6:14; John 5:14; 8:11; Eph. 4:26; 1 John 3:9; 5:18.
7. Saint John of the Cross, *The Complete Works of Saint John of the Cross, Doctor of Church,* trans. and ed. E. Allison Peers from the critical edition of P. Siverio de Santa Teresa, "The Dark Night of the Soul" [c. 1587], (London: Burns and Oates, 1964, 1935), I, ix, x.
8. Wesley's judgment of Roman Catholic piety applied to some mystical teachers in that tradition—for example, the seventeenth-century Jansenists. Most Roman Catholics, however, did not (and do not) hold this somber outlook on the spiritual life.
9. Hab. 1:16.

Introduction to Sermon 47

HEAVINESS THROUGH MANIFOLD TEMPTATIONS

John Wesley was by nature an introspective person. From his years as a member of the Holy Club at Oxford, he kept a journal and a diary that contain elements of self-examination and self-reflection. In January 1739, more than six months after he received the assurance of his salvation, he recorded,

> My friends affirm I am mad, because I said I was not a Christian a year ago. I affirm, I am not a Christian now. Indeed, what I might have been I know not, had I been faithful to the grace then given, when, expecting nothing less, I received such a sense of the forgiveness of my sins, as till then I never knew. But that I am not a Christian at this day, I as assuredly know, as that Jesus is the Christ. For a Christian is one who has the fruits of the Spirit of Christ, which (to mention no more) are love, peace, joy. But these I have not. I have not any love of God.[1]

We can certainly describe this miserable state, even if temporary, as being in "heaviness through manifold temptations." One recalls the often-discussed period of *Anfechtung* (anxiety or depression) experienced by Martin Luther.[2] Times of "heaviness" of spirit are not uncommon among Christian believers.

In Wesley's pastoral work, he encountered other Christians who experienced periods of inward suffering. His sermon register shows that during the years 1775 to 1757, he preached at least sixteen sermons on the text of this sermon—"You greatly rejoice, though now for a season, if need be, you are in heaviness through manifold temptations." The frequent use of this text indicates that the problems of religious struggle and spiritual melancholy were common among the Methodists.

In a letter to Elizabeth Hardy, Wesley wrote,

> Without doubt, it seems to you, that yours is a peculiar case [of sadness]. You think there is none like you in the world. Indeed there are. It may be, ten thousand persons are now in the same state of mind as you. I myself was so a few years ago. I felt the wrath of God abiding on me. I was afraid every hour of dropping into hell. I knew myself to be the chief of sinners. Though I had been very innocent, in the account of others, I saw my heart to be all sin and corruption. I was without the knowledge and the love of God, and therefore an abomination in his sight. But I had an Advocate with the Father, Jesus Christ the Righteous. And so have you. He died for your sins; and he is now pleading for you at the right hand of God. O look unto Him, and be saved! He loves you freely, without any merit of yours. He has atoned for all your sins. See all your sins on Jesus laid! His blood has paid for all. Fear nothing; only believe. His mercy embraces you: It holds you in on every side. Surely you shall not depart hence, till your eyes have seen his salvation.[3]

Wesley made a distinction between being in "the wilderness state" and in "heaviness through manifold temptations." The wilderness state is usually a result of sin; heaviness through manifold temptations is usually due to the heavy burdens we carry. In the New Testament, there are two meanings for the term *temptation*: (1) an *allurement to sin* and (2) a *testing* or *trial*. The two uses of this term have entirely different connotations. In Wesley's *Explanatory Notes upon the New Testament*, he explains the distinction:

> James 1:12: *Happy is the man that endureth temptation*—Trials of various kinds.

James 1:13: *But let no man who is tempted*—To sin.

In the first instance, temptation refers to a *trial*; in the second instance, temptation refers to a *sin.*

Elsewhere, Wesley dealt with on 1 Peter 1:6-7:

> Wherein ye greatly rejoice, though now for a season, if need be, ye are in heaviness through manifold temptations: That the trial of your faith, being much more precious than of gold that perisheth, though it be tried with fire, might be found unto praise and honor and glory at the appearing of Jesus Christ. (KJV)

Commenting on the phrase "heaviness through manifold temptations," Wesley wrote that those to whom St. Peter wrote were "in heaviness—or sorrow; but not in darkness; for they still retained both faith . . . hope, and love; yea, at this very time were rejoicing with joy unspeakable."[4] Here, temptation refers to trials, not to sin. In this sermon, "heaviness through manifold temptations" means being weighed down, or burdened, by trials and testing.

The previous sermon shows that the wilderness state is "a state of darkness" into which those who once walked in the light of God's presence fall through sin, disobedience, or neglect. Again, in this sermon, "heaviness through manifold temptations" refers to suffering under a heavy load. Wesley explained this distinction in a letter to Mary Bishop: "The difference between heaviness and darkness of soul [the wilderness state] should never be forgotten. Darkness [unless in the case of bodily disorder] seldom comes upon us but by our own fault."[5] By contrast, melancholy and sorrow stem from the pain attached to carrying the heavy burdens that Christians sometimes must assume. These trials are an inevitable part of living as Christ's disciples in the present world.

Wesley believed that God uses our times of heaviness through manifold temptations as a necessary part of our sanctification. He wrote to Dorothy Furley,

> It is a happy thing, if we can learn obedience by the things which we suffer. Weakness of body, and heaviness of mind, will, I trust,

> have this good effect upon you. The particular lesson which you have now to learn, is, to be faithful in comparatively little things; particularly in conversation. God hath given you a tongue: Why? That you may praise him therewith; that all your conversation may be, for the time to come, "meet to minister grace to the hearers." Such conversation, and private prayer, exceedingly assist each other. By resolutely persisting, according to your little strength, in all works of piety and mercy, you are waiting on God in the old scriptural way. And therein he will come and save you. Do not think he is afar off. He is nigh that justifieth, that sanctifieth. Beware you do not thrust him away from you. Rather say, "My heart would now receive thee, Lord: Come in, my Lord, come in!"[6]

To summarize: The wilderness state and the state of being weighed down with trials are often confused with each other. However, as Wesley teaches in this sermon, "The two terms are far from being the same. The loss of faith that leads to a 'wilderness state' is one thing; burden-bearing that leads to 'heaviness' is another. There is a wide and fundamental difference between the two."

Wesley wrote Jane Hilton Barton a letter of encouragement during her time of heaviness through multiple trials:

> You have little children; you have worldly care; and, frequently, a weak body. Therefore, you may have far more grace than you had before, though you have not so much joy; nay, though you should for a time have no joy at all, but sorrow and heaviness. . . . And what is at the end? An eternal weight of glory! It is laid up for you both. Taste of it now.[7]

In Wesley's preface to *Hymns and Sacred Poems* (1740), he wrote,

> Whosoever he be, who hath a sure trust and confidence in God, that through the merits of Christ his sins are forgiven, and he reconciled to the favour of God; he is a child of God, and, if he abide in him, an heir of all the great and precious promises. Neither ought he in any wise to cast away his confidence, or to deny the faith he hath received, because it is weak, because hitherto it is only "as a grain of mustard-seed"; or because "it is tried with fire," so that his soul is "in heaviness through manifold temptations."

As noted, Wesley knew that the state of "heaviness" was common among Christian believers. He declares, "Indeed, to a greater or lesser degree, almost all God's children experience this burden." This sermon gives perspective during times of burden bearing and shows the way to joy and victory.

Sermon 47

HEAVINESS THROUGH MANIFOLD TEMPTATIONS

Now for a little while you have had to suffer various trials.
(1 Peter 1:6)

1 In the preceding sermon, I have specially spoken about the wilderness state (or a state of darkness), into which those who once walked in the light of God's presence sometimes fall. Closely related to the loss of faith is the heaviness of soul (or sorrow) that is even more common among Christian believers. Indeed, to a greater or lesser degree, almost all God's children experience this burden. The similarity between these two spiritual disorders is so great that they are often confused with each other. We are prone to say carelessly, "So and so has 'lost his faith,'" or "so and so is 'depressed,'" as if they were equivalent terms that can be used synonymously.

The two terms are far from being the same. The loss of faith that leads to a "wilderness state" is one thing; sorrow that leads to "heaviness" is another. There is a wide and fundamental difference between the two. The difference is so important that all children of God are deeply concerned to understand the matter.

Without proper understanding, it is easy to move from suffering (heaviness) into the darkness that comes from a loss of faith. To prevent this drift from occurring, I will try to explain the following: (1) To whom the apostle said, "You have had to suffer." (2) What kind of suffering they experienced. (3) The causes of spiritual suffering. (4) The results of spiritual suffering. (5) I will end with some conclusions.

I. Who They Are That Are Subject to Spiritual Suffering

1. In the first place, I will explain what kind of people they were to whom the apostle Peter wrote, "You have had to suffer." To begin with, St. Peter undoubtedly wrote to those who were at the time Christian believers. They had *faith*. He specifically said to them, "You are being protected by the power of God through faith for salvation." The apostle also spoke of the testing of "their faith—being more precious than gold that is perishable." He wrote that they "were receiving the outcome of their faith, the salvation of their souls." At the same time that they were in heaviness and sorrow because they had to suffer "various trials," they also certainly had "genuine faith." Their heavy trials did not destroy their faith. They still "persevered as though they saw him who is invisible."

2. Neither did their suffering destroy their *peace*. They possessed the peace of God that "surpasses all understanding," which is inseparable from authentic, living faith. Their possession of true Christian faith is easily demonstrated in the apostle's prayer, not that grace and peace would be given to them, but that *presently* "grace and peace be theirs in abundance." Saint Peter prayed that the blessing they already enjoyed might be more abundantly bestowed upon them.

3. The persons to whom the apostle wrote in this Epistle were also full of a *living hope*. He wrote, "Blessed be the God and Father of our Lord Jesus Christ! By his great mercy he has given us a new birth." This blessing referred both to St. Peter and to those to whom he wrote—that is, all who were "sanctified by the Spirit" and were "sprinkled with Christ's blood into a living hope

for an inheritance that is imperishable, undefiled, and unfading." Even though they "suffered various trials," they still retained a hope for full immortality.

4. They also had *joy*. Those to whom St. Peter wrote still "rejoiced in the hope of sharing the glory of God." They were filled with joy in the Holy Spirit. Saint Peter refers to the time "when Jesus Christ will be revealed" (that is, when he returns to judge the world). Then, the apostle immediately adds, "Although you have not seen him, you love him; and even though you do not see him now, you believe in him and rejoice with an indescribable and glorious joy." Their "suffering various trials" was consistent not only with "a living hope," but also with "indescribable and glorious joy." At the same time that they were suffering, they nevertheless had the joy of the Lord.

5. They also had *love*. In the midst of their heaviness they still enjoyed "God's love poured into their hearts." Saint Peter said, "Although you have not seen him, you love him." Even though they had not yet beheld the Lord face-to-face, yet by faith they knew him and obeyed his word: "My child, give me your heart." The apostle was saying that the Lord was their God, their love, their desire, and their "very great reward." They had sought and found happiness in him; they "took delight in the Lord," and he had given them the "desires of their hearts."

6. Furthermore, although they suffered, they were *holy*. They retained their power over sin. They were still "protected by the power of God." They were "obedient children, not conformed to their former desires." "As Christ who called them is holy, they were holy themselves in all their conduct." They knew that they "were ransomed by the precious blood of Christ, like that of a lamb without defect or blemish." Their faith and hope were set on God, and they had purified their souls in the Spirit.

In sum, their heaviness and trials included *faith*, *hope*, *joy*, and *love* for God and others. Their suffering incorporated the peace of God, joy in the Holy Spirit, and inward and outward holiness. Their trials did not in any way decrease, much less destroy, any part of God's work in their hearts. Their suffering did not in the least interfere with the sanctification of the Spirit that forms the foundation of all true obedience. Nor did their suffering cancel their happiness, which necessarily follows grace and peace reigning in their hearts.

II. The Nature of Spiritual Suffering

1. Second, I will explain the nature of the heaviness (or spiritual suffering) that these Christians endured. The original word for *suffer* is to be "made sorry," or to be "grieved." This translation of the word agrees with the unchanging, literal meaning of the word *suffer*. Therefore, there is no uncertainty about its meaning or any problem related to understanding it. The persons to whom St. Peter wrote were *grieved*. The heaviness or suffering they were experiencing was nothing more or less than *sorrow* or *heartache*. And everyone on earth is familiar with this emotion.

2. It is probable that the translators of the King James Version used the word "heaviness" (although it is not as common a word) to signify two things: (1) the degree of suffering and (2) its duration. Saint Peter's Epistle makes it clear that the suffering of his readers was not a superficial or insignificant kind of suffering. Rather, it was the kind of suffering that makes a strong impression upon our souls and sinks into us deeply. Neither does this suffering appear to be a temporary sorrow, such as the kind that passes away in an hour. Instead, this heaviness had taken a firm grip on their hearts. It was the sort of suffering that cannot be immediately shaken off. It is the kind that continues for a period of time as a permanent emotion. It was not a fleeting emotion, even in those who placed living faith in Christ and had God's genuine love in their hearts.

3. Indeed, faithful Christians can sometimes experience sufferings so deep that they shroud the entire soul. They affect all our emotions in a way that expresses itself in all our conduct. This spiritual suffering can also affect us physically. The corporeal influence of "heaviness" is especially seen in persons with naturally frail bodies, or in those persons whose bodies have been weakened by some accidental ailment, especially of a nervous sort. In many cases, we find that "a perishable body weighs down the

soul."[8] In cases of spiritual suffering (heaviness), the soul weighs down the body and weakens it more and more. I do not hesitate to say that deep and lasting sorrow of heart may sometimes weaken even a strong body and lay the foundation for physical ailments that cannot easily be healed. All the while, this suffering can exist in those who have a measure of "faith working through love."

4. This heaviness, or suffering, may well be called a "fiery ordeal." This testing is not the same as the ordeal spoken of in the fourth chapter of this Epistle of St. Peter. Even so, many of the expressions used there, with reference to physical suffering, can be used to clarify the nature of the heaviness that I am discussing.

These expressions cannot suitably be applied to those who live in the darkness of a wilderness state—that is, to those who have lost their faith. Such people cannot and do not rejoice. Nor can it be said that "the spirit of glory, which is the Spirit of God, is resting on them." However, the Spirit of God frequently rests on those who are "in heaviness." Although "they are sorrowful, yet they are always rejoicing."

III. The Causes of Spiritual Suffering

1. Third, what are the causes of this kind of heaviness in true believers? The apostle tells us clearly: "You have had to suffer various trials." The original word *various* refers to the large number and many-sided varieties of trials and burdens. These testings can be diverse and dissimilar in a thousand ways, depending on the change or addition of numberless circumstances. The large amount of diversity and variety makes it that much more difficult to protect ourselves against them. Among these diverse factors, we can place all bodily disorders—particularly strong diseases and violent pains of every kind, whether they affect the entire body or the smallest part of it.

It is true that some people who have enjoyed constant good health and have felt none of these afflictions may dismiss them. Healthy folk may question whether sickness or physical pain can bring heaviness upon the spirit. Perhaps one person in a thousand has such an unusual constitution that he or she does not feel pain like other people. It has pleased God to reveal his almighty power by producing some of these wonders of nature who seem not to regard pain at all, even the severest kind.

It may be that their disregard for pain is partly due to the power of education and partly to supernatural causes (either the power of good or evil spirits who elevated these people above a natural state). But disregarding these exceptions, in general it is an accurate observation that,

> Pain is perfect misery, the worst
> Of evil, and, excessive, overturns
> All patience.[9]

And even where this suffering is prevented by God's grace, and when "by endurance" people "gain their souls," physical pain can, nevertheless, cause much inward heaviness. The soul sympathizes with the body.

2. All diseases of long duration, even if less painful than others, are likely to produce the same result. When God sends tuberculosis and fever, if they are not quickly removed, they will "waste the eyes and cause life to pine away." This result is especially the case with regard to all those maladies that we call "nervous disorders." Faith does not cancel the course of nature; natural causes still produce natural effects. Faith does not prevent our spirits from suffering an emotional illness any more than faith prevents a faster heartbeat during a fever.

3. Is it a small trial when "calamity comes like a whirlwind" and "poverty comes like a robber"? Is it surprising that this testing causes heaviness and sorrow? These afflictions may seem only small things to those who stand at a distance or to those who look and "pass by on the other side." But they are not small to those who feel them.

"If we have food and clothing" (the original word for *clothing* includes *shelter* as well as what we wear), and if God's love is in our hearts, "we will be content with these." But what will people who have no food, clothing, or shelter do? What about those who, as it were, "cling to the rock for want of shelter"? They have only the earth to lie on and only the sky to cover them. They do not have a dry, warm, or clean dwelling for themselves and their children. Either by day or night, they have no clothing to keep themselves and their immediate loved ones from the biting cold. I smile at the foolish heathen who declares,

> Poverty brings no unhappiness worse than this:
> It exposes men to ridicule.[10]

Does poverty really bring nothing worse than making us subject to taunts? This opinion reveals that the shallow poet only repeated things he did not understand. Is not the lack of food something worse than receiving some taunts? God pronounced it as a curse upon us that we must earn our food "by the sweat of our face." However, there are many people in this Christian country who toil, strive, and sweat, yet they still do not have enough food. They struggle against both hunger and weariness. Is it not depressing after a hard day's labor to return to a poor, cold, dirty, uncomfortable dwelling and find that there is not even the food you need to restore your depleted strength?

Listen, those of you who live comfortably and lack nothing except the eyes to see, ears to hear, and hearts to understand how good God has been to you. Is it not a hardship day by day for one to seek bread and find none? Perhaps a man even finds five or six children crying for what he cannot provide. If it were not that he is restrained by the Lord's unseen hand, would he not soon "curse God and die"? O, the lack of bread! The lack of bread! Who can describe what this hunger means unless they have felt it personally? I am astonished that hunger causes no more than physical suffering in those who believe!

4. Possibly, next to hunger we can place the death of those who are near and dear to us. Perhaps it is the death of a kind parent, someone not yet elderly, a cherished child just beginning life and near to our hearts, or a close friend who was, next to God's grace, the best of heaven's gifts. There are a thousand circumstances that can increase our suffering. Perhaps the child or the friend died in our arms! Perhaps the departed one was snatched away when we were not expecting it! Perhaps in their prime they were cut down like a flower!

In all these cases, we not only *can* be, but also *ought* to be, affected. It is God's intent that we should. He would not have us respond as sticks and stones. He wants us to control our emotions, but not extinguish them. Therefore, "Nature unreproved may drop a tear."[11] One may sorrow without the presence of sin.

5. We may feel a still deeper sorrow for those who are dead while they live. I refer to the unkindness, ingratitude, and apostasy of those who are united to us in the closest ties. Who can express the pain that a lover of souls feels for a friend or a sibling who is dead to God? Perhaps it is a husband, wife, parent, or a child, rushing into sin "like a horse plunging headlong into battle." Despite all discussions and exhortations, they are hastening to forge their own damnation. Our spiritual anguish can increase to an unimaginable degree when the ones who are now speeding toward destruction once ran well in the way of life. Whatever heights they had reached in the past now only serve to make our thoughts about them even more painful and severe.

6. In all these circumstances, we may be assured that our great adversary will not fail to advance his opportunity. He who always "prowls around, looking for someone to devour" will especially, on these occasions, exert all his power and skill in the hope that he can gain some advantage over the soul that is already suffering. Satan will not withhold his flaming arrows that are most suitable to the occasion and most likely to be effective in piercing the heart. He will work to interject unbelieving, blasphemous, or gloomy thoughts. He will suggest that God does not regard or govern the earth. At the least, Satan will suggest that God does not govern according to the principles of justice and mercy. The devil will try to agitate our hearts against God and to revive our natural opposition to him. If we attempt to fight Satan with his own weapons by reasoning with him, increasing heaviness will undoubtedly follow—perhaps even complete darkness.

7. Some people have frequently conjectured that there is another cause of spiritual heaviness (if not loss of faith)—namely, God's withdrawing himself from the soul because it is his sovereign will. Certainly, God will withdraw from us if we grieve his Holy Spirit by outward or inward sin; by doing evil or neglecting

to do good; or by giving in to pride, anger, spiritual sloth, foolish desire, or excessive affections. However, I absolutely deny that God ever withdraws himself from us because it is his will or because it pleases him. There is no text in the entire Bible that gives any support to such a theory. None at all.

This speculation is contrary to many specific biblical texts and to the overall teaching of Scripture. Such a notion is offensive to the very nature of God. It is utterly beneath his majesty and wisdom (as an eminent writer strongly expresses it) "to play bo-peep with his creatures."[12] That is, God does not play teasing games with us. To withdraw from us arbitrarily is inconsistent with God's justice, his mercy, and the invariable experience of all his children.

8. Authors who are called "mystics" mention one additional cause of heaviness and suffering. This notion has crept in (I do not know how) even among ordinary people who have no knowledge of the mystics' writings. I cannot explain this theory better than in the words of a late writer who told about her own experience:

> I continued so happy in my beloved Lord, that although I would have been forced to live as a vagabond in a desert, I would have found no difficulty in it. This state had not lasted long when in effect I found myself led into a type of a desert. . . . I found myself in a forsaken condition, altogether poor, wretched, and miserable. . . . The proper source of this grief is the knowledge of ourselves, by which we find that there is an extreme unlikeness between ourselves and God. We see ourselves the most opposite of him. We see that our inmost soul is entirely corrupted, depraved, and full of all kind of evil and malice. We are full of the world, the flesh, and all sorts of abominations.[13]

From her account, some have concluded that self-knowledge, without which we should perish everlastingly, must, even after we have attained justifying faith, cause the deepest depression and suffering.

9. However, I will say several things about this point of view. (1) In the paragraph that precedes the passage just quoted, this writer says, "Hearing I had not a true faith in Christ, I offered

myself up to God, and immediately felt his love." It may be so, but it does not appear that she experienced justification. It is more probable that she experienced no more than what are usually called the "drawings of the Father." And if so, the heaviness and darkness that followed was nothing more than conviction of sin. In the scheme of things, conviction of sin must precede the faith by which we are justified.

(2) Suppose she was justified at almost the same moment she was convinced that she lacked faith. There was no time for the gradually increasing self-knowledge that usually precedes justification. In her case, it came afterward, and it was probably all the more depressing because she did not expect it.

(3) I acknowledge that after justification there will be a far deeper, clearer, and fuller knowledge of our inbred sin and total corruption than there ever was prior to justification. This knowledge, however, does not need to cause suffering. I refuse to say that it must bring us into depression. If that were the case, in our text the apostle would not have used the expression, "if now for a little while." Otherwise, for us to know ourselves there would be an absolute, indispensable need for us constantly to suffer. In this way of thinking, such continuous suffering would be needed if we are to know the perfect love of God and to be thereby "enabled to share in the inheritance of the saints in the light."

It is by no means the case, however, that God requires such permanent suffering. On the contrary, God can increase our self-knowledge to any degree, while at the same time increasing our knowledge of him and his love. And there is no indispensable requirement for chastisement, misery, or abandonment. Rather, we can experience love, peace, and joy gradually "gushing up to eternal life."

IV. The Results of Spiritual Suffering

1. Fourth, why does God permit suffering to come to so many of his children? The apostle gives us a clear and direct answer to this important question. It is "so that the genuineness of our faith—being more precious than gold that, though perishable, is

tested by fire—may be found to result in praise and glory and honor when Jesus Christ is revealed." There may be a reference to this reason in the well-known passage in the fourth chapter of St. Peter's Epistle (even though, as we have seen, it primarily relates to quite another thing). The apostle wrote, "Do not be surprised at the fiery ordeal that is taking place among you. But rejoice insofar as you are sharing Christ's sufferings, so that you may also be glad and shout for joy."

2. From this statement, we learn the first and chief purpose of God's permitting the trials that bring suffering to his children. Their faith is refined by afflictions, just as gold is purified by the fire. We know that gold tried in the fire is separated from its dross. In the same way, our faith is tested in fiery trials—and the more it is tested, the more it is purified. The soul is not only purified, but also strengthened, confirmed, and profusely enlarged. We grow as we experience the many proofs of God's wisdom, power, love, and faithfulness. Overall, suffering increases our faith—the one gracious purpose of God's permitting various trials.

3. Trials also serve to try, purify, confirm, and increase the "living hope," which "the God and Father of our Lord Jesus Christ by his great mercy has given us through the new birth." Indeed, our hope always grows to the same degree that our faith grows. Faith is the foundation of our hope: Believing in his name and living by faith in the Son of God, we have a confident expectation of "the glory about to be revealed to us." Therefore, whatever strengthens our faith also increases our hope.

At the same time, our hope increases our joy in the Lord, which must accompany our "hope that is full of immortality."[14] With this hope in mind, the apostle encouraged believers: "Rejoice insofar as you are sharing Christ's sufferings," because as you do, "you are blessed, because the spirit of glory, which is the Spirit of God, is resting on you." Even in the midst of sufferings, God enables us to "rejoice with an indescribable and glorious joy."

4. Christians rejoice all the more because the trials that increase their faith and hope also increase their love. Their love heightens their gratitude to God for all his mercies, and their goodwill grows toward everyone. The more deeply aware they become of the

loving-kindness of God their Savior, the more their heart is warmed with love for him who "first loved us." The clearer and stronger assurance they have of the glory that will be revealed, the more they love him who has purchased it for them and "given them a first installment in their hearts." So, the increase of their love is another purpose for the trials that God permits to come upon Christians.

5. Another purpose for trials is for our growth in holiness of heart and conduct (the latter naturally resulting from the former). "Every good tree bears good fruit." All inward holiness is the direct fruit of "faith working through love." The blessed Spirit purifies the heart from pride, self-will, lust, love for the world, senseless and harmful desires, and vile and vain affections. In addition, by God's grace, sanctified afflictions have a clear and direct inclination to increase our holiness. Through the operation of God's Spirit, trials humble the soul more and more before God. Afflictions calm and subdue our turbulent spirit, tame the intensity of our nature, soften our stubbornness and self-will, crucify us to the world, and bring us to expect all our strength from God and seek our entire happiness in him.

6. All these changes lead to God's foremost purpose for our lives. He plans that our faith, hope, love, and holiness may be found to result in praise (from God) and glory (from the Great Judge) and honor (from people and angels) assigned to all who have endured to the end. In the great judgment day, God will "repay everyone for what has been done." This repayment will take place according to the work that God has done in our hearts and the outward works that we have done for him. Also, God will judge us according to what we have suffered. Therefore, our trials are an indescribable gain for us. In many ways our "slight momentary afflictions are preparing us for an eternal weight of glory beyond all measure."

7. To these benefits, we can add the advantage that others can benefit by observing our behavior when we are under afflictions. Experience has taught us that people's examples often make a deeper impression on us than their beliefs. What example other than that of a soul that is calm and peaceful in the midst of storms

has a greater influence on those who have received a faith as precious as ours, as well as those who do not know God! Those who are good examples are "sorrowful, yet always rejoicing." They humbly accept whatever is God's will, however displeasing it may be. They say, "Am I not to drink the cup that the Father has given me?" In deprivation or need they say, "The LORD gave, and the LORD has taken away; blessed be the name of the LORD."

V. Concluding Lessons About Spiritual Suffering

1. I will end this sermon with some conclusions. First, there is a vast difference between the wilderness state (loss of faith) and heaviness (sorrow and suffering). Nonetheless, even experienced Christians commonly confuse the two with each other. The loss of faith (or darkness), which I call the Wilderness State, means a complete loss of joy in the Holy Spirit. Sorrow (or heaviness) does not mean that our joy is gone. Even in the midst of suffering, we can "rejoice with an indescribable and glorious joy." Those who are in a wilderness state have lost the peace of God; those who endure heaviness have not lost their peace. Indeed, they are so far from losing God's peace that in the midst of suffering, "grace and peace are theirs in abundance." In the darkness of the wilderness state, one's love for God has grown cold, if it is not completely gone. In the sorrow of heaviness, love for God retains its full force. Indeed, it increases daily.

Those who are in heaviness through manifold temptations suffer from the testing of their faith. Their assurance and conviction of things not seen, particularly of God's pardoning love, is not as clear or strong as in times past. Their trust in God is proportionally weakened. Although they cannot see God, they still have a certain, unshaken confidence in him and an abiding assurance that God's love blots out their sins. So, as long as we can distinguish faith from unbelief, hope from despair, peace from war, love for God from love for the world, we can infallibly distinguish a state of heaviness, sorrow, and suffering from a state of spiritual wilderness.

2. Second, we can learn that there may be a need for sorrow and heaviness, but there can be no need for being in the darkness of a wilderness state. For a period of time, we may need to suffer so as to fulfill the purposes explained earlier. Sufferings are a natural result of our various trials. And we sometimes need them to test and increase our faith, confirm and enlarge our hope, purify our hearts from all unholy attitudes, and perfect us in love. Sufferings also brighten our crown and add to our "eternal weight of glory."

We cannot say, however, that the wilderness state is needed for any of these purposes. Such darkness is in no way necessary to accomplish God's objective. Surely, the loss of faith, hope, and love is helpful neither for holiness nor for increasing the reward in heaven, which will be in proportion to our holiness on earth.

3. Third, from the apostle's way of speaking, we can conclude that even suffering and sorrow are not always necessary. Saint Peter wrote, "even if now *for a little while* you have had to suffer." These words do not tell us that suffering is necessary for all people at all times. When it pleases God, he has the power, wisdom, and ability to work the same grace in any one by other means. And in some instances he does so. With hardly any heaviness at all, God causes those whom he pleases "to go on from strength to strength," "making holiness perfect in the fear of God." God has absolute power over our hearts, and he moves them according to his will and pleasure.

These cases are rare, however. Generally, God sees that it is good to "test acceptable people in the furnace of humiliation."[15] More or less, heaviness through manifold temptations, sorrow, and affliction is usually the allotment of God's dearest children.

4. Finally, we should stay alert, pray, and use our best efforts to avoid falling into the darkness of a wilderness state and a loss of faith. We should not be nearly as concerned about avoiding suffering as how to become better through suffering. Our main concern in our suffering should be to behave ourselves in such a way as to wait upon the Lord. Our purpose should be that our burdens would completely fulfill all the purposes of God's love when he permits suffering to come upon us.

Suffering can become a means of increasing our faith, confirming our hope, and perfecting us in all holiness. Whenever the heaviness of manifold temptations comes, let us have an eye to the gracious purposes for which God permits them. And let us use all diligence so that we do not "reject the purpose of God for ourselves" and "make void the plans of God." Let us earnestly "work together with God" by the grace that he is continually giving to us: "Let us cleanse ourselves from every defilement of body and of spirit." Daily, let us "grow in the grace and knowledge of our Lord and Savior Jesus Christ," until he receives us into his everlasting kingdom!

Notes

1. Ward and Heitzenrater, *Wesley's Journal and Diaries,* January 4, 1739, 19:29-30.
2. In 1727, Luther wrote, "For more than a week I was close to the gates of death and hell. I trembled in all my members. Christ was wholly lost. I was shaken by desperation and blasphemy of God." (Quoted in Roland H. Bainton, *Here I Stand: A Life of Martin Luther* [New York: Abingdon-Cokesbury Press, 1950], 361.)
3. Telford, *Wesley's Letters,* May 1758, 4:20.
4. *Explanatory Notes upon the New Testament,* 1 Peter 1:6.
5. Jackson, *Wesley's Works,* Letters to Miss Bishop, June 17, 1774, 13:27.
6. Ibid., December 22, 1756, 12:196.
7. Telford, *Wesley's Letters,* December 30, 1774, 6:135.
8. Wisd. of Sol. 9:15.
9. John Milton, *Paradise Lost: An Authoritative Text, Backgrounds, and Sources,* ed. Scott Elledge (New York: Norton, 1975), "All Patience," vi, 462-64.
10. Juvenal, *Sixteen Satires,* iii, 152, 153.
11. Samuel Wesley Jr., "The Parish Priest," *Poems on Several Occasions* (London: Printed for the author by E. Say, 1736), 65.
12. The term *bo-peep* means to tease as one tantalizes another by repeatedly covering one's face and withdrawing one's hands. The OED lists this term as first appearing in 1528 in the writings of William Tyndale: "Mark how he playeth bo-peep with the scripture."
13. The source of this quotation is unknown.
14. Wisd. of Sol. 3:4.
15. Sir. 2:5.

Introduction to Sermon 48

SELF-DENIAL

John Wesley taught that faith and works are inseparable. Right belief must be linked with the worship of God and the service of humankind. The content of his sermons, therefore, was both theological and practical. He preached about proper relationships both with God and with others. This sermon on self-denial is a practical application of an important theological truth: If we are to serve God and neighbor, again and again we must be willing to deny self and accept the crosses that Christ asks us to bear in ministering to others.

The well-known Methodist Covenant Service underscores the traditional Wesleyan emphasis on the duty and privilege of self-denial:

> Christ has many services to be done; some are easy, others are difficult; some bring honor, others bring reproach; some are suitable to our natural inclinations and temporal interests, others are contrary to both. In some we may please Christ and please ourselves; in others we cannot please Christ except by denying ourselves. Yet the power to do all these things is assuredly given us in Christ, who strengtheneth us. Therefore let us make the covenant of God our own. Let us engage our heart to the Lord, and resolve in his strength never to go back.[1]

From its beginning, Methodism has assumed that discipline and self-denial are necessary components of serious Christian discipleship. Wesley saw the need to publish this sermon because a number of his contemporaries renounced the need for self-denial and sought to discredit Wesley for preaching on this subject. Opposition to self-denial came from three sources.

One of these sources was the Enlightenment spirit of human autonomy that had taken root in many upper-class citizens. The English Deists in the Church had dissolved the close links between the Creator and the creation. This approach to religion left humankind in charge of the world and assigned to all people the responsibility for their own lives. The religion of Deism did not focus as much on God as on the present world. The duty of self-denial had given way to the demand for self-expression.

A second source of opposition to self-denial was Antinomianism, which also had insinuated itself into the religion of the day. The Antinomians stressed "faith alone" to the point that many people gathered the impression that they needed only to trust in the imputed righteousness of Christ. This understanding often led them to follow only their personal inclinations and desires. One Antinomian teacher said to Wesley, "We Christians do as we please, and nothing more." Wesley strenuously opposed this kind of religion because it undercut the clear call of Jesus: "If any want to become my followers, let them deny themselves and take up their cross and follow me. For those who want to save their life will lose it, and those who lose their life for my sake will find it" (Matt. 16:24, 25). Concerning the Moravian Antinomians and their rejection of self-denial, Wesley wrote,

> As yet I dare in no wise join with the Moravians: 1. Because their general scheme is mystical, not scriptural; refined in every point above what is written; immeasurably beyond the plain Gospel. 2. Because there is darkness and closeness in all their behaviour, and guile in almost all their words. 3. Because they not only do not practise, but utterly despise and decry, self-denial and the daily cross. 4. Because they conform to the world, in wearing gold and gay or costly apparel. 5. Because they are by no means zealous of good works, or at least only to their own people: For these reasons

> (chiefly) I will rather, God being my helper, stand quite alone than join with them: I mean till I have full assurance, that they are better acquainted with "the truth as it is in Jesus."[2]

In 1743, John and Charles Wesley prepared Methodism's General Rules. In part, their purpose was to answer the accusation that teaching self-denial betrays the doctrine of justification by grace alone. Wesley wrote that the Methodists "[trample] under foot that enthusiastic doctrine of devils, that 'we are not to do good unless *our heart be free to it.*'"[3]

The third reason that self-denial had few eighteenth-century advocates was that, in the past, some had taken perverse delight in excessive self-neglect, extreme mortification, and needless suffering. For instance, some of the early Christian hermits burned away their fingers at candles in order to prevent themselves from sinning with their hands. Certain medieval monks wore hair shirts, flogged their backs with whips, sprinkled ashes on their food, and slept uncovered in the cold. In their misguided efforts to purify their souls, some of the mystics actually *sought* physical suffering.

Wesley, of course, meant something entirely different by self-denial. In this sermon, he defines self-denial as "rejecting or refusing to follow our own will, from a conviction that the will of God is the only rule of action for us." Commenting elsewhere on self-denial, Wesley wrote,

> A rule that can never be too much observed: let [one] in all things deny his own will, however pleasing, and do the will of God, however painful. Should we not consider all crosses, all things grievous to flesh and blood, as what they really are, as opportunities of embracing God's will at the expense of our own? And consequently as so many steps by which we may advance toward perfection? We would make swift progress in the spiritual life, if we were faithful in this practice. Crosses are so frequent, that whoever makes advantage of them, will soon be a gainer. Great crosses are occasions of great improvement: and the little ones, which come daily, and even hourly, make up in number what they want in weight. We may in these daily and hourly crosses make effectual oblations of our will to God; which oblations, so frequently repeated, will soon

> amount to a great sum. Let us remember then (what can never be sufficiently inculcated) that God is the author of all events, that none is so small or inconsiderable, as to escape his notice and direction. Every event therefore declares to us the will of God, to which thus declared we should heartily submit. We should renounce our own to embrace it; we should approve and choose what his choice warrants as best for us. Herein should we exercise ourselves continually; this should be our practice all the day long. We should in humility accept the little crosses that are dispensed to us, as those that best suit our weakness. Let us bear these little things, at least for God's sake, and prefer his will to our own in matters of so small importance. And his goodness will accept these mean oblations; for he despiseth not the day of small things.[4]

Wesley went so far as to say, "That day is lost wherein no cross is taken up."[5]

In this sermon, Wesley states that God calls Christians to deny themselves by surrendering their natural preferences to the will of God and expending their time and energies in serving others. He points out that so long as Christians are unwilling to deny themselves in order to obey Christ, they grieve the Holy Spirit and remain unfruitful. Wesley shows the dangers of ignoring self-denial and stresses the importance of making it a central Christian attitude and way of life. The final section of the sermon discusses the errors of those teachers who opposed self-denial.

Here, Wesley teaches that unconverted people will remain outside God's kingdom until they are willing to practice self-denial. He declares, "It is always due to one's failure to deny self or take up one's cross that one does not completely follow Christ and therefore cannot be his disciple." Wesley insists that one cannot put Christ first until one is willing to subordinate self-will to God's will.

Wesley found great personal joy in self-denial because it led to many blessings in his life. In 1744, he wrote in a letter,

> I plainly see every hour produces occasions of self-pleasing: And this I apprehend is a sufficient call for, and rule of, self-denial. For instance: In the morning, it is a great self-denial to rise out of a warm bed; but if I do not, I am immediately condemned as a

> slothful servant: If I do, I find a great inward blessing. . . . If I deny myself for Christ's sake, his consolations abound with me.[6]

In a letter to Miss March, Wesley wrote, "To use the grace given is the certain way to obtain more grace. To use all the faith you have will bring an increase of faith. But this word is of very wide extent: it takes in the full exercise of every talent wherewith we are entrusted. . . . I believe it would help you, to read and consider the Sermon on Self-Denial."[7]

In 1790, a year before he died, Wesley noted in his journal,

> This week I visited the classes in Bristol. I wonder we do not increase in number, although many are convinced, many justified, and a few perfected in love. I can impute the want of increase to nothing but want of self-denial. Without this, indeed, whatever other helps they have, no believers can go forward.[8]

Wesley opens this sermon by referring to self-denial as "this grand doctrine of Christianity." He closes the sermon by saying, "Practice self-denial everywhere, on every one of the thousand occasions that will occur in all circumstances of life. Practice it daily, without stopping—from the hour you first set your hand to the plow, and diligently endure in self-denial until your spirit returns to God."

Sermon 48

SELF-DENIAL

Then he said to them all, "If any want to become my followers, let them deny themselves and take up their cross daily and follow me." (Luke 9:23)

1 People have often speculated that Jesus addressed the words of our text primarily, if not entirely, to the apostles. At the least, many have assumed that these words were meant for the Christians of the first ages or for those under persecution. However, this assumption constitutes a regrettable mistake. Certainly, in this text our blessed Lord intended his message more directly for his apostles and those other disciples who followed him in the days of his flesh. Nevertheless, in these words he also speaks to us and to all humankind, without any exception or condition.

Reason confirms that the duty commanded here is not unique to the apostles or to the Christians of the early ages. This commandment is no more restricted to a particular group of people than to a specific nation. Rather, Christ's call to self-denial applies universally to all times and all people. This call relates to all aspects of life—not just to food, drink, and those things pertaining to the senses. The meaning is, "If *any* man (of whatever rank, station, circumstances, in any nation, in any age of the world) be willing to come after me, let him deny himself, and take up his cross daily (of whatever kind), and follow me."[9]

2. In the full extent of its meaning, the expressions, "denying ourselves" and "taking up one's cross" are of great importance. This command is not applicable only to some of the details of religion. It is unconditionally and fundamentally necessary to becoming or remaining Christ's disciple. In the very nature of the matter, self-denial is absolutely necessary to becoming Christ's disciple and following him. To the extent that we do not practice it, we are not his disciples.

If we do not constantly "deny ourselves," we are not learning from him, but from other teachers. If we do not "take up our crosses daily," we do not "become his disciples." Instead, we become followers of the world, or of the prince of the world, or of our own "human way of thinking." If we are not walking in the way of the cross, we are not following Christ. We are not following in his steps; instead, we are retreating from him or avoiding him.

3. It is because of the importance of Christ's call to self-denial that so many ministers of Christ in almost every age and nation (especially since the reformation of the Church from the innovations and corruptions that had gradually crept into it) have written and spoken so amply on this important duty. They have done so in their public discourses and private exhortations. This subject has prompted them to distribute widely many tracts on the subject. Some of these tracts have appeared in our own country. From the Bible and from the witness of their own experience, these ministers knew both how impossible it is to avoid denying our Master unless we are willing to deny ourselves, and how hopelessly we attempt to follow the crucified Christ, unless we take up our cross daily.

4. But does not the quantity of these previous writings raise a fair question: "If so much has already been said and written on the subject, what need is there to say or write any more?" I answer that there are many people, even among those who revere God, who have not had the opportunity to hear or read what has been

said about self-denial. And perhaps if they had read much of what has been written, they would not have benefited significantly. Many who have written on this subject (some of them composed large volumes) do not at all appear to have understood it. Either they had imperfect views about the nature of self-denial (so they could not explain it to others), or they were unfamiliar with the full range of the subject. Possibly, they did not see how exceedingly comprehensive this command is, or they were not aware of the absolute and essential need for self-denial.

Others have spoken on the subject in an obscure, complex, and mysterious way. They have communicated in a style that seems intended more to conceal their thoughts from ordinary people than to clarify them. Others speak commendably well and with great clarity and power on the necessity of self-denial. But, they deal only with generalities, without speaking to specific issues. Their efforts, therefore, have little relevance for the majority of the people who have ordinary abilities and education. Furthermore, even if some of these teachers do get down to specifics, their "specifics" do not affect most of the people because they seldom, if ever, occur in daily life.

I am referring to such self-denial as enduring imprisonment or torture, or literally losing houses, lands, spouses, children, or even life itself. We are not called to this kind of self-denial, nor are we likely to be—unless God would allow times of public persecution to return. All the while, I do not know of any writer in the English language who has described the nature of self-denial in simple, clear, and relevant terms, relating self-denial to the lesser details of our daily life. To this day, we still need such a discourse. It is needed all the more because in every stage of the spiritual life, we fail either to deny ourselves or to take up our crosses. There are many particular hindrances to our acquiring grace or growing through self-denial. These hindrances can be listed under the general categories that I will discuss in this sermon.

In order to meet the need for a better understanding of self-denial, I will try to explain the following points: (1) The meaning of self-denial and taking up one's cross. (2) If one is not fully a disciple of Christ, it is always due to the lack of self-denial or taking up one's cross. (3) I will conclude with some encouragements to self-denial and cross-bearing.

I. The Meaning of Self-Denial and Cross-Bearing

1. First, I will try to explain what it means for people to "deny themselves and take up their cross daily." Above all other points, this one must be considered and understood completely. Many strong enemies oppose self-denial more than any other thing. Everything within human nature rises up against self-denial, even to argue against it. The world and those who are guided by nature instead of grace despise the very sound of the word *self-denial.*

Also, the great enemy of our souls knows well the importance of self-denial and moves every stone against it. Likewise, opposition comes even from those who, to some extent, have shaken off the devil's yoke and have recently experienced a genuine work of grace in their hearts. Despite their profession of Christ, they are not friends of this important doctrine of Christianity, even though their Master specifically insisted on it. Some of these Christians are as deeply and completely ignorant of self-denial, as if there were not one word about it in the Bible.

Others are farther off still. Without realizing it, they have absorbed strong prejudices against self-denial. They have received this bias partly from superficial Christians whose pleasing speech and *form* of religion reveal that they lack nothing of godliness except its power. They lack nothing of religion except from its *spirit.* Misguided Christians have also been partly influenced by those who no longer taste "the powers of the age to come."

Some teachers fail to practice self-denial, and they discourage others from practicing it. If you doubt that this statement is true, you are not well acquainted with people. Entire groups declare war against self-denial. Go no farther than London and observe the whole body of Predestinarians. They believe that by God's free mercy they have recently been called out of the darkness of nature into the light of faith. But are they patterns of self-denial? How few of them even profess to practice it at all! How small a number of them recommend self-denial to others or delight in those who do recommend it! Rather, do they not continually cast self-denial in the most detestable light? They equate self-denial with seeking salvation by works or "seeking to establish our own righteousness."

Furthermore, how readily do Antinomians of all kinds, from the cultured Moravian leader[10] to the boisterous, foul-mouthed Ranter,[11] join the cry against self-denial. They engage in silly, empty talk about self-denial as being "legalism" and "preaching the law." If you are not deeply grounded in the gospel, you are in constant danger of being entreated, nagged, or ridiculed out of this important gospel doctrine by false teachers or false brothers and sisters. They are more or less charmed away from the simplicity of the gospel. Therefore, let fervent prayer precede, accompany, and follow what you are now about to read. Let the finger of God write it on your heart, so that it will never be erased.

2. What then is self-denial? In what way are we to deny ourselves? And from what source does the need for self-denial arise? I answer that God's will is the supreme, unalterable rule for every intelligent being. The will of God is equally binding on every angel in heaven and every person on earth. It cannot be otherwise. Obeying God's will is the natural and necessary consequence of the relationship between the Creator and those he has created. And if God's will is our one rule of action in everything great and small, it follows as an undeniable outcome that we are not to do our own will in anything.

In the following proposition, we immediately understand the nature of self-denial, as well as its basis and reason: *Self-denial is rejecting or refusing to follow our own wills, from a conviction that the will of God is the only rule of action for us.* And we understand the reason for self-denial because we are God's creation. "It is he that made us, and we are his."

3. This reason for self-denial is the same whether for the angels of God in heaven or for Adam and Eve, as innocent and holy as the hands of their Creator who formed them. But an additional reason for self-denial arises from the condition of all people since the Fall. We were born guilty sinners when our mothers conceived us. In every ability and capacity, our natures are altogether

corrupt. Our wills, which are equally depraved with the rest of our being, are entirely inclined to pamper our natural sinfulness. On the other hand, it is the will of God that we resist and counteract that corruption—not only at some times or in some things, but at all times and in all things. Our natural depravity, therefore, is an additional reason for constant and universal self-denial.

4. I will illustrate a little further our need for self-denial. The will of God is a path leading straight to him. The human will, which, before the Fall, ran parallel to God's will, now follows another path. Our wills are not only different from God's will, but also in our present state they are directly contrary to it. Our paths lead away from God. So, if we walk in our own way, it is necessary for us to leave God's way. We cannot walk on both pathways. Indeed, those with "timid hearts and slack hands" may "walk a double path"—one path and then the other.[12] We cannot walk in two ways at the same time, however. We cannot simultaneously follow our own wills and the will of God. We must choose one path or the other. We must either deny God's will to follow our own, or else deny ourselves to follow God's will.

5. Undoubtedly, for the present, it is pleasing to ourselves to follow our own wills by indulging the corruption of our natures on every occasion that arises. Yet when we follow our own choices in anything, we strengthen the stubbornness of our wills. By indulging our self-will, we continuously increase the corruption of our sinful natures. To illustrate: by the food that is agreeable to the taste, we often increase a bodily disease. In the same way, self-will gratifies the desires, but it irritates the disorder. Self-will brings pleasure, but it also brings death.

6. In sum, to deny ourselves is to reject our own desires (however pleasing they may be) if those desires do not accord with the will of God. Self-denial is to refuse ourselves any pleasure that does not spring from, and lead to, God. In effect, it is to refuse to depart from God's way, even if tempted by a pleasant, flowery path. Self-denial is to refuse what we know to be deadly poison, although it may be agreeable to the taste.

7. All who want to follow Christ and be his genuine disciples must not only "deny themselves," but also "take up their crosses."

A "cross" is anything contrary to our wills, everything displeasing to our natures. Taking up our cross goes somewhat further than denying ourselves, and it rises even higher. It is more difficult for flesh and blood to abstain from pleasure than to endure pain.

8. Now, in "running the race that is set before us," according to the will of God, often we find a cross lying on the way. I am speaking of something that not only lacks joy, but is also painful. It is contrary to our wills and displeasing to our natures. At this point, what are we to do? The choice is clear: Either we must "take up our cross," or we must turn aside from the way of God and "the holy commandment that was passed on to us." Either we stop our way altogether, or we turn back to everlasting perdition.

9. For the healing of our corruption (that evil disease that everyone brings into the world) it is often necessary, as it were, to "tear out one's right eye" or to "cut off one's right hand." This illustration tells us that often the thing that needs to be done and the means of doing it are painful. It is painful to part with "senseless and harmful desires." Often, we can rid ourselves of evil desires only by extinguishing that upon which they are fixed.

Tearing away a desire or affection when it is deeply rooted in the soul is often like the piercing of a sword. Yes, it is as "the separation of soul and spirit and the joints and marrow." The Lord then rests upon the soul "as a refiner's fire" to burn up all its dross. This process indeed involves a cross. It is necessarily painful—in the very nature of the thing it must be so. The soul cannot be torn asunder and pass through the fire without undergoing pain.

10. The ways to heal a sin-sick soul and cure a senseless desire or an excessive affection are often painful because of the nature of the disease. Our Lord said to the rich young man, "Go, sell your possessions, and give the money to the poor." Jesus knew that this action was the only means of healing the young man's covetousness. But the very thought of doing what the Lord asked gave him so much anguish that "he went away grieving." The young man chose to part with his hope for heaven rather than to give up his earthly possessions. Christ's command was a burden that the young man would not agree to carry; it was a cross that he refused

to bear. In one way or another, every follower of Christ will surely need to "take up his cross daily."

11. "Taking up a cross" differs somewhat from "bearing a cross." We are properly said to "bear our cross" when with meekness and resignation we endure what is laid upon us without our choice. On the contrary, we "take up our crosses" when we voluntarily suffer what is in our power to avoid. We take up a cross when we willingly embrace the will of God, although it is contrary to our own wills. It is when we choose what is painful because it is the will of our wise and gracious Creator.

12. Every disciple of Christ is obligated to "take up a cross" as well as to "bear a cross." Indeed, in one sense, a cross is not ours alone. A cross belongs to us and to many others as well. We know that "no testing has overtaken us that is not common to everyone." Our crosses belong to our common humanity, and they are a part of life in the present world. Yet, in another sense, in the overall scheme of things, our crosses are individually our own.

God prepared your cross for you and gave it to you as an expression of his love. If you receive it as such (after using the means to remove the pressure that Christian wisdom directs) and become as clay in the potter's hand, your cross is inclined and directed by God for your good. God's cross for you is to your advantage with respect to its quality, quantity, degree, and duration. It is good in every way.

13. In all our self-denial, we can easily understand that our blessed Lord acts as the physician of our souls. "He disciplines us for our good, in order that we may share his holiness." If God causes us pain by probing our wounds, it is only to heal them. He cuts away what is decayed or diseased in order to protect what is good. If we voluntarily choose the loss of a limb, rather than the entire body perishing, how much more should we choose (figuratively and spiritually) "to lose one of our members than for our whole body to go into hell"!

14. We can clearly understand both the nature and basis for "taking up our cross." As some teach, it does not imply mortification—the literal slashing of our own flesh or wearing haircloth, iron girdles, or anything else that would impair our bodily

health.[13] (We do not know what allowance God may make for those who do these things because of involuntary ignorance.) Taking up our cross involves embracing God's will, even if it is contrary to our own wills. It means choosing beneficial, although bitter, medicines. It means willingly accepting temporary discomforts of whatever kind or degree, when doing so is fundamentally or incidentally necessary for our eternal pleasure.

II. The Need for Self-Denial and Cross-Bearing

1. Second, I will explain that it is always due to our failure to deny ourselves or take up our crosses that we do not completely follow Christ and therefore cannot be his disciples.

It is true that in some cases a lack of self-denial and cross-bearing can be partly due to our lack of access to God's established means of grace. That is, we may not have the opportunity to hear the true word of God spoken with power, to partake of the sacraments, or to benefit from Christian fellowship. However, when these means of grace are available, the main obstacle to our receiving or growing in God's grace is always our lack of self-denial or the failure to take up our cross.

2. A few illustrations will make this fact apparent. Suppose people hear the word that is able to save their souls. They delight in what they hear, acknowledge the truth, and are somewhat affected by God's word. Yet, they remain apathetic and asleep, "dead through trespasses and sins." Why do people assume this attitude? It is because they refuse to part with their cherished sins, although they know that they are an abomination to the Lord.

People come to hear God's word; but because they are full of lusts and unholy desires, they will not part with them. Consequently, no deep impression is made upon them. Instead, their senseless minds stay darkened. They remain apathetic and unawakened because they are not willing to deny themselves.

3. Suppose people begin to awaken from spiritual sleep, and their eyes are somewhat opened. Why do they so quickly close them again? Why do they once more sink into the sleep of spiritual death? Because they yield again to their cherished sins and

drink again of their pleasing poison. It is impossible, therefore, for any lasting impression to be made upon their hearts. They slip back into their fatal indifference because they will not deny themselves.

4. However, one person's response is not true of everyone. We have many illustrations of people who were once awakened and sleep no more. God's impressions on their souls did not fade away. God's workings were deep and permanent. Still, many of these people have not yet found what they seek. They mourn, but they are not comforted.

Why is it so? It is because they do not "bring forth fruit worthy of repentance." According to the grace they have received, they do not "cease to do evil" and "learn to do good." They do not turn away from the "sin that clings so closely"—the sin that is inherent in their physical nature, education, or profession. Or, they fail to do the good that they can and should do, because some disagreeable circumstance is connected with it. They fail to attain faith because they will not deny themselves or take up their crosses.

5. Suppose that other people did receive "the heavenly gift" and tasted "the powers of the age to come." They saw "the light of the knowledge of the glory of God in the face of Christ." The "peace that passes all understanding" did "rule their hearts and minds." "God's love was poured into their hearts through the Holy Spirit, which was given to them." Yet now, they have become as weak as any other person. They once more enjoy the things of earth, and they have more taste for the things that are seen than for those things that are unseen. The eyes of their hearts are closed again, so that they cannot "see him who is invisible." Their love has grown cold, and the peace of God no longer rules in their hearts.

It is no wonder, because they have once more given an "opportunity to the devil" and "grieved the Holy Spirit of God." They have turned again to folly or to some pleasing sin. If it is not an outward act, it is a sin of the heart. They have given a place to pride, anger, lust, self-will, or stubbornness. Or, they failed to "stir up the gift of God that was in them." They gave in to spiritual sloth and would not pay the price of "praying always and watching thereunto with all perseverance." So it is, for the lack of self-denial and cross-bearing, they made shipwreck of the faith.

6. Perhaps some have not made shipwreck of the faith. Assume that they have still a measure of the Spirit of adoption that continues to witness with their spirits that they are children of God. Yet they are not "going on to perfection." They no longer hunger and thirst after righteousness as formerly. They do not seek for the full image and enjoyment of God, as "a deer longs for flowing streams." Instead, they are weary and faint in their minds, spiritually hovering between life and death.

Why are they in this condition? Because they have forgotten the word of God: "Faith is completed by works." They do not exercise full diligence in "working the works of God." In "patient suffering," they do not "persevere in prayer," private and public. They fail to take Communion, listen to God's word, meditate, fast, and meet with other Christians.

If they do not completely neglect some of these means of grace, at least they do not use all of them with their full ability. Or they are not zealous for good deeds and works of piety. They are not as merciful as possible, using the full ability that God gives them. They do not fervently serve the Lord by doing good to the souls and bodies of others in every way and to every degree they are able.

Why do they fail to "devote themselves to prayer"? Because in times of spiritual dryness, it is painful and vexing for them. They do not continue in hearing God's word at all opportunities, because sleep is sweet or because the weather is cold, or dark, or rainy. Why have they discontinued doing works of mercy? Because they are unwilling to feed the hungry or clothe the naked. Serving others would require them to lessen the costs of their own clothing or use less expensive and less pleasing food.

In addition, visiting the sick or imprisoned involves many disagreeable circumstances. And so are most works of spiritual mercy, particularly exhorting others. They would speak to their neighbors, but sometimes embarrassment or fear stops them. Doing this work requires exposing ourselves to ridicule and even more demanding inconveniences. Because of these considerations and others like them, they omit one or more, if not all, works of mercy and works of piety. Therefore, their "faith is not brought to completion." Neither can they grow in grace because they are unwilling to "deny themselves and daily take up their crosses."

7. It clearly follows that it is always due to the lack of self-denial or cross-bearing that people do not completely follow their Lord as his dedicated disciples. This failure is the reason that those who are dead in sin do not awaken, even though "the trumpet has blown." This spiritual collapse is also the reason that those who begin to awaken from sleep do not retain a deep or lasting conviction of their state. It is why the ones who are deeply and lastingly convinced of their transgressions do not receive remission of sins.

The failure to deny self and bear a cross is also the reason that some who have received this heavenly gift do not retain it. Instead, they "suffer shipwreck in the faith." It is for this reason that others, if they do not "draw back unto perdition," yet "grow weary or lose heart." They fall short of reaching "the goal for the prize of the heavenly call of God in Christ Jesus."

III. Encouragements to Self-Denial

1. How easily we can identify those who directly or indirectly, in public or in private, oppose the doctrine of self-denial and daily cross-bearing! They "know neither the Scriptures nor the power of God." These teachers are completely ignorant of a hundred specific texts, as well as of the general message of the entire Bible! And how completely unacquainted they are with authentic, genuine Christian experience! They are ignorant of the way the Holy Spirit has always worked and even now continues to operate in human souls! Indeed, they may talk very loudly and confidently (a natural fruit of ignorance!) as though they were the only people who understand the word of God or the experience of his children. Yet, in every way they speak "deceptive words." "They have been weighed on the scales and found wanting."

2. Second, we can learn the real reason that many individuals and even entire groups of people who were once burning and shin-

ing lamps have now lost both their heat and light. If they did not hate and oppose this precious gospel doctrine, at the least they had small regard for it. If they did not boldly say, "We trample all self-denial under foot, and we assign it to destruction," they neither value self-denial as a matter of great importance nor take any pains to practice it. One of their important (but uninformed) leaders said, "The mystics teach self-denial." I answer that the inspired *biblical writers* teach it. And God teaches self-denial to every soul that is willing to hear his voice.

3. Third, we can learn that it is not enough for a minister of the gospel to avoid opposing self-denial and yet say nothing about it. Indeed, ministers cannot fulfill their duty by mentioning only a few words in favor of self-denial. If they want to be free from the blood of all people, they must speak about this subject frequently and thoroughly. They must instill the need for it in the clearest and strongest way. With all their might, they must urge self-denial on all persons, at all times, and in all places. They must set down "precept upon precept, precept upon precept, line upon line, line upon line." In this way, they will "have a clear conscience toward God and all people." They will save their own souls and those of their hearers.

4. Finally, see that you apply self-denial to your own soul. Meditate upon it when you are in private. Ponder it in your heart. Be careful both to understand it completely and to remember it to the end of your life. Cry unto the mighty God for strength, that as soon as you understand self-denial you will begin to practice it. Do not delay. This very hour, begin to deny yourself. Practice self-denial everywhere, on every one of the thousand occasions that will occur in all circumstances of life. Practice it daily, without stopping—from the hour you first set your hand to the plow—and diligently endure in self-denial until your spirit returns to God.

Notes

1. *Methodist Book of Worship* (Nashville: The Methodist Publishing House, 1944, 1945, 1952), 52.
2. Ward and Heitzenrater, *Wesley's Journal and Diaries*, April 21, 1741, 19:191.
3. Davies, *The Methodist Societies*, General Rules of the United Societies, 9:72.
4. *Notes upon the New Testament,* Matt. 16:24.

5. Ibid., Luke 9:23.
6. Jackson, *Wesley's Works,* 1:469.
7. Telford, *Wesley's Letters*, September 15, 1770, 5:200.
8. Jackson, *Wesley's Works,* 4:481.
9. Wesley's translation of Luke 9:23.
10. Here, Wesley is referring to Count Nikolaus Ludwig Graf von Zinzendorf [1700–60], the founder of the *Hernhutter Brudergemeine.*
11. The Ranters were a seventeenth-century sect of fanatical Antinomians. They appealed to inward experiences of Christ but denied the authority of the Bible and rejected the creeds of Christendom.
12. Sir. 2:12.
13. Mortification is an ecclesiastical term describing the practice of "killing" or "numbing" the flesh and its lusts by inflicting bodily pain so as to conquer bad habits or sin.

Introduction to Sermon 49

THE CURE OF EVIL-SPEAKING

Many of Wesley's converts had come from the poorer and less educated segments of society, and Methodism had brought them from despair to hope. As Christians, they had received the assurance that they possessed the treasures of Christ and the riches of grace, spiritual knowledge and wisdom. They knew that they were partakers of eternal life and that they would enter the bountiful bliss of heaven. Having become new persons in Christ, they had changed their ways of living, and their finances began to improve. The Methodist converts were both grateful and humbled by their new life. However, they faced the temptation to gossip about those who had formerly regarded them as inferior people. The lure to speak evil about others was ever present.

Furthermore, Methodism's system of class meetings provided opportunities for class members to learn about the personal and intimate details of one another's lives. The possibility of careless gossip was constant. Because of the evils of irresponsible talk, Wesley was determined that the Methodists would not engage in "backbiting, tale-bearing, and whispering."[1] In his sermon "The More Excellent Way," he said,

> Let us consider a little in what manner the generality of Christians usually converse together. What are the ordinary subjects of their conversation? If it is harmless (as one would hope it is), if there be nothing in it profane, nothing immodest, nothing untrue, or unkind; if there be no talebearing, backbiting, or evil-speaking, they have reason to praise God for his restraining grace.[2]

In 1752, John and Charles Wesley, along with eleven Methodist lay preachers, signed the following circular letter, which was then sent to all the Methodist preachers:

> It is agreed by us whose names are underwritten (1) That we will not listen, or willingly inquire after any ill concerning each other. (2) That if we do hear any ill of each other, we will not be forward to believe it. (3) That as soon as possible we will communicate what we hear, by speaking or writing to the person concerned. (4) That till we have done this we will not write or speak a syllable of it to any other person whatsoever. (5) That neither will we mention it after we have done this to any other person. (6) That we will not make any exception to any of these rules, unless we think ourselves absolutely obliged in conscience so to do.[3]

By the example of leaders who followed these rules, Wesley hoped to curtail jealousy, disunity, and the injurious effects of backbiting among the Methodists. Often we read such journal entries as the following: "I earnestly exhorted the society to beware of speaking evil of each other, and of censuring those who followed not with us."[4]

The Methodists, however, were sometimes guilty of evil-speaking. And when they fell into this practice, many problems infected their societies. For instance, Wesley wrote the following account in his journal:

> A year ago there was such an awakening here [in Bath] as never had been from the beginning. And in consequence of it, a swift and large increase of the society. Just then Mr. McNab, quarrelling with Mr. Smyth, threw wildfire among the people and occasioned anger, jealousies, judging each other, back-biting, and tale-bearing without end. And in spite of all the pains which have been taken, the wound is not healed to this day.[5]

Wesley was so opposed to speaking evil about others that he cautioned the Methodists even against disparaging those who persecuted them. In his *Advice to the People Called Methodists* he counseled,

> [Do not] *talk much of what you suffer,* "of the *persecution* you endured at such a time, and the wickedness of your *persecutors.*" Nothing more tends to exasperate them than this; and therefore (although there is a time when these things must be mentioned, yet) it might be a general rule to do it as seldom as you can with a safe conscience. For (besides its tendency to inflame them) it has the appearance of evil, of ostentation, of magnifying yourselves. It also tends to puff you up with pride, and to make you think yourselves some great ones, as it certainly does to excite or increase in your heart ill will, anger, and all unkind tempers. It is, at best, loss of time; for instead of the wickedness of men, you might be talking of the goodness of God. Nay, it is, in truth, an open, wilful sin: it is talebearing, backbiting, evil-speaking,—a sin you can never be sufficiently watchful against, seeing it steals upon you in a thousand shapes. Would it not be far more profitable for your souls, instead of speaking against them, to pray for them? To confirm your love towards those unhappy men whom you believe to be fighting against God by crying mightily to him in their behalf, that he may open their eyes and change their hearts?[6]

In this sermon, Wesley declares,

> I call upon all of you who suffer the abuse of Christ and are derisively called *Methodists.* Will you set an example for the so-called Christian world, at least in this one matter! Shun evil-speaking, gossiping, and spreading rumors. Let none of these things come out of your mouths. Be careful that you "speak evil of no one." Speak nothing but good of those who are absent. If you must be distinguished by any mark (whether or not you wish to be) let the absence of evil-speaking be the characteristic mark of you as Methodists. By this fruit you can know Methodists: They censure no one behind his back. What blessed effects of this kind of self-denial we would quickly feel in our hearts! How eminently would our "prosperity become like a river," when in this way we "pursued peace with everyone."

Sermon 49

THE CURE OF EVIL-SPEAKING

If another member of the church sins against you, go and point out the fault when the two of you are alone. If the member listens to you, you have regained that one. But if you are not listened to, take one or two others along with you, so that the evidence of two or three witnesses may confirm every word. If the member refuses to listen to them, tell it to the church; and if the offender refuses to listen even to the church, let such a one be to you as a Gentile and a tax collector. *(Matthew 18:15-17)*

1 "Speak evil of no one," says the eminent apostle Paul. This directive is as clear as "You shall not murder." Still, who even among Christians observes this injunction against evil-speaking? Indeed, how many Christians even understand the command?

What is "evil-speaking"? It is not the same as lying or slandering (as some suppose). Everything one says can be as true as the Bible, and yet just saying it can be speaking evil of another. Evil-speaking is nothing more or less than speaking ill of an absent person. It is reporting something evil that was actually done or said by one who is not present at the time of the report.

Suppose after I have seen a man drunk or heard him curse or blaspheme, I report this fact in his absence. My words would be evil-speaking. In our language, this kind of talk has a very accurate name—*backbiting*. There is no substantial difference between backbiting and what we usually call *rumor*. If the report is given in a soft and quiet manner (perhaps with expressions of goodwill to the person and hope that things may not be quite as bad), we call it *gossiping*. Regardless of the manner in which the report is given, it is the same thing. At least in substance (if not in style) it is still evil-speaking. We trample under foot the command "speak evil of no one" if we relate to another person the failing of a third person when that one is not present to respond.

2. This sin is extremely common among all types and ranks of people. The high and low, rich and poor, wise and foolish, educated and uneducated fall into this sin constantly! People who differ from one another in everything else, nonetheless agree that evil-speaking is common. Few people can testify before God that they are innocent and can say,

> I have set a watch, O Lord, before my mouth;
> And keep the door of my lips. (Ps. 141:3 KJV)

What conversation do you hear of any considerable length in which evil-speaking is not a component? This practice is found even among people who for the most part have "the fear of God before their eyes" and truly desire to "have a clear conscience toward God and all people."

3. The very frequency of this sin makes it difficult to avoid. Evil-speaking surrounds us on every side. Consequently, if we are not deeply aware of the danger and constantly guarding against it, we are liable to be carried away by its flood. In this matter, almost the whole world, as it were, is part of a conspiracy against our escaping this sin. The actions of others influence us in ways that we do not recognize; and without realizing it, we follow their examples.

In addition to the influence of others, the tendency toward evil-speaking comes from within ourselves. There is hardly a bad inclination within us that cannot be nourished by this wrong. Therefore, we are constantly inclined toward evil-speaking. It feeds our pride to report the faults of others, faults of which we think we are not guilty. We indulge anger, resentment, and all unkind attitudes when we speak against those with whom we are displeased. Often, when we report the sins of our neighbors, we are actually indulging our own "senseless and harmful desires."

4. Evil-speaking is all the more difficult to avoid because it frequently comes to us in disguise. We speak evil of others out of a virtuous and general (it is best if we do not say "holy") "indignation" against these repulsive people! We commit sin out of our mere hatred of sin! We serve the devil out of our pure zeal for God! It is only to punish the wicked that we plunge into this wickedness. One writer has said, "The passions all justify themselves."[7] So, we believe that our emotions excuse our actions. In this way, under the guise of holiness, our strong feelings impose sin upon us!

5. Is there no way to avoid the snare of evil-speaking? Certainly there is. In the words of our text, our blessed Lord has marked out a clear way for his followers. No one who cautiously and steadily walks in this path will ever fall into evil-speaking. This command of Christ is an infallible safeguard against, or a certain cure for, evil-speaking. In the verses preceding our text, the Lord said, "Woe to the world because of stumbling blocks [or offenses]!" Indescribable misery will arise in the world from this deadly fountain. (Stumbling blocks, or offenses, consist of those things that turn aside or hinder people in the ways of God.) Jesus said, "Occasions for stumbling are bound to come." Such is the nature of this world because of the weakness, foolishness, and wickedness of humankind. Jesus also said, "Woe to the one by whom the stumbling block comes! If your hand or your foot causes you to stumble [or your dearest pleasure or most loved and useful friend], cut it off and throw it away."

How can we avoid becoming a stumbling block to others, and how can we ourselves avoid stumbling because of others? Suppose another person is definitely in the wrong, and we see the wrong. Here, our Lord teaches us how definitely to avoid becoming a stumbling block to others:

> If another member of the church [a sister or brother] sins against you, go and point out the fault when the two of you are alone. . . . If you are not listened to, take one or two others along with you, so that the evidence of two or three witnesses may confirm every word. If the member refuses to listen to them, tell it to the church; and if the offender refuses to listen even to the church, let such a one be to you as a Gentile and a tax collector. (Matt. 18:15-17)

I. Exhorting Another in Private

1. First, "if another sins against you, go and point out the fault when the two of you are alone." When it is possible, the most literal way of following this first rule is the best. Therefore, if you see a fellow Christian undeniably commit a sin or hear about it so that it is impossible for you to doubt the fact, then your duty is clear. Take the very first opportunity to go to him. And if you can see him, "point out the fault when the two of you are alone." Of course, you must take great care that you have a right spirit and speak in the right way. The success of a reproof greatly depends on the spirit in which it is given. Therefore, pray earnestly that God will enable you to give your reproof with a humble spirit.

Admonish others with a deep, penetrating conviction that it is God alone who causes you to differ with them and that if any good is accomplished by what you say, it is God's work. Pray that God will watch over your heart, enlighten your mind, direct your tongue, and guide your words so that he will bless them. See that you speak in a gentle and humble spirit, because "your anger does not produce God's righteousness." "If anyone is detected in a transgression," that person can be restored only "in a spirit of gentleness."

If others oppose the truth, they can only be brought to know the truth when they are corrected with kindness. Always speak in a spirit of tender love, "which many waters cannot quench." If love is not overcome, it will conquer everything. Who can describe the force of love?

Love can bow down the stubborn neck,
The stone to flesh convert;
Soften and melt and pierce, and break
An adamantine heart.[8]

Therefore, confirm your love toward others, and you will thereby "heap burning coals of fire upon their heads."

2. Also, see to it that the manner in which you speak to others is according to the gospel of Christ. Avoid everything in appearance, gesture, word, and tone of voice that is tinged with pride or self-sufficiency. Diligently avoid everything that is domineering, overbearing, arrogant, or presumptuous. Beware of the slightest hint of scorn, haughtiness, or contempt. With equal care, avoid every appearance of anger. Although you speak with great clarity, let there be no insult. Do not show insolent denunciation or indications of passion. Have only the passion of love.

Above all, let there be no suggestion of hate or ill will, no bitterness or irritability of expression. Rather, demonstrate the attitude and language of affection and gentleness, so that everything will come from a heart of love. Your affection need not keep you from speaking in the most serious and solemn manner. As far as possible, speak in the very words of Scripture, for there are none like them. Speak as one who lives under the eye of him who is coming to judge the living and dead.

3. If you have no opportunity to speak to the other person or if you cannot reach him, you can communicate through a messenger. Perhaps you can use a common friend whose discretion and fairness you can trust completely. Such a person, speaking in your name and in the spirit and manner I have described, can promote the same purpose and adequately serve in your stead. Take caution, however, that you do not pretend a lack of opportunity in order to avoid the burden. And do not take it for granted that you cannot reach the other person without trying to do so. Whenever you can speak personally, it is far better. Still, it is better to speak through another person than not to speak at all. That arrangement is better than doing nothing.

4. What if you cannot speak yourself or find a suitable messenger that you trust? If such is really the case, you can write a letter

to the other person. There may be some circumstances that make written communication the most advisable way of communicating. One of these circumstances is when the other person has an excitable and impulsive disposition that does not easily bear correction, especially coming from an equal or subordinate. Your words can be softened in writing in a way that makes them far more acceptable to the other person.

Furthermore, many will read the very same words that they could not bear to hear. Written communication does not bestow as intense a shock to pride or as emotionally have an effect on self-respect. Suppose at first your letter makes only a slight impression. Perhaps the other person will give it a second reading, and on further consideration take to heart what he or she previously disregarded. If you sign your name, it is almost the same thing as going to the other person and speaking personally. And you should always sign your correspondence, unless special circumstances make it improper.

5. It should be strongly noted that our Lord absolutely commands us first to go alone to the one who sins against us. He also commands us to take this step to start with before undertaking any other measure. Christ allowed no alternative approach—"This is the way; walk in it." If the need requires, it is true that Christ directs us to take two other steps. However, he instructs us to take them successively *after* this first step, and we are to take neither of them before it. We must not take any other step either prior to or instead of this one. To do anything else or not to obey this command is equally inexcusable.

6. Do not rationalize or excuse yourself for taking an altogether different approach. Do not say, "Well, I did not speak to anyone until I was so burdened that I could not refrain from speaking." You were "burdened," you say! Unless your conscience was seared, it is no wonder that you should speak this way. You were under the guilt of sin for disobeying a clear commandment of God. Immediately, you should have "gone and pointed out the fault when the two of you were alone." Unless your heart was utterly hardened, how could you be anything *other* than burdened?

You were trampling under foot the command of God and "devising evil in your heart against another person." And what way have you found to unburden yourself? God reproves you for a sin of omission—for not telling your brother or sister his or her fault. And then you comfort yourself while under God's rebuke by committing a sin of commission—telling the other person's fault to a third person! Comfort bought by sin is an expensive purchase! I trust God that you will have no peace, but that you will be burdened so much the more until you go to the other person and tell him and no one else.

7. I know of only one exception to this law. In order to protect the innocent, there may be an unusual case when one finds it necessary to accuse guilty people without informing them. For instance, suppose you are aware of a plan that someone has against the property or life of a neighbor. If so, the case may be such that there is no other way of stopping that plan from taking effect except by immediately making it known to the intended victim. In this instance, the command of the apostle—"Speak evil of no one"—is set aside. It is lawful, indeed it is our honor-bound duty, to speak evil of absent persons in order to prevent them from doing evil both to others and to themselves.

All the while, remember that evil-speaking is by nature a deadly poison. Therefore, if you are sometimes compelled to speak evil as a "medicine," use it with fear and trembling. Evil-speaking is such a dangerous medicine that nothing but absolute necessity can justify its use. Accordingly, use this medicine as seldom as possible, and only when it is completely necessary. Even then, use as little of it as possible. Use only as much as is essential to accomplish your purpose. At all other times, "go and point out the fault when the two of you are alone."

II. Exhorting in the Presence of Witnesses

1. What if the others "will not listen"? What if they "repay evil for good"? What if they become enraged rather than convinced? What if they listen without heeding and continue in their evil ways? We must anticipate that this very thing will often be the

case. Sometimes, our most gentle and sensitive reproof will have no effect, and the blessing we wished for another will be rejected. What are we to do when the other person will not listen?

Our Lord has given us clear and complete directions. If the other person will not listen, then Christ instructs us to "take one or two others along with us." This action then is the second step: Take one or two whom you know to be of a loving spirit, lovers of God and of their neighbors. Make sure that they are persons of a meek spirit and that they are "clothed with humility." Let them also be such as are meek and gentle, patient and longsuffering; not inclined to "repay evil for evil or abuse for abuse; but, on the contrary, disposed to answer with a blessing." Let them be wise people—those who are endowed with wisdom from above. They should be fair, unbiased, and free from any kind of intolerance. Also, you should see to it that the person you visit is well acquainted with those whom you take with you. Choose, above all others, people who are acceptable to the one to whom you seek to minister.

2. According to the nature of the case, love will dictate the manner in which you are to proceed. There is no single course of action prescribed for all instances. Before opening up the subject at hand, in general, we can advise that the witnesses should assure the person that they have no animosity or prejudice against him or her. They should clarify that only goodwill motivates them to become involved in other person's affairs. Before attempting to settle anything, Christians should clarify the purpose of their visit and perhaps calmly review the substance of your former conversation with them and what they said in their defense. After sharing these things, your friends will be better able to determine how to proceed, "so that every word may be confirmed by the evidence of two or three witnesses." Whatever you have said will have its full force by the additional weight of their authority.

3. In order to accomplish the purpose of their visit, the witnesses can consider the following points. (1) Briefly repeat what you reported and how the person answered. (2) Discuss and confirm the reasons you first went to him or her. (3) Support your reproof, showing how fair, kind, and how appropriate it was.

(4) Uphold the counsel and exhortation that you added to your reproof. Later, if necessary, these witnesses can testify to what was said.

4. Concerning this rule and the one preceding it (going privately to the other person), our Lord gives us no choice and leaves us no alternative. He specifically commands us to take witnesses with us, and nothing else will substitute. Christ also directs us when to engage witnesses. We are to take others with us *after* we have taken the first step of going to the offending person in private, and *before* we have taken the third step of going to the entire church. Take witnesses with you neither sooner nor later.

Only after we have followed these guidelines does Christ authorize us to report another person's evil to the church—the people we want to involve in this great example of brotherly love. Let us be careful not to report the evil to any other person until we have taken both of these steps. If we neglect these measures or if we take any others, it is no wonder that we are still burdened! In failing to follow Christ's instruction, we sin against God and our neighbors. And however favorably we may present our actions, if we have any conscience, our sin will find us out and bring a burden upon our souls.

III. Taking a Concern to the Entire Church

1. So that we can be completely instructed in this important matter, our Lord has given us an additional instruction: "If the member refuses to listen to the witnesses, [only then] tell it to the church." Taking this action is the third step. The main question is how we are to understand "the church." Beyond all reasonable doubt, the context will determine the answer. You cannot tell it to the *national* Church (the entire body of people called the Church of England). Even if you were able to inform them all of the matter, it would not serve a good Christian purpose. Reporting the sin to the total Church is not the intent of our Lord.

Neither should you to tell it to the entire body of Christian people in England, with whom you have a more direct connection. Such an act would not accomplish any good. Jesus was not referring to this body of people. It would not accomplish any useful purpose to report the faults of every particular member to the congregation or society united together in London.

You should report the sin to the elder or elders of the church, who are overseers of the Christian flock to which you both belong. These leaders "are keeping watch over your souls and will give an account." If possible, make your report in the presence of the person concerned. Make your statement clear, yet show all the kindness and love that the situation will allow. It is appropriately the leaders' responsibility to judge the behavior of those under their care. Their task is to "reprove with all authority," regarding the discipline that is appropriate to the offense. Therefore, when you have followed these steps, you have done everything required of you by the word of God or the law of love. You are not a participant in others' sins, and if they perish, their blood is "on their own heads."

2. At this point, it should be noted that this third step (and no other step) is the one that we are to take. We are to take it in its proper order, after the other two steps have first been followed. Unless in some very special circumstance, do not let this third step come before the second step, much less prior to the first one. Indeed, in some cases the second step may coincide with the third, when they are the same. The elder or elders of the church may be so connected with the offending brother that they may set aside the need for the second step and serve as the "one or two witnesses." Therefore, it may be enough to report the sin to them after you have first gone to the offending person "when the two of you are alone."

3. When you have followed Christ's directions, you have saved your own soul. "If the offenders refuses to listen even to the church" and continue in sin, "let such ones be to you as Gentiles or tax collectors." You are under no obligation to concern yourself with them, except when you entrust them to God in prayer. You need not speak about them any more. Leave them to their own Master. Indeed, you still owe the offenders (what you owe to all heathen people) ardent and compassionate goodwill. You owe them courtesy and all the duties of kindness, as occasions arise.

But have no fellowship or intimacy with them—no other dealings than you would have with an obvious heathen.

4. Although Christians are required to walk by this rule of Christ, where can you find an assembly of believers that obeys it? Perhaps you might find a few Christians scattered here and there who make it a matter of conscience to observe Christ's command. However, there are very few of them! How thinly they are scattered across the face of the earth! But where is there any Christian community that steadfastly walks by this command? Can we have such a group in Europe? Or, to go no farther, in Great Britain or Ireland? I fear not. I fear that we can search throughout these kingdoms and yet search in vain. I am alarmed for the Christian world! I am alarmed for Protestants, for Reformed Christians!

> Who rises up for me against the wicked?
> Who stands up for me against evildoers? (Ps. 94:16)

I ask you, "Are *you* the man of God?" By God's grace, will you be one who is not carried away by the flood? From this very hour, are you—God being your helper—completely determined to "set a guard over your mouth and to keep watch over the door of your lips"? From this hour, will you walk by Christ's command, "to speak evil of no one"? If you see your brother or sister do evil, will you "go and point out the fault when the two of you are alone"? Afterward, will you "take one or two others along with you," and only in the end "tell it to the church"?

If the single purpose of your heart is to obey the Lord, then learn one lesson well: *Listen to no evil report about anyone.* If there were no listeners, there would be none to report evil. According to the common proverb, "Is not the receiver as bad as the thief?"[9] So, if others begin to report evil in your hearing, halt them immediately. Refuse to "hear the voice of charmers or cunning enchanters," even though they speak so sweetly. Refuse to listen, even if those who engage in evil-speaking use ever so mild a manner or tone and offer ever so many declarations of goodwill for those that they are stabbing in the dark. Resolutely refuse to listen, although the evil-speakers complain of being "burdened" until they give their evil report. Burdened, you say? You foolish person! Do "pangs and agony seize you in anguish like a woman in labor"? If so, go and be released from your burden in the way that the Lord has established.

First, "go and point out the fault when the two of you are alone." Next, "take one or two common friends along with you and reprove the offenders in their presence." If neither of these steps take effect, then "tell it to the church." At the peril of your soul, report the sin to no one else, either before or after, unless in that one exceptional case that it is necessary to protect the innocent. Why should you burden other people by making them partakers of your sin?

5. I call upon all of you who "suffer the abuse of Christ" and are derisively called *Methodists*. Will you set an example for the so-called Christian world, at least in this one matter? Shun evil-speaking, gossiping, and spreading rumors. Let no such words come out of your mouths. Be careful that you "speak evil of no one." Speak nothing but good about those who are absent. If you must be distinguished by any mark (whether or not you wish to be), let the absence of evil-speaking be the characteristic mark of you as Methodists. By this trait, you can know the Methodists: They censure no others behind their backs.

What blessed effects of this kind of self-denial we would quickly feel in our hearts! How eminently would our "prosperity become like a river," when in this way we "pursued peace with everyone"! How greatly God's love would abound in our own souls, as in this way we confirmed our love for our sisters and brothers! And what a good effect it would have on all who are united together in the name of the Lord Jesus! How significantly would brotherly love continuously increase when this principal hindrance to it is removed! All the members of Christ's mystical body would then regularly care for one another. If one member suffers, all suffer together with that one; if one member is honored, all rejoice together. Sisters and brothers, "love one another deeply from the heart."

These benefits are not all that would come to us. Shunning evil-speaking would have a significant effect on the wild, unthinking world! How soon would others discover in us what they could not find among all the thousands of their own friends. They would cry out, even as Julian the Apostate [332–63] declared to his heathen escorts: "See how these Christians love one another!" By this witness, God would especially convince the unbelievers in the world and prepare them for his kingdom.

We can easily discover this truth from those remarkable words in our Lord's last solemn prayer:

> I ask not only on behalf of these, but also on behalf of those who will believe in me through their word, that they may all be one. As you, Father, are in me and I am in you, may they also be in us, so that the world may believe that you have sent me. (John 17:20, 21)

May the Lord hasten the time! May Christ enable us to love one another, not only "in word or speech, but in truth and action," just as Christ has loved us.

Notes

1. In the eighteenth century, *whispering* meant what today is meant by *gossiping.*
2. Outler, *Wesley's Sermons,* "The More Excellent Way" (IV, 3), 3:271.
3. Baker, *Wesley's Letters,* 26:490. A facsimile of this circular letter appears in Nehemiah Curnock's edition of *Wesley's Journal,* 4:9.
4. Curnock, *Wesley's Journal,* November 20, 1743, 3:111.
5. Ward and Heitzenrater, *Wesley's Journal and Diaries,* July 17, 1780, 23:181.
6. Davies, *The Methodist Societies,* "Advice to the People Called Methodists," 9:131.
7. Francis Hutcheson, *An Inquiry into the Original of Our Ideas of Beauty and Virtue in Two Treatises,* enl. and corr. 2nd ed. (London: Printed for J. Darby, 1726), 152.
8. Charles Wesley, "Against Hope, Believing in Hope," stanza 6, *Poet. Wks.*, 1:329.
9. Philip Dormer Stanhope, Earl of Chesterfield [1694–1773], *Advice to His Son: Rules for Conversation,* "On Scandal." Quoted in *The Oxford Dictionary of Quotations,* 2nd ed. (Oxford University Press, 1959), 139. In its original form, this proverb reads, "In scandal, as in robbery, the receiver is always thought as bad as the thief."

Introduction to Sermon 50

THE USE OF MONEY

Four years before John Wesley's death, he wrote *Thoughts Upon Methodism.* In that work he said,

> I fear, wherever riches have increased, (exceeding few are the exceptions,) the essence of religion, the mind that was in Christ, has decreased in the same proportion. Therefore, I do not see how it is possible, in the nature of things, for any revival of true religion to continue long. For religion must necessarily produce both industry and frugality; and these cannot but produce riches. But as riches increase, so will pride, anger, and love of the world in all its branches.[1]

Wesley often warned both the unconverted and the converted against the dangers of riches, and he frequently preached about the proper stewardship of material resources. This sermon contains one of his most articulate statements about the use of money.

In the previous two sermons, Wesley dealt with the stewardship of time and the stewardship of the tongue. This sermon deals with the stewardship of treasure. Here, he develops his famous formula: *Gain all you can; save all you can; give all you can.*[2] Furthermore, Wesley insists that we are not *owners* of our assets, but *stewards.*

God puts money into our hands only temporarily, and he takes it away whenever it pleases him. Wesley's opposition to the hoarding of wealth and to needless personal consumption is second only to his preaching on justification and sanctification. A biblical outlook on money and its use radically clashes with the natural inclinations of humankind.

Wesley worried that the Methodists would fall prey to "the deceitfulness of riches." In his sermon *Causes of the Inefficacy of Christianity*, he stated,

> But why is self-denial in general so little practised at present among the Methodists? Why is so exceeding little of it to be found even in the oldest and largest societies? . . . The Methodists grow more and more self-indulgent, because they *grow rich*. Although many of them are still deplorably poor, . . . yet many others, in the space of twenty, thirty, or forty years, are twenty, thirty, yea, a hundred times richer than they were when they first entered the society. And it is an observation which admits of few exceptions, that nine in ten of these decreased in grace in the same proportion as they increased in wealth.[3]

In another of Wesley's sermons, "The Wisdom of God's Counsels," he declared,

> Of all temptations none so struck at the whole work of God as "the deceitfulness of riches"—a thousand melancholy proofs of which I have seen within these last fifty years. Deceitful are they indeed! For who will believe they do him the least harm? And yet I have not known threescore rich persons, perhaps not half the number, during threescore years, who, as far as I can judge, were not less holy than they would have been had they been poor. By riches I mean, not thousands of pounds; but any more than will procure the conveniences of life.[4]

Wesley was so convinced of the dangers of undedicated possessions that until the end of his life, he continued to preach and teach on the use of money. In 1790, less than a year before he died, he preached at Bristol a sermon titled *The Danger of Increasing Riches*. In part, he said,

> After having served you between sixty and seventy years; with dim eyes, shaking hands, and tottering feet, I give you one more advice before I sink into the dust. Mark those words of St. Paul: "Those that desire" or endeavour "to be rich," that moment "fall into temptation," yea, a deep gulf of temptation, out of which nothing less than almighty power can deliver them. "They fall into a snare"—the word properly means a *steel trap*, which instantly crushes the animal taken therein to pieces—"and into divers foolish and hurtful desires, which plunge men into destruction and perdition." You, above all men, who now prosper in the world, never forget these awful words! How unspeakably slippery is your path! How dangerous every step! The Lord God enable you to see your danger, and make you deeply sensible of it. O may you "awake up after his likeness," and "be satisfied with it!"[5]

What Wesley preached, he modeled. It is estimated that he gave away at least £30,000 during his lifetime (mostly profits from his books), an enormous amount of money by that day's standards. In his sermon "The Danger of Riches," Wesley testifies,

> Permit me to speak as freely of myself as I would of another man. I "gain all I can" (namely, by writing) without hurting either my soul or body. I "save all I can," not willingly wasting anything, not a sheet of paper, not a cup of water. I do not lay out anything, not a shilling, unless as a sacrifice to God. Yet by "giving all I can" I am effectually secured from "laying up treasures upon earth." Yea, and I am secured from either desiring or endeavouring it as long as I "give all I can." And that I do this I call all that know me, both friends and foes, to testify.[6]

The present sermon is Wesley's most concise articulation of his views on gaining, saving, and giving money. In 1778, concerning this message, he wrote, "I cannot write a better [sermon] on *The Use of Money* than I did near thirty years ago."[7]

Sermon 50

THE USE OF MONEY

And I tell you, make friends for yourselves by means of dishonest wealth so that when it is gone, they may welcome you into the eternal homes. *(Luke 16:9)*

1 Our Lord's beautiful parable of the prodigal son especially applied to those who grumbled that he conversed with tax collectors and sinners. Following this parable, Jesus taught about a different kind of relationship, and he addressed this teaching to the children of God. Jesus spoke not to the scribes and Pharisees, but to his disciples:

> There was a rich man who had a manager, and charges were brought to him that this man was squandering his property. So he summoned him and said to him, "What is this that I hear about you? Give me an accounting of your management, because you cannot be my manager any longer." (Luke 16:1, 2).

After describing the method that the bad steward used to prepare for the day of need, our Savior added, "His master commended the dishonest manager because he had acted shrewdly" (that is, he exercised prudent precaution). Then Jesus said, "The children of this age are more astute in dealing with their own generation than are the children of light."

Those who seek nothing beyond the present age "are more astute in dealing with their own generation than are the children of light." (Of course, they are not *really* wiser because they are the greatest of fools and the most conspicuous lunatics under heaven.) Yet, *in their own generation* and *in their own way,* they are wiser than the children of light. Those who live only for the present are truer to their acknowledged principles and more consistently pursue their goals than those who see "the light of the knowledge of the glory of God in the face of Jesus Christ." Therefore, give heed to the words that I have already quoted: "Give me an accounting of your management, because you cannot be my manager any longer."

God is saying, "I, the only begotten Son of God, the Creator, Lord and Master of heaven and earth and everything in it, am the Judge of all people; and you will give an account to me. I advise you to learn from the dishonest manager who made friends for himself by means of dishonest wealth. He exercised well-timed precaution. It is called dishonest wealth because of the unrighteous way it is frequently procured and because of the way even honest wealth is generally used. Prepare for the future by doing as much good as you can, particularly to the children of God. Then, when you die and have no more place on earth, those who died before you 'may welcome you into the eternal homes.'"

2. Here, our Lord imparted a superb segment of Christian wisdom to all his followers. It pertains to the proper use of money. People of the world customarily speak a great deal about money, but those whom God has chosen out of the world do not adequately consider its use. In general, they do not give this important matter the attention it deserves. Neither do Christians understand how to use money to its best advantage.

God's introduction of stewardship into the world is a worthy example of his wise and gracious providence. In almost all ages and nations, it has surely been the tendency of poets, orators, and philosophers to revile money as the main corrupter of the world. People often regard money as the scourge of virtue and the bane of human society. Consequently, nothing is so commonly heard as:

Gold is more mischievous than the sharpest iron.[8]

Based on that assumption, we hear the lamentable complaint,

Wealth is dug up, and it is an incentive to all evil.[9]

Indeed, in order to banish all vice immediately, one famous writer solemnly exhorts his countrymen:

Throw all your money into the nearest sea.[10]

In truth, are not these views merely empty ravings? Is there any good sense in this advice? None at all. Let the world be as corrupt as it will. Are we to lay all the blame on gold or silver? We know that it is the *love* of money that is a root of all kinds of evil. The fault does not lie in the money, but in those who use it.

Money can be used wrongly—and what cannot be misused? However, money can also be used properly. Money is equally suited to the best as well as to the worst uses. Money is of indescribable benefit to all civilized nations in all the common affairs of life. It is a most condensed means to transact all kinds of business and of doing all kinds of good (if we use it according to Christian wisdom).

If humankind were in an uncorrupted state or if all people were filled with the Holy Spirit, there would be no misuse of money. In the infant church at Jerusalem "no one claimed private ownership of any possessions." Money "was distributed to each as any had need." In paradise, the use of money will be outmoded, and we cannot imagine that there is anything like money among heaven's inhabitants.

In our present state, though, money is an excellent gift from God, working toward the most elevated purposes. In the hands of God's children, money is food for the hungry, drink for the thirsty, and clothing for the naked. For the pilgrim and stranger, money provides a place to lie down to rest. By the right use of money we can provide for others. Money can serve as a husband for the widow and as a father to the orphans. We can supply protection for the oppressed, a means of health for the sick, and comfort for those in pain. Money can become as "eyes to the blind, and feet to the lame"; and, indeed, money can "lift up others from the gates of death."

3. Therefore, it ranks among our highest concerns that all who fear God know how to use this valuable gift. It is important that we be instructed in how money can serve admirable ends to the highest degree. Perhaps all the instructions necessary for this goal can be reduced to three simple rules. By observing them, we can become faithful managers of money. These rules are *gain all you can*, *save all you can*, and *give all you can*.

I. Gain All You Can

1. The first of these simple rules is: *Gain all you can*. As Jesus said, "Listen and understand." Here, we can speak like the children of this age. We meet them on their own ground. It is our obligation and duty to follow this rule. We ought to gain all we can without paying more for gold than it is worth.

Of course, it is certain that we should not gain money at the expense of life or health (which is in effect paying too high a price for gold). Therefore, no gain whatever should prompt us to enter into, or to continue in, any lengthy or difficult work that will damage our health. Neither should we begin or stay with any business that deprives us of appropriate times to eat and sleep as our bodies require. Indeed, there are great differences here. Some vocations are absolutely and totally unhealthy, such as those that deal too much with arsenic or other equally harmful chemicals. We should not work in a place in which we breathe air that is polluted with the fumes of molten lead. In time, breathing these vapors will destroy the strongest constitution.

Other vocations might not be completely unhealthy, except to people with weak constitutions. Such occupations are those that require one to spend many hours writing, especially if one writes while sitting and leaning upon his or her stomach or remaining in an uncomfortable posture for long periods. We must not engage in any work that reason or experience shows to be injurious to health or strength. Jesus said, "Life is more than food, and the body more than clothing." If we are already engaged in such work, as soon as possible we should exchange it for some other work. If it reduces our income, it will not degrade our health.

2. Second, if we are not to harm our bodies, neither are we to harm our minds. Whatever the circumstance, we must maintain a healthy mind. Therefore, we cannot begin or continue in any sinful occupations, any of which are contrary to the law of God or the nation. Illegal occupations certainly include robbing or defrauding the government of lawful taxes. It is at least as sinful to defraud the government as it is to rob our fellow citizens. The government has fully as much right to taxes as we have to our houses and clothing.

There are businesses that are untainted in themselves, but in which we cannot innocently participate (at least, not in our country). For instance, we cannot any longer engage in certain occupations without cheating, lying, or conforming to a practice that is not consistent with a good conscience. We must devoutly avoid these jobs, regardless of the income they might provide. In gaining money, we must not lose our own souls.

There are other vocations that many other people can pursue with perfect innocence and without harming either their bodies or minds. Yet it is possible that *you* cannot follow after them. Those jobs might involve you with others who would destroy your soul. Through repeated experiences it might become clear that you cannot separate the job from evil influences. Or perhaps there might be a characteristic particularity in your soul (as there is in the *physical* constitution of others) that makes that job spiritually fatal to you, although someone else can safely hold that job.

For example, experience has taught me that I cannot study mathematics, arithmetic, or algebra to any degree of perfection without thinking as a Deist, if not an atheist. Yet others may study these subjects all their lives without suffering any harm. Therefore, no one can decide for another. We must all judge for ourselves and abstain from whatever we personally find harmful to our souls.

3. Third, in gaining all we can, we must never harm others. Naturally, we will not and cannot do so if we love our neighbors

as ourselves. If we love all people as ourselves, we cannot deprive them of what belongs to them. We cannot take the produce of their land, the land itself, or the land and buildings. Therefore, we cannot despoil a neighbor through gambling, collecting a debt owed to us (whether on account of medical problems, law, or anything else), or extracting interest in excess of what the law allows. Therefore, we prohibit all loans based on pledged collateral. Whatever temporary good such loans might bring, all unbiased people see with sorrow that this kind of lending leads to more evil than good. Even if good would come from these kinds of loans, we are not allowed to "do evil that good may come."

Consistent with brotherly love, we must not sell our goods below the market price. We cannot scheme to undercut our neighbor's trade in order to advance our own. And it is even more certain that we cannot lure away or take possession of any of the servants or workers that our neighbors need. None of us can advance our self-interests by means of swallowing up our neighbor's substance without earning the damnation of hell.

4. We must not gain more by harming our neighbors' bodies. Therefore, we cannot sell anything that tends to impair the health of others. At the forefront of such activity is the selling of that liquid fire commonly called "drams"[11] or "spirituous liquors."[12] It is true that alcohol has a place in medical treatments. It can be of use in some bodily disorders (although there would rarely be occasions for it, if it were not for untrained practitioners). Therefore, those who prepare and sell alcohol for medical purposes can keep their conscience clear.

Who are those, however, who prepare and sell alcohol only for medical reasons? Do you know ten such distillers in England? If so, then absolve them from blame. Ordinarily, though, all who sell alcohol to anyone who will buy it are masters of poison. They murder our citizens indiscriminately, and they do not pity or spare anyone. They drive others to hell like sheep. And what do they gain? Is it not the blood of these people?

Who, therefore, would envy their large estates and sumptuous mansions? Damnation is in the midst of these mansions. God's curse clings to their very stones, woodwork, and furniture. God's denunciation is on their gardens, walkways, and woodlands. God's displeasure is a fire that burns to the lowest hell. Blood is in these mansions. The foundations, floors, walls, and roofs are stained with blood!

O, you men and women of blood, do you have any hope? Although you are "dressed in purple and fine linen and feast sumptuously every day," can you hope to pass down your "fields of blood" to the third generation? You will not! There is a God in heaven. Therefore, your name will soon be rooted out. Just as those whom you have destroyed body and soul, "your very memory has perished."

5. There are others who are equally guilty, although to a lesser degree. These are unscrupulous surgeons, medicine makers, and healing practitioners who trifle with the life or health of others in order to increase their incomes. Some purposely lengthen the pain or disease that they are able to remove quickly. They prolong the cure of their patients' bodies in order to plunder their assets. Can those be innocent before God who fail to shorten every physical disorder as much as possible and remove all sickness and pain as soon as they can? Those who do not help others in these ways cannot be innocent. Nothing can be more obvious: they do not "love their neighbors as themselves." It is clear that they do not do to others what they would want in return.

6. This way of gaining money demands a high price. And so does everything that we acquire by harming our neighbors' souls. We harm others when we directly or indirectly promote their immorality or debauchery. Certainly, no one who does these things fears God or has any genuine desire to please him. This truth closely pertains to all who have anything to do with establishments that sell alcohol—restaurants, music halls, theaters, or any other places of fashionable public entertainment.

If these places of business benefit people's souls, they are innocent. Their work is good and their profits are untainted. However, if any of these establishments are in themselves sinful or natural channels of different kinds of sin, then I fear that they await an unhappy accounting. O be careful that on the day of judgment

God will not say, "Those wicked persons shall die for their iniquity; but their blood I will require at your hand!"

7. Observe these cautions and restrictions: It is the solemn duty of all who engage in worldly business to notice the first and principal rule of Christian wisdom with respect to money: *Gain all you can.* Gain all you can by honest industry, and exercise all possible diligence in your calling. Make the most of the time. If you understand yourself and your relationship to God and others, you know that you have no hours to spare. If you understand your particular calling as you should, you will not have any time to waste.

Every vocation will provide enough work for every day and hour. Wherever you are placed, if you earnestly do your work, there will be no spare time for inane and empty amusements. Always, you have something better to do—things that will in some way benefit you. "Whatever your hand finds to do, do with your might." Do it as soon as possible. Let there be no delay or putting off your tasks from day to day or from hour to hour. Never leave anything until tomorrow that you can do today.[13]

Furthermore, do your work as well as possible. Do not sleep or yawn over it. Put your whole strength into your labor. Spare no pains. Let nothing be done by halves or in a superficial and careless manner. Let nothing in your business be left undone if labor or patience can do it.

8. In gaining all you can, use common sense. That is, employ all the intelligence that God has given you. It is astonishing to observe how few people use all that God has given them. It is surprising how many people continue on in the same dull track that their ancestors took. The ways of those who do not know God are not your guide. It is shameful for Christians not to improve on the work of others, regardless of the work at hand. From the understanding of others and from your own experience, reading, and thinking, you should continuously learn in everything to do better today than you did yesterday. See to it that you put into practice whatever you learn, so that you can take full advantage of everything in your hands.

II. Save All You Can

1. Here is the second rule of Christian prudence: As you gain all you can, by honest wisdom and tireless diligence, *save all you can.* Do not throw your precious gains into the sea. Leave that foolishness to heathen philosophers. Do not waste your resources on trivial expenses, which is the same as throwing your money into the ocean. Spend none of your money merely to gratify "the desire of the flesh, the desire of the eyes, and the pride in riches."

2. Do not waste any of your precious resources merely in gratifying the desires of the flesh. Do not try to obtain any kinds of physical pleasures, especially in cultivating a taste for various foods. I am not only referring to gluttony and drunkenness. An honest heathen would condemn these things. There is, however, an ordinary, reputable kind of sensuality, which is a sophisticated kind of Epicurean pleasure that does not directly upset the stomach or impair the reason (at least, you are not aware that it does). Yet, you cannot retain these pleasures without considerable cost (not to mention other effects as well). Cut out all these unnecessary expenditures. Despise delicacies and variety, and be content with the simple food that nature requires.

3. Do not waste any part of your valuable resources gratifying the desire of the eye with extravagant or expensive clothing or needless accessories. Waste no part of your money fancifully adorning your houses with unnecessary or expensive furniture. Avoid expensive paintings, portraits, decorations, books, and elegant (rather than useful) gardens. Let your neighbors who do not know any better buy these things. Jesus said, "Follow me, and let the dead bury their own dead." With regard to doing what others do, Jesus also said, "What is that to you? Follow me!" Are you *willing* to follow him? If so, you are *able* to follow him.

4. Spend no money to gratify the pride of life or to gain the admiration and praise of others. This reason for spending money is often connected with the lust of the flesh and the lust of the eye. It is not only to delight their appetites or to gratify their eyes and fantasies that people spend too much money on expensive food, clothing, and furniture. They also have an eye to their own vanity. "Others praise you when you prosper." As long as you are

"dressed in purple and fine linen and feast sumptuously every day," no doubt many will applaud your elegant taste, generosity, and hospitality. However, do not buy their applause at such a great price. Instead, be content with "the glory that comes from God."

5. Would we spend anything to gratify these desires if we realized that when we cater to them we only increase them? Nothing can be more certain than this truth. Daily experience reveals that the more we indulge our desires, the more our requirements grow. Therefore, whenever you spend anything to please your tastes or your other senses, you are paying only to satisfy your sensuality.

When you lay out money to please your eyes, you are spending to increase your curiosity. You spend money to develop a stronger attachment to these pleasures, whereas they will only "perish with use." While you are buying things to gain human applause, you are paying for more vanity. Did you not have enough pride, sensuality, and curiosity when you began? Do you really need more things, and then be forced to support them with your own money? What kind of wisdom is this? Would it not be a less devilish folly for you literally to throw your money into the sea?

6. Why should you throw away money upon your children any more than upon yourself? Why indulge them in delicate food and pretentious or costly clothing or any other kinds of excesses? Why should you pay your money for them to develop even more pride, lust, vanity, or "senseless and harmful desires"? They do not need any more of these kinds of things because they have enough of them already. Human nature has made ample provision for their pride! Why should you go to further expense only to increase their temptations and snares? You work to "pierce them with many pains."

7. Do not leave them money to squander. Do you have good reason to believe that they would waste what is now in your possession by gratifying and therefore increasing the desires of the flesh, the desires of the eye, or the pride of life? Do not set traps in their way. Such actions jeopardize your soul and theirs. Do not offer your sons or daughters to the satanic god Belial, any more than you would offer them to Moloch, the god of child sacrifice.

Have pity on your children, and remove from their paths whatever you can easily foresee will increase their sins and consequently plunge them deeper into everlasting destruction. How amazing it is to see the obsession of those parents who think that they can never leave their children enough money. Think of that folly! Can you not leave them enough "arrows, live coals, and death"? Can you not scheme enough to impart to them "foolish and harmful desires"? Are you afraid that you cannot give them enough pride, lust, ambition, and vanity? Do you fear that you cannot give your children enough of the everlasting flames? You poor, miserable creature! You fear where fear is inappropriate. Surely both you and them, when you are lifting up your eyes in hell, will have more than enough of the "worm that never dies, and of the fire that is never quenched."

8. Someone may ask the question, "What then would you do if you were in my situation? What would you do if you had a considerable fortune to leave?"

I answer that whether I would do it or not, I know what I *should* do. My answer cannot be refuted. If I had one child, younger or older, who knew the value of money, a child that I believed would put it to the right use, I think it would be my absolute, indispensable duty to leave most of my fortune to that child. I would leave to the other children only as much as would enable them to live in the manner to which they had become accustomed.

Someone might ask, "But what if all your children were equally ignorant of the right use of money?"

I answer in the words of Christ's disciples: "My teaching is difficult; who can accept it?" I would give to each what would keep him above need and give all the rest in a way that I thought would work best for God's glory.

III. Give All You Can

1. Do not imagine that you have done anything merely by *gaining* and *saving* all you can. Do not stop here. Making and saving money is nothing if we fail to go forward to the final purpose.

People cannot rightly be said to save money if they only store it away. You might just as well throw your money into the sea as bury it in the ground. And you might as well bury it in the ground as store it in your money chest or in the Bank of England. Not to use your money is essentially to throw it away. Therefore, if you really want to make friends for yourselves by means of earthly treasures, add the third rule to the preceding two rules. First, having gained all you can and, second, having saved all you can, then *give all you can.*

2. In order to see the basis and objective of this rule, consider the following point. When the owner of heaven and earth brought you into being and placed you in this world, he positioned you here not as an owner. He placed you on earth as a steward or manager. As such, for a time he deposited various kinds of goods with you. But the sole *ownership* of these things still rests in God, and they can never be taken from him. Because you are not your own, neither are the possessions that you enjoy.

Even your soul and body are not yours—they belong to God. And your possessions in particular do not really belong to you. In the most clear and explicit terms, God has revealed how you are to employ yourself and your possessions. You are to use them in a way that becomes a "spiritual sacrifice acceptable to God through Jesus Christ." Moreover, God has promised to reward this "light burden and easy yoke" with "an eternal weight of glory."

3. The directions that God gave us on the use of our worldly substance may be summed up in the following specific ways. If you want to be a faithful and wise steward of the things that God has presently put into your hands (with the right to take them back whenever it pleases him), do the following things. First, provide for your basic needs—food, clothing, and what is necessary to keep yourself in health and strength.

Second, provide these things for your spouse, children, servants, or any others related to your household. When you have done these things, if you have any surplus, do good for "those of the family of faith." If you still have a surplus, "whenever you have an opportunity, work for the good of all." In doing so, you are giving all you can. Indeed, in a real sense, you are giving all you have. Everything that you give in this way is actually given to God. You are "giving to God the things that are God's." This gift to God includes what you give to the needy and what you give to provide for your own needs and those of your household.

4. If at any time a doubt should arise concerning what sum you should spend on yourself or any part of your family, there is an easy way to resolve the doubt. Calmly and seriously ask these questions: (1) In spending this money, am I acting according to my character? Am I acting not as an owner, but as a steward of my Lord's goods? (2) Am I giving this money in obedience to God's Word? In what scripture does God require me to spend this money? (3) Can I offer up this action or expenditure as a sacrifice to God through Jesus Christ? (4) Do I have reason to believe that for this very work I will receive a reward at the resurrection of the righteous? You will seldom need anything more than these questions to remove any doubt that may arise. By this fourfold consideration, you will receive clear light as to what you should do.

5. If any doubt still remains, you can further examine yourself by prayer according to each of these four questions. Consider whether you can pray the following prayer to the Searcher of Hearts, without your conscience condemning you.

> Lord, you see that I am ready to expend this amount on this food, clothing, or furniture. You know that I do this with a single eye as a steward of your property. I want to spend this money for the purpose you planned when you gave me these resources. You know that I do this in obedience to your Word, *as* you command it and *because* you command it. I pray that you will allow this expenditure to become a "spiritual sacrifice acceptable to God through Jesus Christ" (Phil. 4:18; I Pet. 2:5)! And give me an inner witness that for this labor of love I will have a reward when "you will repay everyone for what has been done." (Matt. 16:27)

If your conscience bears witness to you in the Holy Spirit that this prayer pleases God, then you have no reason to doubt that the expenditure is right and good. As such, it will never make you ashamed.

6. Now, you can understand what it means to "make friends for yourselves by means of worldly treasure," and in what way "when it is gone, others will welcome you into the eternal homes." You can see the nature and extent of genuine Christian prudence, as it relates to the use of the important gift of money. By applying yourself with perpetual diligence, and by using all the understanding that God has given you, gain all you can without harming yourself or your neighbor in soul or body. Save all you can by cutting off every expense that only serves to indulge the foolish desires of the flesh, the lust of the eye, or the pride of life.

In your living and dying, waste nothing on sin or on foolishness for yourself or for your children. And finally, give all you can. In other words, give to God everything you have. Do not confine yourself (as a Jew rather than as a Christian) to this or that percentage of your income. Give to God not a tenth, a third, or a half. Be it more or less, give God all that belongs to God. Give to yourself, your household, the family of faith, and all humankind in such a way that you can render a good account of your stewardship when you can no longer be God's steward. Use your money in the way that Scripture directs in its general and specific principles. Use your money in such a way that whatever you do may be "a fragrant offering and sacrifice to God." Spend so that every act will be rewarded in that day when the Lord comes with all his saints.

7. Brothers and sisters, can we be either wise or faithful stewards without managing the Lord's goods in this way? No, we cannot. Both the Bible and our own consciences bear witness. Why, then, should we delay? Why should we any longer consult with flesh and blood or with people of the world? Our kingdom, our wisdom "is not from this world." Heathen custom means nothing to us. We follow others no further than they follow Christ. Listen to the Lord. Indeed, while it is still today, hear and obey God's voice. Today and from now on, do the will of God. Fulfill God's work in the use of money and in everything else.

I appeal to you in the name of the Lord Jesus, lead a life worthy of the dignity of your calling. Let there be no more sloth! "Whatever your hand finds to do, do with your might." Let there be no more waste! Cut off every expense demanded by fashion, whim, or flesh and blood. Let there be no more greed! Instead, use whatever God has entrusted to you for the family of faith and for all people to do all possible good of every kind and amount.

The right use of money is no small part of "the wisdom of the righteous." Give all you have and all you are as a living sacrifice to him who did not withhold his only Son from you. In doing so, you are "storing up for yourselves the treasure of a good foundation for the future, so that you may take hold of the life that really is life."[14]

Notes

1. *Arminian Magazine* (1787): 10, 100-102, 155-56.
2. See also Sermon 28, "Upon our Lord's Sermon on the Mount," Discourse 8.
3. Outler, *Wesley's Sermons,* "Causes of the Inefficacy of Christianity," §16, 4:95.
4. Ibid., "The Wisdom of God's Counsels," §16, 2:560.
5. Ibid., "The Danger of Increasing Riches," §16, 4:185-86.
6. Ibid., "The Danger of Riches," II, 6, 3:237-38.
7. Ward and Heitzenrater, *Wesley's Journal and Diaries,* September 1, 1778, 23:104-5.
8. Ovid [43 B.C.–A.D. 18 or 17], *Ovid in Six Volumes,* "Metamorphoses" (Cambridge, Mass.: Harvard University Press; London: W. Heinemann, 1969, 1977), I, i, 141.
9. Ibid., 140.
10. Horace, *Odes,* III, xxiv, The Loeb classical library (Cambridge, Mass.: n.p., 1927), 33:47-49.
11. "Drams" was the eighteenth-century word for mixed drinks.
12. "Spirituous liquors" refers to distilled alcohol.
13. Benjamin Franklin [1706–90], *Poor Richard's Almanack* (New York: Random House; London: Hi Marketing, 2000), Maxims Prefixed to Poor Richard's Almanack [1757], "Never leave that till to-morrow which you can do to-day."
14. 1 Tim. 6:19

Introduction to Sermon 51

THE GOOD STEWARD

Less than a year before John Wesley died, he concluded a letter to a bishop of the Church with these words: "I am on the brink of eternity! Perhaps so is your Lordship too! How soon may you also be called to give an account of your stewardship, to the great Shepherd and Bishop of our souls! May He enable both you and me to do it with joy!"[1] Faithful stewardship had occupied Wesley's mind throughout his entire adult life. During his student days at Oxford, he made a lifetime commitment to exercise good stewardship of his life. In his mature years, Wesley recalled his decision to serve God:

> In the year 1725, being in the twenty-third year of my age . . . I resolved to dedicate all my life to God, all my thoughts, and words, and actions; being thoroughly convinced, there was no medium; but that every part of my life (not some only) must either be a sacrifice to God, or myself, that is, in effect, to the devil. Can any serious person doubt of this, or find a medium between serving God and serving the devil?[2]

For more than two thirds of a century thereafter, with remarkable consistency, he maintained this attitude of accountability to God. This sermon articulates Wesley's theological understanding of the stewardship of one's time, talent, and treasure.

The style of this discourse differs from most of Wesley's other sermons. In 1769, he preached *The Good Steward* in Edinburgh at Holyrood House to a gathering of the aristocracy. Wesley remarked that it was "a noble pile of building."[3] James Boswell tells us that at this site lay buried "the remains of many of the kings of Scotland, and of many of our nobility."[4] Wesley's journal gives the following summary of his preaching this sermon to the eminent congregation assembled that day: "In the evening our House was sufficiently crowded, even with the rich and honourable. 'Who hath warned these to flee from the wrath to come?' O may they at length awake and 'arise from the dead!'"[5] This company of "the rich and honourable" probably consisted of the highborn friends of the Countess Dowager of Buchan. The formal style of this sermon and its somewhat higher intellectual tone reflect his sensitivity to the aristocratic literary tastes of those who had gathered to hear him preach.

Wesley begins the message by distinguishing a *debtor* to God from a *steward* of God: Although *debtors* are obligated to return what they have received, up until the time of repayment they are free to choose how they use what they have. The case is not the same with *stewards*. They are not at liberty to use the things entrusted to them as they please. They have no right to deal with anything in their charge, except according to the will of their master.

This sermon explains that, as God's stewards, Christians are not the owners of the things entrusted to them. Stewards are only temporary custodians. For a short time, God grants us stewardship of our souls, bodies, possessions, abilities, and opportunities—all of which we temporarily have from God. As managers of these things, we must eventually give an accounting of how we used them. Wesley emphasizes the brief span of time allotted to us as the stewards of what God has entrusted into our care. He reminds the reader, "We have this trust only during the short, uncertain interval that we live here below." When life ends, we can no longer use and develop what God has given us in the same way that is possible while we are on the earth.

The sermon discusses the great judgment and the final accounting that we all must give of our stewardship. Wesley writes, "God, the judge of all, will then ask, 'How did you use your life? I entrusted you with an immortal spirit, endowed with various powers and abilities. I gave you comprehension, imagination, memory, will, and emotions.'" This message moves on to explain that at death our eternal destiny is sealed and unchanging. At that point we enter into either heaven or hell. In a sobering sentence, Wesley's journal sums up the life of a certain man who had recently died: "In the year 1759, having eat, and drank, and forgotten God, for eighty-four years, he went himself to give an account of his stewardship."[6]

The sermon ends with a reminder of the value of time: "How precious, beyond all understanding and description is every moment of time! . . . How greatly important it is for us all, as long as we have God's breath within us, to waste no time, but use it for the highest of God's purposes!" Wesley reinforces the truth that none of our work is indifferent or unimportant: "Everything we do is either good or bad, because all our time, as is the case with everything we have, is not our own." This eloquent discourse constitutes a powerful application of the truth that all the things we are and have belong to God. During our short time on earth, God expects us to expend our lives for others and for his glory. For the present, the Lord grants us time, talent, and treasure. In the final judgment to come, we will give a full account of our stewardship, at which time we will receive everlasting punishments or rewards.

Sermon 51

THE GOOD STEWARD

Give me an accounting of your management, because you cannot be my manager any longer. *(Luke 16:2)*

1. The relationship that we, the created, have to God, the Creator, is disclosed to us in the Bible in different ways. Picturing us as sinners and fallen beings, Scripture shows that we are *debtors* to our Creator. The Bible also pictures us as *servants*, which is an appropriate status for created beings. Furthermore, this designation was also given to the Son of God in his state of humiliation when he "took the form of a slave, being born in human likeness."

2. No description more precisely defines humankind in its present state than the designation of a *steward* (or *manager*). Our blessed Lord frequently identifies us in this way, and there is a special appropriateness in this designation. It is only in our particular state of sinfulness that we are called "debtors." And when we are called "servants," the designation is broad and vague. But a "steward" is a specific kind of servant. In every respect, we human beings are stewards. This term precisely describes our status in the present world. The word "steward" specifies the kind of servants we are and the kind of service God expects from us.

It may be useful, therefore, thoroughly to consider this matter and fully to develop it. We will consider (1) in what respects we are presently God's stewards, (2) the brief duration of our stewardship, (3) the final accounting of our stewardship, and (4) the precious nature of time.

I. The Nature of Our Stewardship

1. First, we will consider in what respects we are now God's stewards. We are indebted to God for all that we have. Although *debtors* are obligated to return what they have received, up until the time of repayment they are free to choose how they use what they have. The case is not the same with *stewards*. They are *not* at liberty to use as they please the things entrusted to them. They have no right to deal with anything in their charge, except according to the will of their master. Stewards are not the owners of any of the things entrusted to them by another. Their stewardship requires them to use what they have received according to their masters' orders.

This arrangement is exactly the case regarding all of us in our relationship with God. We are not at liberty to use as we wish what he has put in our hands. We are obligated to do what *he* pleases. God alone is the "maker of heaven and earth," and he is Lord over every one of us. Because we are not the owners of the things we have, we have no right to use them except in accordance with his will. As our Lord states, everything we have "belongs to another."

Strictly speaking, "in the land in which we reside as aliens," nothing is our own. We will not receive "private ownership of any possessions" until we arrive in our own country—heaven. In the present, the only things that belong to us are eternal things. God, who is the Manager and Lord of everything, merely entrusts us with temporal things. And he puts them into our care with the explicit condition that we use them only as belonging to our Master and according to the specific directions that he has given us in his Word.

2. On this condition, God has entrusted us with our souls, bodies, possessions, and whatever abilities we have received. Now, in

order to impress this important truth on our hearts, it is necessary to deal with some specific points. First, God has entrusted us with our *souls*, which are immortal spirits (together with all their powers and abilities) made in the image of God. We have comprehension, imagination, memory, will, and a sequence of affections. All these are either included in the soul or closely dependent on it. In the present, with regard to good and evil, we possess love and hate, joy, and sorrow. With respect to the future, we possess desire, aversion, hope, and fear. Saint Paul seems to include all these things in two words—hearts and minds: "The peace of God, which surpasses all understanding, will guard your hearts and your minds in Christ Jesus." Perhaps the term *minds* could be translated "thoughts," provided we understand the word in its most extensive sense to mean every active and passive perception of the mind.

3. It is certain that we are only stewards of all these things. God has entrusted us with these powers and the ability to employ them not according to our own wills but according to the explicit directions he gave us. Now, it is true that in doing God's will we most effectively obtain our own happiness. It is only in doing the will of God that we can be happy in time or eternity. Therefore, we should use our intelligence, imagination, and memory entirely for the glory of God who gave them.

In this way, we are to give our wills completely to him, and all our affections must be guided as he directs. We are to love and hate, rejoice and grieve, desire and shun, and hope and fear according to the rule prescribed by the one to whom we belong and whom we are to serve in all things. In the sense that they are not ours to use as we please, even our thoughts are not our own. We are accountable to our Great Master for every deliberate action of our minds.

4. Second, God entrusts us with our *bodies*—these incomparably formed instruments that are so "fearfully and wonderfully made" with all their abilities and components. God has entrusted us with the senses of touch, sight, hearing, and all our other abilities. However, he gave none of these things as our own to use according to our own wills. None of these abilities are loaned to us for a time with the freedom to employ them as we please. No,

we have received them on the condition that as long as we have them we must exercise them in the exact way that God directs, and no other.

5. On these same conditions, God has given us the most superior capacity for speech. An ancient writer said, "You have given me a tongue with which I can praise you."[7] God gave each of us the power of speech to be used to glorify him. Consequently, nothing is more ungrateful or absurd than to think or say, "My tongue is my own." That claim is not true, unless we have created ourselves and are therefore independent of the Most High God. No, "it is he who made us, and we are his." Because God created us, it is obvious that he is still Lord over us in our speech as he is in all other respects. It follows that there is not a word that we say for which we are not accountable to God.

6. We are equally accountable to God for the use of our hands and feet and all the members of our bodies. Our bodies are comprised of a certain number of abilities, which God has entrusted to us until the termination date set by the Father. Until then, we have the use of all these things—but as stewards, not as owners. God conferred abilities upon us so that we would "present our members to God as instruments of righteousness."

7. Third, God has consigned to us an allotment of *worldly goods*—food to eat, clothing to wear, and places to live. He has provided us with the necessities and the comforts of life. Above all, God has committed to our charge that precious gift that contains all the rest—*money*. Indeed, financial assets are indescribably precious if we are "faithful and prudent managers." Money is good only if we use it all for those purposes that our blessed Lord has commanded.

8. Fourth, God has entrusted us with several gifts that do not appropriately come under any of the categories already mentioned. I refer to such gifts as *physical energy; health, favorable appearance*, or *a good speaking voice*. We can also include such things as various degrees of *education* and *knowledge*, along with all their advantages. We have influence over others, whether due to their love and respect for us or to our ability to hurt or help them in life's circumstances.

Added to these gifts is the invaluable gift of *time*, which God entrusts to us moment by moment. Finally, we have a gift, on which all else depends and without which they would all be curses, not blessings. I am referring to the *grace of God* and *the power of his Holy Spirit* who alone works in all of us what is acceptable in his sight.

II. The Duration of Our Stewardship

1. In all these ways, we are managers for the Lord who is "the maker of heaven and earth." He has assigned to our stewardship a large portion of his various gifts. However, our standing as stewards will not continue forever (or indeed for any substantial amount of time). We have this trust only during the short, uncertain period in which we live here below. We are stewards only as long as we remain on earth, while this fleeting breath is in us. The hour is swiftly approaching (it is almost at hand) when we "cannot be his managers any longer." The moment "the dust returns to the earth as it was, and the breath returns to God who gave it," we will be no longer stewards. Then, the time of our stewardship will end. We will no longer have a part in those things that God entrusted to us. At least, as far as we are concerned, we no longer manage them. And those things that remain with us can no longer be used and developed as when we were on the earth.

2. As far as we are concerned, part of what God entrusts to us ends. After this life, what will we have to do with food, clothing, houses, and earthly possessions? "The food of the dead is the dust of the earth." The dead are clothed only with worms and decay. They live in "the house appointed for all living." Their lands have nothing more to do with them. All their worldly goods are transferred into other hands, and they "have no share in all that happens under the sun."

3. The same circumstances apply to the body. The moment the spirit returns to God, we are no longer stewards of this instrument. At death, it is "sown in weakness and dishonor." All the body's parts and members lie disintegrating in the clay. The hands no longer have strength to move; the feet have forgotten their pur-

pose; the flesh, tendons, and bones are all fast dissolving into ordinary dust.

4. Death also ends the combined gifts of strength, health, beauty, eloquence, and speech. We no longer have the ability to please, persuade, or convince others. Death also ends all the honors that we once enjoyed, all the power that God placed in our hands, and all the influence that we once had over others because of the love or esteem they had for us. Then, "our love, hate, and envy have already perished." People no longer regard how we once related to them. They look upon the dead as able neither to help nor to hurt them, "for a living dog is better than a dead lion."[8]

5. Perhaps there is doubt remaining about some of the other talents with which we are now entrusted as stewards. When our bodies return to dust, will they cease to exist or only cease to improve? Indeed, there is no doubt that when our organs of speech are destroyed, the kind of speech we now use will cease. It is certain that the tongue will no more cause any vibrations in the air. Neither will the ear convey these pulsating motions to the eardrum.

Even the "still small voice" that the poet supposes he hears from a separate spirit has no existence.[9] It is a mere flight of imagination. Indeed, we cannot doubt that departed spirits have some way to communicate their thoughts with one another. But can flesh and blood communicate in this way? The dead cannot have what we call "speech." Consequently, when we take our place among the dead, we can no longer be stewards of the gift of earthly speech.

6. It is also doubtful that our senses will exist when the organs of sense are destroyed. Is it not probable that the lower senses such as feeling, smell, and taste will cease? They have a more direct relationship to the body. Are they not mainly (if not completely) intended for its preservation?

Will not some kind of sight remain, however, even though the eye is closed in death? Will there not be something in the soul that is equivalent to the present sense of hearing? Indeed, is it not probable that these faculties will not only exist after death, but also continue in a far greater degree and in a more conspicuous manner than now? When the soul, free from its clay, is no longer as

> A dying sparkle in a cloudy place; [when it no longer]
> Looks through the windows of the eye and ear.[10]

After death, in a way that we cannot conceive, the soul is entirely eyes, ears, and consciousness.

Do we not have clear proof of the possibility of seeing without the use of the eye, and hearing without the use of the ear? Yes, we have a continuous sign of it. Does the soul not see in the clearest way when the eye is not in use—that is, in our dreams? In our dreaming, does the soul not enjoy the ability to hear without any help from the ear? In whatever way this kind of perceiving might take place, it is certain that after death, none of our senses will be entrusted to us in the way they now are.

7. We cannot say how much the knowledge or wisdom we have gained by education will remain. King Solomon said, "There is no work or thought or knowledge or wisdom in the grave, to which you are going." It is obvious, though, that his words cannot be understood in an absolute sense. The claim that we have no knowledge after we die is so far from being true that the doubt lies on the other side.

Will there be any such thing as real understanding until *after* we die? It is more likely a clear, solemn truth and not merely a poetic fiction that

> All these shadows which for things we take,
> Are but the empty dreams which in death's sleep we make.[11]

The only exceptions are those things that God himself has been pleased to reveal to us.

I will speak for myself. After having sought for truth with some diligence for half a century, I am now hardly sure of anything except what I learn from the Bible. I absolutely affirm that I know nothing else so certainly that I would dare to stake my salvation upon it.

This much, however, we can learn from King Solomon: "There is no work or thought or knowledge or wisdom in the grave" that will be of any use to unsaved souls.[12] After death, there are no means by which we can use those talents that God entrusted to us.

There will be no more time, and the period of our trial for everlasting happiness or misery is past. Our day will be over. The "day of salvation" will have ended. Nothing will remain but the Day of the Lord, which will usher in a vast and unchangeable eternity.

8. When our bodies have disintegrated into dust, our souls will retain all their faculties, because they are imperishable and immortal. They are of a nature that is "a little lower than God," even if we are to understand that phrase to refer to our original nature, which may well be doubtful. Our memory and comprehension will certainly not be destroyed or impaired by the disintegration of the body. On the contrary, we have reason to believe that they will be unimaginably strengthened.

Do we not have the clearest reason to believe that after death our souls will be completely freed from those defects that are now a consequence of the union of our souls with corruptible bodies? It is highly probable that from the time our souls and bodies are separated, our memories will forget nothing. Indeed, they will faithfully disclose everything that ever occurred in our lives.

It is true that in the Old Testament the invisible world is called "the land of forgetfulness." It is still more strongly stated in an old translation, "the land where all things are forgotten."[13] They are forgotten, but by whom? Not by the inhabitants of eternity, but by the inhabitants of the earth. It is with regard to people *on earth* that the unseen world is "the land of forgetfulness." All things in the next world are too frequently forgotten by people on earth, but not by disembodied spirits. From the time "the earthly tent we live in is destroyed," we can hardly suppose that the dead forget anything.

9. In the same respect, our comprehension will undoubtedly be freed from its present defects. For many ages, there has been an unquestioned maxim: "Ignorance and mistakes are inseparable from human nature." But this assertion is true only of the living and for as as long as "a perishable body weighs down the soul."[14] Ignorance is indeed a part of every finite person. We acknowledge that no one but God knows everything. (Mistakes, however, are not inevitable.) When we lay aside our bodies, we forsake ignorance forever.

10. What then can we say to "enlightened" persons who have recently made the "discovery" that disembodied spirits have no senses? According to them, the dead have no sight, hearing, memory, comprehension, thought, or recognition—not even a consciousness of their own existence! An ancient poet has said that we can call this state "a near kinsman of death," if it is not the same thing as death.[15] I can only conclude that speculative people sometimes dream strange things and then mistake their dreams for realities.

11. But let us return to our subject. Because the soul *will* retain its comprehension and memory even though the body disintegrates, without doubt the soul also retains the full vigor of its will and affections. If our love, anger, hope, or desire perish, it is only with regard to those that we leave behind. It does not matter to the departed whether they are the objects of our love, hate, desire, or dislike. However, we have no reason to believe that departed spirits have lost the capacity to think, sense, and feel. It is more probable that they function with far greater force than when the soul was limited by flesh and blood.

12. Although all these faculties (knowledge, thought, memory and comprehension, volition, love, hate, and all our affections) remain after the body is laid aside, in one respect we do not retain them. We are no longer stewards of them. These faculties continue, but our stewardship of them does not. We are no longer the stewards that once we were. Even the grace that was formerly given to us to enable us to be faithful and wise stewards is no longer granted to us for that purpose. In sum, the days of our stewardship will have ended.

III. The Final Accounting of Our Stewardship

1. After death, because we are no longer stewards we will "give an accounting of our management." Some people have assumed that this accounting will take place immediately after death, as soon as we enter into the world of spirits. The Church of Rome absolutely asserts this view and even makes it an article of faith. We can acknowledge this much: The moment a soul leaves the

body and stands exposed before God, it will certainly know where it shall be for all eternity. It will have a full view of either everlasting joy or everlasting torment. At the time of death, it is no longer possible to be deceived concerning the judgment that we have brought upon ourselves.

Scripture gives us no reason to believe that God will immediately sit in judgment upon us at that time. There is no passage in the Bible that affirms any such thing. Those scriptures that have often been used to support this idea actually prove the opposite. One such scripture is the following: "It is appointed for mortals to die once, and after that the judgment." Reason confirms that the word "once" applies both to judgment as well as to death. Therefore, the objective inference to be drawn from this text is not that there are *two* judgments—a general judgment and a particular judgment. Instead, the text states that we are once to die and once to be judged.

We will not be judged once immediately after death and again after the general resurrection. Rather, we are judged "when the Son of Man comes in his glory, and all the angels with him." Therefore, those who make the written Word of God the entire and only standard of their faith cannot accept the speculation that there is one judgment at death and a second judgment at the end of the world.

2. We are to give the account of our stewardship when the "great white throne and the one who sat on it come down from heaven, and the earth and the heaven flee from God's presence, and no place is found for them." At that time "the dead, great and small, will stand before the throne, and books will be opened." The "books" spoken of are the *scriptures* (for those to whom the Bible has been entrusted) and the *conscience* of all humankind.

In addition, the "book of remembrance" (to use another scriptural expression) will then be laid open to the view of everyone. This volume has been written from the foundation of the world. The book of remembrance will be opened before the entire human race, the devil and his demons, innumerable holy angels, and God, the Judge of all. Without any shelter, covering, or disguise, you will appear at this judgment to give a particular account of the way you have used all your Lord's goods.

3. God, the judge of all, will then ask, "How did you use your life? I entrusted you with an immortal spirit, endowed with various powers and abilities. I gave you comprehension, imagination, memory, will, and emotions. I gave you complete and explicit directions as to how you were to use these endowments. Did you use your comprehension, as far as it was capable, according to my directions?"

God will ask, "Did you come really to know yourself and me? Did you come to understand my nature, attributes, and works—whether of creation, providence, or grace? Did you become familiar with my Word? Did you use every means to increase your knowledge of Scripture? Did you meditate on it day and night? Did you use your memory according to my will? Did you retain whatever knowledge you acquired that might promote my glory, your own salvation, and the benefit of others? Did you accumulate in your memory not worthless things of no value, but whatever instructions you learned from my Word and whatever experience you gained of my wisdom, truth, power, and mercy? Did you use your imagination to conceive empty dreams or plans that fed senseless and harmful desires?"

The Lord will inquire, "Did you use your imagination to think about those things that would benefit your soul and nourish your pursuit of wisdom and holiness? Did you follow my directions with regard to the use of your will? Was it completely surrendered to me? Was your will absorbed in mine, so that you never opposed my purpose, but always lived in harmony with it?"

God will also ask, "Were your affections directed and ordered in the way that I designated in my Word? Did you give me your heart? Did you reject the world and the things of the world? Did you make me the object of your love? Was all your desire for me and for the remembrance of my name? Was I the joy of your heart, the delight of your soul, and the chief among ten thousand? Did you sorrow over nothing except the things that grieved my spirit? Did you fear and hate nothing but sin? Did the entire stream of your affections flow back into the ocean from which they came? Were your thoughts directed according to my will—not in ranging to the ends of the earth to think about foolishness and sin? Rather, were your thoughts fixed on 'whatever is true, whatever is honorable, whatever is just, whatever is pure, whatever is pleasing, and whatever is commendable'? Did you focus on what contributed to my glory and to 'peace among those whom I favor'?"

4. In that day, your Lord will ask you, "How did you use the body I entrusted to you? I gave you a tongue with which to praise me. Did you use it for this purpose? Did you refrain from using your tongue in evil or idle-speaking and unkind or empty conversation? Instead, did you use your tongue in ways that were good, substantive, and beneficial to yourself and to others? Directly or indirectly, did your words always give grace to those who hear? Together with your other senses, I gave you those wonderful avenues of comprehension, sight, and hearing. Did you use them for the righteous purposes for which I intended? Did these faculties bring you more and more training in true righteousness and holiness?

"I gave you hands, feet, and various members with which to accomplish the works I prepared for you to do. Did you refrain from using these faculties, by doing 'the will of the flesh,' the will of your evil nature, or your own will—the things to which your reason or whims led you? Or, did you use your body to do the will of him who sent you into the world, which is to work out your own salvation? Did you present all the members of your body, not to sin as instruments of unrighteousness, but to me alone through my beloved son as instruments of righteousness?"

5. Next, the Lord of all will ask, "How did you use the worldly goods that I placed in your hands? Did you use your food, not primarily as a means for your pleasure, but as a means to preserve your body in health, strength, and stamina—a healthy instrument for your soul? Did you use clothing to nourish pride, feed self-esteem, or tempt others to sin—or, did you use your clothing appropriately and fittingly to protect yourself from harmful weather? Did you arrange and use your house and all other conveniences with a single eye to my glory? In every way, did you seek your own honor, or did you seek my honor?[16] Did you do your best not to please yourself, but to please me?

"Again, how did you use that important gift of money? Did you refrain from using it to gratify the desire of the flesh, the desire of the eye, or the pride of life? Did you refrain from wasting it on worthless expenses, which is equal to throwing your money into the sea? Did you refuse to hoard it up in order to leave it behind you, which is the same as burying it in the earth? Did you first provide for your own reasonable needs and then the needs of your family? Then, did you return the rest to me by providing for the poor that I appointed to receive it?

"Did you regard yourself as only *one* of the poor whose needs were to be supplied out of that part of my provisions that I put into your hands? God has left you the right to be supplied first, and then to know the blessedness of giving rather than receiving. Accordingly, were you a general benefactor of humankind? Did you feed the hungry, cloth the naked, comfort the sick, assist the stranger, and relieve the sick according to their various needs? Were you 'eyes to the blind, and feet to the lame'? Were you 'a father to the fatherless, and a husband to the widow'? Did you work to use all outward acts of mercy as a means of 'saving souls from death'?"

6. Your Lord will also ask: "Have you been a wise and faithful steward of the combined gifts that I loaned to you? Did you refrain from using your health and strength in foolishness or sin—those pleasures that 'perish with use'? Did you refrain from 'making provision for the flesh, to gratify its desires'? Did you zealously seek the better things that cannot be taken away from you? Did you use for me what was pleasing in your appearance or voice? Did you employ your educational advantages, learning, and understanding of people and things to promote virtue in the world and to increase my kingdom? Did you use whatever share of power and influence you had (due to people's love or respect of you) to increase their wisdom and holiness? Did you use the priceless gift of time with caution and prudence, carefully considering the value of every moment, knowing that every minute is numbered in eternity? Above all, were you a good steward of my grace that preceded, accompanied, and followed you?"

When we stand before God, he will also ask, "Did you properly recognize and carefully employ all the influences of my Spirit? Did you use every good desire, measure of light, and the Spirit's sharp or gentle rebukes? How did you benefit from 'a spirit of slavery and fear' that preceded 'the Spirit of adoption'? Did you stand firm in the glorious liberty that I gave you when I made you a partaker of the Holy Spirit who cried 'Abba! Father!'? From that time forward, did you present your soul and body, and all your thoughts, words, and actions in one flame of love as a holy sacrifice, glorifying me with your body and your spirit?"

If so, God will declare, "Well done, good and trustworthy servant; enter into the joy of your Master." For both the faithful and unfaithful stewards, the decision of the righteous Judge will be carried out. This judgment will assign you to a state that allows no change through the everlasting ages. It only remains for you through all eternity to receive the results of the works you did on earth.

IV. The Value of Time

1. From these clear considerations we can learn, first, the importance of this short, uncertain day of life! How precious, beyond all understanding and description, is every moment of time!

> The least of these a serious care demands;
> For though they are little, they are golden sands![17]

How very important it is for us all, for as long as we have God's breath within us, to waste no time but to use it for the highest of God's purposes!

2. Second, we learn that in using time, no word or deed is truly unimportant. Everything that we do is either good or bad. All our time, as is the case with all that we have, is not our own. As our Lord said, everything that we have "belongs to another"—God our Creator. What we have either is or is not used according to his will. If our minutes are engaged in good things, everything is good. If our minutes are not engaged in good things, all of them are evil.

Again, God wills that we should continually grow in grace and in the living knowledge of our Lord Jesus Christ. Consequently, every thought, word, and deed by which we increase this knowledge and grow in grace is good. Everything that does not improve us in this way is positively and properly evil.

3. Third, we learn that there are no works of supererogation (works that produce "excess merit"). We can never do more than our duty, because everything we have belongs not to us, but to God. All that we are able to do depends on him. We have not received just *some* things from God. The whole of life comes from him, and we owe the entire sum to him. God who gives us everything has a right to everything.

Therefore, if we give him anything less than all that we are and all that we have, we cannot be "faithful stewards." We know that "each will receive wages according to the labor of each." So, we cannot be wise stewards unless we labor to the utmost of our energy, not leaving anything undone that we can possibly do, but expending all our strength.

4. Brothers and sisters, "who is wise and understanding among you?" Let us all bring to light the wisdom from above by living in wisdom's ways. If we consider ourselves as stewards of God's many gifts, let us make sure that all our thoughts, words, and deeds conform to the calling that God has assigned to us.

It is not an easy thing to give back to God all that we have received from him. This work will require all our wisdom, perseverance, patience, and faithfulness. Good stewardship requires more than we naturally have within ourselves, but not more than we receive from grace. God's grace is sufficient for us, and we know that "all things can be done for the one who believes." Therefore, by faith "put on the Lord Jesus Christ." "Put on the whole armor of God," and he will enable you to glorify him in all your words and deeds. You will be able to "take every thought captive to obey Christ."

Edinburgh
May 14, 1768

Notes

1. Telford, *Wesley's Letters*, June 26, 1790, 8:225.
2. Jackson, *Wesley's Works*, "A Plain Account of Christian Perfection," §2, 11:366.

3. Ward and Heitzenrater, *Wesley's Journals and Diaries,* May 14, 1768, 22:133.

4. James Boswell, *The Life of Samuel Johnson, LLD. Comprehending an Account of his Studies and Numerous Works, in Chronological Order; a Series of his Epistolary Correspondence and Conversations with Many Eminent Persons; and Various Original Pieces of his Composition, Never Before Published: the Whole Exhibiting a View of Literature and Literary Men in Great Britain, for Near Half a Century, During which he Flourished,* 4 vols., 3rd rev. and augmented ed. (London: Printed by Henry Baldwin for Charles Dilly, 1799).

5. Ward and Heitzenrater, *Wesley's Journals and Diaries,* May 15, 1768, 22:134.

6. Ibid., November 5, 1771, 22:296.

7. Augustine, *Confessions,* Book 5, §1. *Nicene and Post-Nicene Fathers,* First Series, 14 vols., ed. Philip Schaff (Peabody, Mass.: Hendrickson Publishers, 1994), 1:79. Augustine wrote, "Accept the sacrifice of my confessions by the agency of my tongue, which Thou has formed and quickened, that it may confess to Thy name."

8. Eccles. 9:4.

9. The phrase "still small voice" first appeared in 1 Kings 19:12. The poet to whom Wesley refers may be Thomas Gray (1716–71), who used this phrase in his work *Ode for Music,* v, l. 8.

10. John Davies [1569–1626], *The Original, Nature, and Immortality of the Soul: A Poem: With an Introduction Concerning Human Knowledge,* 2nd ed. (London: Printed by S. Keimer for Hammond Banks, 1714), *Know Thyself,* Part 1, stanza 17.

11. Abraham Cowley [1618–67], *The Poems of Abraham Cowley,* 3 vols. (Chiswick, England: Press of C. Whittingham, 1822), "Pindarique Odes" (1656), II, 22, 23.

12. Eccles. 9:10.

13. Book of Common Prayer, 1662 edition, Ps. 88:12.

14. Wisd. of Sol. 9:15.

15. Virgil, *The Aeneid of Virgil,* trans. John Dryden (Franklin Center, Pa.: Franklin Library, 1982), vi, 278.

16. Sir. 47:20.

17. John Gambold, "Upon Listening to the Vibrations of a Clock," in John Wesley, *A Collection of Moral and Sacred Poems from the Most Celebrated English Authors,* 3 vols. (Bristol: Printed by Felix Farley, 1744), 3:195.

Introduction to Sermon 52

THE REFORMATION OF MANNERS

Although John Wesley was noted for the widespread development of Methodist societies, he did not originate religious societies. They existed in the Church of England before he was born. As early as 1678, Dr. Anthony Horneck, Dr. William Smythies, and Dr. William Beveridge had pioneered the establishment of small religious societies within the Anglican Church.[1] John Wesley's father, Samuel, had been a member of one of these societies. Members met weekly for prayer and Christian fellowship. The groups also gathered regular collections for the needy and did good works among the poor. These religious societies suffered a temporary setback during the reign of the unsympathetic Roman Catholic James II, who ruled in England from 1685 to 1688. After he fled to France, England's religious societies again flourished. National societies also emerged, including the Society for Promoting Christian Knowledge (1698) and the Society for the Propagation of the Gospel in Foreign Parts (1701).

Another of these pre-Wesleyan societies was the Society for the Reformation of Manners, organized in the late seventeenth century. In 1701, an early account of these societies states,

> The *Societies for Reformation* bent their utmost Endeavours from the first to supress *publick Vice*; whilst the *Religious Societies*

> endeavour'd chiefly to promote a due sense of *Religion* in their own Breasts, tho' they have since been eminently instrumental in the publick Reformation.[2]

In 1691, Archbishop John Tillotson and Bishop Edward Stillingfleet had convinced Queen Anne to write letters to public officials, admonishing them to enforce existing laws against public vices. Practices of particular concern were public drunkenness, prostitution, open swearing, and operating businesses on Sundays. In 1692, the members of England's religious societies founded several local chapters of the Society for the Reformation of Manners for the explicit purpose of curbing public vice. The Lord Mayor of London and the city's aldermen prepared and distributed a summary of the city's statutes prohibiting public immoralities. To enforce existing moral standards, civil authorities drafted rules for the conviction and punishment of those who engaged in open immorality. Because of these efforts, civic leaders shut down several businesses and public markets that operated on Sunday. Civil authorities also prosecuted and punished a number of proprietors of brothels. Christian workers in these societies helped hundreds of prostitutes find respectable employment and led many public offenders to faith in Christ. At the end of the seventeenth century, Thomas Bray evaluated the results of this work:

> [The society for the Reformation of manners] had prospered to a degree exceedingly great, beyond what human wisdom did or could expect. . . . More than twenty thousand persons had been convicted of swearing, cursing, and profanation of the Lord's day in and about London and Westminster. . . . About three thousand lewd and disorderly persons had been punished within the same limits.[3]

Customarily, an annual sermon was preached before the national meeting of the local chapters of the Society for the Reformation of Manners. In 1698, Samuel Wesley, the father of John and Charles Wesley, delivered the sermon. For his text Samuel chose Psalm 94:16, "Who will rise up for me against the wicked?"[4] In 1763, John Wesley was called on to preach this annual sermon, and he used the same text that his father had used sixty-five years earlier. Indeed, much of the content of the two sermons is similar.

The present sermon first traces the history of the Society for the Reformation of Manners and then details some of the vices publicly practiced in Wesley's day. (Pictorial illustrations of these immoralities were graphically drawn in the popular eighteenth-century engravings of William Hogarth in such pictures as *Gin Lane*, *Beer Street*, and *Industry and Idleness*.) This sermon also recalls the immense public good done by the Society for the Reformation of Manners. Wesley writes, "Taking an open stand against all the ungodliness and unrighteousness that cover our land as a flood is one of the noblest ways of confessing Christ." The sermon speaks of the enormous benefits to a nation's culture when public immoralities are eliminated. Wesley goes on to defend the activities of the Society as entirely appropriate work for serious Christians.

Wesley moves on in this message to talk about the qualifications of those who wish to become members of the Society for the Reformation of Manners:

> Whoever lives in any known sin is not fit to engage in the work of reforming sinners. These people have no part in the society, especially if they are guilty in any sense or degree of profaning the name of God, or buying, selling, or doing any unnecessary work on the Lord's day. They should not be members if they are guilty of anything else that the society is particularly organized to reform. No! Let none who need to be reformed presume to intrude into the work of the reformation of public manners. First, let them "take the log out of their own eyes." Let them in all things be without blame.

Finally, Wesley advises and exhorts the society to exercise care and caution in the choice of those they admit as members:

> Examine carefully whether the proposed member is a person of flawless bearing and faith, courage, patience, and balance. Insist that new members love God and humankind. If they possess these qualities, they will add to your strength as well as membership. If you admit unqualified persons, you will lose more than you will gain.

Wesley concludes the sermon by reminding the members to do all their work in the love of Christ and with goodwill toward all to whom they minister. The sermon contains principles to keep in mind if one intends to become actively involved in addressing public vice and improving the morals and manners of society.

Sermon 52

THE REFORMATION OF MANNERS

Who rises up for me against the wicked? (*Psalm 94:16*)

1 In all ages, those "who neither feared God nor had respect for people" have joined to form alliances to carry on the works of darkness. In their work, they have shown themselves wise in their generations. Through their shrewd organization, they have promoted the kingdom of their father, the devil, more effectively than they could otherwise have done individually.

On the other hand, in every age, those who feared God and desired the well-being of others have found it necessary to join together to oppose the works of darkness, spread the knowledge of God their Savior, and promote his kingdom in the world. Indeed, the Lord himself has instructed us to work to establish his kingdom on earth. From the time that God created humankind, he has instructed us to join in his service, and he has bound us together in one body by one spirit. God has united us in order "to destroy the works of the devil." First, God acts to destroy Satan's labors in those who are already joined in Christ. Then, God works through his unified people to minister to those around them.

2. God's original plan was for the church of Christ to function as a body of those who are linked together in order, first, to save their own souls. Then, God instructs the members of this body of God's people to help others to work out their salvation. And thereafter, by overthrowing the kingdom of Satan and establishing the kingdom of Christ, they are, as far as possible, to save everyone else from present and future misery. This task should be the continuing responsibility and work of all members of his church. Otherwise, we are not worthy to be called constituents of the church because we are not truly active members of Christ's body.

3. Accordingly, this work should be the unceasing responsibility and work of all those who are united together in our realm in the Church of England. Believers are united together for the very purpose of opposing the devil and all his works. Christians are to wage war against the world and the flesh, which are Satan's constant and faithful allies.

Do the members of the church fulfill their callings as parts of this body? Are all who call themselves "members of the Church of England" heartily engaged in opposing the works of the devil and fighting against the world and the flesh? I fear that we cannot say that they do this work. Some of them (I fear most of them) are so far from fulfilling their calling that they themselves belong to the world. They are joined with those who do not know God in a saving way. Day after day, they are indulging themselves instead of "crucifying the flesh with its passions and desires." They are doing those very works of the devil that God specifically commissioned them to destroy.

4. Therefore, even in this "Christian country" (as we politely call Great Britain), there is still a clear need in our Christian church (if we can give that title to the mass of our nation). We need Christians who will "rise up against the wicked" and "band together to stand against evildoers." Indeed, there has never been a greater need than there is today for "those who revere the LORD to speak with one another" on the very subject of how they can lift up a banner against the iniquity that covers the land. There are many reasons for all the servants of God to join together against the works of the devil. With united hearts, deliberations, and

labors, they need to take a stand for God and, to the best of their abilities, restrain the "torrents of perdition."

5. For this purpose, toward the close of the seventeenth century, a few persons in London came together and formed the Society for Reformation of Manners. For nearly forty years, this society accomplished incredible good. Then, most of the original members went to their eternal reward, and those who followed them "grew weary and lost heart," and they left the work. A few years ago, the society came to an end, and none of its work remained in our country.

6. Recently, a similar society has been formed. In this sermon, I intend to clarify (1) the plan of the society members and the steps they have already taken, (2) the excellence of their effort and the objections raised against it, (3) the kind of people who should be engaged in this work, and (4) the spirit and manner with which we should proceed with this enterprise. I will conclude with an encouragement for them and for all who honor God.

I. The Rise and Development of the Society

1. First, I will explain the nature of the work of the Society for the Reformation of Manners and its history. On a Lord's Day in August 1757, a small company met for prayer and religious conversation. At that meeting, there was discussion of the flagrant and open desecration of the Lord's Day. On Sunday, people were buying and selling; keeping their shops open; drinking in alehouses; and standing or sitting in the streets, roads, or fields; and selling their wares just as if it were not the day of rest.

These practices were outrageous, especially in Moorfields, in which every Sunday was full of these vices. Those present at that meeting of concerned Christians discussed the steps they could take to remedy these evils. They agreed that in the morning, six of those present would visit Sir John Fielding for guidance.[5] They did so, and Mr. Fielding approved of their plan and advised them on how to implement it.

2. First, they delivered petitions to the right honorable Lord Mayor, the Court of Aldermen, and the Justices sitting at Hicks's

Hall and in Westminster Hall. They received from all these honorable offices much encouragement to proceed.

3. Next, it was judged appropriate to disclose their plan to many persons in high positions, to the body of the clergy, and to the ministers of other denominations in and around the cities of London and Westminster. The organizers of the Society were gratified with the enthusiastic consent and general approval they received from those with whom they conversed.

4. Then, at their own expense they printed and distributed to sheriffs and other parish officials several thousand instruction books that recommended duties for them. These books encouraged their cooperation in this work. As far as possible, these organizers sought to avoid the need to enforce the laws. Therefore, they printed and distributed throughout the city exhortations against the desecration of Sunday, extracts from Acts of Parliament against profaning the Lord's Day, and notices to the offenders.

5. The effort to restore respect for the Lord's Day was paved by the preparations mentioned above. Those who profaned the day received repeated notices, which again and again they ignored. Then, in the beginning of 1758, the Society reported to the magistrates the names of those who profaned the Lord's Day. By this means, they first cleared the streets and fields of those notorious offenders who, without any regard either for God or for the king, sold their wares on Sunday from morning to night.

Next, the Society progressed to the more difficult task of preventing drinking alcohol by those who spent time in alehouses that ought to have been spent in the direct worship of God. In this effort, the members of the Society were exposed to much criticism, invectives, and every kind of abuse. Opposition came from the heavy drinkers, the alehouse keepers who served them, and the rich and distinguished people (including the landlords of the alehouse keepers) who supported the sale of alcohol. In general, everyone who profited by these sins objected to the Society's efforts to stop the drinking of alcohol on Sunday.

Some of those who opposed Sunday observance were not only people of wealth but also people in authority. Indeed, those opposed to Sunday observance were often the very people before whom the guilty were taken. These officials gave the members of the Society for the Reformation of Manners such ill treatment that they naturally encouraged those citizens who lived like animals to follow their example and treat members of the Society as people who were not fit to live upon the earth. These mobs did not hesitate to abuse Society members with disgraceful language. They threw at them mud, stones, or whatever they had. Many times they beat them without mercy and dragged them over the stones or through the gutters of the street. That these mobs did not murder some of the members of the Society was not due to their lack of desire. Only the threat of penalties stopped them.

6. God helped the Society in its work, and the members also organized to stop the bakers from spending so much of the Lord's Day in their work. Many of the bakers were more virtuous than the tavernkeepers. They did not resent the work of the Society or regard it as a nuisance. Several of the bakers who had been pressured by custom to act against their consciences sincerely thanked the Society members for their work and acknowledged it as a genuine kindness.

7. In clearing the streets, fields, and alehouses of Sabbath-breakers, the Society discovered other kinds of offenders equally harmful to society. These people played various games of chance. Some of these citizens were of the lowest and vilest class, commonly called "gamblers." They made a business of preying on young and inexperienced men and cheating them out of all their money. After they made them destitute, they frequently taught them the same "mystery of lawlessness." The Society for the Reformation of Manners rooted out several nests of gamblers and caused some of them to earn their bread honestly by the sweat of their brow and the labors of their hands.

8. As the Society increased in numbers and strength, it enlarged its mission and began to suppress profane public swearing and to remove from the streets another public nuisance and scandal to Christians—common prostitutes. Many of these women, although still active, were persuaded to stop their brazen wickedness. In order to get to the root of this plague, many of the houses of pros-

titution were discovered, prosecuted according to law, and closed. Some of these poor, forlorn women, although having fallen to "the lowest line of human infamy," have acknowledged the gracious providence of God, and by lasting repentance they have left their sins. Several of these women have been successfully placed into Magdalen Hospital, a home for reformed prostitutes.

9. If a little digression can be permitted, who can adequately appreciate the wisdom of divine providence in arranging times and seasons to meet particular needs as they arose? For instance, at the very time that many of these poor women were rescued from their life of sin and came to desire a better life, they faced a difficult matter. They asked, "If I abandon prostitution, what can I do for a living? I am not skilled in any trade, and I have no friends who will take me in." At this very time, God has provided Magdalen Hospital. Here, those prostitutes who have no trade or friends to take them in are received with all kindness. They can live there in comfort, being provided with "everything needed for life and godliness."

10. Now to return to this history of the Society for the Reformation of Manners, the numbers of people brought to justice are as follows:

From August 1757 to August 1762	9,596
From that time to the present:	
For unlawful gambling and blasphemous swearing	40
For Sabbath-breaking	400
Lewd women and keepers of houses of prostitution	550
For offering to sell pornographic pictures	2
Total	10,588

11. The Society accepts into its membership people from any religious denomination or political party. Whoever on examination is found to be a good person is freely admitted. None who have selfish or monetary concerns will remain members very long because they can gain nothing through their membership. They will soon lose money, for they must become subscribers as soon as they become members.

The common cry is: "These are all *Whitfelites.*" That notion is mistaken, however. Only about twenty of the regularly subscribing members are connected with Mr. George Whitefield. About fifty are connected with me. About twenty members, who are members of the established Church, have no connection with either Mr. Whitefield or me; and about seventy members are dissenters,[6] bringing the total membership to 160. There are indeed many more people who assist in the work by their occasional subscriptions.

II. The Excellence of the Society

1. The steps that I have described have been taken by the Society. Now, in the second place, I will clarify the value of the Society, despite the objections that others have raised against it. Several considerations will demonstrate the value of the Society. First, one of the noblest ways of confessing Christ in the presence of his enemies is by taking an open stand against all the ungodliness and unrighteousness that cover our land as a flood. This testimony brings glory to God and witnesses to everyone that, even in these depraved times,

> All are not of thy Train; there be, who Faith
> Prefer, and Piety to God.[7]

What is more admirable than to "ascribe to the LORD the glory due his name"? What is more noble than to affirm by suffering and risking every hazard (a stronger evidence than words)?

> Surely there is a reward for the righteous;
> Surely there is a God who judges on earth.[8]

2. How worthy is this plan to prevent in any degree possible the dishonor of God's glorious name and the contempt poured out on his authority! How noble it is to stop the scandal brought upon our holy religion by the outrageous, flagrant wickedness of those who are still called by the name of Christ! No greater plan can possibly be conceived in a human heart than to any degree to stop

the flow of wickedness, to restrain the floods of ungodliness, and in any measure to remove those causes that "blaspheme the excellent name that was invoked over us"!

3. Because this intention obviously tends to bring "glory to God in the highest heaven," it no less evidently assists in establishing "peace on earth." By openly defying him, all sin tends directly to destroy our peace with God, expel peace from our own hearts, and set people's swords against their neighbors. Therefore, to the same degree, whatever prevents or removes public evil tends to promote peace in our own souls, peace with God, and peace with one another. We see these genuine fruits of the Society for the Reformation of Manners in our nation today.

Why should we confine our survey to the narrow confines of time and space? Instead, let us look also into eternity. What fruit of the Society will we find there? Let the apostle James speak: "My brothers and sisters, if anyone among you wanders from the truth and is brought back by another [not to this or that opinion, but to *God*!], you should know that whoever brings back a sinner from wandering will save the sinner's soul from death and will cover a multitude of sins."

4. The benefits of this Society do not extend just to individuals such as those who mislead others into sin or those who are likely to be betrayed and destroyed by them. The benefits of the work of the Society come to the entire community of which we are members. Is it not certain that "righteousness exalts a nation, but sin is a reproach to any people"? Indeed, is it not true that sin brings down the curse of God upon nations?

For that reason, to the extent that any kind of righteousness is promoted, the national interest is advanced. So far as sin (especially open sin) is restricted, its curse and condemnation are removed from us. Therefore, those who labor to restrain sin are general benefactors of the nation. They are the truest friends of their government and country. To the degree that their plans succeed, God will doubtless grant national prosperity in fulfillment of his reliable word, "Those who honor me I will honor."

5. Someone may object, "However excellent a plan you may have, public morality is not really your concern. Are there not

people whose formal responsibility is to control public offenses and to punish the offenders? Are there not sheriffs and other public officers that are bound by oath to do this very work?"

I answer, "Yes, there are." In particular, sheriffs and church superintendents are pledged by solemn oaths to give appropriate testimony against those who profane the Lord's Day and against all other scandalous sinners as well. However, some neglect their work and, despite their promises, they do not trouble themselves with fulfilling their responsibilities.

It follows that this enterprise concerns all who honor God, love humankind, and wish for the well-being of their government and nation. They should pursue the work with the very same energy as if there were no such officers. If people do not do their assigned work, it is the same as if they did not exist.

6. Some may object, "The work of the Society for the Reformation of Manners is only a pretext. The members' true intent is to get money by informing on others."

I answer that this charge has been made frequently and widely, but without the slightest shadow of truth. A thousand instances prove the very opposite. No member of the Society takes any part of the money that the law allots to the informers. From the beginning, they have never done so, and none of them have ever received any money to conceal or reveal information. This charge is a mistake (if not willful slander), for which there is not the slightest foundation.

7. Another might object, "But the plan is unworkable. Corruption has risen to such heights that it is impossible to restrain it, especially by the means used by the Society. What can a handful of poor people do in opposition to all the world?"

I answer, "For mortals it is impossible, but for God all things are possible." The members of the society trust not in themselves, but in God. However strong the patrons of wickedness may be, to God they are no more than grasshoppers. All their resources make no difference to God. "Nothing can hinder the LORD from saving by many or by few." Therefore, the small number of those who are on the Lord's side is nothing to God, and neither is the great number of those who are against him. God still does whatever pleases him. "No wisdom, understanding, or counsel can prevail against the LORD."

8. Still another critic might say, "If the goal you seek is really to reform sinners, you are choosing the wrong means. The Word of God, and not human laws, must lead to this goal. Furthermore, saving souls is the work of ministers, not of public judges. Therefore, your methods can produce only an outward reformation. The offenders have no change of heart."

I respond to this point of view by saying that ordinarily it is true that the Word of God is the chief means by which God changes the hearts and lives of sinners, and he does this mainly by ministers of the gospel. It is likewise true that public judges are also "the ministers of God." God ordained that "rulers are a terror not to good conduct, but to bad" by enforcing human laws upon the wicked. Even if the enforcement of the law does not change the heart, a valuable purpose is gained when outward sin is prevented. As public sins decline, there is less insult to God, less scandal to our holy religion, less curse and condemnation upon our nation, and less temptation laid in the way of others. Indeed, for the coming day of wrath, there is less condemnation heaped up by the sinners on themselves.

9. Some may object and say, "No. Sinners lay up for themselves *more* condemnation. Public laws only make hypocrites out of many of them because they pretend to be what they are not. Others of them who are ashamed and caused to lose money become insolent and dangerous in wickedness. So, in reality none of the sinners are any better off. They may be worse than they were before."

I answer that this view is full of mistakes: (1) Where are these hypocrites you speak about? We do not know any who pretend to be what they are not. (2) Putting obstinate offenders to shame and causing them to lose money does not make them dangerous offenders; it causes them to become afraid of transgressing the law. (3) Some of them, far from becoming worse, have become significantly better, and the entire direction of their lives has changed. (4) Indeed, some have inwardly changed "from darkness to light and from the power of Satan to God."

10. The critic may say, "Many people are not convinced that buying or selling on the Lord's Day is a sin."

I answer that if they are not convinced, they *ought* to be. It is high time that they should. The matter is as clear as it can be. If an open, willful violation of the law of God and the law of the land is not sin, I ask what sin is. Furthermore, if a violation of divine and human laws is not to be punished because a person is not convinced it is a sin, that state of affairs brings to an end all implementation of justice. People would then live as they please.

11. Someone may say, "But first we should try easygoing methods."

I reply that we should, and we do. A mild admonition is given to every offender before the law is implemented against him or her. People are never prosecuted until they are specifically notified that this will be the case, unless they halt their prosecution by stopping the sin that causes it. In every case, the mildest warning that the case will allow is given to the offenders. More severe means are never used, except when they are absolutely necessary to stop the transgression.

12. Someone may complain, "After all this excitement about reformation, what real good has been done?"

I reply that indescribable good is done. Considering the small number of workers and the difficulties they must encounter, abundantly more good is accomplished than anyone could have expected in such a short time.

The Society for the Reformation of Manners has prevented and removed much public evil. Many sinners have been outwardly reformed, and some have been inwardly changed. The honor of God, whose name we bear, has been openly ignored, and it has been openly defended. It is not easy to determine how many important blessings may already have come upon our entire nation due to this small stand made for God and his cause against his shameless enemies. On the whole, despite all the objections that can be made, reasonable people can still conclude that a better method for addressing public immoralities could hardly ever enter into the human heart.

III. The Membership of the Society

1. What kinds of people are needed to accomplish the plan of the Society for the Reformation of Manners? Some may think that any who are willing to assist in this work should immediately be admitted. They assume that the greater the number of members, the greater will be their influence. But this assumption is not at all true. The facts undeniably prove the opposite. When the former Society consisted only of selected members (even though most of them were not rich or powerful), they overcame all opposition and were exceptionally successful in every aspect of their endeavor. When a number of less carefully chosen people were accepted into the Society, however, they grew less and less useful. Gradually, the original Society dwindled into nothing.

2. The number of members, therefore, is no more of a consideration than riches or rank. This work belongs to God, and we undertake it in his name and for his sake. Consequently, people who neither love nor fear God "have no part or share" in this work. God can say to these people: "What right have you to recite my statutes or take my covenant on your lips? For you hate discipline, and you cast my words behind you."[9]

Whoever lives in any known sin is not fit to engage in the work of reforming transgressors. Such people have no part in the Society, especially if they are guilty in any sense or degree of profaning the name of God, or buying, selling, or doing any unnecessary work on the Lord's Day. They should not be members if they are guilty of anything that the Society is particularly organized to reform. No! Let none who need to be reformed presume to intrude into the work of the reformation of public manners. First, let them "take the log out of their own eyes." Let them in all things "be without blame."

3. Even this qualification is not enough for membership in the Society. All those who engage in this work should go beyond being innocent people. They should be persons of *faith*. At the least, they need some measure of a "conviction of things not seen." Because of their faith, they "look not at what can be seen, but at what cannot be seen; for what can be seen is temporary, but what cannot be seen is eternal." They need a faith that produces a steadfast fear of God and, by his grace, an enduring resolve to

abstain from all that he has forbidden. Also, they need a determination to do everything that he has commanded.

Members of the Society more especially need a faith that maintains "confidence in God." This kind of faith "removes mountains," "quenches the raging fire," and breaks through all opposition. This faith enables "one to put to flight a thousand." People with this kind of faith know in whom their strength lies, and even when they have "received the sentence of death they do not rely on themselves but on God who raises the dead."

4. Those who have faith and confidence in God will become people of *courage*. Bravery is necessary for everyone who engages in this work. In undertaking the ministry of the Society, many things will occur that are offensive to human nature. Indeed, the challenges are so frightful that all who seek human counsel will fear to face the public offenders. This work requires an authentic courage of the highest degree. This kind of bravery comes only through faith. A true believer can say,

> I fear no denial;
> No danger I fear:
> Nor flee from the trial;
> While Jesus is near.[10]

5. The virtue of courage is closely connected to *patience*. While courage faces future challenges, patience faces present challenges. Those who join in carrying forward the purpose of the Society will greatly need persistence and fortitude. Although they are without blame, they will find themselves precisely in the situation of Ishmael: "with their hands against everyone, and everyone's hands against them."[11]

It is not surprising that opposition will come. It is a fact that "all who want to live a godly life in Christ Jesus will be persecuted." This reality is especially the case with those who are not content just to live godly themselves, but who also admonish the ungodly to do so (or at least to refrain from public ungodliness). Is not this work a declaration of war against the entire world system? Are not worldly people setting all the children of the devil in opposition to those who do the work of the Society?

Will not Satan himself, "the prince of this world" and "the ruler of the darkness" in the world, work to exert all his cleverness and energy in support of his tottering kingdom? Who can expect the "roaring lion" tamely to submit to having his prey plucked from his teeth? "You need endurance, so that when you have done the will of God, you may receive what was promised."

6. You need to be firmly established, so that you can "hold fast to the confession of your hope without wavering." All who unite in this Society must also be *steadfast*. The work is not a job for the "double-minded," because such people are "unstable in every way." Those who are as "a reed shaken by the wind" are not suitable for this warfare. The struggle demands a firm purpose of soul and a constant and determined perseverance. Those who are lacking in fortitude can "set their hands to the plow," but how soon they will look back! They might indeed endure for a while, but when trouble and persecution (public or private) arise because of the work, immediately they fall away.

7. Of course, it is hard for people to persevere in such unpleasant work, unless their pain and fear are conquered by *love*. Therefore, it is highly advantageous for all who are involved in this work to have "God's love poured into their hearts." They should all be able to proclaim, "We love because God first loved us." The presence of him whom their soul loves will then make their labors light. Because of God's love within them (not from the eagerness of a heated imagination, but with the utmost truth and seriousness), they can testify:

> With thee conversing, I forget
> All time, and toil, and care;
> Labor is rest, and pain is sweet
> While thou, my God, art here.[12]

8. Christian love for our neighbors adds a still greater sweetness even to labor and pain. When people "love their neighbors as themselves" (that is, *everyone*), and when "the love of Christ urges them on" to love one another just as he loved us, they will be ready to endure any kind of suffering to save just one soul from everlasting flames. As Christ "tasted death for everyone,"

Christians are "ready to lay down their lives for one another"—including everyone for whom Christ died. Christian love will not be turned aside from its fixed determination by continuing labor, disappointment, or pain. These Christians will be

> 'Gainst all repulses steeled, nor ever tired
> With toilsome day, or ill-succeeding night.[13]

Thus, love both "hopes all things and endures all things." "Love never ends."

9. There is also another reason that love is necessary for all the members of the Society: Love is not "boastful or arrogant." Love not only generates courage and patience but also leads to *humility*. Oh, how greatly needed is this virtue for all who engage in the work of the Society! What can be of greater importance than that the members should be subordinate, lowly, humble, and unworthy in their own eyes? Nothing could more directly tend to overthrow the entire purpose of the Society than workers who regard themselves as self-important, take credit for anything, or show a hint of the self-righteous spirit of a Pharisee. Society members should never "trust in themselves that they are righteous" or "regard others with contempt."

If Christians become arrogant, they would not only clash with the entire world. They would also have to contend with God. The Lord "opposes the proud, and gives grace only to the humble." Therefore, the members of this Society should be deeply conscious of their own defects, weaknesses, and powerlessness. They should constantly rest their souls upon him who alone has wisdom and strength. They need the indefinable conviction that God himself is the source of "all the help that comes to the earth." It is God alone who "is at work in us, enabling us both to will and to work for his good pleasure."

10. There is one other thing that those who engage in this project should have deeply impressed on their hearts: "Our anger does not produce God's righteousness." Therefore, let our workers "learn from him who was gentle and humble in heart." Let them live *meekly* and *humbly*. Let them "lead a life worthy of the call-

ing to which they have been called, with all humility and gentleness." For their own sakes, the sake of others, and the sake of Christ, let them be "kind to everyone," whether they are good or bad.

Are others "ignorant and wayward"? Let our workers "deal gently with them." Do others oppose the word and work of God? Do they indeed set themselves in battle array against it? So much the more, we need to "correct opponents with gentleness." God may perhaps grant that they will repent and come to know the truth and that they may "escape from the snare of the devil" and no more be "held captive by him to do his will."

IV. The Spirit and Work of the Society

1. Fourth, I will turn from the qualifications of those who are suitable for engaging in this undertaking to explain with what spirit and manner they should attempt this work. First, we will consider the spirit with which we should proceed. To begin with, we must reflect on the *motive* that is to be maintained in every step of the work. Jesus said, "If your eye is healthy, your whole body will be full of light; but if your eye is unhealthy, your whole body will be full of darkness. If then the light in you is darkness, how great is the darkness!" We must constantly remember this truth and carry it into all our words and deeds. Nothing great or small is to be spoken or done with a view to any earthly advantage. We must do nothing with the intention of gaining the favor, honor, love, or praise of people. Instead, our goal (the eye of the mind) is always to be fixed on the glory of God and the good of others.

2. The spirit with which we do everything affects our attitudes and motives. We have already described these properties. The same courage, patience, and steadfastness that *qualify* us for the work are also to be *demonstrated* in the work. In everything, "take the shield of faith, with which you will be able to quench all the flaming arrows of the evil one." In every trying hour, let our workers exercise all the faith that God has given them. "Let all that you do be done in love," and never allow love to be taken from you. "Do not allow many waters to quench your love or the

floods of ingratitude to drown it."[14] Also, "let the same mind be in you that was in Christ Jesus." Yes, and "clothe yourselves with humility." Let this virtue fill your hearts and adorn all your conduct.

At the same time, "clothe yourselves with compassion, kindness, humility, meekness, and patience." Avoid the slightest appearance of hostility, bitterness, anger, or resentment. Understand that our calling is "not to be overcome by evil, but to overcome evil with good."

In order to maintain this humble and gentle love, it is necessary to do everything while controlling our spirits and guarding against all haste and evil thinking. We must also protect ourselves from pride, anger, and rudeness. We can keep from these things only by "persevering in prayer"—before and after we go into a field of service and during all our work. We must do everything in the spirit of sacrifice, offering all things to God through his beloved Son.

3. With regard to your outward course of action, a general rule is to let your exterior conduct express your interior attitudes. In particular, your behavior should reflect the following points: Let every society member be careful never to "do evil so that good may come." Therefore, "putting away falsehood, let all of us speak the truth to our neighbors." Use no deceit or trickery to detect wrongdoing or to chastise anyone. Instead, "with frankness and godly sincerity," "commend yourselves to the conscience of everyone in the sight of God." It is likely that by adhering to these rules, fewer offenders will be convicted. Nonetheless, much more of God's blessing will accompany the entire work of the Society.

4. Let purity of heart be balanced with the right kind of prudence. I do not mean that spawn of hell, which the world calls prudence. Worldly "prudence" is sheer deceit and cunning pretense. Instead, I am speaking about the kind of good sense that is informed by "wisdom from above," which our Lord highly recommends to all who want to promote his kingdom upon earth. "Be wise as serpents and innocent as doves." God's wisdom will instruct you how to adapt all your words and conduct to the persons with whom you deal. This wisdom will help you with regard

to the time, place, and all other circumstances of your work. Wisdom will teach you to avoid all occasions of offending others and to do those things of the most disagreeable nautre in a manner that is as least disagreeable as possible.

5. Your way of speaking, particularly to offenders, should at all times be deeply serious, so that you do not appear as those who insult others or seek to control them. Rather, your words should incline toward sorrow. Demonstrate to others that you pity them for what they do and sympathize with them in what they endure. Let your behavior, tone of voice, and words be unperturbed, calm, and gentle. Indeed, you should not appear hypocritical, but kind and friendly. In some cases, in which it will probably be received as you mean it, you can affirm the goodwill you have for the offenders. At the same time (so that you do not appear to be fearful or insincere), affirm your self-confidence and steadfast resolution to oppose and punish vice to the uttermost.

V. Exhortation and Advice for the Members of the Society

1. It remains for me only to make some applications of what has been said. I am speaking partly to those of you who are already engaged in this work, partly to everyone who respects God, and more particularly to those who love and fear God.

Concerning you who are already engaged in this work, the first advice I would give you is calmly and profoundly to consider the nature of your endeavor. Understand your mission and become completely familiar with all your strengths. Consider the objections that others make to the work you are doing. Before you continue, be satisfied that their objections have no real weight. Then, every one of you can act as you are "fully convinced in your own minds."

2. Second, I advise you not to be in haste to increase the number of members of the Society. And when you do add members, do not add them with an eye to their wealth, rank, or any other outward consideration. Keep to the qualifications that I have already described. Examine carefully whether the proposed member is a person of flawless bearing, as well as faith, courage, patience, and balance. Insist that new members love God and humankind.

If they possess these qualities, they will add to your strength as well as to your membership. If you admit unqualified people, you will lose more than you will gain. You will have displeased God. Furthermore, do not be afraid to purge out from among you any who do not satisfy the qualifications that I have given. By reducing your numbers, you will increase your strength. You will become "special vessels, dedicated and useful to God."

3. Third, I advise you to discern carefully from what motive you act or speak at any time. Be careful that your intentions are not stained with any concern for profit or praise. Do everything "as for the Lord" and as the "servants of Christ." At any point, do not attempt to please yourselves. Rather, seek to please God "to whom you belong and whom you worship." From start to finish, let your eye be healthy, and in every word and deed look to God alone.

4. In the fourth place, I advise you to make sure that you do everything with the right attitude. As those who are worthy of the gospel of Christ, do your work with humility, meekness, patience, and kindness. Trust God in every step, working in the most compassionate and loving spirit that you can.

Meanwhile, constantly guard against all hurry and waste. Always pray earnestly and persistently, so that your faith does not fail. Let nothing interrupt that spirit of sacrifice, which you show in everything that you have and are, and maintain this spirit in all that you suffer and do. Then, through Jesus Christ your service will be "a fragrant offering and sacrifice to God."

5. As to your manner of acting and speaking, I advise you to serve with purity of heart, simplicity, prudence, and seriousness. Add to these virtues all possible calmness and gentleness. Indeed, demonstrate all the kindness that the case will allow. You are not to behave as butchers or hangmen. Instead, serve as surgeons who inflict on the patient no more pain than is necessary to accomplish a cure. For this work, each of you will also need "a lady's hand with a lion's heart."[15] With this spirit, many of you who are compelled to punish public offenders will "glorify God when he comes to judge."

6. I also admonish all of you who fear God. I speak to you if you hope to find mercy at his hands, and if you dread "being

found fighting against God," although you did not know it. For any purpose, reason, or pretense whatsoever, do not directly or indirectly oppose or hinder this Society, which continues to contribute so much to God's glory.

But this advice is not all that I have for you. I speak to you if you love humankind and desire to lessen the sins and miseries of your fellow human beings. Can you satisfy yourselves, and can you be innocent before God just by not opposing his work? Are you not also bound by the most sacred ties that call us to this task: "Whenever we have an opportunity, let us work for the good of all"? Is there not in the work of the society an opportunity to do the highest kind of good to many people? Therefore, in the name of God, embrace the opportunity. Assist this good work, even if in no way other than by your fervent prayers for those who are directly engaged in it. According to your ability, help them to defray the expenses that necessarily attend this ministry.

Without the help of charitable persons, the work would be a burden that the Society could not sustain. If without inconvenience you can help, assist these workers by quarterly or yearly gifts. At the very least, help them today. In this very hour give what God puts on your heart. Let it not be said that you saw your brothers and sisters laboring for God and would not lift a finger to help them. By your help you are actually "coming to the help of the LORD against the mighty."[16]

7. I have a higher request of you that love and fear God. He whom you reverence and adore has qualified you for promoting his work in a more excellent way. "Those who love God must love their brothers and sisters also." You who truly love God, love not only your friends, but also your enemies. "As God's chosen ones," you have put on "all humility and gentleness, with patience, bearing with one another in love."

You have faith in "the only true God and Jesus Christ whom he has sent." This faith "overcomes the world." By faith, you conquer the "fear of others that lays a snare." By faith you "will stand with great confidence in the presence of those who have oppressed you and those who make light of your labors."[17] Therefore, prepared as you are and armed for the fight, will you be as "the

Ephraimites, armed with the bow, who turned back on the day of battle"? Will you leave a few of your brothers and sisters to stand alone against all the hosts of the aliens?

O, do not say, "This is too heavy a cross, and I do not have the strength or courage to endure it." It is true that you do not have adequate strength within yourselves. You who believe "can do all things through him who strengthens you." "If you are able to believe, all things can be done for the one who believes." No cross is too heavy for these kinds of Christians to bear. They know that "if we endure, we will also reign with him." Do not say, "No, I cannot bear to be single-minded." Then you cannot enter into the kingdom of heaven. No one enters there except through the "narrow gate." And all who walk on the "hard road" *must* be single-minded.

Do not say that you cannot endure the disapproval and defamation that come to those who testify against public evil. Has anyone whose name was not a "byword and an object of reproach" ever been saved?[18] Neither can you ever be saved, unless you are willing for others to "utter all kinds of evil against you falsely on Christ's account."

Do not say, "But if I become active in this work I will lose my reputation, my friends, my customers, my business, and my livelihood. I will be reduced to poverty." You will not and cannot experience this consequence. It is completely impossible, unless God himself chooses it for you. "God's kingdom rules over all," and "even the hairs of your head are all counted."[19] If the wise and gracious God chooses poverty for you, however, will you grumble or complain? Instead, will you not say, "Am I not to drink the cup that the Father has given me?" "If you are reviled for the name of Christ, you are blessed, because the spirit of glory, which is the Spirit of God, is resting on you."

Do not say, "I am willing to suffer all things, but my spouse will not consent to it." Assuredly, "a man shall leave his father and mother and be joined to his wife." This way of life is true of everyone, excepting God and his son, Jesus Christ. We are not to leave God in favor of a spouse, and we are not to neglect any duty toward God for the sake of our dearest relative. In this very regard, our Lord himself said, "Whoever loves father or mother more than me is not worthy of me; and whoever loves son or daughter more than me is not worthy of me."

Do not say, "I am willing to forsake everything for Christ. However, one duty must not obstruct another. The work of the Society would frequently keep me from attending public worship." Sometimes this work probably *will* keep you from going to church. Jesus said, "Go and learn what this means, 'I desire mercy, not sacrifice.'" And whatever you lose by demonstrating this mercy to others, God will repay you sevenfold.

Do not say, "But I will harm my own soul. I am a young man, and by working with loose women I would expose myself to temptation." Yes, you would be exposed to temptation if you did this work in your own strength or for your own pleasure. But that is not the case. You trust in God, and you aim at pleasing him only. Even if God called you into the middle of a burning fiery furnace, "when you walk through fire, you shall not be burned, and the flame shall not consume you."

You may reply, "That is true, *if* God called me into the furnace. But I do not see that I am called to this kind of trial." I answer that perhaps you are not willing to *recognize* God's call. If you were not previously called, now, in the name of Christ, I call you. "Take up your cross and follow him." Argue no more with flesh and blood. Resolve now to join with the most despised and rejected of his followers, who are counted as "the rubbish and dregs of the world."

Especially, I call you that once strengthened the hands of God's servants, but afterward drew back. Take courage! Be strong! Make their joy complete by returning to their sides with heart and hand. Let it appear that you "separated from them for a while, so that they might have you back forever."[20] O, "do not be disobedient to the heavenly vision."

As for all of you who know what God has called you to do, "regard everything as loss," so that you can save one soul for whom Christ died. In this work, "do not worry about tomorrow," but "cast all your anxiety on him because he cares for you." Entrust your souls, bodies, and possessions to God "as unto a merciful and faithful Creator."

Notes

1. John H. Overton, *Life in the English Church, 1660–1714* (London: Longmans, Green, and Co., 1885), 204-14.

2. Josiah Woodward [1660–1712], *An Account of the Rise and Progress of the Religious Societies, in the City of London & c. and of their Endeavours for Reformation of Manners*, 3rd enlarged ed. (London: Printed for the author, 1701), 64.

3. Thomas Bray, *A Short Account of the Several Kinds of Societies, Set up of Late Years, for Carrying on the Reformation of Manners, and for the Propagation of Christian Knowledge* (London: Printed by J. Brudewell, 1700). Cited by John H. Overton, *Life in the English Church, 1600–1714* (London: Longmans, Green, and Co., 1885), 214.

4. Samuel Wesley's sermon was later printed in the *Methodist Magazine* (1814), 648-65, 727-36.

5. Sir John Fielding [1721–80], the half-brother of the novelist Henry Fielding, was a prominent English police magistrate who helped restrain professional crime. He reformed the administration of London's criminal justice system. Although Fielding was blind, he was said to have been able to recognize three thousand thieves by their voices.

6. Dissenters are those who separate themselves from the established Church. At one time, the term referred to Roman Catholics; but by Wesley's day, it was used to designate Protestant dissenters. Some dissenters belonged to denominations, and opposed all churches.

7. John Milton, *Paradise Lost: A Poem Written in Ten Books* (London: Printed by Peter Parker, Robert Boulter, and Matthias Walker, 1667), 4:143-44.

8. Ps. 58:11.

9. Ps. 50:16, 17.

10. Charles Wesley, "The Good Fight," stanza 2, *Poet. Wks.*, 2:197.

11. Gen. 16:12.

12. Charles Wesley, "On a Journey," stanza 3, *Poet. Wks.*, 1:304.

13. Samuel Wesley, Jr., "The Battle of the Sexes," in *A Collection of Moral and Sacred Poems From the Most Celebrated English Authors*, ed. John Wesley, 3 vols. (Bristol: Printed by Felix Farley, and sold by the booksellers of London, Newcastle, Bristol, Bath, Exeter, & c., 1744), 3:27.

14. Song of Sol. 8:7.

15. Leonard Wright, *A Display of Dutie, deckt with sage sayings, pithy sentences, and proper similies, pleasant to read, delightfull to heare, and profitable to practise* (London: Printed by V. S. for Nicholas Lyng, 1602).

16. Judg. 5:23.

17. Wisd. of Sol. 5:1.

18. Tob. 3:4.

19. Ps. 103.19; Additions to Esther 16:18, 21; 3 Maccabees 5:28; Matt. 10:30; Luke 12:7.

20. Philem. 15.

Introduction to Sermon 53

ON THE DEATH OF GEORGE WHITEFIELD

George Whitefield was arguably one of the most renowned preachers in English history. Luke Tyerman evaluated him as "one of the greatest Christian orators that ever lived—a man who, though often heavily afflicted, preached, in four-and-thirty years, upwards of eighteen thousand sermons, many of them in the open air, and often to enormous crowds, and in the teeth of brutal persecution."[1] During one of his numerous evangelistic trips to America, on September 30, 1770, in Newburyport, Massachusetts, Whitefield died of exhaustion and complications from asthma. Weeks later, on November 10, 1770, Wesley wrote in his journal,

> I returned to London and had the melancholy news of Mr. Whitefield's death confirmed by his executors, who desired me to preach his funeral sermon on Sunday, the 18th. In order to write this, I retired to Lewisham on Monday and on Sunday following went to the chapel in Tottenham Court Road. An immense multitude was gathered together from all corners of the town. I was at first afraid that a great part of the congregation would not be able to hear. But it pleased God so to strengthen my voice that even

> those at the door heard distinctly. It was an awful season. All were still as night. Most appeared to be deeply affected. And an impression was made on many, which one would hope will not speedily be effaced.
>
> The time appointed for my beginning at the Tabernacle was half-hour after five. But it was quite filled at three, so I began at four. At first the noise was exceeding great, but it ceased when I began to speak. And my voice was again so strengthened that all who were within could hear, unless an accidental noise hindered here or there for a few moments. O that all may hear the voice of him with whom are the issues of life and death! And who so loudly by this unexpected stroke calls all his children to love one another![2]

John Wesley preached Whitefield's funeral sermon under awkward circumstances. The major factor contributing to the tense atmosphere was the well-known fact that Whitefield and Wesley had theological differences. Whitefield was a Calvinist who believed in predestination, election, and "irresistible grace"—doctrines that precluded both free will and the earthly probation of Christians. Despite the fact that Wesley and Whitefield differed on these points of doctrine, they had agreed to maintain their friendship. Their theological differences, however, prevented them from working together.

Whitefield's friends and supporters asked Wesley to preach Whitefield's memorial sermon only because Whitefield had made it clear that he wanted Wesley to do so. Contributing further to the strained situation was the fact that in 1770, the year of Whitefield's death, Wesley's conference of preachers had issued a summary of the differences between Methodism and Calvinism. These differences focused on Calvinism's doctrine of a limited atonement, predestination to salvation and damnation, and the unconditional security of believers. Given the theological differences between Wesley and the followers of George Whitefield, the atmosphere of the memorial service was strained.

In the days following the sermon, several Calvinists severely attacked Wesley's sermon because it contained no mention of the doctrines of election and final perseverance. In the January 1771 *Gospel Magazine,* the Rev. William Romaine harshly criticized

Wesley's sermon. Romaine objected, first, to Wesley's sermon text: "Let me die the death of the righteous, and let my last end be like his" (Num. 23:10). Romaine criticized, "How improper to apply the words of a mad prophet [Balaam] to so holy a man as Mr. Whitefield!"

In a letter to the editor of *Lloyd's Evening Post,* Wesley replied that he had not intended to apply this text to Whitefield, but to *himself.* Wesley wrote, "Others imagine nothing could be more suitable, than for Balaam junior to use the words of his forefather; especially as he did not apply them to Mr. Whitefield, but to himself: Surely a poor reprobate may, without offense, wish to die like one of the elect. I dare say every one understood me to mean this, the moment he heard the text: If not, the very hymn I sung showed to whom I applied the words."[3]

Romaine's second and most violent attack against Wesley's sermon was to criticize him for stating that the grand fundamental doctrines that Mr. Whitefield everywhere preached were those of the new birth and justification by faith. Romaine grumbled,

> No, not at all: The grand fundamental doctrines he everywhere preached, were the everlasting covenant between the Father and the Son; and absolute predestination flowing therefrom. . . . Mr. Whitefield everywhere insisted on other fundamental doctrines, from the foundation of which, the new birth and justification take their rise, with which they are inseparably connected: These are, the everlasting covenant which was entered into by the Holy Trinity, and God the Father's everlasting, unchangeable election of sinners; these doctrines are not of a less essential nature than either regeneration, or justification. No, by no means; they are to the full equally essential to the glory of God. Yea, there is an inseparable connexion between them. This is a most essential, a most fundamental point.

Wesley responded,

> 1. He did not everywhere preach the eternal covenant, and absolute predestination. I never heard him utter a sentence on one or the other. Yea, all the times he preached in West-street chapel, and in our other chapels throughout England, he did not preach those

> doctrines at all, no, not in a single paragraph; which, by the by, is a demonstration that he did not think them the fundamental doctrines of Christianity. 2. Both in West-street chapel, and all our other chapels throughout England, he did preach the necessity of the new birth, and justification by faith, as clearly as he has done in his two volumes of printed sermons: Therefore, all I have asserted is true, and provable by ten thousand witnesses.[4]

Whitefield was the better orator of the two friends, although his printed sermons are seldom, if ever, read. He addressed the heart more than the head. Without his oral delivery, his sermons now have little interest. John Wesley was a vastly superior thinker, and his messages of enduring quality will be read until Christ returns. Despite the difficult circumstances attending this sermon, Wesley paid due tribute to his fallen friend in Christ and called for Christian unity in the Lord. The sermon is both a fitting acknowledgment of Whitefield's saintliness and a positive demonstration of Wesley's dignity and grace under challenging circumstances.

Sermon 53

ON THE DEATH OF GEORGE WHITEFIELD

Let me die the death of the upright, and let my end be like his! *(Numbers 23:10)*

1 "Let my end be like his!" How many of you join in this wish? Perhaps even in this large congregation, there may be few of you who do not hold this desire. Oh, I hope that this wish rests upon your minds! I pray that this aspiration will not fade away until your souls reside "where the wicked cease from troubling, and where the weary are at rest."

2. An elaborate exposition of the sermon text will not be expected on this occasion. It would keep you too long from the melancholy thought of your beloved brother, friend, and pastor, Mr. George Whitefield. Indeed, he was also your father in Christ because many are present today for whom Mr. Whitefield is "your father through the gospel"! Will it not then be more suitable to your preferences, as well as to this solemn occasion, directly to speak about this man of God whom you have so often heard speaking in this place? You know the aim of his preaching: "Jesus Christ is the same yesterday and today and forever."

Therefore, let us (1) comment on a few circumstances of his life and death, (2) look at his character, and (3) consider how we can make the most of the severe providence of his sudden removal from us.

I. The Circumstances of Mr. Whitefield's Life and Death

1. In the first place, we will consider some of the details of Mr. Whitefield's life and death. In December 1714, he was born at Gloucester, where he was placed in a grammar school when about twelve years old. At the age of seventeen, he became seriously religious, and he served God to the best of his understanding. At about the age of eighteen, he was admitted into Pembroke College at the University of Oxford. About a year later, he became acquainted with the Methodists (so called) whom, from that time onward, he loved as his own soul.

2. The Methodists convinced him that we must be born again, or otherwise outward religion gains us nothing. Mr. Whitefield joined with the Methodists in fasting on Wednesdays and Fridays, visiting the sick and imprisoned, and in the disciplined use of every moment, so that no time would be wasted. Then, he changed the course of his studies, mostly reading those books that focused on the heart of religion. These actions led him directly to an experiential knowledge of "Jesus Christ and him crucified."

3. He was soon tried as by fire. Not only did he lose his reputation (because of the gospel), and some of his dearest friends forsook him, but also he struggled with inward trials of the severest kind. Many nights he lay sleepless on his bed, and numerous days he prostrated himself on the ground. After he had agonized several months under "the spirit of slavery," God was pleased to remove the heavy load by giving him "the spirit of adoption." God enabled him, through a living faith, to lay hold on God's beloved son.

4. For the recovery of his greatly impaired health, however, it was considered necessary for him to go into the country. Accordingly, Mr. Whitefield went to Gloucester, where God enabled him to awaken several young persons to their need for

God. These people soon formed themselves into a little society, and they became some of the first fruits of his labor. Shortly thereafter, he began to read to some poor people in the town two or three times a week. Daily, he read to, and prayed with, the prisoners in the county jail.

5. He was now about twenty-one years old, and he was urged to enter into holy orders. He was acutely fearful of taking this step because he deeply felt his own insufficiency. The bishop himself sent for him and said, "Although I had intended to ordain no one under the age of three and twenty, yet I will ordain you whenever you come."[5] Several other providential circumstances confirmed this decision, and Mr. Whitefield was ordained a deacon on Trinity Sunday in 1736. The following Sunday, he preached to a crowded assembly in the church where he had been baptized. The next week, he returned to Oxford and received his bachelor's degree. Then, he became a full time Christian worker, ministering primarily to the prisoners and the poor.

6. It was not long until he was invited to London to serve as a parish priest for a friend who went into the country. Mr. Whitefield continued there two months, lodging in the Tower of London. Twice weekly, he read prayers in the chapel, and once a week he catechized the young and preached. Also, each day, he visited the soldiers in the barracks and the infirmary. In addition, he read prayers every evening at Wapping Chapel and preached at Ludgate Prison every Tuesday. While he was in London, letters came from his friends in Georgia, which made him yearn to go to America and help them. However, he did not see a clear way to go; so at the appointed time, he returned to his little charge at Oxford. There, several young people met daily in his room to "build themselves up on their most holy faith."

7. Soon, he was called from there to serve as the curate of the parish of Dummer in Hampshire. There, he read prayers twice daily, early in the morning and in the evening after the people returned from work. Daily, he catechized the children and visited from house to house. In Dummer, he divided the day into three parts: eight hours for sleep and meals, eight hours for study and private time, and eight hours for reading prayers, catechizing, and

visiting the people. Is there a more excellent pattern for a servant of Christ and his church? If there is not a better way, who will "go and do likewise"?

8. His mind still continued to ponder going to America. On becoming fully convinced that God was calling him there, Mr. Whitefield set all things in order; and in January 1737, he went down to bid farewell to his friends in Gloucester. It was on this journey that God began to bless his ministry in an extraordinary manner. Wherever he preached, unexpected multitudes of hearers flocked together—in Gloucester, Stonehouse, Bath, and Bristol. The excitement of the churches was hardly contained. No less extraordinary was the influence that he made on the minds of many people.

After his return to London, for week after week and month after month he was occupied in conversations with James Oglethorpe.[6] During this time, it pleased God to bless his word still more. Mr. Whitefield was untiring in his labors. Ordinarily, on Sunday he preached four times to exceeding large audiences. He also read prayers two or three times a week. His ministry required him to walk from place to place, often distances of ten or twelve miles.

9. On December 28, 1737, he left London, and on December 29, he first preached without sermon notes. On December 30, he went on board a ship bound for America, but it was more than a month before they sailed. The voyage was very slow, but there were advantages. In April of 1738, he wrote,

> Blessed be God. We now live very comfortably in the great cabin. We talk of little else but God and Christ. . . . And when we are together hardly a word is heard among us except what has reference to our fall in the first Adam and our new birth in the Second Adam, Jesus Christ.[7]

It seems also to have been a particular providence that Mr. Whitefield should spend a little time at Gibraltar, where both citizens and soldiers, high and low, young and old, acknowledged the day of God's coming among them.

10. From Sunday May 7, 1738, until the end of August, in Georgia, and particularly in Savannah, he "carried out his ministry fully." He read prayers, preached twice a day, and daily visited the sick. On Sundays, he preached at five and ten in the morning, and at three in the afternoon he read prayers and preached. Then, at seven in the evening he explained the Church catechism. How much easier is it for our brethren in the ministry in England, Scotland, or Ireland to find fault with such a laborer in our Lord's vineyard than to follow in his steps!

11. At this time, Mr. Whitefield saw the deplorable condition of many children in Savannah, and God put into his heart the first thought of founding an orphanage. He determined that if God would give him a safe return to England, he would raise money for the project. The following December, he returned to London; and on Sunday, January 14, 1739, he was ordained a priest at Christ Church, Oxford. The following day, he came again to London. And on Sunday, January 21, he preached twice. Although the churches were large and exceedingly crowded, many hundreds stood in the churchyard; and for the lack of room, hundreds more were forced to return to their homes.

This experience planted within him the first thought of preaching in the open air. However, when he mentioned the idea to some of his friends, they considered it to be sheer insanity. So he did not carry out his idea until after he had left London. On Wednesday, February 21, 1739, in Bristol, he found that all the church doors were locked shut against them. Moreover, no church in Bristol was able to accommodate one half of his congregation. So, at three in the afternoon, he went to Kingswood and preached outdoors to almost two thousand people.

On Friday, he preached there to four or five thousand; and on Sunday, it was estimated that he preached to ten thousand. During the time he stayed at Bristol, the numbers constantly increased. His preaching lit a flame of holy love that will not easily be extinguished. The same kind of fire was also later kindled in different parts of Wales, Gloucestershire, and Worcestershire. Indeed, wherever Mr. Whitefield went, "God abundantly confirmed the word of his messenger."

12. On Sunday, April 29, 1739, he preached outdoors for the first time in Moorfields and on Kennington Common. The thousands of hearers were as quiet as if they had been inside a church. Because Mr. Whitefield was again detained in England for several months, he made short excursions into several counties, in which willing multitudes gave him contributions for an orphanage in Georgia. The embargo, which was then laid on shipping, gave him free time for more journeys through various parts of England. And many will have reason to bless God to all eternity for these preaching tours.

Finally, on August 14, 1739, he set sail, but he did not land in Pennsylvania until October 30. Afterward, he toured Pennsylvania, New Jersey, New York, Maryland, Virginia, and North and South Carolina. He preached along the way to immense congregations, with fully as great a result as in England. On January 10, 1740, he arrived in Savannah.

13. On January 29, he added three desolate orphans to the almost twenty children he had brought to his house during his first trip to Savannah. The next day, about ten miles from Savannah, he laid out the ground for the orphanage. On February 11, he took in four more orphans and set out for Frederica (on St. Simons Island, Georgia) in order to gather in the orphans who were in the southern parts of the Georgia colony. On his return, he established a school for children and adults at Darien. He also collected four more orphans from that place.

On March 25, Mr. Whitefield laid the first stone for the orphanage, to which, with great decorum, he gave the name *Bethesda*. This orphanage is a work for which children yet unborn will praise the Lord. Mr. Whitefield now had about forty orphans, so that there were almost a hundred mouths to feed daily. However, he "did not worry about anything." Instead, he cast his care on him who "gives food to the young ravens when they cry."

14. In April, he made another tour through Pennsylvania, New Jersey, and New York. Incredible multitudes flocked to hear him, among whom were many Negroes. Everywhere he preached, most of the hearers were affected to an amazing degree. Large numbers were deeply convinced of their lost condition, and many were

truly converted to God. In some places, thousands cried out aloud, and many of them were as in the agonies of death. Most cried freely, and some turned as pale as death. Others wrung their hands, fell to the ground, or sank into the arms of their friends. Almost all the people lifted up their eyes and cried out for mercy.

15. On June 5, Mr. Whitefield returned to Savannah. The next evening during the public service, the entire congregation, young and old, melted into tears. After the service, several of the parishioners and their families, particularly the little children, returned home, crying as they went. Some could not help praying aloud. The groans and cries of the children continued all night and through most of the next day.

16. In August, he set out again, preaching through various provinces until he arrived in Boston. While he was there and in nearby places, he became extremely weak in body. Yet the multitudes of hearers were so vast and the effects wrought on them so astonishing that the oldest people then alive in the town had never seen anything like this religious revival.

The same power accompanied his preaching in New York, particularly on Sunday, November 2. Almost as soon as he began to preach, the sounds of crying, weeping, and wailing were heard everywhere. Innumerable people were cut to the heart and fell to the ground. And many were filled with divine consolation. Toward the close of his preaching tour, he wrote in his journal:

> It is the seventy-fifth day since I arrived at Rhode Island, exceeding weak in body. Yet God has enabled me to preach a hundred and seventy-five times in public, beside exhorting frequently in private. Never did God give me greater comforts. Never did I perform my journeys with less fatigue, or see such a continuance of the divine presence in the congregations to whom I preached.[8]

In December, he returned to Savannah; and in the following March, he arrived in England.

17. You can easily detect that the preceding account is mainly drawn from Mr. Whitefield's own journals. Their genuine and natural simplicity may rival any writings of this kind. During the next thirty years, his journals are an accurate account of his work in

Europe and America for the honor of his beloved Master. They also correctly tell about the uninterrupted showers of blessings with which God was pleased to prosper Mr. Whitefield's labors!

It is greatly to be lamented that he did not continue this account of his ministry, at least until near the time when his Lord called him to heaven to enjoy the fruit of his labors. If Mr. Whitefield did leave any such papers of this kind and his friends account me worthy of the privilege, it would be my honor and joy to organize, transcribe, and prepare them for public reading.

18. A gentleman from Boston gave a particular account of the last scene of his life:

> After being about a month with us in Boston and its vicinity, and preaching every day, he went to Old York, preached on Thursday, September 27, there; proceeded to Portsmouth and preached there on Friday. On Saturday morning he set out for Boston; but before he came to Newbury [Massachusetts] where he had engaged to preach the next morning, he was urged to preach an unscheduled sermon. The house not being large enough to contain the people, he preached in an open field. But having been infirm for several weeks, preaching this sermon so exhausted his strength that when he came to Newbury he could not get out of the ferryboat without the help of two men.
>
> In the evening, however, he recovered his spirits and appeared with his usual cheerfulness. He went to his chamber at nine, his fixed time for private prayer, from which he could not be diverted. He slept better than he had done for some weeks. He arose at four in the morning, September 30, and went into his closet [for prayer]; and his companion observed he was unusually long in private. He left his place of prayer, returned to his companion, threw himself on the bed, on which he laid about ten minutes. Then he fell upon his knees and prayed most fervently that, if it was consistent with God's will, he might that day finish his Master's work. He then asked his helper to call Mr. Parsons, the clergyman at whose house he was staying. However, in a minute, before Mr. Parsons could reach him, Mr. Whitefield died without a sigh or groan.
>
> On the news of his death, six gentlemen set out for Newbury in order to move his remains, but he could not be moved, so that his precious ashes must remain at Newbury. Hundreds would have gone from this town to attend his funeral had they not expected he

would have been interred here. . . . May this stroke be sanctified to the church of God in general, and to this province in particular![9]

II. The Character of Mr. Whitefield

1. In the second place, we will look into Mr. Whitefield's character. A little sketch of his character was published in the *Boston Gazette* soon after his death. Here, I will add an extract from that article:

> Little can be said of him but what every friend to vital Christianity who has sat under his ministry will attest. In his public labors he has for many years astonished the world with his eloquence and devotion. With what divine pathos did he persuade the impenitent sinner to embrace the practice of piety and virtue! Filled with the spirit of grace, he spoke from the heart, and with a fervency of zeal perhaps unequalled since the days of the apostles, adorned the truths he delivered with the most graceful charms of rhetoric and oratory. From the pulpit he was unrivalled in the command of an ever-crowded auditory [audience]. Nor was he less agreeable and instructive in his private conversation: happy in a remarkable ease of address, willing to communicate, studious to edify. May the rising generation catch a spark of that flame which shone with such distinguished luster in the spirit and practice of this faithful servant of the highest God![10]

2. A more particular and equally accurate assessment of his character appeared in one of the English papers. It may be enlightening also to add the substance of this assessment of Mr. Whitefield:

> The character of this truly pious person must be deeply impressed on the heart of every friend to vital religion. In spite of a tender and delicate constitution he continued to the last day of his life preaching with a frequency and a fervor that seemed to exceed the natural strength of the most robust. Being called to the exercise of his function at an early age, when most young men are only beginning to qualify themselves for it, he had not time to make a very considerable progress in the learned languages. But this defect was

amply supplied by a lively and fertile genius, by fervent zeal, and by a forcible and most persuasive delivery. And though in the pulpit he often found it needful by "the terrors of the Lord to persuade men," he had nothing gloomy in his nature, being singularly cheerful, as well as charitable and tenderhearted. He was as ready to relieve the bodily as the spiritual necessities of those that applied to him. It ought also to be observed that he constantly enforced upon his audience every moral duty, particularly industry in their several callings, and obedience to their superiors. He endeavored by the most extraordinary efforts of preaching in different places, and even in the open fields, to rouse the lower class of people from the last degree of inattention and ignorance to a sense of religion. For this and his other labors the name of George Whitefield will long be remembered with esteem and veneration.[11]

3. That both these accounts are fair and impartial will readily be acknowledged—that is, as far as they go. However, they go little further than statements about the outward qualities of his character. They reveal the public preacher, but not the private man, the Christian and saint of God. May I be permitted to add a little commentary on this matter from a personal knowledge of nearly forty years? Indeed, I am thoroughly aware of how difficult it is to speak on such a critical subject. Prudence is required to avoid both extremes—saying too little or too much. Some will seriously think that I say too little, and others will think that I have said too much. But without paying attention to critics, I will speak just what I know. And I speak before God, to whom we are all to give an account.

4. I have already mentioned Mr. Whitefield's unparalleled zeal, tireless activity, kindness to the sick, and generosity toward the poor. Shall we not also mention his deep gratitude toward everyone that God used as instruments of good to him? Even to his dying day, he did not cease to speak about them in the most respectful manner. Should we not mention that he had a heart inclined to the most generous and tender friendships? Of all the distinguishing marks of his character, I have frequently thought that this quality was the most defining mark of George Whitefield. How few people we have known have had such a kind disposition and such abundant and far-reaching affections!

Was it not primarily by this quality of gratitude that the hearts of others were so strangely drawn to, and bonded with, him? Can anything other than love generate love? Love radiated from his very appearance, and love continually came through all his words, whether in public or private. Was it not love, which was as quick and piercing as lightning, that leaped from heart to heart? Was it not love that gave life to his sermons, his conversation, and his letters? You are witnesses.

5. Let us set aside the depraved misunderstandings of corrupt people who know only of love that is "earthly, unspiritual, and devilish." At the same time, let it be remembered that Mr. Whitefield was endued with the most refined and unblemished kind of modesty. His ministerial office called him to converse very frequently and at length with both women and men of every age and condition. His entire behavior toward all of them was a practical commentary on the advice of St. Paul to Timothy: "Speak to older women as mothers, to younger women as sisters—with absolute purity."

6. All the while, the friendliness of his spirit was evident in the sincerity and honesty of his conversation! His talk was as far removed from rudeness, on the one hand, as it was from dishonesty and deception, on the other hand. Was this honesty not at the same time a fruit and a proof of his courage and poise? Armed with these qualities, he did not fear others. He "acted with great boldness" toward persons of every rank and condition, high and low, rich and poor. "By the open statement of the truth, he commended himself to the conscience of everyone in the sight of God."

7. He did not fear labor, pain, or "what anyone could do to him." He was equally "patient in bearing ill and doing well."[12] This quality was evident in the steadfastness with which he pursued whatever he undertook for his Master's sake.

One example speaks for them all—the orphanage in Georgia. He began and completed this orphanage despite all the obstacles he faced. Indeed, in whatever concerned him, he was adaptable and flexible. He was "willing to yield" and easy to be convinced or persuaded. However, he was immovable in the things of God, or whenever it was a matter of conscience. No one could persuade or frighten him to waver in the least point from the integrity that was inseparable from his entire character. It governed all his words and actions. In matters of integrity, Mr. Whitefield did

> Stand as an iron pillar strong,
> And steadfast as a wall of brass.[13]

8. If it is asked what was the foundation of such integrity, sincerity, courage, patience, and every other valuable and amiable quality, it is easy to give the answer. It was not the excellence of his natural disposition or the power of his intelligence. It was not the strength of his education or the counsel of his friends. Mr. Whitefield's qualities came from no other source than his faith in a bleeding Lord—it was his "faith in the power of God." It was "a living hope" of "an inheritance that is imperishable, undefiled, and unfading." It was "God's love poured into his heart through the Holy Spirit that was given to him."

This love filled his soul with kind, impartial affection for everyone. From this source of love came that flood of eloquence that frequently swept everything before it. Love was the source of his astonishing power of persuasion, which the most hardened sinners could not resist. It was love that often made his "head a spring of water, and his eyes a fountain of tears."[14] Love enabled him to pour out his soul in prayer in a unique manner. Love empowered him to pray with fullness and ease united together and with strength and variety of emotion and eloquence.

9. I will close this part of the sermon by observing what a great honor God bestowed upon his faithful servant by allowing him to declare his everlasting gospel in so many various countries. He preached to masses of people and with great effect on many of their precious souls! Since the apostles, have we read or heard of any person who witnessed to the gospel of God's grace in so many different places throughout such a large part of the habitable world? Have we read or heard of any person who called so many thousands and so many multitudes of sinners to repentance?

Above all, have we read or heard of anyone who has been such a blessed instrument in God's hand to bring so many sinners "from darkness to light and from the power of Satan to God"? It is true that if we were to talk this way to the pleasure-loving world, we would be judged as speaking in a foreign language. However, you understand the language of the country to which you are going and to which our dear friend has gone a little ahead of us.

III. Lessons Learned on the Occasion of Mr. Whitefield's Death

Third, we will consider how we can benefit from Mr. Whitefield's lamentable death. The answer to this important question is easy, and may God write it on all our hearts! We can benefit by keeping close to the grand doctrines that he delivered and by partaking of his godly spirit.

1. First, let us keep close to the grand scriptural doctrines that he delivered everywhere. There are many doctrines that are not of an essential nature, about which even the sincere children of God are, and have been, divided for many ages. Such is the present frailty of human comprehension! In these minor doctrines, we can think and let think; we may agree to disagree. All the while, however, let us cling to the essentials of "the faith that was once for all entrusted to the saints." This faith is what our champion of God so strongly insisted on at all times and in all places.

2. His fundamental message was to give God all the glory for everything that is good in humankind. And in the matter of salvation, Mr. Whitefield set Christ as high as possible and humankind as low as possible. This assumption was the one that he and his friends at Oxford, the original Methodists (so called), started with in their work. Their main principle was that there is no natural ability or saving merit in humankind.

The original Methodists insisted that all ability to think, speak, or act rightly is due to the Spirit of Christ. All merit is not in us, but in the blood of Christ. However much grace we may have, our merit is not due to ourselves. It is due to God's grace. Mr. Whitefield and the Methodists taught that until given to us from above, there is no power in us to do a single good work, speak one good word, or form one good desire. It is not enough to say that we are *sick* from sin. No, we are all "*dead* through trespasses and sins." It follows that all of us are "by nature children of wrath." We are all "held accountable to God," and we are in danger of temporal and eternal death.

3. Moreover, we are all helpless to overcome the power and guilt of sin. "Who can bring a clean thing out of an unclean thing?" No one except the Almighty. Who of us can raise those who are spiritually dead in sin? No one except the One who raised us from the dust of the earth. But on what basis will God do this work?

God will not free us from spiritual death "because of any works of righteousness that we have done." "The dead do not praise the LORD." The dead cannot do anything to merit being raised up into life. Therefore, whatever God does, he does only for the sake of his well-beloved Son. "He was wounded for our transgressions, crushed for our iniquities." "He himself bore our sins in his body on the cross." Jesus Christ "was handed over to death for our trespasses and was raised for our justification."

The work of Christ, then, is the sole meritorious cause of every blessing we do or can enjoy—especially our pardon and acceptance with God and our full and free justification. Now, by what means do we partake of what Christ has done and suffered? It is "not the result of works, so that no one may boast." Rather, it is by faith alone. The apostle Paul said, "We hold that a person is justified by faith apart from works prescribed by the law." "To all who received him, who believed in his name, he gave power to become children of God, who were born, not of the will of man, but of God."

4. Moreover, as Jesus said, "No one can see the kingdom of God without being born from above." All who are in this way "born of the Spirit" have "the kingdom of God within them." Christ sets up his kingdom in their hearts, and it consists of "righteousness and peace and joy in the Holy Spirit." "The same mind is in them that was in Christ Jesus," enabling them to "walk as Christ also walked." Christ's indwelling Spirit makes them both

holy in heart and righteous in conduct. Because salvation is a gift through the righteousness and blood of Christ, eternally we all have one thing to remember: "Let the one who boasts, boast in the Lord."

5. You are not unaware that these are the fundamental doctrines that Mr. Whitefield constantly insisted on. They can be summed up, as it were, in two terms—the *new birth* and *justification by faith*. With all boldness and at all times and in all places, let us insist on these two doctrines. Let those of us who are called into the gospel ministry champion these doctrines in public, in private, and at every opportunity.

Even if they are out of fashion, let us keep close to these good and ancient truths, regardless of how many people may deny or blaspheme them. Remain steadfast, my brothers and sisters, and be "strong in the Lord and in the strength of his power." With all care and diligence, "guard what has been entrusted to you," knowing that "heaven and earth will pass away, but Christ's words will not pass away."

6. Will it be enough to keep close to Mr. Whitefield's beliefs, however pure they are? Is there not a point of still greater importance than maintaining correct doctrine—namely, to drink of a *righteous spirit*? In this regard, be imitators of him, as he was of Christ. Without partaking of the Spirit of Christ, as our departed brother did, our good doctrines would only increase our condemnation. Therefore, the principal thing to learn from George Whitefield is his spirit of devotion to Christ. We confess that in some points we must be content to admire what we cannot imitate. Yet, through the same free grace, in many other points we can partake of the same blessings that he received.

Being conscious of your own needs and of the abundant love of God who gives to all generously and ungrudgingly, call to him who works everything in everyone for a measure of the same precious faith. Ask God for the identical zeal and vitality, the same kindness, love, and compassion. Wrestle with God for a measure of the same grateful, friendly, affectionate disposition. Seek the identical honesty, simplicity, godly sincerity, and genuine love. Continue to pray until the power from on high works in you the same steadfast courage and patience. Above all, because it is the crown of everything else, seek the same unwavering integrity.

7. Was George Whitefield endowed with any other fruit of God's grace that is lacking in us (a lack he frequently and passionately lamented)? There is one—universal love. This catholic spirit is a sincere and kind affection that is due to all those we have reason to believe are children of God by faith. In other words, this love accepts all those of every theological persuasion who "fear God and work righteousness." Mr. Whitefield longed to see all who had "tasted the goodness of the word of God" joined together in one catholic spirit. *Catholic spirit* is a term little understood and still less experienced by many people who frequently use these words.

Who are those that have this characteristic? Who is the man or woman of a "catholic spirit"? People with a catholic spirit love others who jointly partake of the present kingdom of heaven as friends, brothers, and sisters in the Lord They love them as fellow heirs of God's eternal kingdom. The catholic spirit accepts those (of whatever opinion, mode of worship, or congregation) who believe in the Lord Jesus and who love God and others.

All the while, they rejoice to please God and fear to offend him. They are careful to abstain from evil and are zealous for good deeds. Those who have a catholic spirit keep all people on their hearts. They have an indescribable affection for them and maintain an earnest desire for their welfare. They do not cease to commend others to God in prayer and to defend them before everyone.

They speak kindly to others and, through their words, labor to strengthen their hands in God. To the utmost of their power, they assist everyone in all things spiritual and temporal. Those with a catholic spirit are ready "to spend and to be spent" for others. Yes, they are willing to "lay down their lives for their sisters and brothers."

8. How appealing is the characteristic that I have described! How desirable it is for every child of God! Then why is a catholic spirit so rarely found? Why are there so few examples of it? If we

have tasted God's love, how can any of us rest until we have this love for others in our hearts? There is a subtle way by which Satan persuades thousands of Christians that they can stop short of love and still be blameless. It is good if many people present here are not in this "snare of the devil and held captive by him to do his will."

Someone may say, "O yes, I have all this kind of love for those whom I believe to be children of God. But I will never believe that another person who belongs to that wretched congregation is a child of God!"

You think that someone cannot be a child of God if he or she holds what you regard as "detestable opinions" or participates in such "senseless and superstitious, if not idolatrous, worship"? In this way, we justify ourselves in one sin by adding a second sin to it! We excuse our lack of love by laying the blame on others. To add to our own devilish disposition, we declare that our brothers and sisters are children of the devil.

O, take care to avoid this attitude! If you are already caught in this snare, escape from it as soon as possible. Strive to develop that truly catholic love that is not "irritable or resentful." Gain that kind of love that "believes all things, hopes all things, and endures all things." Seek the love that makes all the possible allowances for others that we want them to make for us. Then, we will recognize the grace of God that is in all Christians, whatever may be their opinions or modes of worship. With the compassion of Christ Jesus, everyone who fears God will become near and dear unto us.

9. Was this kind of love not characteristic of the spirit of our dear departed friend? Why should this love not also be ours? O God of love, how long will your people remain "a by-word among the nations"? How long will they laugh us to scorn and say, "Look at the way those Christians love one another"? Lord, when will you "roll away our disgrace"? Will the "sword keep devouring forever"? At least, now "order your people to turn from the pursuit of their kinsmen."

My brothers and sisters, whatever others do, let all of us hear the voice of him who "being dead, still speaks." Imagine that you hear Mr. Whitefield say: "Now, at least 'be imitators of me, as I am of Christ.' Let brother 'no more lift up sword against brother,' 'neither shall you learn war any more'! Rather, 'as God's chosen ones, holy and beloved, clothe yourselves with compassion, kindness, humility, meekness, and patience. Bear with one another in love.'" Let the time past suffice for conflict, envy, controversy, and for "biting and devouring one another." Blessed be God that you have not long ago been "consumed by one another"! From this time on, "make every effort to maintain the unity of the Spirit in the bond of peace."

10. O, God, with you no work is impossible! You do whatever pleases you! O, that you would cause the mantle of your prophet George Whitefield, whom you have taken to yourself, now to fall upon us who remain! "Where is the LORD, the God of Elijah?" Let his spirit rest upon these your servants!

Show us that you are the God who answers by fire! Let the flame of your love fall upon every heart! As we love you, let us love one another with a "love stronger than death." "Take away from us all bitterness and wrath and anger and wrangling and slander." Let your Spirit so rest upon us that from this hour we may "be kind to one another, tenderhearted, forgiving one another, as God in Christ has forgiven us"!

The following hymn by Charles Wesley was most likely sung at the time that John Wesley preached this funeral sermon.

A Hymn by Charles Wesley

I

Servant of God, well done!
   Thy glorious warfare's past,
The battle's fought, the race is won,
   And thou art crowned at last;
   Of all thy heart's desire
   Triumphantly possessed,
Lodged by the ministerial choir
   In thy Redeemer's breast.

II

In condescending love
  Thy ceaseless prayer He heard,
And bade thee suddenly remove
  To thy complete reward:
  Ready to bring the peace,
  Thy beauteous feet were shod,
When mercy signed thy soul's release
  And caught thee up to God.

III

With saints enthroned on high
  Thou dost thy Lord proclaim,
And still to God Salvation cry,
  Salvation to the Lamb!
  O happy, happy soul!
  In ecstasies of praise,
Long as eternal ages roll,
  Thou seest thy Saviour's face.

IV

Redeemed from earth and pain,
  Ah! when shall we ascend,
And all in Jesus' presence reign
  With our translated friend!
  Come, Lord, and quickly come!
  And when in thee complete,
Receive thy longing servants home,
  To triumph—at thy feet![15]

Notes

1. Luke Tyerman, *The Life and Times of John Wesley*, 3 vols. (London: Hodder and Stoughton, 1870), 3:78.
2. Ward and Heitzenrater, *Wesley's Journal and Diaries*, November 10, 1770, 22:259.
3. Jackson, *Wesley's Works*, 13:401.

4. Ibid., 13:401-2.

5. Luke Tyerman, *The Life of the Rev. George Whitefield,* 2 vols. (London: Hodder and Stoughton, 1876), 1:42.

6. James Edward Oglethorpe [1696–1785] founded the British colony of Georgia in America. In 1733, he established Savannah, where later John and Charles Wesley and George Whitefield ministered for a short time.

7. Iain Murray, ed., *George Whitefield's Journals* (London: Banner of Truth Trust, 1960), 149.

8. Murray, *Whitefield's Journals,* December 1, 1740, 499.

9. Probably from one of three letters sent from Boston to Mr. Robert Keen of London, a friend of George Whitefield.

10. Condensed from an editorial that appeared October 1, 1770, in *The Massachusetts Gazette, Boston Post-Boy,* and *The Advertizer,* #684, 3.

11. Condensed from the article that appeared November 10, 1770, in *The London Evening Post,* #1607, 4.

12. Samuel Wesley Jr., "The Battle of the Sexes," stanza 25, in John Wesley, *A Collection of Moral and Sacred Poems* (1744), 3:33.

13. Charles Wesley, Hymn on Acts 4:29; last two lines of stanza 7, *Poet. Wks.,* 1:180.

14. Jer. 9:1.

15. Charles Wesley, "An Hymn on the Death of the Rev. George Whitefield," *Poet. Wks.,* 4:316-17.

Index

Made in the USA
Middletown, DE
12 July 2016